THE MARRIAGE COLLECTION

THE MARRIAGE COLLECTION

*Keys to Make
Your Marriage Better*

Fritz Ridenour

Zondervan Publishing House
Grand Rapids, Michigan

THE MARRIAGE COLLECTION
Copyright © 1989 by Zondervan Corporation

Pyranee Books
are published by Zondervan Publishing House
1415 Lake Drive, S.E.
Grand Rapids, MI 49506

Library of Congress Cataloging-in-Publication Data

The Marriage collection : keys to make your marriage better /
  compiled by Fritz Ridenour.
     p. cm.
   "Pyranee books."
   ISBN 0-310-20961-7
   1. Marriage—Religious aspects—Christianity. I. Ridenour,
Fritz.
BV835.M236   1989
248.4—dc20   89–34342
                                                       CIP

Printed in the United States of America.

89 90 91 92 93 94 / AF / 10 9 8 7 6 5 4 3 2 1

1644

CONTENTS

HOW DO WE GROW A GOOD MARRIAGE?

By FRITZ RIDENOUR, Editor/Compiler

It's a fair question for young couples—and older ones, too.

And it's a complex question that can only be answered fully by both partners. The stereotype pictures the wife having concerns about the state of the marriage, while hubby pursues more "manly" interests. The reality, however, is that a marriage grows best in the fertile soil of mutual concern when *both* partners ask:

♥ Are we growing closer, stronger, more secure in our love for each other every day?

♥ Or are we slowly (possibly swiftly) drifting apart—daily becoming weaker in our commitment to one another?

The plight of a marriage that has grown in the wrong direction is vividly pictured in the following poem:

THE WALL

Their wedding picture mocked them from the table,
　these two,
whose minds no longer touched each other.

They lived with such a heavy barricade between them
that neither battering ram of words
nor artilleries of touch could break it down.

Somewhere, between the oldest child's first tooth
and the youngest daughter's graduation,
they lost each other.

Throughout the years each slowly unraveled
that tangled ball of string called self,
and as they tugged at stubborn knots,
each hid his searching from the other.

Sometimes she cried at night
and begged the whispering darkness to tell her
    who she was.

He lay beside her, snoring like a hibernating bear,
unaware of her winter.

Once, after they had made love,
he wanted to tell her how afraid he was of dying,
but, fearing to show his naked soul,
he spoke instead about the beauty of her breasts.

She took a course in modern art,
trying to find herself in colors splashed upon a canvas,
complaining to other women about men who
    are insensitive.

He climbed into a tomb called "The Office,"
wrapped his mind in a shroud of paper figures,
and buried himself in customers.

Slowly, the wall between them rose,
cemented by the mortar of indifference.

One day, reaching out to touch each other,
they found a barrier they could not penetrate,
and recoiling from the coldness of the stone,
each retreated from the stranger on the other side.

For when love dies, it is not in a moment of angry battle,
nor when fiery bodies lose their heat.
It lies panting, exhausted,
expiring at the bottom of a wall it could not scale.[1]

It takes time for a wall like this to separate two people who
have begun their marriage with the same glowing expectations as
all the other couples who have met at the altar on that magic day of
"I do's." What is the secret of preventing such a wall from growing
bit by bit until it seems unscalable and impenetrable? Or is it a
"secret"? Could it be simple truth, applied to married life with hard
work and determination?

Marriage is the most rewarding,
and the most difficult
relationship known to man.[2]

Cecil Osborne

FOUR MARKS OF TRUE LOVE

The marriage that draws two people closer into oneness is God's mystery (Eph. 5:22–33). We try to describe it with words like *commitment, faithfulness, loyalty*—and that many-faceted favorite, *love.* In their latest book, written to newly married couples, Dr. Ed Wheat and co-author Gloria Okes Perkins, describe falling in love as a "powerful emotional event." The two lovers have a sense of wonder and thrill of newness that puts everything in a different light. According to Wheat and Perkins, there are four significant marks of genuine love:

1. *The lovers want to be together—all the time.* As one bride put it: "I used to hate having to say good-bye to him. It had nothing to do with wanting to be with him for sexual reasons. I just wanted to be with him! For me marriage means not having to part at the end of the evening, but being together, whatever we're doing and wherever we happen to be."

2. *They see each other as unique.* For lovers there is *no one* like the one loved. One husband said: "My wife sees a side of me that no one else sees. I feel as though she knows the true me, and her love filters out all the faults that other people might notice."

3. *They want to be committed to one another.* They are willing to give up precious "independence" to gain something far more valuable—belongingness. One man commented: "When I fell in love with her, I knew it meant changing the direction of my life. I had planned on a life of travel . . . alone. I valued fast cars and my airplane. But that was worth nothing compared to the value of knowing her and building our life together."

4. *They want to be married—"for keeps."* The jet setter who formerly valued traveling fast and alone admitted he had a brief passing regret as he put all that behind him, but he said

nonetheless, "I realize that genuine happiness for me meant loving this girl and being loved by her for the rest of my life. And I haven't been sorry!"[3]

GOOD NEWS AND BAD NEWS FOR MARRIAGE

As we moved through the mid-1980s, there was good news and bad news for marriage. On the good news side, some marriage therapists noted a nation-wide trend among baby boomers and yuppies—exchanging "living together" for marriage and having children.[4]

The four marks of "true love" weren't as evident in the 60s and 70s as they began to be in the 80s. Fifteen and twenty years ago, the catch phrases (and Catch 22's) were "living together" and "open marriage." But as the 80s dawned, more and more women discovered that living-together arrangements were really for the convenience of men who didn't want to make commitments. As for open marriage, that option went quietly and almost completely bankrupt because its advocates forgot one basic principle: Marriage is an exclusive, not an inclusive, relationship.[5]

Also on the good news side, marriage not only became fashionable once more, but couples tried much harder to make it work. By 1984, the National Center for Health Statistics released figures that showed the divorce rate on the way *down* for the first time in twenty years. Usually expressed as the number of divorces per 1,000 Americans, the "divorce rate" in 1986 was 4.8 per 1,000, a significant drop from its peak figure of 5.3 in 1981. According to the NCHS, the 4.8 figure for 1986 was the lowest since 1975. It was only the second time in twelve years that the rate had dropped below 5.0.[6]

But at least one researcher of the marriage scene is not "wildly optimistic" about the modest drop in the divorce rate. Francine Klagsbrun, author of *Married People: Staying Together in the Age of Divorce* (Bantam Books, 1985), points to at least two possible reasons for a lower divorce rate: fewer marriages in the mid-1970s; hence, fewer divorces in the 1980s. In addition, she believes that our inflationary economy has also affected divorce, making it "a luxury fewer people can afford."[7]

And while there is a new interest in getting married and sticking together, the divorce rate remains relatively high for certain segments of the population. In a census bureau study published in 1987, researchers Arthur Norton and Jeanne Moorman predicted that up to sixty percent of women from age thirty to thirty-nine will become victims of divorce. One reason for this ominous forecast is that women in their thirties are at the center of the vast social changes that have taken place in the last two decades. Arthur Norton commented: "They (women in their thirties) delayed marriage, they went to college in larger numbers, they invested in their careers. The demands of extreme change have been a burden for these women."[8]

In other words, women in their thirties have been caught in the tug-of-war between career versus homemaking and mother- hood. They are trying to have it all and are winding up saying, "I've had it!"

Statistics also reveal that up to eighty-five percent of those who are divorced remarry within five years, but only forty percent of these remarriages last. Sixty percent fail, usually within five years.[9]

One major reason for the high rate of failure in second marriages is that one (or both partners) hasn't resolved issues from a first marriage. According to The American Academy of Family Mediators, it's not unusual for people in their thirties and forties, who are ten or fifteen years into a marriage, to suddenly call it quits and get a divorce. Then they leap into a second marriage almost immediately, convinced that all the problems in their first one were the fault of the other spouse![10]

As we move toward the final decade of the twentieth century, surveys continue to show that people get married for the same reason they always have: They believe married people are happier than single ones. Ninety-five percent of Americans eventually marry, though today's brides and bridegrooms are a little older and, hopefully, a little wiser. The average bride is now more than twenty-three years old compared with an average age of just under twenty back in the 1960s. The average bridegroom is now twenty- five and a half years old, while back in the 60s he was only twenty- two.[11]

Statisticians and researchers sound a hopeful but cautious note that points toward a continuing drop in divorce rates in the 1990s. Once thought to be a way to creativity, growth, and "expanding yourself emotionally," divorce is now recognized as a major cause of chaos, heartbreak, and financial ruin, especially for women. Many more couples are realizing that it is much better to make up than to break up, but the underlying problem that faces all marriages has resurfaced with new clarity.[12] People still have no problem with falling in love and wanting to get married. *The real challenge is staying in love and growing together.* In other words, how do you make the marriage work?

TEN MYTHS THAT CAN CAUSE FAILURE

In his long career of counseling married couples, Dr. David Mace has organized and taught marriage programs, classes, and seminars around the world. Until the 1960s he and his wife, Vera, emphasized the development of marriage counseling for couples in serious trouble. But with the growing availability of well-trained counselors, the Maces shifted their emphasis to the *prevention* of marital discord and became interested in the marriage enrichment movement. Since their first weekend retreat for couples in 1962, they have worked with many people who want to make their relatively satisfying marriages even better.

In the course of these programs, the Maces began to see tremendous possibilities for cultivating marital growth. This was a radical departure from the popular view that the marriage relationship is static: Couples were expected to get married and "settle down." But the Maces began teaching that marriage is a dynamic relationship that must adapt to individual changes in partners and the cultural environment as well as the successive stages of the life cycle. As Mace says, "Few marriages stand still. Most are either getting better or getting worse."[13]

The Maces also gained insight into the real reason for so many marriage failures: Couples simply don't understand what a challenging task marriage is and how to go about making it work. Even in the latter part of the twentieth century, marriage is still shrouded in myths that have little to do with reality. According to Dr. Mace, the following are ten commonly accepted misconceptions about marriage:

1. *Marriages are made in heaven.* This is the romantic illusion that just because two people are attracted to each other and go through a wedding ceremony, some special dispensation spares them the toil and effort normally necessary for success in most other human undertakings. All couples awaken from this rosy but deceptive dream sooner or later—usually by the end of the first six months.

2. *A wedding is a marriage.* We often use the words *wedding* and *marriage* interchangeably, talking about "getting married" when we should say "getting wedded." A wedding is only the *beginning* of the task of achieving a marriage. In the U.S. today, about two-and-a-half million men and women annually report to a court of law that they have had a wedding but have failed to achieve a marriage, and they now want their agreement canceled.

3. *Married couples must accept what happens to them "for better or for worse."* These words imply that some impersonal fate decides the issue for them. Not at all. Whether their marriage turns out to be better or worse than the average is decided by what the couple themselves make of the resources they bring to the union.

4. *Couples must be "compatible" for a marriage to succeed.* There is some truth in this. But the idea, first started by Plato, that the "right" couples fit each other like pieces of a jigsaw puzzle, is nonsense. Every marriage involves a long process of mutual adaptation, which may take most of a lifetime.

5. *Don't expect behavior changes in your marriage partner.* It

is true that putting pressure on your spouse to change will be ineffective. But couples who *work together* can achieve remarkable changes. It is now known that even very old people can change their behavior if they are effectively motivated and suitably rewarded.

6. *Happily married couples never disagree.* All couples have disagreements. Happy couples are those who have developed the skills necessary to resolve their differences amicably, while couples who avoid and suppress disagreements are not happy.

7. *Couples who stay together must be happily married.* The view that "stable" marriages are necessarily successful is now unacceptable. Many couples who don't divorce might have more and better reasons for doing so than many who do split up.

8. *Don't unload your personal problems on your spouse—keep them to yourself.* If marriage partners can't seek sympathy and support from each other in the ups and downs of life, who can they turn to? A loving, caring relationship involves everything that concerns the couple.

9. *Married couples should never discuss their marital difficulties with other couples.* We call this the "intermarital taboo," and it deprives couples of all kinds of mutual support and help, which they could otherwise be giving each other.

10. *You don't need marriage counseling until you are in really serious trouble.* By that time it may be too late, because alienation has undermined the couple's motivation to work at the relationship. The counselor can do most for those who seek help early.[14]

HOW THE AUTHORS OF THIS BOOK CAN HELP

When it comes to making a marriage work, the questions don't change much. Husbands and wives want to know:

Why isn't marriage more what I expected it to be?
Am I losing him/her?
Why can't he share his feelings?
Where did all the romance go?
Why is she so hard to understand?
Why does he work so much?
How can we grow closer?
Why do I have fantasies about other members of the opposite sex?
Is there a way to disagree without getting angry?
Whatever happened to "Please," "Thank you," and "You look great, honey"?
Must I always do the dirty work around here?
Why do we pay more attention to the children than to each other?

Why doesn't he want to talk?
Shouldn't we do more praying together?
Why don't we make love more often?
Where does the time go? We never have time for each other.

In the following pages, some of today's best counselors and writers on the subject of marriage will tell you how to grow a marriage that is alive, vibrant, fulfilling, and healthy. All contributors are Zondervan authors, including Dr. Ed Wheat, Counselor Gloria Okes Perkins, Dr. David Mace, Counselor Gary Smalley, Dr. Cecil Osborne, The Reverend Tim LaHaye, and Counselor Larry Crabb. I have collected their wisdom, as well as the advice of other Zondervan authors, around the theme of "growing a great marriage."

A quick look at the contents shows that this book does not follow a "passages" or "seasons" approach to marriage. Rather, the concept of growth is centered on the marital bond itself. Every marriage passes through familiar periods, such as courtship, adjustment in the early years, child-rearing, mid-life, the empty nest. At all stages, however, the *relationship* of the partners is the key.

OCCASIONALLY—A GEM OF GREAT PRICE

No matter where you or your partner are in your own relationship, *The Marriage Collection* offers valuable insights, practical ideas, worthwhile observations and—occasionally—a gem of great price. Of course, no two couples will always find the same gem. Because all of us are unique, we have different needs and interests. To paraphrase Tolstoy, "While all happy marriages are happy in the same way, all growing marriages grow in their own way, according to the special needs of each partner."

What can authors like Wheat, Perkins, Smalley, Mace, Osborne, LaHaye, Crabb, and others do to help you grow closer to one another?

On the "cognitive" side, they give insight regarding:

... The importance of oneness and intimacy
... The difference between mature love and self-
centeredness
... The vital need to understand and accept basic differences
between you
(These subjects are dealt with in Parts I, II, and III.)

On the "practical," action-oriented side, these authors can help you:
... Communicate at deeper, more meaningful levels

... Deal with anger and conflict in constructive, creative ways

... Make sexual love that fulfills both partners

... Grow together spiritually

... Improve your "love-showing skills"—not sexual techniques, but the dozens of ways to make your mate feel cherished, secure, respected, and admired.

(These topics are covered in Parts IV to VIII.)

THREE KEYS TO STAYING IN LOVE

One of the chief goals of this book is to help you stay in love with your spouse. As Ed Wheat and Gloria Okes Perkins explain, staying in love involves at least three major areas of effort:

1. Concentrate on building an intimate relationship; nurture each other emotionally. Touch lovingly, share thoughts and feelings, spend focused time together in privacy, so that you can continue to feel most secure and at home in each other's presence.

2. Avoid the negatives that could change the way you see each other. Live in an atmosphere of approval and forgive quickly and generously.

3. Live out your commitment to one another in such a way that strong links of trust are established and maintained. Build your marriage on a solid, biblical base.[15]

HOW DOES YOUR MARRIAGE RATE?

No relationship remains static, especially marriage. The following quiz can help you measure your growth as marriage partners in nine major areas, all of which will be covered in this book.

1. We seek to be one with each other through a lifelong commitment to meet each other's deepest needs.
____ Always   ____ Often   ____ Sometimes   ____ Never

2. We treat each other with unconditional love, seeking to give to each other rather than to receive from each other.
____ Always   ____ Often   ____ Sometimes   ____ Never

3. We constantly seek to understand and accept one another.
____ Always   ____ Often   ____ Sometimes   ____ Never

4. We strive to communicate with each other by sharing our feelings and listening carefully to what the other person is trying to say.
____ Always   ____ Often   ____ Sometimes   ____ Never

5. We deal constructively with anger and conflict, working on the problem rather than on each other.
____ Always   ____ Often   ____ Sometimes   ____ Never

6. Our sex life is fulfilling and enjoyable.
____ Always ____ Often ____ Sometimes ____ Never

7. We both know Jesus Christ as Savior and seek to grow spiritually by praying and reading Scripture together.
____ Always ____ Often ____ Sometimes ____ Never

8. We work at showing love for each other in many simple, practical ways.
____ Always ____ Often ____ Sometimes ____ Never

A common problem with a quiz like the one above is that one partner may be able to answer "Always" or "Often" to many of the questions, while the other partner may not. If you feel that you are alone in your struggle to keep your marriage going and growing, don't give up. The authors contributing to this book have a great deal to say to the spouse who is trying to save his or her marriage.

Granted, however, this book will be most effective for the couple who can read it, discuss it, and use its ideas together. It takes two to grow a good marriage, but it only takes one uncooperative, wayward, or disinterested spouse to ruin a marriage or to stunt its growth. (If you suspect you need professional help beyond the scope of this book, read the following "How to Locate a Qualified Marriage Counselor.")

HOW TO LOCATE A QUALIFIED MARRIAGE COUNSELOR

1. A couple in need of a marriage counselor should go first to their own pastor. If the pastor is a qualified marriage counselor, he will give thorough and understanding counsel. If not, he will be the first to say so and will know how to help locate such a service. His advice will be dependable.

2. If for any reason a couple feels they cannot go to their pastor, write the American Association of Marriage and Family Therapy and ask for the name and location of one or more marriage counselors in your geographical area. That address is:

American Association of Marriage and Family Therapy
924 West 9th Street
Upland, California 91786

3. If a couple cannot locate a member of the American Association of Marriage and Family Therapy in their area, then contact a local family social service agency. In larger cities there are private family agencies, sometimes called Children's Bureaus, that offer professional help in marriage counseling. Most social workers are not professional marriage counselors. Yet, most all family social service agencies will have a qualified marriage counselor on staff.

If there is no private family service agency in the area, the couple could ask for help at the local County or City Social Welfare Office or mental health clinics.[16]

AND HOW DOES YOUR MARRIAGE GROW?

Like a plant that needs food, water, and sunlight in order to thrive, a marriage grows best when the partners have practical relating skills, understanding and insight, plus spiritual faith and discernment. The following eight sections of this book provide help in all three areas. Husbands, for example, will learn:

... How to attract your wife instead of driving her away
... Why intimacy involves much more than physical love-making
... Why affection is so important to your wife (and how it leads to better sex)
... Why your wife needs comfort, not lectures
... Why your wife has such different needs from yours—and how to meet those needs
... How to deal with disagreements and process anger rather than attack one another
... What no woman can resist
... Why you may need a refresher course on sexual techniques
... What wives admire most in husbands
... How to develop soul communication—the spiritual side of your marriage
... How to get your wife to stop neglecting you
... A sure-fire method for avoiding arguments
... How to have a perfect wife
... How to be her best friend

Many of the benefits for men listed above apply equally to wives, but, in addition, this book will be especially helpful to women regarding:

... Why men act the way they do
... Why your husband needs your encouragement and admiration
... How to help your husband become more sensitive
... How to get your husband to really listen to you
... How to send him "I" messages to communicate how you feel without attacking him
... How to help your husband decide to change
... How to gain his undivided attention
... How to actively listen to him and get him to actively listen to you

... How to get him to help with the children and the household responsibilities
... How to have a more satisfying sex life—for both of you
... How to teach him to be affectionate, not just passionate
... How to get him to spend more time with you
... How to be his best friend

THERE ARE NO INSTANT SOLUTIONS

While all of the above is a tall order, the answers are here, waiting to be discovered one at a time. In many marriages, some problems seem complex, others overwhelming. Oddly enough, most of the answers are simple, but not simplistic. There are literally dozens of ways to revive a dying marriage, strengthen a struggling marriage, enliven a dull marriage, or make a growing marriage even healthier and more fulfilling.

Dr. Ed Wheat speaks for all contributors to this book when he says:

> As a Christian marriage counselor who accepts the Bible as the final authority, I do not offer my patients mere sympathy or set forth pet ideas that may or may not work. The principles I offer are solid biblical principles that will always work when applied properly to individual problems. I have found God's Word, the Bible, to be eternally true and totally dependable. . . . Because neither God nor man has essentially changed since the dawn of time, the principles of living spelled out in the Bible are completely relevant to marriage today.[17]

How does a good marriage grow? Slowly, as a rule, like a giant redwood that takes decades to reach its towering potential.

Looking back over his career and fifty-two years of marriage, Dr. David Mace observes, "One of the ironies of the decade is that young people talk about intimacy and relating skills, and yet their marriages are flying apart at an alarming rate. Older people never thought in those terms, and their marriages lasted a lifetime."

Mace says today's typical young couple comes for counseling, but doesn't want to hear anything like, "Be patient. With time, the problems will work themselves out." They want instant solutions. "But the fact is," says Mace, "recent studies have proven that after a number of years together, couples learn to appreciate each other in ways they never ever could before."[18]

And how does a marriage die? Some marriages wither in the shade of their own boredom, while others starve in the thin arid topsoil of self-centeredness as each partner smolders with anger or wallows in self-pity. Other marriages are trampled by the hobnailed boots of adultery. But no marriage is terminal, unless the partners will it so. Marriage is amazingly resilient, if given any care at all.

In *A Healing Season*, Karen Kuhne shares a poem written by her husband, Gary, as they struggled through a long period of healing following her extramarital affair.

YOUR FRIENDSHIP

I reached you,
when I realized the depth of need
within my heart.

I touched you,
when barriers crumbled
and pain permitted
befriending of "self."

I love you,
at last understanding
the joy of knowing
and being known.

I like you,
sensing anew the wonder
of walking together
united in heart.[19]

Reaching, touching, loving, liking—you need all four to nourish your marriage so that it will grow stronger, straighter, and truer through the years. The following pages are a veritable feast of insights, ideas, and encouraging guidance. *Bon appetit!*

Marriage becomes a great adventure, a continuous discovery both of oneself and of one's mate. It becomes a daily broadening of one's horizon, an opportunity of learning something new about life, about human existence, about God.[20]

Paul Tournier

PART I

INTIMACY:
IT TAKES TWO TO HAVE ONENESS

For a great number of the two million Americans who marry each year, marriage means, "Why not give it a try? If it doesn't work, there is always divorce."

Some people joke about their first marriage, calling it a trial run in preparation for the "real thing," which is supposed to happen on the second or, possibly, the third try. Perhaps the only other experience for which many couples are less prepared is parenthood. Unfortunately, couples marry with no idea of what is involved in being a husband, wife, or parent, except "being in love."

When Adam got married, he had no formal preparation, but he did possess a God-given understanding of the basic idea:

"This is it!" Adam exclaimed. "She is part of my own bone and flesh! Her name is 'woman' because she was taken out of a man." This explains why a man leaves his father and mother and is joined to his wife in such a way that the two become one person (Gen. 2:23–24 LB).

In these verses is a scriptural provision for one of the most basic needs in a marriage—intimacy. Couples divorce for various reasons—incompatibility, adultery, no communication—but what they really lack is intimacy, oneness that *binds* them together with the super glue of commitment.

Lawrence J. Crabb, Jr., clinical psychologist and author of several excellent books on counseling from a biblical and Christian perspective, continually observes the destructive patterns that prevent real intimacy in marriages. As Crabb speaks to Christian groups across the country, he sees husbands and wives sharing hymnals and singing praises to God, but suspects that "very few are experiencing substantial intimacy."[1]

He wonders why marriages are "so often filled with tension, bitterness, distance, shallow satisfactions, routineness, and short-lived moments of romance? Why do I sometimes face a problem within my own marriage and, after earnest prayer and brutal self-examination, remain unsure how to respond to my wife in a way that will deepen our oneness?"[2]

Crabb believes that the lack of intimacy in many homes can be traced to several dangerous trends in our thinking about Christian marriage. In his extensive counseling of married couples, he has discovered four incorrect ideas that are influencing husbands and wives:

1. A misreading of the Bible that reduces complicated issues to a few easily solved problems
2. An increasing emphasis on becoming happy and fulfilled
3. A trend toward focusing on psychological needs in marriage
4. A fragmented approach to understanding the family[3]

These errors aptly picture today's cultural traps. We are bombarded twenty-four hours a day with pitches, arguments, and appeals, all designed to help us take "the easy way out," or find the "quick fix" to a problem. But there is no quick and easy way to achieve intimacy between a man and a woman. Couples may marry, believing that moonlight and roses will make them one, but they soon discover that they face a challenge that will take a lifetime of daily effort and understanding.

There are no slogans or Bible memory verses to quote that result in "instant intimacy." Indeed, the words of Scripture all too clearly reveal the thoughts and intents of the heart that has not yet learned the hard lessons of humility and unselfishness, which are part of what intimacy is all about.

As Crabb observes, there is too much emphasis on meeting psychological needs and personal fulfillment and not enough on obeying the biblical blueprint for marriage. Instead of the ultimate authority for marriage, the Bible is considered by many as an optional guidebook. Even in Christian circles, the premise for marriage rests on a humanistic foundation with two false doctrines: (1) the needs of people are of supreme importance; (2) biblical truth can be useful in meeting those needs.

Crabb writes, "The error is subtle, but serious. In this line of thought, needy people march onto center stage, the spotlight bathes them in absorbing attention, and the God of the Bible remains in the wings, calling out directions as they search for fulfillment."[4]

But in a biblical approach to marriage, it is Jesus Christ who stands in the spotlight, beckoning us to find fulfillment in him alone.

According to one survey of marriage counselors, one of the great desires of most wives is that they feel true intimacy with their husbands.[5] Many wives only know their marriage lacks those feelings of closeness that they long for. In the following chapters, you will discover the biblical meaning of intimacy and oneness, and how to achieve it in your own marriage:

In chapter 1, Dr. Ed Wheat and Gloria Okes Perkins (*Love Life for Every Married Couple*) compare the scriptural view of a truly intimate marriage with the pseudo-truths or outright falsehoods that are offered through television, films, magazines, and the opinions of misinformed parents or friends.

In chapters 2 and 3, Dr. Lawrence Crabb (*The Marriage Builder*) shares the secret of finding true intimacy: by meeting your personal needs for security and significance, not through your spouse, but through the Lord himself, and then committing yourself to ministering to the needs of your spouse without depending on a positive response in return.

In chapter 4, Anne Kristin Carroll (*Together Forever*) shares the poignant account of the bittersweet years of her second marriage, recreated, after divorce, on an entirely new foundation of biblical values. Far from a simplistic example of how "we got right with God, prayed, and everything came together magically," this is the story of a woman who searched for oneness with two different husbands, only to find intimacy at its very source—in the reality of Jesus Christ.

In chapter 5, Shirley Cook talks about what you can do when your "I do's" seem to be coming undone.

Dr. Ed Wheat has observed that there are basically two views of the meaning of marriage. The human perspective says, "I'll try as long as I see it's working for me." The divine perspective says, "I'll do it, till death do us part, and always give my very best to my partner."

Only in the divine perspective can you and your mate find true intimacy.

Marriage involves nothing more than a lifelong commitment to love just one person—to do, whatever else one does, a good thorough job of loving one person. What could be simpler than that?[6]

Mike Mason

Chapter 1

YOUR MARRIAGE: TRUE OR FALSE?

BY DR. ED WHEAT AND GLORIA OKES PERKINS
Love Life for Every Married Couple

When Dr. Ed Wheat became a Christian, he began his study of the Bible systematically; as a mathematics major in college, he had learned that unless you start with the right premise, it is impossible to solve any problem correctly. In his search for foundational principles, Dr. Wheat spent more time in the first three chapters of Genesis than in any other part of Scripture because "these chapters form the foundation for everything else."

It was here—in Genesis 1–3—that he discovered the essence of God's truth concerning man and woman, their relationships to their Creator and to each other. It was here that he began to understand himself, as well as his wife, and to find God's perfect design for marriage. He says, "Like a mathematician, I plunged into the painstaking study of these seed chapters, knowing that I had to build my marriage and life on the right premises in order to come out right in the end. The outcome has been more wonderful than I expected—a beautiful marriage, a godly home, and a life ministry with the opportunity to show many other couples how to find happiness together by following God's original plan."[7]

An earnest search of scriptural truth may mean unlearning concepts picked up elsewhere. What are the underlying attitudes that have shaped your thinking about marriage? Are they really biblical, or are they a mixture of pseudo-truths and outright error that you've absorbed from our culture? Which of these premises are correct and which are false and ultimately unworkable, or even harmful to your marriage? Dr. Wheat opens this chapter with the story of Dean and Carol, active Christians in a large evangelical church, whose marriage appeared to be sound but had to be rebuilt from the ground up when disaster struck.

SHORING UP A SHAKY MARRIAGE THROUGH GOD'S WORD

Carol regarded her husband as "a wonderful, gentle man" and a good father to their teen-age sons. Their life together was "comfortable." If the thrill seemed to be gone from their relationship, Carol attributed that to twenty years of marriage and their age—a bit past forty.

Then her world was shaken on its foundations when Dean admitted his involvement in an affair with a young woman who worked with him in the church's music ministry. Dean said the affair had ended, but a close Christian friend counseled Carol to divorce him without delay because, as she warned, "Adultery kills a marriage. And it's not right to let yourself be used as a doormat."

While Carol, feeling bewildered and betrayed, withdrew from Dean, the young woman kept on actively pursuing him. Dean had met with the deacons to confess his wrongdoing, but now he became reluctant to attend church with his wife and sons. The church leaders regarded this as proof of Dean's insincerity, and they predicted to Carol that the marriage could not be saved because "Dean is just not right with God."

Dean, deeply depressed, began considering a job transfer to another part of the country for a period of ten months or more. He explained to Carol, "The separation will help us to know if we really love each other, or not." Carol's confidante reacted with angry advice, saying, "Just pack his bags and leave them on the front steps. The sooner he goes, the better!"

When Carol told me her story, I was impressed by the fact that all the people involved in this painful situation claimed to be believers in Jesus Christ and recognized his Word as truth: the wife, the husband, the other woman, the counseling friend, and the church leaders. Yet each of these, in his or her own way, had displayed a lack of knowledge of the biblical principles that could preserve and heal this marriage. So many important biblical principles concerning marriage, love, forgiveness, and restoration were violated or ignored that it is no wonder that Dean and Carol both felt "frozen" into the tragic event and were unable to move on beyond it.

Unfortunately, this is a typical story. I have heard it many times with minor variations on the basic theme. I share it with you because so much can be learned from it.

As I worked with Carol, she began taking a long look at her

own thinking and behavior patterns. How valid were her actions and reactions during the crisis and what had prompted them? Were her decisions being shaped by faulty human advice or by the eternal counsels of God? What basic assumptions were guiding her thinking? Were these premises true or false?

Then something very interesting happened to Carol. When she turned to the Word of God, determined to follow his counsel wherever it led, and to leave the results with him, the unbiblical advice she had received faded out of her thinking, and she began to see clearly the false and the true. She found that there was total disagreement between the Bible and the world's system of thinking on marriage and divorce, and that she had almost been tricked by Satan, the master hypocrite, into believing his lies concerning her marriage. She discovered that Satan can work through even the most well-meaning Christian who takes the human viewpoint on marriage instead of God's clear scriptural teaching. She also learned that when men and women react according to their natural inclinations, they will usually make the wrong decision.

As she described it, both she and Dean had fallen into a pit of muddled thinking, mixed-up feelings, and wrong reactions. Only the truth could set them free. Together they began the relearning process, and they started with Genesis 1–3.

Every married couple needs to know the real truth concerning marriage, but it will never be found in the teachings or examples of the present world system. The best this world can offer is a low-cost, no-fault divorce obtained through the local department store—a new convenience for thousands of people blundering in and out of marriage as though it were a revolving door. It took the words of one social critic to put the situation into clear, hard perspective. He said, "In the 1970s, divorce became the *natural outcome* of marriage!"

If divorce is now accepted, even expected, as the natural result of marriage, this is a chilling heritage for the 80s and 90s. But we certainly do not have to adopt it in our thinking. Bible-believing Christians in every culture, in every age, have found the wisdom and strength to move upstream against the current of prevailing lifestyles. Note that the scriptural wisdom comes first: then the strength to go against popular opinion, no matter how powerful.

Let me take you on the scriptural tour that Dean and Carol took in their search for foundational truth on which to build their marriage. We'll begin at the beginning with the creation of male and female. Our purpose: to understand marriage as God ordained it in contrast to the opinions of the world around us. We need to look at these verses in Genesis as though we have never seen them before; we will look at them not as clichés but as truth for our individual lives.

The idea of male and female was God's idea.

"So God created man in his own image, in the image of God created he him; male and female created he them" (Gen. 1:27).

Genesis 1 declares the fact of man's creation while Genesis 2 reveals the process by which this occurred. Here in the first chapter we find the fundamental truth that is so essential to the appreciation of marriage—that God made male and female for his own good purposes. It seems too obvious to mention, but perhaps it should be pointed out that the creation of two kinds of people— men and women—was not a dark conspiracy to thwart the ambitions of the women's liberation movement. It was scarcely a put-down for women. Indeed, it became a testimonial, for creation was incomplete without woman. In a loving, amazing, creative act, the almighty God conceived the wonderful mysteries of male and female, masculinity and femininity, to bring joy into our lives. Think how colorless, how one-dimensional a world would be in which there was only your sex! Who would want to live in an all-male world or an all-female world? Or, for that matter, in a unisex world where all signs of gender were ignored or suppressed? The person who refuses to see and rejoice in the fundamental differences between male and female will never taste the divine goodness God planned for marriage.

Marriage was designed to solve loneliness.

> And the Lord God said, It is not good that the man should be alone; I will make him an help meet for him. And out of the ground the Lord God formed every beast of the field, and every fowl of the air; and brought them unto Adam to see what he would call them: and whatsoever Adam called every living creature, that was the name thereof. And Adam gave names to all cattle, and to the fowl of the air, and to every beast of the field; but for Adam there was not found an help meet for him. And the Lord God caused a deep sleep to fall upon Adam, and he slept; and he took one of his ribs, and closed up the flesh instead thereof; and the rib, which the Lord God had taken from man, made he a woman, and brought her unto the man (Gen. 2:18–22).

Picture this one man in a perfect environment, but alone. He had the fellowship of God and the company of birds and animals. He had an interesting job, for he was given the task of observing, categorizing, and naming all living creatures. But he was alone. God observed that this was "not good." So a wise and loving Creator provided a perfect solution. He made another creature, like the man and yet wondrously unlike him. She was taken from him, but she complemented him. She was totally suitable for him—spiritually, intellectually, emotionally, and physically. According to God, she was designed to be his "helper." This term *helper* refers to a beneficial relationship where one person aids or supports another person as a friend and ally. Perhaps you have thought of a helper as a subordinate, a kind of glorified servant. You will see the woman's calling in a new light when you realize that the same Hebrew word for *help* is used of God himself in Psalm 46:1 where he is called our *helper*, "a very present help in trouble."

Marriage always begins with a need that has been there from the dawn of time, a need for companionship and completion that God understands. Marriage was designed to relieve the fundamental loneliness that every human experiences. In your own case, to the degree to which your mate does not meet your needs— spiritually, intellectually, emotionally, and physically—and to the degree to which you do not meet your mate's needs, the two of you are still alone. But this is not according to the plan of God and it can be remedied. His plan is *completeness* for the two of you together.

Marriage was planned to bring happiness.

"And Adam said, This is now bone of my bones, and flesh of my flesh; she shall be called Woman, because she was taken out of Man" (Gen. 2:23).

Here is the world's first love song! Hebrew experts tell us that Adam was expressing a tremendous excitement, a joyous astonishment. "At *last*, I have someone corresponding to me!" His phrase, "bone of my bones, and flesh of my flesh," became a favorite Old Testament saying to describe an intimate, personal relationship. But the fullness of its meaning belongs to Adam and his bride. Dr. Charles Ryrie makes the interesting suggestion that the Hebrew word for woman, *ishshah*, may come from a root word meaning "to be soft"—an expression, perhaps, of the delightful and novel femininity of woman.

So, when the Lord brought the woman to Adam, the man expressed his feelings in words like these: "I have finally found the one who can complete me, who takes away my loneliness, who will be as dear to me as my own flesh. She is so beautiful! She is perfectly suited to me. She is all I will ever need!"

Can you imagine the emotion that must have flamed within both the man and the woman as they realized what they could mean to each other? Can you grasp the purpose with which God created woman for man? All the tired jokes to the contrary, marriage was designed for our joy, our happiness. And God's purpose has never changed.

Marriage must begin with a leaving of all others.

"Therefore shall a man leave his father and his mother, and shall cleave unto his wife: and they shall be one flesh" (Gen. 2:24).

God gave this three-part commandment at the beginning as

he ordained the institution of marriage. It remains the most concise and comprehensive counseling session ever presented on marriage. If you will notice, the words are mostly one-syllable words in the English—plain words, easily understood, in spite of their infinite depth of meaning. These twenty-two words sum up the entire teaching of Scripture on marriage. All else that is said emphasizes or amplifies the three fundamental principles originated here, but never changes them in the slightest. They deserve your careful consideration, for any real problem you face in marriage will come from ignoring some aspect of God's Genesis commandment.

We must understand, first of all, that marriage begins with a *leaving:* leaving all other relationships. The closest relationship outside of marriage is specified here, implying that if it is necessary to leave your father and mother, then certainly all lesser ties must be broken, changed, or left behind.

Of course the bonds of love with parents are lasting ones. But these ties must be changed in character so that the man's full commitment is now to his wife. And the wife's full commitment is now to her husband. The Lord gave the man this commandment, although the principle applies to both husband and wife, because it is up to the man to establish a new household that he will be responsible for. He can no longer be dependent on his father and mother; he can no longer be under their authority, for now he assumes headship of his own family.

Scripture makes it clear that the adult must continue to honor his parents and, now that he is independent, he needs to care for them when necessary and to assume responsibility *for* them rather than responsibility *to* them. (See Matthew 15:3–9 and 1 Timothy 5:4–8.) But a leaving must occur, for neither parents nor any other relationship should come between husband and wife.

This means that you and your mate need to refocus your lives on each other, rather than looking to another individual or group of people to meet your emotional needs. This also means giving other things a lesser priority—your business, your career, your house, your hobbies, your talents, your interests, or even your church work. All must be put into proper perspective. Whatever is important to you in this life should be less important than your marriage.

The wife of a successful businessman who has poured all his energies into his business shed some bitter tears in my office, saying, "He keeps giving me *monetary rewards,* and every time he does it, I think how much better it would be to have his time and love. Dr. Wheat, I don't want all those *things.* I just want him to pay some attention to me."

In more than twenty-five years of counseling I have observed that when a man consistently puts his business or career ahead of his wife, nothing he can buy with money will really please her.

There are many different ways of failing to leave something and thus failing to build a real marriage. I have seen women so involved with their jobs or advanced education that they became more like roommates than wives, and other women whose preoccupation with meticulous housekeeping marred what could have been good marriages. I have known men who could not leave the ties with their hunting or golfing buddies long enough to establish love relationships with their wives. Some cannot even tear themselves away from televised sports long enough to communicate with their wives. I have observed situations where either husband or wife became excessively involved in church work to the serious detriment of their marriage. And I have known sad cases where the mother or sometimes the father gave the children top priority. When those children grew up, nothing was left. The marriage was emotionally bankrupt.

The first principle we can learn from Genesis 2:24 is that marriage means leaving. Unless you are willing to leave all else, you will never develop the thrilling oneness of relationship that God intended for every married couple to enjoy.

Marriage requires joining for life.

"Therefore shall a man leave his father and his mother, *and shall cleave unto his wife:* and they shall be one flesh" (Gen. 2:24).

The next principle to be learned from this ordinance is that it is no use leaving unless you are ready to spend a lifetime *cleaving.* Again, notice that the Lord directs this to the husband especially, although the principle applies to both partners.

What does it mean to cleave? The word sometimes causes confusion because in the English it has two opposite definitions and the most common of these is "to divide, to split, to open." Thus, butchers use a cleaver to cut meat into various pieces. Splitting and dividing is precisely *not* what is meant here, so picture the reverse. *Cleave* (derived from the Anglo-Saxon and German) also means: "to adhere, to stick, to be attached by some strong tie." This verb suggests determined action in its essential meaning, so there is nothing passive about the act of cleaving. For example, the word *climb* is said to be closely akin to *cleave.*

The same feeling of action accompanies the Hebrew word *dabaq* which the King James Bible translates as "cleave." Here are some definitions of *dabaq:* "To cling to or adhere to, abide fast, cleave fast together, follow close and hard after, be joined together, keep fast, overtake, pursue hard, stick to, take, catch by pursuit." Modern Bible translators usually change "cleave" to "cling to" or "hold fast to." When we come to the Greek New Testament, the word means to cement together—to stick like glue—or to be welded together so that the two cannot be separated without damage to both.

From this, it is obvious that God has a powerful message for both marriage partners and a dynamic course of action laid out for the husband in particular. The husband is primarily responsible to do everything possible and to be all he should be in order to form ties with his wife that will make them inseparable. And the wife must respond to her husband in the same manner. These ties are not like the pretty silken ribbons attached to wedding presents. Instead, they must be forged like steel in the heat of daily life and the pressures of crisis in order to form a union that cannot be severed.

The best way to comprehend the force of meaning in the word *cleave* is to consider how the Holy Spirit has used the word *dabaq* in the Book of Deuteronomy. These four prime examples all speak of cleaving to the living God.

"You shall fear the Lord your God; you shall serve him and *cling to him*, and you shall swear by his name" (Deut. 10:20 NASB).

"To love the Lord your God, to walk in all his ways and *hold fast to him*" (Deut. 11:22 NASB).

"You shall follow the Lord your God and fear him; and you shall keep his commandments, listen to his voice, serve him, and *cling to him*" (Deut. 13:4 NASB).

"By loving the Lord your God, by obeying his voice, and by *holding fast to him;* for this is your life" (Deut. 30:20 NASB).

This indicates that in the eyes of God cleaving means wholehearted commitment, first of all spiritual, but spilling over into every area of our being, so that the cleaving is also intellectual, emotional, and physical. It means that you will have unceasing opportunity to cleave to your partner even in the smallest details of life. In fact, anything that draws the two of you together and cements your relationship more firmly will be a part of cleaving. Anything that puts distance between you—mentally or physically—should be avoided because it breaks the divine pattern for marriage.

Much of the practical counsel in this book will show you how to cleave to your partner under varying circumstances and in many different ways. However it is expressed, cleaving always involves two characteristics: (1) an unswerving loyalty; (2) an active, pursuing love that will not let go.

If you want to test an action, attitude, word, or decision against the biblical standards of cleaving, ask yourself these questions. Will this draw us closer or drive us apart? Will it build our relationship or tear it down? Will it bring about a positive response or a negative response? Does it express my love and loyalty to my partner or does it reveal my self-centered individualism?

Remember that God's plan for you and your partner is an inseparable union that you bring about as you obey his commandment to cleave to each other.

Marriage means oneness in the fullest possible sense.

"Therefore shall a man leave his father and his mother, and shall cleave unto his wife: *and they shall be one flesh*. And they were both naked, the man and his wife, and were not ashamed" (Gen. 2:24–25).

We see now that the pattern for marriage that God established at Creation will produce something quite remarkable if it is followed. Two will actually become one. This is more than togetherness! No writer, teacher, or theologian has ever yet explained all that it means for two people to become "one flesh." We only know that it happens!

Several elementary requirements should be noted. For this to take place, the marriage must be *monogamous* (for two people only). At the same time all adultery and promiscuity are ruled out, for, as the Lord Jesus emphasizes in the New Testament, *the two* become one. The Bible graphically portrays the miserable long-term effects of polygamous marriage and the deadly results of adultery. Proverbs 6:32, for instance, says: "The one who commits adultery with a woman is lacking sense; he who would destroy himself does it" (NASB). Certainly none can plead ignorance as an excuse! The marriage must also be *heterosexual*. God made one *woman* for one *man*. The homosexual "marriage" being promoted in some quarters today is a pathetic, squalid distortion of the Creator's plan for holy union between one man and one woman.

Although it goes far deeper than the physical, becoming one flesh involves intimate physical union in sexual intercourse. And this without shame between marriage partners. Shame in marital sex was never imparted by God! Instead, the biblical expression for sexual intercourse between husband and wife is *to know*, an expression of profound dignity. "Adam *knew* Eve his wife; and she conceived" (Gen. 4:1). "Then Joseph . . . took unto him his wife: and *knew* her not until he had brought forth her firstborn son" (Matt. 1:24–25).

This word *know* is the same word used of God's loving, personal knowledge of Abraham in Genesis 18:19: "For I *know* him, that he will command his children and his household after him, and they shall keep the way of the Lord, to do justice and judgment."

Thus, in the divine pattern of marriage, sexual intercourse between husband and wife includes both intimate physical knowledge and a tender, intimate, personal knowledge. So the leaving, cleaving, and knowing each other results in a new identity in which two individuals merge into one—one in mind, heart, body and spirit. This is why divorce has such a devastating effect. Not two people are left, but two fractions of one.

In the New Testament, the Holy Spirit uses the Genesis mystery of becoming one flesh with its dimension of sexual intercourse to picture an even deeper mystery: that of the relationship between Jesus Christ and his bride, the church. "For this cause shall a man leave his father and mother, and shall be joined unto his wife, and they two shall be one flesh. This is a great mystery: but I speak concerning Christ and the church" (Eph. 5:31–32).

Here is the marriage design as ordained by God at the very beginning—a love relationship so deep, tender, pure, and intimate that it is patterned after that of Christ for his church. This is the foundation for the love life you can experience in your own marriage, a foundation on which you can safely build.

♥ TAKE THE CLEAVING TEST ♥

Talk together about what this chapter says to each of you regarding basic truths for marriage in Genesis 1–3. What insights have each of you gained? In particular, what does the word *cleave* mean to each of you? Review Dr. Wheat's tests for any action, attitude, word, or decision that affects cleaving to one another:

- ♥ Will this draw us closer or drive us apart?
- ♥ Will it build our relationship or tear it down?
- ♥ Will it bring about a positive response or a negative response?
- ♥ Does it express my love and loyalty to my partner, or does it reveal my self-centered individualism?

Understanding the foundations of marital oneness is the first step, but others must follow. Just what is oneness as experienced by a man and a woman? Many couples can describe "lack of oneness" better than they can the warm feelings of intimacy they can only long for. In the next two chapters Dr. Lawrence Crabb describes a strategy for building oneness and intimacy.

Chapter 2

WHY IS INTIMACY SO SCARCE?

BY DR. LAWRENCE CRABB, JR.
The Marriage Builder

In doing research for her book, *Married People: Staying Together in the Age of Divorce*, Francine Klagsbrun conducted an intensive interview of eighty-seven couples who had been married fifteen years or longer. According to Klagsbrun, the "secrets" of these lasting marriages fall into several categories that include:

- ♥ Enjoying one another
- ♥ Being able to choose to change
- ♥ Accepting one another, warts and all
- ♥ Assuming that marriage is for life
- ♥ Trusting each other
- ♥ Sharing and cherishing the "history" they have written together—their private stories, jokes, code words, and rituals[8]

All of these "secrets" could be described as aspects of intimacy or oneness. There is much more to intimacy than is listed here, but this is a good start toward beginning to define what Larry Crabb calls "the illusive goal of marriage." In the following chapter, he describes oneness—what it is and why it is so important. As you read, think about these questions:

- ♥ Why is intimacy so important to any marriage?
- ♥ Why is intimacy so illusive to so many married couples?
- ♥ How much intimacy do we enjoy in our marriage? How can we cultivate more?

ONENESS: WHY IT IS IMPORTANT

Several months ago I was working on a rough draft of a book during a flight to New York City. A flight attendant noticed the words "The Goal of Marriage" written at the top of a yellow pad of paper resting on the tray table in front of me. She asked what I was writing. When I told her I was starting a book on marriage, she said, "Well, I'm glad, because I really believe in marriage. After six years of living with a man, I decided that I wanted to be married. Since the fellow I was living with liked our no-strings-attached arrangement, I found somebody else who was willing to tie the knot, and we got married two months ago. So far it's great!"

I asked her why she preferred a marriage commitment to merely living together. She thought for a few seconds, then said, "I think it's the commitment part I wanted. I married a man who seems to be really committed to loving me and working on a relationship. I never felt secure enough to really open up and try to get close with a man who wouldn't make any promises."

This incident prompts two questions: (1) What was this woman's purpose in exchanging her live-in boyfriend for a husband? (2) How was she hoping to reach her objective?

Consider a second example.

A husband in his early thirties complained to me that his wife was a disappointment to him. She was pretty and personable, a good cook, and a devoted mother to their two small children. But these qualities were offset by her constant criticizing, her impatient corrections and rebukes, and her negative attitude. Nothing he did seemed to satisfy her and, he added with a touch of noble frustration, he was the sort of husband many women would be delighted to have.

This man's wife had been staring dejectedly at the floor the whole time he was speaking. When he stopped talking, she spoke without raising her head. "What he says is true. I'm an awful nag, and I do complain a lot. I just feel so unloved by Jimmy."

When she raised her head, there was anger in her eyes.

"Sometimes he explodes at me, calling me awful names. He'll never pray with me. Sure, he smiles at me a lot, and he thinks that makes him a great husband, but I know he doesn't really accept me. His smiles always turn into pushy demands for sex; and when I won't give in to him, he throws a fit."

Reflect on this couple and ask the same two questions: (1) What was each partner longing for from the other? (2) What were their strategies for gaining their desires?

Think about one more illustration.

A middle-aged couple—Christians, attractive, talented, financially comfortable, faithful, active church members—admitted that their marriage was in trouble.

"I feel like such a hypocrite," the wife stated. "If you asked the people in our church to list the ten most happily married couples they know, our names would probably appear on every list. We're sociable, we entertain church people frequently in our beautiful home, we sing in the choir together. We really play the role—but our relationship is miserable.

"We get along—but from a distance. I can never tell him how I really feel about anything. He always gets mad and jumps at me, or he clams up for a couple days. I don't think we've ever had a really close relationship."

Her husband responded, "I don't think it's all that bad. We've got a lot going for us: the kids are doing fine, my wife teaches Sunday school, the Lord is blessing my business. That's better than a lot of—"

I interrupted. "How much do you really share yourself—your feelings, hopes, and dreams—with your wife?"

"Well," he replied, "whenever I try she usually doesn't seem all that interested, so I just don't bother."

"I'd listen if you'd really share with me!" his wife blurted. "But your idea of sharing is to lecture me on how things should be. Whenever I try to tell you how I feel, you always say something like 'I don't know why you feel like that.' I think our communication is awful."

Once more, consider the same two questions: (1) What do these emotionally divorced partners want from their marriage but have so far been unable to develop? (2) How are they trying to achieve what they both so deeply desire?

THE NEED FOR INTIMACY

Let's deal with the first question: *What was each of these people seeking?*

It is apparent that the flight attendant married in the hope that a relationship of mutual commitment would provide the intimacy she lacked with her live-in boyfriend.

The frustrated husband wanted to feel a sense of oneness with his wife but believed her critical and rejecting spirit was getting in the way. He felt angry with her, much as I would feel toward someone who, after I had gone without food for several days, blocked my path to a table spread with good things to eat. His wife felt unable to give herself warmly to a man who seemed to use rather than accept her. She desperately wanted to be close to her husband, but felt a sense of dread at the prospect of moving toward a man who perhaps didn't really love her.

The couple whose marriage was a well-decorated but empty package felt completely blocked from touching one another emotionally. The absence of real intimacy left a void for them—

which she freely and bitterly acknowledged, but which he ignored by focusing on the external trappings of family success.

The newlywed flight attendant, the explosive husband and his critical wife, and the couple who could not communicate were all pursuing the same elusive goal: *a deep experience of personal intimacy through relationship with a person of the opposite sex.*

Nothing reaches so deeply into the human personality as relationship. The fabric of biblical truth is woven from Genesis to Revelation with the thread of relationship:

- *Perfect relationships* within the Trinity
- *Broken relationships* between God and man, Adam and Eve, and Cain and Abel
- *Loving relationships* between Aquila and Priscilla, Ruth and Naomi, and Jesus and John
- *Oppositional relationships* between Jezebel and Elijah, and Jesus and the Pharisees
- *Strained relationships* between Abraham and Lot, and Paul and John Mark

The kinds of emotions that develop within relationships are also vividly portrayed in Scripture:

- *Agony over lost relationships*—David weeping for Absalom; Jesus crying out, "My God, why have you forsaken me?"
- *Bitter remorse from grieving a loved one*—Peter after the cock crowed the third time
- *The joy of reunion*—Jacob meeting Joseph in Egypt; Jairus's daughter restored to her father
- *The relaxed enjoyment of a comfortable relationship*—Christ at the home of Mary and Martha

The list is endless. Clearly, the biblical story presents the drama of relationship in all its fullness.

Why is the theme of relationship so prominent in the Word of God? Because only within the context of relationship can the deepest needs of human personality be met.

People everywhere long for intimate relationships. We all need to be close to someone. Make no apology for your strong desire to be intimate with someone; it is neither sinful nor selfish. Don't ignore the need by preoccupying yourself with peripheral satisfactions such as social achievement or acquiring knowledge. Neglecting your longing for relationship by claiming to be above it is as foolish as pretending you can live without food. Our need for relationship is real, and it is there by God's design.

God created us in his image, personal beings unlike all other creatures, and like him in our unique capacity for relationship. As dependent personal beings, we cannot function as fully as we are designed without close relationships. I understand the Scriptures to teach that relationship offers two elements which are absolutely essential if we are to live as God intended: (1) the *security* of being truly loved and accepted, and (2) the *significance* of making a substantial, lasting, positive impact on another person.*

These needs are real and must be satisfied before thoroughly biblical action is possible. It makes no sense to exhort people whose needs for security and significance are not met to live responsibly before God any more than it does to instruct someone with laryngitis to speak up. If a woman knows nothing of inward security and sees no hope of finding it, she cannot give herself to her husband in the way the Bible commands. To submit willingly to a man who is selfish and inconsiderate in his decisions, to become vulnerable to a husband who through weakness or indifference will not provide love, requires some already existing security.

Consistently loving a woman who communicates disrespect for his thinking and keeps a critical, angry, rejecting distance is impossible for a man who lacks a convinced sense of his own significance and worth. We were not intended to function according to the Master's plan without first equipping ourselves with the Master's provisions.

THE PROBLEM OF FEELINGS

To avoid misunderstanding, let me state that we do not need to *feel* secure or significant in order to function as we should. I may not *feel* worthy or accepted, but I am still responsible to *believe* what God has said. His Word assures me that in Christ I am both secure in his love and significant in his plan. A wife who *feels* desperately insecure is quite capable of giving herself to her husband if she *believes* she is secure in Christ. A husband who *feels* threatened by his wife's rejection is responsible for lovingly accepting her because he can *believe* that he is a worthwhile Christian regardless of her response.

Christ has made me secure and significant. Whether I feel it or not, it is true. I am instructed by God to believe that my needs are already met, and therefore I am to live selflessly, concerned only with the needs of others. The more I choose to live according to the truth of what Christ has done for me, the more I will come to sense the reality of my security and significance in him.

Sin has made an utter wreck of things. God's original design was that man and woman should live in fellowship with him and in a selfless relationship of mutual giving to each other. In such a

---

*See the next chapter for a fuller discussion of these two needs.

relationship my love would so thrill my wife that I would feel deeply *significant* as I realized the joy that my love creates in her; I would exult in the *security* that her love provides me. She too would find her *significance* in touching my deepest needs and would enjoy the *security* of my love for her.

But something has gone wrong in our marriage. I no longer believe that my needs are already met. I seem to think that I need my spouse to give me security and significance *before* I can respond as I should. I now *wait* for her to fill me first, *then* I give of myself to her. If she fails to come through in a way that satisfies me, I back away or perhaps attack her. To the degree that I trust her to accept me fully, I will be open and loving with her. But now my love for her depends on her love for me. And she approaches our relationship in exactly the same way. *If* I love her in a way that brings her security, *then* she gives herself in loving subjection to me. Otherwise she establishes enough distance to numb the pain of rejection.

A terrible situation results. Because I have asked my spouse to meet my needs, she now has the power to withhold what I need— and thereby to destroy me. *Fear* has entered our relationship. We have become afraid of each other. We play cat-and-mouse, wait-and-see games. Neither of us can find what we desperately need in our relationship because of fear.

Yet God intends that I become one with my wife in a relationship that deeply touches her need for security. And she is to become one with me in a way that satisfies my longing for significance and worth. God planned for our marriage to develop into an intimate relationship in which we experience the truth that our deepest personal needs for significance and security are genuinely met in Christ. When God presented Eve to her husband, the Bible tells us, they became one flesh, that is, they fully experienced a relationship of *Oneness*. Developing this kind of relationship is the goal of marriage.

The goal of oneness can be almost frightening when we realize that God does not intend that my wife and I find our personal needs met in our marriage. He also wants our relationship to validate the claims of Christianity to a watching world as an example of the power of Christ's redeeming love to overcome the divisive effects of sin. In John 17:21, Jesus poured out his heart to the Father: "I pray . . . that all of them may be one, Father, just as you are in me and I am in you. May they also be in us so that the world may believe that you have sent me." Our relationships with all fellow believers were in mind in Christ's prayer for oneness; but marriage, with its unique opportunity for intimacy, offers a convincing demonstration of the power of Christ's love to enable people to experience true relationship.

The first of our two questions can now be answered more

completely. What were the flight attendant and the two unhappy couples seeking? A relationship in which their deepest needs for security and significance could be substantially met.

Now, the second question: How were they trying to develop such a relationship?

Whatever strategies the two couples had followed were woefully ineffective. Neither am I confident that the flight attendant had a more successful game plan for achieving the oneness she desired.

What is an effective strategy for building a good relationship? Should you start by telling your partner everything you feel? Do you make a list of "ways to be nice this week" and do your best to follow it? Will getting up earlier to spend more time with God in devotions be helpful? Perhaps counseling or attending another seminar will do the trick. Or is the solution simply to repent of your selfishness and promise God to really do your part?

There are no simple answers. But there are answers— difficult to accept because they cut across the grain of our fallen human nature, authoritative because they come from God's Word.

♥ A GROWING MARRIAGE NEEDS A STRATEGY ♥

Talk together about the flaws in the thinking of the people Crabb refers to in this chapter: the flight attendant, the husband in his early thirties, the middle-aged Christian couple who feel hypocritical about the image they are presenting to the world. What is missing in each case? What are basic elements in an effective strategy for building a truly intimate marriage?

A key to oneness is understanding the needs of both marriage partners. Most spouses try to meet their needs in each other, and when that doesn't work they are frustrated in their search for intimacy. But there is a better way, which Dr. Crabb describes in the next chapter.

No other human relationship is fraught with so many possibilities of failure. There are no perfect marriages for the simple reason that there are no perfect people, and no one person can satisfy *all* of one's needs.[9]

Cecil Osborne

Chapter 3

WAIT A MINUTE! WHO MEETS *MY* NEEDS?

BY DR. LAWRENCE CRABB, JR.
The Marriage Builder

In another study of long-term marriages, Jeanette and Robert Lauer, faculty members at the United States International University, San Diego, California, discovered this common theme among the couples they interviewed: "The things they really liked in each other were qualities of caring, giving, integrity and a sense of humor. In essence, they said, 'I am married to someone who cares about me, who is concerned about my well-being, gives as much or more than he or she gets, is open and trustworthy and is not mired down in a somber, bleak outlook on life.'"[10]

Deep inside, all of us say, "Wait a minute! Who's going to meet *my* needs?" The husbands and wives in this study are obviously able to meet each other's needs, but the question is, What motivates them? Are they living in a *quid pro quo* situation in which each gives in order to get something in return? According to Larry Crabb, this self-serving approach is certainly not the way to real oneness and intimacy. In a Christian marriage, he reminds us, there is only one way to find security and significance. Sadly, it is often overlooked. As you read, think about the following:

- ♥ How much are you depending on your spouse to meet your needs?
- ♥ Is this approach working very well? If not, why not?
- ♥ Where does the author believe each of us must go to have our needs met? Is his idea practical?

WHO'S GOING TO MEET MY NEEDS?

A man in his middle forties complained to me that his wife was cold, angry, and argumentative. I interrupted his recitation of her faults to say, "It sounds as if you think that because your wife is failing you so badly, you are therefore justified in your bitter attitude toward her. The Bible, however, instructs you to love your wife though she may be thoroughly disagreeable, to love her the way Christ loves his people."

The man was incredulous.

"Wait a minute! Maybe I am supposed to love her—I'm sure I should. But I need a little love and respect, too. She's giving me nothing but criticism and a cold shoulder, and you tell me to love her? Who's going to meet *my* needs?"

His question must not be lightly dismissed with exhortations to stop such self-centered fussing and to trust the Lord with whatever emotional bruises result from his wife's neglect. Truth reduced to the level of cliché ("Trust the Lord," "Pray about it," etc.) rarely promotes conviction or healing. This man has substantive needs that cry for satisfaction and will not quiet down under glib scolding and the reminder that "Jesus is all you need."

He was distraught and irritated as a result of his wife's failure to love him. The marriage relationship was not meeting his emotional needs. The solution to his problem seemed obvious to him: to change his wife so that she would give him what he needed.

Picture the dilemma of the marriage counselor. Suppose he were to tell this man's wife that she should become more loving to her husband. Can you predict her response? "But I have needs too, and I don't feel very loved in this relationship, either. Who's going to meet *my* needs for love and affection?"

To understand God's design for marriage, we must begin with the fact that both husbands and wives have legitimate personal needs which press for satisfaction.

PERSONAL NEEDS   PERSONAL NEEDS

These *personal* needs are as real as our *physical* needs. It is impossible to function effectively if these needs are not met. In this chapter I show that no marriage can ever follow the biblical pattern unless both partners have experienced satisfaction at the deepest level of their personal needs. These needs can only be met in the context of a relationship with someone else; no person can satisfy his own needs.

THE DILEMMA OF NEEDS

This state of affairs creates a dilemma. Both my wife and I have real personal needs for love and respect that must be met if we are to treat each other as we should. It follows that I cannot fully love her until I sense that I am a loved, worthwhile person. It also follows that she cannot truly love me until she knows that she is a deeply secure woman. What are we to do?

Can I rightly rebuke my wife and exhort her to do better? But I really cannot expect her to treat me properly until she feels loved. Yet I am unable to provide her with the love *she* needs until someone meets *my* needs. This situation between husband and wife is rather like two bankrupt businessmen depending on each other for the capital to begin a new partnership.

Perhaps we are both supposed to rely exclusively on the Lord to respond adequately to our longings. This answer seems sound, but it has its own set of problems. The spiritual maturity required to experience Christ's love as continually sustaining amid real emotional pain is a distant goal for many Christians. The Lord sometimes seems far off and removed from the reality of our pressing, human needs. A thirty-five-year-old woman whose husband has coldly neglected her for years has, understandably, a difficult time turning down a man who offers her a warm, close relationship that includes sexual relations. To console her with words about God's unfailing love seems rather like encouraging a starving woman by showing her magazine pictures of a well-spread dinner table; to exhort her to remain obedient to God's Word may somehow seem to deny or understate her legitimate hunger.

But suppose we commit ourselves to trusting fully in the sufficiency of Christ to meet our needs. What role, then, should our spouses assume? Is my wife to be only a concerned bystander watching from a distance as I struggle to deepen my walk with the Lord? Will her efforts to become close to God be so personal and private that I will be excluded from the realm of her innermost emotional nature? Exactly how are we to become deeply one?

Before we deal with these questions, we need to consider in greater detail the nature of personal needs.

PERSONAL NEEDS

People are more than physical bodies. The Bible clearly teaches that our skin and bones and hair and organs constitute a home in which our personal selves temporarily live. When our hearts stop beating and our bodies decompose, that identifiable entity I know as "Me" continues in a conscious and personal existence. Who is this "Me"?

Genesis 1:27 states that mankind was created in God's image. In some sense, people are like God. But God is a non-corporeal being; that is, he does not have a physical body (except, of course, through the incarnation of the Second Person of the Godhead). His essential being is not matter. Therefore our similarity to God cannot be found in our flesh and bones. My *physical* being is not like God.

But I am a *personal* being, and that is like God. God is a loving, purposeful *Person* who thinks, chooses, and feels. I, too, am a *person* capable of love and purpose who thinks, chooses, and feels. The Bible uses various words to describe the personal character of man, such as *soul, mind, heart* and *will.* The biblical term *spirit,* however, seems to refer to the deepest part of man's essential nature as a person. When I think about the deepest part of me— the part that has the capacity for fellowship with God—I am reflecting on my spirit. Let us consider the characteristics of this person or spirit who resides in the body.

I recently asked a group of people to close their eyes and meditate on these questions: What do I really want? What are my deepest longings? What do I most desire that would bring me the greatest joy? As they meditated, I asked them to choose one word that best expressed their longings. Among the words they offered were *acceptance, meaning, love, purpose, value,* and *worth.*

Most of us, when we look within, can put our fingers on a strong desire to love and be loved, to accept and be accepted. When we sense that someone genuinely cares about us, or when we ourselves sense a deep compassion for someone else, something profound is stirred within us. I suggest that our longing for love represents one set of needs that partly defines what it means to be a person or spirit.

If you continue to reflect on your inner desires, you may notice something else. Do you experience an intangible sense of wholeness, a feeling of vitality and fullness, when you do something important to you? Washing dishes or mowing the lawn may bore us, but wrestling with decisions of major consequence or responding to a medical emergency extends into deeper parts of our personality. We sense an urgent meaningfulness to what we are doing—nerve-shattering perhaps, but meaningful. Thus, to be a person involves a second set of needs—needs for meaning and value.

The intangible identity that I know as "Me" has two real and profound needs, which are substantive personal realities not reducible to biological or chemical analysis. They have a personal existence, independent of the physical body, that constitutes the core of what it means to be a spirit.

The image of God is reflected in these two needs. God is a personal being who in his essential nature is *love* and who, as a God of design and purpose, is the author of *meaning*. We are also personal beings, but unlike our infinite, self-sufficient, and perfect God, we are limited, dependent, and fallen. God *is* love; we *need* love. Whatever God does *is* significant; we *need to do* something significant.

We can state these needs succinctly:

Security: A convinced awareness of being unconditionally and totally loved without needing to change in order to win love, and loved by a love that is freely given, that cannot be earned and therefore cannot be lost.

Significance: A realization that I am engaged in a responsibility or job that is truly important, whose result will not evaporate with time but will last through eternity, that fundamentally involves having a meaningful impact on another person, a job for which I am completely adequate.

Thus, being a person (or spirit) centrally involves an identity that requires security and significance to function effectively. When both these needs are met, we experience ourselves as *worthwhile* people.

My wife, too, is a spirit being; that is, she also needs to find security and significance. If we as a married couple are to become one at the level of our spirits—achieve what I call Spirit Oneness—then we must find some way to meet at the level of our deepest needs.

But how? And here we are back to the question posed at the beginning of this chapter: How can husband and wife become deeply one at the level of their personal needs? It would appear that as we seek to meet our personal needs in marriage, essentially four courses of action are open to us. We may:

1. Ignore our needs.
2. Find satisfaction in achievement.
3. Attempt to meet our needs in each other.
4. Depend on the Lord to meet our needs.

Option 1: Ignore our needs.

The first option can be quickly rejected. If, as I believe the Scriptures teach, these personal needs are as real as our physical needs for food, water, and shelter, then to ignore them is to invite catastrophe. When physical needs remain unmet, we move toward *physical death*. When personal needs for security and significance are neglected and go unsatisfied, we move toward *personal death*. The symptoms of approaching personal death include feelings of worthlessness, despair, morbid fears, loss of motivation and energy, a turning to drugs or sex or alcohol to numb the pain of dying, and a sense of emptiness and boredom. We have been created with real personal needs and, to be faithful stewards of our lives, we must not ignore them.

Option 2: Find satisfaction in achievement.

Operating through a fallen world, Satan has taught us to believe a lie. Our culture encourages us to measure a person's value by his or her achievement. The world has squeezed many Christians into the mold of believing that our need for a sense of worth can be met without entering into a deep relationship with the living God.

In our society, a man's value is typically measured in terms of earning power; prestige of occupation; the location, cost, and size of his home; social personality and physical attractiveness; cars; clothing; education; and athletic talent or musical ability. In a religious context, his ministry abilities in the church (singing, teaching Sunday school, etc.) are additional standards of measurement.

For women, worth is often evaluated according to social circles; the husband's job or position; charm, poise, and graciousness; the style, brand name, and cost of clothing; home and furnishings; and public abilities (entertaining, speaking to women's groups, etc.).

Too many couples have unwittingly bought Satan's lie. The "beautiful people" who have been blessed with money, good looks, and talent may experience a counterfeit sense of worth that provides some satisfaction of their needs. Because the pain of their unmet needs is dulled, they may never enter into the difficult struggle of finding real security and significance. Their lives may appear happy, vital, and trouble-free—no morbid wrestling matches with deep inner conflict. Whenever discomfort reaches the threshold of awareness, these people anesthetize it with more activities, purchases, trips, or whatever else they enjoy.

I wonder how many Christian couples with comfortable means and interesting lives never come together at the deepest level of their personalities, but bury their inward longings for love and purpose under a mountain of success instead. How sad! How empty! Better to struggle with substance than to comfortably accept a shadow.

Following Option 2—attempting to find satisfaction in achievement rather than in the struggles of relationship—will reliably result in a shallow relationship that may feel very pleasant but will fail to unite husband and wife at their deepest level.

Option 3: Attempt to meet our needs in each other.

If ignoring our needs is dangerous and if finding counterfeit satisfaction in achievement results in shallow relationships, then what should we do with our needs? A large majority of people turn to their marriage partners for the answer.

Consider what may really be happening when a couple gets married: Two people, each with personal needs pressing for fulfillment, pledge themselves to become one. As they recite their vows to love and respect each other, strong but hidden motivations stir inside them. If a tape recorder could somehow tune in to the couple's unconscious intentions, I wonder if perhaps we would hear words like these:

> *Bridegroom:* I need to feel important and I expect you to meet that need by submitting to my every decision, whether good or bad; by respecting me no matter how I behave; and by supporting me in whatever I choose to do. I want you to treat me as the most important man in the world. My goal in marrying you is to find my significance through you. An arrangement in which you are commanded by God to submit to me sounds very attractive.

> *Bride:* I have never felt as deeply loved as my nature requires. I am expecting you to meet that need through gentle affection even when I'm growling, thoughtful consideration whether I am always sensitive to you or not, and an accepting, romantic sensitivity to my emotional ups and downs. Don't let me down.

A marriage bound together by commitments to exploit the other for filling one's own needs (and I fear that most marriages are built on such a basis) can legitimately be described as a "tick on a dog" relationship. Just as a hungry tick clamps on to a nourishing host in anticipation of a meal, so each partner unites with the other in the expectation of finding what his or her personal nature demands. The rather frustrating dilemma, of course, is that in such a marriage there are two ticks and no dog!

Inevitably, as the years pass, husband and wife will occasionally touch at deep levels. One woman told me how desperate she felt when the doctor emerged from the operating room to inform her that her four-year-old daughter had just died. In that moment she knew a terrible pain that penetrated to the core of her being.

When she fell into her husband's arms, he coldly pushed her away and left the hospital. She was alone at a time when she needed to know that life still had purpose. When she needed to feel the love of someone close, her husband failed her. There is no greater torment than to expose your needs so fully and receive no help. And *every* husband and wife, no matter how godly, has many times failed to provide what the other has needed.

Reflect on your marriage for a moment. Is there a feeling of hurt that you are reluctant to share directly with your spouse or perhaps a subject (like sex or time together or annoying habits) that you carefully avoid? Why? Why do we sometimes have difficulty telling our spouses how we feel or what concerns us?

Every person alive has experienced sometime the profound hurt of finding rejection when he or she longed for acceptance. We come into marriage hoping for something different, but inevitably we soon encounter some form of criticism or rejection. The pain that results is so intense that it *demands* relief. So we retreat behind protective walls of emotional distance, angry with our partners for letting us down so badly, unwilling to meet again at the level of deep needs for fear of experiencing more pain.

Perhaps this situation can be diagramed as in the next chart. Protective layers are designed to prevent the rejection from getting "inside" where we feel the hurt.

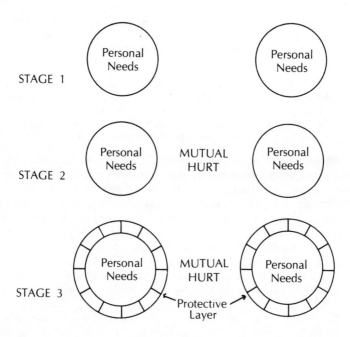

A variety of behaviors can function as protective layers. Some of the more common ones follow:

- Unwillingness to share deep feelings
- Responding with anger when real feelings are hurt
- Changing the subject when the conversation begins to be threatening
- Turning off, clamming up, or other maneuvers designed to avoid rejection or criticism
- Keeping oneself so busy with work, social engagements, entertainment, church activities, or endless chatter that no deep sharing is possible

Again, the point of each of these layers is to protect oneself from vulnerability to hurt at the hands of a spouse.

I am persuaded that most couples today live behind thick protective walls of emotional distance that block any hope for developing substantial oneness at the level of our deepest personal needs. What is to be done? Shouldn't we learn to be more loving and sensitive to each other? Can't we break down the barriers that separate us by accepting each other as God for Christ's sake has accepted us? Of course we should. The Bible tells us to and therefore we can. But we can never do it perfectly.

The most accepting wife in the world cannot meet her husband's need for significance. Because she is a sinner, my wife will not always minister to me as she should; even if she were to do so, she does not have the power to make me adequate for an eternally important task—and that alone will satisfy me.

The most loving husband in the world can never meet his wife's need for security. The stain of self-centeredness has discolored every motivation within us. We are utterly incapable of providing our wives with the unconditional and selfless acceptance they require. We simply are not enough for each other.

Let me briefly restate the problems with Option 3. If I look to my wife to meet my needs, then our relationship is corrupted by (1) *manipulative efforts* to acquire what I think I need; (2) *fear* that my manipulations may not be effective; (3) *anger and pain* when they do not succeed; and (4) a nagging (perhaps unconscious) sense of *guilt* because my approach to marriage is fundamentally selfish. We will inevitably retreat from each other behind protective layers that block the development of oneness.

I am therefore forced to conclude that if my wife and I are to become one at the level of our spirit (the deepest level of our being), then we must *not* depend on each other to meet our personal needs. What are we to do?

Option 4: Depend on the Lord to meet our needs.

Our personal needs for security and significance can be genuinely and fully met only in relationship with the Lord Jesus Christ. To put it another way, all that we need to function effectively as persons (*not necessarily to feel happy or fulfilled*) is at any given moment fully supplied in relationship with Christ and in whatever he chooses to provide.

1. We need to be secure. He loves us with a love we never deserved, a love that sees everything ugly within us yet accepts us, a love that we can do nothing to increase or decrease, a love that was forever proven at the Cross, where Christ through his shed blood fully paid for our sins to provide us with the gift of an eternally loving relationship with God. In that love, I am secure.

2. We need to be significant. The Holy Spirit has graciously and sovereignly equipped every believer to participate in God's great purpose of bringing all things together in Christ. The body of Christ builds itself up through the exercise of each member's gifts. We are enabled to express our value by ministering to others, encouraging our spouses, training our children, enduring wrong without grumbling, and faithfully doing everything to the limits of our capacity for the glory of God. We can live in the confidence that God has set out a path of good works for us to follow (Eph. 2:10) and that our obedience will contribute to fulfilling the eternal plan of God. These truths, when realized and acted upon, provide unparalleled significance.

THE PLATFORM OF TRUTH

Our fourth option, then, is to depend on the Lord to meet our personal needs. We really have no other rational choice. But there are problems. Our dulled eyes of faith strain to keep these spiritual realities in clear focus. We have a remarkable capacity for failing to lay hold of ideas that I suppose would seem so clear to undiluted faith.

Spiritual truth can be compared to a balance beam, a narrow platform from which we can easily fall off either side. The central truth that serves as the platform for Christian marriage—and for all Christian relationships—is that in Christ we are at every moment eternally loved and genuinely significant.

Too often Christians fall off this platform of truth into error. When key relationships (marriage, family, friendship) or life events (job, health, prestige) fail to make me *feel* secure or significant, it may be difficult to hold firmly onto the fact that I remain a worthwhile person. When a wife communicates disrespect for her husband or when a husband emotionally withdraws from his wife,

In Christ, I am significant and secure; therefore I can live responsibly before God no matter what happens.

PLATFORM OF TRUTH

it is not easy for the rejected partner to grasp with warm conviction the truth of acceptance and worth in Christ.

In Christ, I am significant and secure; therefore I can live responsibly before God no matter what happens.

PLATFORM OF TRUTH

Error 1: Rejection and failure mean that I am a less worthwhile person.

Rejection and failure can easily nudge us off the platform of truth into Error 1: *Because someone has rejected me or because I have failed, I am less worthwhile as a person.*

It is also possible to slip from the platform of truth into error on the other side. The truth that "Christ is all I need" may sometimes degenerate into a defensive posture to avoid personal hurt by maintaining a safe emotional distance in relationships. I once heard a lonely but proud man say to a Christian colleague, "Because I have Jesus, I am worthwhile with or without you. Your criticism, therefore, doesn't get to me at all. Nor does your acceptance really matter to me. It would represent a lack of faith in the Lord to let you affect me emotionally." He fell headlong into Error 2: *Hiding behind the truth of our worth in Christ to avoid feeling pain in relationships.*

Regardless of our spiritual maturity, we will acutely feel the pain of loss and rejection. And rightly so. Although our central relationship is with the Lord, we should enter into relationships with others deep enough to cause profound hurt when they fail. To say that Christ is sufficient does *not* imply that he is to function as some sort of asbestos cover protecting us from the pain of interpersonal fire. Rather, his resources make it possible for us to continue responding biblically in spite of the great pain we may feel, because the hurt, though great, will never be enough to rob us of our security and significance. And all we need to live as Christians, no matter what our circumstances, is the security of his love and the significance of participation in his purpose. We must never claim that our relationships with others do not affect us deeply: they do. But Christ's resources are enough to keep us going.

We can now complete the diagram.

In Christ, I am significant and secure; therefore I can live responsibly before God no matter what happens.

PLATFORM OF TRUTH

Error 1: Rejection and failure mean that I am a less worthwhile person.

Error 2: Christ is all I need; therefore I can avoid intimate relationships with others.

In the rest of this chapter we will think through how a Christian couple can become spiritually one by remaining atop the platform of truth.

Consider first how we can avoid falling into Error 1.

What are Christian husbands and wives to do when they keenly feel the insensitivity or disrespect of their spouses? How can they handle the acute pain or feel insecurity or insignificance that seeks relief behind the protective layers of emotional distance? How can a spouse who *feels* hurt realistically hang onto the truth of personal worth in Christ and thus avoid falling into the first error?

A woman I was counseling came to realize that for years she had been turning to her children for emotional fulfillment. Her husband shut her out of his life, leaving her hungry for affection and loving response. She found what she wanted in her children. This led to a stubborn reluctance to approach her husband with love and warmth, and the source of her reluctance was a profound fear that he would react coldly to her overtures.

I suggested that she was depending on her husband to meet her personal needs and that her relationship was essentially selfish and manipulative. She shook her head and answered, "I know God is supposed to meet my need for love, but what am I supposed to do with all this hurt and fear? I believe God loves me, but I can't get it to really work inside me."

I recommended that she follow three steps to help her find solid footing on the platform of the truth that because Christ loves her, she can be obedient to all that Scripture commands.

Step 1: Fully acknowledge all your feelings to God.

Christians are often trained to pretend that they feel joyful and happy when they are really miserable. Because we "shouldn't" feel unhappy, we pretend we don't. Yet Hebrews 4:15 teaches that our Great High Priest can sympathize with us when we experience weakness. How wrong it is, then, to hide our emotional weaknesses from him and to deny ourselves the comfort of noncritical understanding.

I encouraged this woman to fully acknowledge her hurt and pain before God, to literally and openly express what she was feeling in God's presence. So often people respond to such advice by reciting in contrite tones a prayer like: "Lord, please forgive me for feeling hurt." But this misses the point entirely. We are not to pretend that we feel *penitent* when we feel *hurt*. When our stomachs churn with grief or anger or pain, we must humbly acknowledge to the One-who-sees-everything whatever we really feel. My client eventually prayed like this: "Lord, right now I am hurting more than I think I can endure. I feel like screaming, running away, hitting somebody! I don't want to feel this way, but I do. I feel worthless, empty, sad, and angry. Thank you for loving me exactly as I am."

Step 2: Reaffirm your security and significance in Christ.

One of the central truths of the Christian life is that our feelings need never determine how we believe or what we do. I exhorted this woman to remind herself that in Christ she is a fully loved and worthwhile woman despite her husband's rejection. To grasp this truth better, I asked her to picture her mind as a tape recorder. We observed that whenever her husband in some form rejected her, she immediately "played a tape" that said, "When my husband rejects me, my need for love cannot be met. I am dependent on my husband to make me feel loved."

The belief that Christ is not sufficient for our personal needs is a lie of Satan. I wrote a new "tape" on a card and asked her to play it (to repeat it to herself) the next time she perceived rejection from her husband. The new tape read: "My husband may reject me. If he does, I will hurt, perhaps a lot. But no matter how he treats me, I am at this moment totally and wonderfully loved by Christ. Because of Christ's love, I am a secure woman."

Step 3: Commit yourself to ministering to your spouse's needs.

Because faith (playing the right tapes) is dead without works, the final step in helping my client to stand on the platform of truth was to encourage her to live out the implications of her new tape. Because she really is secure in Christ, she can make herself vulnerable to her husband's rejection by giving herself fully to him. The fact that she has not done so is sin and must be confessed as such. Repentance must follow.

I asked her to picture a cliff. In her imagination she was to see herself standing on its edge looking down into the abyss. The abyss represents what she fears would destroy her: her husband's rejection. While she remains on the cliff, she is safe; she cannot experience the deep pain of her husband's rejection so long as she keeps her distance from him. Every time she backs away from him or lashes out at him or hides behind a protective layer, she is choosing to remain on the cliff of emotional safety.

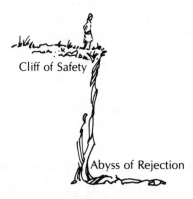

Cliff of Safety

Abyss of Rejection

We discussed the biblical model of marriage that requires her to give herself fully to her husband for the purpose of helping him feel valuable and important. To obey the Lord, she would need to jump off the cliff of safety and distance into her husband's rejecting arms. She looked at me with terror in her eyes: "If I give myself to him I'll get hurt again. And I just can't handle any more rejection!"

I then asked her to visualize a strong rope tied securely around her waist, a rope that represents God's love and is held by the Lord from his position directly over the abyss. As long as she remains on the cliff, the rope hangs limply because it is not challenged by her weight. The cliff, not the rope, is supporting her.

It was apparent to my client that from her position on the cliff she could never *feel* the strength of the rope. To develop the conviction that "Christ's love really does make me secure," she would have to jump, to leave the cliff of safety by committing

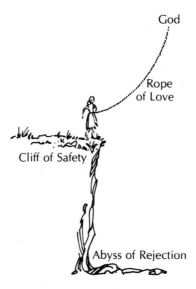

herself to meeting her husband's needs no matter what the cost. She cannot meaningfully claim that she is trusting the Lord for all needs until she leaps from the cliff. Until she is dangling over the abyss of rejection, held only by the love of God—and not until then—will she deeply know that Christ can meet her need for security. Her fear of rejection keeps her on the cliff. "Perfect love drives out fear" (1 John 4:18). But we will never know that love until we depend on it to preserve us from destruction.

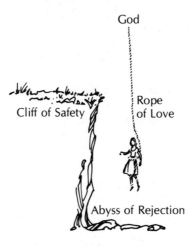

My client studied the diagram. "I can really see what you

mean. But it doesn't take away the fear. Even thinking about making that jump terrifies me."

Her comment triggered one more addition to the sketch. After a fearful person jumps from the cliff of safety, there is an *interval of time* before the rope of love extends fully to support the person's weight over the abyss. The situation is similar to skydiving. When a skydiver steps from the plane, he or she experiences a few moments of sheer, unsupported falling until the parachute opens. For the scared Christian who makes the "leap of faith," the moments before Christ's love is experienced as real personal security may last an hour, a day, a week, a year, or longer. During this interval between the jump and the felt reality of security in Christ, the Christian will likely sense a fear more profound than any known before. At this time, relying on the Word of God is absolutely indispensable. "Underneath are the everlasting arms" (Deut. 33:27). "My flesh and my heart may fail, but God is the strength of my heart" (Ps. 73:26).

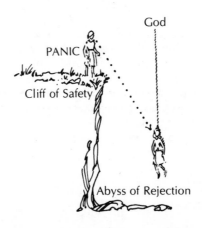

Let me summarize. When times of testing lead us into fierce personal struggles to maintain a sense of our worth as persons, it is easy to lose sight of the basis of our worth. To avoid the error of regarding ourselves as less worthwhile because of rejection or failure, we must—

Step 1: Openly acknowledge our painful feelings of hurt and worthlessness before the Lord.

Step 2: Reaffirm and continually remind ourselves of the truth that in Christ our security and significance are eternally intact.

Step 3: Act on the basis of this truth by squarely facing whatever we fear (rejection, failure, looking foolish, disapproval, etc.), depending on the strong love of God to conquer our fears.

THE PROBLEM OF EMOTIONAL WITHDRAWAL

Now consider how we can keep from slipping into Error 2. Falling from the platform into the second error ("Since Christ is all I need, I can withdraw from you emotionally") will destroy any hope of developing Spirit Oneness. Although it is true that our needs are fully met in Christ, it is also true that the Lord normally uses husbands and wives as his instruments to develop within each other a conscious awareness of personal worth. It is Christ alone who grants us security and significance, but it is often (by no means always) our spouses who help us to *feel* worthwhile.

God commands husbands and wives to submit to one another, that is, to put each other's *needs* first. I am to touch my spouse's deepest needs in such a way that I produce in her a conscious taste of what it is like to be deeply loved and respected.

Now, if we are to do our jobs well, we must explore how our behavior affects each other's awareness of our security and significance in Christ. In doing so, we will necessarily expose very private aspects of our personality. Nothing gives me a deeper sense of oneness with my wife than to share with her some of my struggles—the disappointments, hurts, fears, and unmet longings.

To know that she is aware of my most central struggles initially creates an incredible fear: I stand exposed and naked before her. Will she pass off my concerns lightly? Will she lose respect for me? Will she laugh or criticize? If she does reject me, I must depend on Christ's love as my basis for a sense of worth. But when she listens to me—really listens—and accepts me with my problems and frustrations, a closeness develops between us that can help me to regain the perspective to believe that I really am worthwhile in Christ. The kind of closeness that results from revealing to my wife parts within me which I share with no one else is a central element in Spirit Oneness.

To remain atop the platform and to develop this kind of oneness, husbands and wives need to regard problems, not as a cause to withdraw, but rather as an opportunity to learn how to minister better to each other. Let me illustrate this truth with a personal example.

A PERSONAL EXAMPLE

Some weeks ago, as my wife and I got into our car after a Bible study, she said in a voice mixed with anger and pain, "I really felt hurt tonight when you said . . . and now I'm so furious I can't even talk about it."

Exactly how does a person move from that beginning toward spirit oneness? Consider a few of my options and select the one that you think would best develop closeness.

1. *I could have ignored her,* knowing that by morning she would settle down and speak politely and perhaps by the next evening become warm again. Why discuss a subject that will just develop into an argument and make matters worse? After all, regardless of whether I failed her or not, I am still accepted by Christ.

2. *I could defend myself:* "Whatever I did, I didn't mean to hurt you." Or I could attack her: "Well, you hurt me, too" or "You are really sensitive. You ought to trust the Lord more" or "All right, tell me what you're mad about now."

3. *I could apologize,* attempting to cut short an anticipated painful conversation.

If you selected any of these options as good bets to improve your marriage, you need this book.

Regretfully, although I know better, I chose to respond with the second option of defense and attack. The conversation went something like this:

> *Me:* "What on earth did I do now?" (Subtle attack on her oversensitivity)
>
> *She:* "You put me down in front of the whole group when you said . . ."
>
> *Me:* "Honey, that was not a put-down! You completely misunderstood what I meant!" (Defend and attack)
>
> *Silence for three seconds*
>
> *She:* "Well, it really hurt and I'm feeling mad!"
>
> *Me:* "Okay, I'm sorry! What else can I say?" (A shift to Option 3: the conversation-ending apology)
>
> *Silence for thirty minutes*

During the second, longer silence, I became acutely aware that I had somewhere missed the road to Spirit Oneness. My wife and I were not experiencing a deep sense of our worth in Christ that enabled us to be mutually and sensitively responsive to each other's needs. I reflected on the fact that I really am a worthwhile person because of the Lord's love and purposes for me, whether or not I have been a success as a husband, and that my worth in Christ should be expressed not in retreat, but in an effort to minister to my wife. I approached her again, this time with a *different goal.* Before, I wanted to avoid pain by defending myself; now I determined to understand better what had happened and how I had hurt her in order to love her better in the future. Our second interchange went as follows:

Me: "Honey, I really hurt you tonight. I guess I don't understand why what I said was so painful—but I want to. Will you talk to me about it?"

She: "I'm not sure I can. It still hurts a lot."

Me: "I can accept that. I want to do a better job of making you feel loved. I failed you badly tonight, and I want to learn from it."

She: "I know you love me and are committed to making me feel good—but sometimes you seem so insensitive. I guess I really need to feel . . ."

And we talked for nearly an hour about our deepest needs and how we can be used of God to touch each other with healing rather than hurt. As we did so, we moved toward Spirit Oneness, the kind of profound closeness that results from meeting at the level of deepest needs.

CONCLUSION

Let us summarize the main points of the chapter:

1. We all have deep personal needs for security and significance that cannot be met outside of a relationship.
2. Many people deal with their needs wrongly by—
   a. Ignoring their existence and looking for satisfaction of *personal* needs with *physical* pleasures.
   b. Settling for counterfeit personal satisfaction through achievement, recognition, affluence, and the like which can never provide real security or significance.
   c. Turning to their marriage partners for security and significance. The result is a manipulative relationship designed to use each other for personal satisfactions. Because no marital partner is fully adequate to meet another's personal needs, such an exploitative relationship will inevitably experience conflict.
3. Only Christ can meet our needs, that is, provide us with eternal security and legitimate significance. We must, therefore, depend on him to give us what our personal natures require.
4. It is difficult for us to grasp deeply the reality of our worth in Christ. To become subjectively and convincingly aware of our security and significance in Christ, we must—
   a. Trust his love enough to give ourselves fully to our spouses in an effort to minister to their needs

and choose to continue our efforts to minister regardless of our spouses' response to us.

b. Honestly explore the impact we make on each other's experience of self-acceptance as worthwhile persons.

Spirit Oneness can be defined as a relationship between husband and wife in which both partners—

1. Turn individually to the Lord in complete dependence upon him for the satisfaction of their personal needs, and

2. Turn to each other in mutual commitment to—

a. Give themselves to one another to be used according to God's purposes in each other's lives, and

b. Openly explore the impact they make on one another's subjective experience of security and significance.

♥ HOW YOU CAN MINISTER TO EACH OTHER ♥

This chapter could be the most important in the entire book. Talk with your spouse about what Larry Crabb is really saying. Consider how each of you feels about his premise: A person must meet his or her needs for security and significance first in God, and then seek to minister to a spouse's needs without fearing rejection.

In this chapter, Dr. Crabb writes from the wife's point of view. Is it just as true that the husband has to leap off the cliff of safety and depend on God's rope of love as well? Some husbands may have difficulty admitting this, but they need to do so if progress is to be made toward real intimacy.

Each of you should choose ways you could minister to one another's needs and test how secure and significant you feel in Christ.

Vowing to have God meet your needs is an excellent but difficult goal. Anne Kristin Carroll suffered through two broken marriages before she learned to jump off the cliff of safety and trust in God only. Her story follows.

Chapter 4

FROM THE BITTER TO THE SWEET: REBIRTH OF A MARRIAGE

BY ANNE KRISTIN CARROLL
Together Forever

Although the mounting divorce statistics of the 1970s and early 80s have abated somewhat, thousands of couples annually face the failure of what should be the most fulfilling relationship in all of life. Anne Kristin Carroll wrote *Together Forever* for one reason: to help "save marriages wavering on the brink of divorce."

She writes, knowing that while many couples are ready to throw in the towel, there is hope, whatever may be ripping and tearing at the fabric of the marriage. Not just temporary patches, but a real and permanent solution.

If her answers were based on her own ideas and views alone, or even on the graphic personal experience she shares, she could not be convincing. But the answers she offers are God's answers, discovered at the most hopeless point in her life—after she had been divorced from her husband Jim for well over a year.

THE FINAL DECREE

In a few minutes it would all be over. Soaked with fear, pain, disappointment and rejection, I shivered as I stood in the judge's chambers. My eyes wandered over the walls covered with books, the cold leather chairs, past the secretary busily taking notes, and back to the judge's face. He was speaking, but his words were like the monotonous grinding of a motor, and my mind simply couldn't register them clearly.

Is this what divorce is—one man rhythmically reading legal

terms, with obviously no awareness or feeling for the cutting finality of his words?

Running from the horrid reality around me, I began to recall all the dreams, the plans for the boys, the schools they hoped to attend, the fine young men they were becoming, and our expectations for a fulfilling future. I had to swallow the urge to scream: "What happened? I don't understand. When did it start to fail? What did I do wrong? Dear God, this isn't the way it was supposed to be!"

A small piece of white paper—what power it had, how deadly it was. It said that in the eyes of the world Jim and I were no more! All the love, memories, hopes and dreams of a lifetime were dissolved. On a flight from the solidarity of the moment, my mind whirled back to the beginning.

THE YESTERDAY OF OUR LOVE

Only a few days after my divorce from my childhood sweetheart, as the mother of a young son, I found myself sitting in a smoke-filled bar. My date had suggested we come here, but as the evening wore on, I became more and more uncomfortable. I sat on the edge of my chair, doing my best to look "hip," but I had only been in a bar once before and I was sure everyone was aware of my insecurity.

I wandered from my table into an adjoining room. A very attractive young man walked up to me and said, "Hi, Anne." My mind spun, wondering how he knew my name. Noticing my confusion, he said, "I'm Jim. We met last week. Don't you remember?"

"Oh yes," I said, trying to recall who he was and who had introduced us. Before I could visualize the previous weekend, he said, "How about going to a party?"

The idea did appeal to me. Grant, the guy I was with, had a severe case of octopus hands and I wasn't in the mood to spend the evening trying to outmaneuver him. Jim had a happy, warm smile, sort of reminded me of a big puppy. His all-American-boy looks, broad shoulders and wavy brown hair, I felt, would be a vast improvement over Grant.

I mustered my courage and said, "Love to."

When we arrived at the party, Jim was a bit surprised when he discovered I neither danced, smoked, nor drank! I still think that that was the main fascination for a long time. He had never met a twenty-one-year-old, especially a divorcee, who acted like an escapee from the Victorian Era.

That evening, he did his best to teach me the current rage in dancing, the Twist. He'd explain and I'd attempt. Someone should have had a camera. Finally, in *total* desperation, he went to the bathroom, got a towel, and returned saying, "It is sort of like drying off after a shower." I started to tell him I didn't take showers, but I knew I had given him enough shocks for one evening, so I picked up the dumb towel and tried, and tried, and tried. But all the patience in the world wouldn't coordinate my feet, my bottom, or any of the rest of me.

After that evening, Jim and I became inseparable. I was working for Mitsubishi International, and modeling for a large fashion house. I think Jim enjoyed sharing my limelight; I know I enjoyed having him there.

But I was running from the failure of my first marriage, and sick with the knowledge that my father, with whom I was extremely close, was dying of cancer. My whole being cried for love and security, and I had a desperate desire to belong to someone again.

Six weeks after Jim and I met, we were wed in a simple ceremony at the county courthouse! Certainly, neither of us was ready for marriage: I was running scared and Jim was just playing a fascinating new game. Obviously, the depth of the commitment he had made had not registered, because the next day, while swimming, he introduced me as "one of his friends"!

When the marriage game became boring, Jim desperately tried to regain his status with the swingles. He was more captivated with pads, partying, and playing than he was with the permanent live-in he'd acquired.

I'll admit, when he did come home he was met with a dramatic display of tears, insinuations, and accusations. There wasn't a peace-filled moment for either of us during that time. Even with the birth of our precious son Michael, I was still doing my best to win the "martyr of the year" award.

My daddy died two weeks before Michael was born. In my agonizing search for *real* answers to my tormented existence, and with the passionate hope of reaching my father in the life beyond, I became deeply involved with the dark world of the occult. Particularly in the readings of Edgar Cayce, I felt I'd found the answers to my intellectual Christianity. Of course, like anything the Devil plagiarizes, there were no lasting solutions here, but I continued to mix my intellectual Christianity with my occult beliefs for a long time. Unfortunately, the few real Christians I knew never suggested that I consult the Scriptures to see what they had to say about horoscopes, mediums, etc. The experience would have been a rude awakening for me. You see, before my marriage to Jim, I had already attended one college and studied theology, and you would have thought I'd have known better, but at this point I was too desperate. I would have reached out to anything. All along I wanted to know God, to follow his will for my life. I just didn't understand how.

The next few years were filled with a few ups, but many, many downs. Then Jim's employer transferred us to Atlanta, Georgia. After our move, we were happy for a short time, but having had a live-in maid all my mothering days, I had never had to be responsible for the children. Jim wasn't much help; he was as immature as I.

If Women's Lib had existed in the early sixties, I would have been a choice candidate. I hated housework, but more than that I "felt" that I was wasting my time and talent being a wife and mother. I wanted a maid, a job, freedom, and money of my own. During this time I felt I had desires that Jim just couldn't fill. In fact, looking back, I can see we had almost switched places. As I relied on him less, he began to search for someone who did need him.

THE GAP GREW WIDER AND WIDER

Soon the problem of "other women" had to be faced. Audaciously, I felt the solution to this new problem was relatively simple; all I had to be was smarter, prettier, or sexier than my assumed competition. I say "assumed," since I blatantly accused Jim of more entanglements than the six-million-dollar man running in high gear could have accomplished. Proverbs 14:1: "Every wise woman builds her house, but the foolish one tears it down with her own hands." That was me.

As my solutions failed to produce the expected results, I became more desperate. I became a master at checking for lipstick stains on Jim's shirts, inspecting his car for hairpins of the wrong color, or a carelessly dropped earring. Of course, I kept a perpetual surveillance on the address book, watching for the entry of any unfamiliar female names.

Occasionally, while trying to track him down, I would call the old bar where we had met, ask for Jim, only to hear him yell from the background and hear the bartender say, "Anne, he says he ain't here!"

Naturally, when I found concrete evidence, heartbroken and crying, I would flaunt it in his face. The gap between us became wider.

In my race to conquer my competition, I took stock of myself in the mirror. I made arrangements with a plastic surgeon to take the patrician out of my nose. I was working so hard on that outer beauty that I never even considered my inner ugliness!

A cute nose didn't do it. A new hairstyle didn't work, and neither did all the new fashions. Many nights I lay in bed listening until the wee hours of the morning for his car. I was consumed with thinking about who he was with, where they were, and what they were doing. Night after night, I lay there with the same old thoughts running through my tormented brain, crying, dying as each hour slipped by. I was forever wondering where I had failed, why I'd failed, what Jim wanted, what it would take to make him happy.

A cold chill would run through me when I heard the car pull into the drive. I'd lie there, torn, as if two women possessed my body. One of them wanted to reach out, touch, forgive. She was filled with happiness because he was home; her whole being wanted to run to him and enfold him in the arms of love. The other woman was filled with bitterness, hostility, despair; she felt cold and icy inside and could only turn away, wanting only to hurt him as she had been hurt.

As the heartbreak continued, I happened to drop in to see my neighborhood physician. As I shared with him some of the upsets in my life, he said, "What you need, Anne, is a pill."

"Well, I sure need something, and anything that will stop this torment and anguish would be a blessed relief," I responded.

I was a prime candidate for the pill habit. Problems that I couldn't solve, questions with no apparent answers, and a desire to escape the pain of the whole thing. It didn't take long for me to like the escape the pills provided. In a short time, I took anything that I could *legally* get my hands on. Uppers to wake up, barbiturates to relax or sleep, antidepressants to keep from facing my ever-mounting problems, and a lovely variety of tranquilizers thrown in for good measure. It finally reached the point that even if there were no pressing problems in our lives, I still took my precious pills just in case one came up! I was totally intent on treating the feelings instead of the cause. In true southern, Scarlett O'Hara fashion, as far as problem-solving was concerned, there was always tomorrow!

I WAS READY FOR SUICIDE WHEN ...

After four years, an article in a local newspaper caught my attention. I read that I was taking twice the dosage used to treat persons who are institutionalized. Right then and there, I decided that I should either be off the pills or in an institution. You can't play detective in a hospital, so I chose to kick the pills and, miracles of miracles, I did.

Of course, there was the issue of what would happen when I was confronted with another crisis. Without my pills, with no hope, having searched the world for answers, suicide seemed beautifully tempting.

I didn't want to do something dramatic, or to cause my children more pain and embarrassment than need be, so I quietly sat down one evening to make suicide plans. That must have been the longest, loneliest night of my life.

When morning came, I had almost finalized my plans when the phone interrupted me. The call was from Xara Ward, a woman I hardly knew. During the course of the conversation, she asked me to attend a women's Bible class with her.

She wanted *me* to go to hear some housewife teach the Bible! I almost laughed, but since I hated to hurt her feelings, I agreed to go.

When we arrived, there was a young woman teaching in the basement of a neighbor's home. I had never heard *anyone* speak with such knowledge and authority about the Scriptures. When she spoke of Jesus, she just radiated, and you *knew* immediately that she was talking about her best friend.

Taken as I was with Darien Cooper, I wasn't at all sold on the merchandise she was pushing. *That "Christ is the answer" stuff is all right,* I thought, *if your biggest problem is getting your husband to take the garbage out, or persuading your children to hang up their clothes, but if she had problems like mine, it wouldn't work.*

The Lord is so gracious. He held me together for another week so I could get another dose of truth. This time everything was different. It was as if Darien had prepared her message especially for ME!

She said that God had a plan for *my* life. She explained how much God loved *me personally.* I understood for the first time why I had never experienced the abundant life Christ promised. I learned that *I* was sinful, and that sin separated me from God. But God in his merciful love sent his Son, Jesus Christ, to span the chasm between a perfect God and sinful Anne. All these years I had been trying to be good enough for God. At that moment, I realized that I could never be good enough to fellowship with a holy God, but that through my acceptance of Christ's payment on the cross for *my* sin, I could then have a personal relationship with Jesus. I, Anne, could have a living, moment-to-moment personal relationship with the Son of God!

Of course, the answer had been there all along. I had just never clearly understood before. I knew at that moment that this was the answer for which I had been searching all my life.

I ran home, glowing with my new-found friend, Jesus, but laden with my total ignorance of his Word. Naturally, that didn't stop me; I politely began to stuff Jesus Christ down Jim's throat.

After nine months of living with a female Billy Graham, Jim had had it, and he demanded a divorce! I thought I had all the answers and I couldn't believe what I was hearing.

"Mrs. Carroll, Mrs. Carroll," the judge called. "You didn't answer my question."

"I'm sorry, Your Honor, I was thinking of something else." Here I was again. It wasn't a nightmare from which I would awaken; Jim had actually asked for a divorce, and in a few minutes it would be all over.

I wondered frantically how this could be happening. When I became a Christian I thought that all my problems were solved. Those I couldn't manage to patch up myself, I *presumed* God would fix. But that wasn't, and isn't, how it works.

LORD, WHY DIDN'T IT WORK?

In the past, once I got a taste of a new idea, I took it and ran, never bothering to read the directions which are enclosed. Christ had something to teach me, but he patiently waited. Feeling I had made a royal mess of my past life and hurrying to establish a new one, I revisited the singles circuit. I realized I was seeing the same lonely faces at every gathering, every party, every "political" meeting. When I'd tried everything, when all my bright ideas had burned out and my brilliant schemes had failed, then I discovered I was almost back where I had begun.

I fell on my knees and prayed to my Father in Heaven: "Dear God, I have tried everything. I did everything I thought was right. I did my best. Why didn't it work? Lord, I'm so tired of trying. I appreciate your help and friendship in the past, but from now on, you can just count me out. I quit." You know, this is what he had been waiting for. I could almost hear him say: "Great! Now, Anne, I can begin my work."

A year and a half *after* our divorce, after seeking help through friends or counseling and finding only discouragement, frustration, and a million unanswered questions, the Lord led me to a dedicated Christian counselor. This wise woman of God showed me Anne as she truly was! She took me directly to the Scriptures to explain the problems Jim and I had faced and failed. After an insight into the problems, from the Word of God, she shared *the answers*.

But now, before I go any further with my story, I'd like you to read Jim's impressions of our life together.

JIM TELLS HIS SIDE

I had never met anyone twenty-one who was so wide-eyed and innocent. I found her lack of worldly sophistication fascinating. I found her high-school-type loyalty embarrassing. But there were so many things special about her that in a few weeks I asked Anne to marry me.

It wasn't your usual wedding ceremony. But I wasn't taking the whole thing very seriously anyway. We dropped down to the courthouse one afternoon and were married. I even forgot that I had an Army Reserve meeting that night. Later, on our wedding night, I went off to the meeting and sent Anne out with some of our friends to celebrate without me!

The following weekend we went apartment hunting. We found the apartment we wanted. There was only one problem— we couldn't move in until the first of the month.

The solution seemed simple enough to me. I'd just shove my roommates into another bedroom and move Anne in with us! Anne was none too thrilled about the idea, but she didn't make too much fuss.

We did get that new place and for a short time playing house was fun. But now there was always Anne home waiting for me, always Anne to account to for my time, for my actions. In due time the fun wore thin.

I missed the free life of a single man, so I returned to my former friends. Making the rounds with the guys, partying, and playing were more exciting than the same person and the same routine every night.

Anyway, by now Anne was pregnant, and she was moody and cranky much of the time.

If I did happen to get home before she went to bed, it was always the same scene:

"Where did you go after work?"

"Nowhere."

"Nowhere! I guess you were nowhere for the last four hours. . . . Are you listening to me? I asked you where you've been! Don't you realize that I'd like to get out of this place sometimes? Good grief, you never think of anyone but yourself!"

She'd start crying. I'd feel like a dirty heel for upsetting her. But, of course, I easily forgot all that by the next afternoon.

Our lives pretty much followed that pattern until I was promoted and given a large territory in the Southeast. For a short time after we moved to Atlanta, things changed between us. I had made a commitment to myself that if I took Anne to Atlanta, I was going to make some dramatic changes in my behavior.

Atlanta seemed to have the magic touch for a time. I was perfectly satisfied learning to be a good husband and father.

Slowly things began to change again. After the initial fun of playing mother wore off, Anne became frustrated, confused, and unsatisfied. In time, she arranged for a live-in, then secured a job.

Anne had never been away from home, so she was experiencing her first taste of independence. She became more and more involved in her work, and spent less and less time with the children and me.

I'd just find someone who wanted to be with me, someone who needed me. Obviously, Anne didn't.

Our lives revolved back to the nightly scenes. By this time, Anne realized that she wasn't as interested in work and a career as she had thought. In time, she became aware that she wasn't the only female on my mind—and boy, that did it.

No Nazi general could have held better interrogation sessions than Anne. Everywhere I went, I expected to turn around and find Anne standing there with that accusing look. Finally, I decided if I was going to be accused of everything in the book, I might as well try to live up to the reputation.

What did she want? When I tried to be a good husband, she ignored me. When I reverted, she harassed me. Women! The only thing I really knew and believed about Anne was that, in her own way, she sincerely and deeply loved me, but she sure had funny ways of showing it.

AND THEN ANNE GOT RELIGION!

I thought, after almost eight years of marriage, that I knew Anne pretty well. But one day, right out of the blue, she came home, grinning from ear to ear and sounding like a tent preacher. I certainly wasn't prepared for this.

She'd almost force me to sit down while she read to me how to become a Christian from a little booklet she always carried around. I couldn't understand it. I had been raised in such a formal religious atmosphere, and all this "saved and new birth" business was foreign to me. Anyway, I went to church a couple times a year, and I didn't see any real effect that had on my life. I couldn't imagine why she thought some miracle could be wrought with this "Christianity" she'd found.

If she wasn't talking religion, she was sending out tracts. The next thing I knew, she began to speak publicly! That's when I let her know I had had it.

Surprise covered her face. She had actually believed that all this Jesus stuff would miraculously solve all the problems in our relationship.

I don't recall too much about the actual day our divorce was final. I just wanted to escape the pressure, responsibility, condemnation, and pain.

During the next year or so, things didn't dramatically change between us. I still took her to all the big business functions. She had become so close to many of my important customers that to show up with anyone else would have been the kiss of death.

About a year and a half after our divorce, I began to notice a change in Anne. I couldn't believe it. When we were together, there were no more sermons, no more questions, just a smiling face. When I'd leave, I'd sense that Anne really liked me just the way I was!

I'd seen Anne go through some pretty tricky forms of manipulation before, so I just backed off and waited for this new spell to run its cycle. Occasionally, I'd push her just a bit to see how far she was willing to carry this new approach. But as time passed, and I tested and tested, she remained consistent. It wasn't a game. She was really different. The inner beauty which radiated from her became a magnet.

Finally, I realized what a jerk I was. I wasn't the only man in the world who could see what a striking, intelligent, caring woman she was. If I didn't start playing my cards right, I might end up losing her.

Two and a half years after our divorce, I asked Anne to marry me again. This time there was no quick civil ceremony . . . and I didn't run off to an Army Reserve meeting that night.

After our remarriage, things were different. Home was a fantastic place to return to, and I found that more and more I wanted to be there with my family.

Anne was so different. She made me feel so important, so needed. I encouraged Anne to begin speaking to women's groups. This time Anne had something to say. She'd discovered God's concepts for herself and for a happy marriage, and she was busy sharing them with anyone who would listen.

Anne talks away from home, but at home she seldom says anything. I haven't seen that little tract she used to preach to me from in a number of years. Anne learned the truth of 1 Peter 3:1. The less she said, the more I saw and accepted the truth through the life she was leading.

It is clear, though, that the truths Anne found in the Scriptures have totally remolded our existence. I am firmly convinced that without that I would never have accepted Jesus Christ as my personal Savior, nor understood his eternal plan for me as a husband, father, and a man.

JIM CHANGED WHEN I DID

All of life's problems were not solved when we were remarried. It has and will always be a process of working in and through God's concepts for Anne as a wife, a mother, and a woman; and for Jim as a husband, a father, and a man.

Daily I claim the promise in Psalms which says: "Delight yourself also in the Lord, and he will give you the desires and secret petitions of your heart. Commit your way unto the Lord— roll and repose (each care of) your load on him; trust . . . also in him, and he will bring it to pass" (Ps. 37:4–5).

I don't question Jim's comings and goings any longer. When he gets home I just let him know how glad I am to have him here with me. The Inquisition is out and love is in. Now I sometimes wonder what to do when, instead of being out late, he is home early and in town as much as possible. I told him the other day I thought I would write a book someday on how to adjust to a transformed husband!

We have a deeper, sweeter relationship now than we ever had before. Often I recall these words in Song of Solomon: "Many waters cannot quench love, neither can floods drown it." First Corinthians 13:8 also speaks about the everlasting qualities which God intended for marital love.

Jim has grown before my very eyes. He has become everything I ever wanted in a man, not by my forcing him to change, but by my allowing Christ to change ME!

I hope no one reading this feels that Jim and I are special, isolated cases. Believe me, it wasn't luck that reunited us, but the application of God's laws. Through them we learned to love again, trust again, share and communicate.

We are still growing in our relationship; I hope that we always will be. Believe me, there are no pills to take, no instant cures for an ailing marriage. Whatever state of decay your marriage is in, it didn't happen overnight; and, depending on the number or severity of your problems, it usually can't be turned around in a day, either. Oh, there are those rare exceptions. I have counseled with some who were so intent, so ready, that they saw changes occurring almost every day. But that is not the norm. Usually a marriage on the brink of divorce needs a firm dose of God's eternal concepts, applied with patience, work, and firmly grounded in a personal trust in God, a day at a time.

What an opportunity, possibly the *greatest* you will ever have—the opportunity to save your marriage, to save your relationship, to save your family! How could you possibly excuse yourself if you closed this book and never tried?

Just think what wonderful things, what marvelous new experiences, may be waiting for you. The decision is up to you. *You* can accept failure without trying, or *you* can reach out, trusting, and put into practice God's eternal concepts and promises.

There was a song which was often played when Jim and I were divorced. It used to tear my heart apart. Even now when I hear its sad refrain, there is a silent tug, a reminder to hold close the love we almost lost. Those have to be the saddest words in the world: "We Almost Made It This Time." Don't make them yours.

I'm sure you will be encouraged by this precious promise: "Now glory be to God who by his mighty power at work within us is able to do far more than we would ever dare to ask or even dream of—infinitely beyond our highest prayers, desires, thoughts or hopes" (Eph. 3:20 LB).

♥ IS IT EVER REALLY SIMPLE? ♥

In the eyes of some, the strength of Anne Carroll's story can be its weakness. Many sincere Christians may read it with appreciation but say, "That's great for *her*. Somehow it all came together and Christ made the difference in their marriage, but even though we're both committed Christians, it just isn't that easy for us."

Fair enough. Honest admissions deserve an honest response. Marriage is *never* simple. Problems are *always* complex when you try living successfully in the most intimate relationship known to mankind. Sometimes the "I do's" can become undone when the "I will's" turn into "I won'ts" or "I can'ts." Shirley Cook closes this section of *The Marriage Collection* by sharing how she and her husband decided, a month before their wedding date, to put each other first.

Chapter 5

TO KEEP THE "I DO'S" FROM BECOMING UNDONE

BY SHIRLEY COOK
The Marriage Puzzle

How do you achieve intimacy in marriage? According to Mrs. Cook, the pieces of the puzzle include God, plans, patterns, and the ability to say "I do." But there is one more thing: To say *I will*, even in those moments when loving your mate isn't convenient or even particularly desirable. As you read, keep these questions in mind:

- ♥ What are our goals as husband and wife? Have we ever really spelled them out?
- ♥ Is our pattern for marriage taken from the Bible? How can we tell?

"I DO"

I started knitting an afghan (was it five years ago?) that still droops, half-finished, out of the knitting basket. I ought to do something with it, but I don't, and besides it does give a nice homey look to our bedroom corner. Dusty, but homey. I guess I'm just not "crafty." I also noticed that in the process of shifting the big blue thing from one place to another, some stitches slipped, and I don't know how to pick them up and start again. Never should have begun such a long-term project without knowing more about finishing it.

Like some marriages, my afghan is falling apart because I didn't plan ahead, (or) I didn't know how to fix my mistakes, (or) I don't have staying power.

But marriage is not an afghan to be cast into the corner to gather dust and slipped stitches. It is a God-planned creation, individually patterned and woven together to bring happiness and warmth to men and women—and joy and glory to the Creator.

Did you catch those two words: planned and patterned? Let's look at them first, then we'll consider the most important word in that sentence: God.

DOES YOUR MARRIAGE HAVE A PLAN?

The dictionary says a plan is a "detailed scheme or method for the accomplishment of an object; a proposed or tentative project or goal."

When Les and I decided to marry, we talked over our goals like other couples (we called them "dreams" in those days). We were not Christians at the time, but I remember our frequent references to wanting God in our marriage. To accomplish this, we decided to attend church on those Sundays it didn't interfere with our trips to the mountains or our game of tennis at the neighborhood park. That worked out to be about once every two months, which was fine with us. (We didn't want to be fanatics!) Besides, the church we attended was so liberal in its theology and dead in its worship that we felt as religious on the courts as in the pews.

Another goal we discussed was to stay married. Regardless. My mother and father were divorced when I was thirteen, and I was determined to have a long and lasting marriage. We agreed that we would never toss the word *divorce* at each other or threaten to split when things got tough. (I'm sure those thoughts crept into both our minds after particularly stormy sessions, though.) Maybe the experience of living with a divorced mother and observing her problems of loneliness and lack of fulfillment were good medicine for an impatient, willful, only child.

Another subject we discussed, which amazes me now as I think about it, was the way we decided to put each other first in our relationship, sexually and otherwise.

The astonishing thing about our premarital discussion was that we were both so naïve. Without going into detail about our wedding night, let's say we met each other unprepared and untried.

We grew up without the television "soaps" and the classes in sex education our kids are getting. Besides that, talk about S–E–X was strictly taboo in mixed groups. And we were a mixed group. About a month before our wedding day, we read an article in *Reader's Digest* about sex in marriage. It stressed the importance of bringing satisfaction to one's partner instead of focusing on your own pleasure. Because we really wanted happiness for each other, we adopted that philosophy for our marriage—both in and out of bed.

So we came up with three major goals:

1. To go to church
2. To go through life together
3. To go out of our way to please each other

These *plans* for our future were made before we said "I do," and I'm excited as I think back over the last thirty-four years to realize that most of the time we tried to incorporate them in practical living. I said *most* of the time.

DOES YOUR MARRIAGE HAVE A PATTERN?

Let's move on to the word *pattern,* "an ideal worthy of imitation. A model. A sample."

We all know people who become our models, or ideals, and that's good if their standards are worthy. Unfortunately, my family didn't provide a positive pattern for a lasting marriage. But Les had parents who had been married for many years and still loved each other. Moreover, as we came to know and involve ourselves in others' lives, and more particularly as we found God's pattern for marriage in the Bible, our individualized model for marriage has grown stronger and easier to follow over the years.

If you don't have a clear pattern for your life, take a long, hard look at Jesus. He is our perfect example.

Plans and patterns. So necessary. But now we come to God, the all-important ingredient. He is the permanent glue that bonds the pieces of the picture puzzle together. After all, marriage is God's idea from the beginning, all the way through the middle, right to the end.

After the heavens and the earth were formed and populated with birds, fish, and animals, God made a man in his own image. Someone he could talk with, someone to give love and be given love. What a beautiful friendship between God and man! Surely such a relationship would totally satisfy Adam. Who could possibly need human companionship with God as a friend?

Adam did. God saw his creature's loneliness and said, "It is not good for the man to be alone. I will make a helper suitable for him" (Gen. 2:18).

So the Lord God performed a unique act of creation. Instead of speaking forth another human or forming her, like Adam, from the dust of the ground, the Divine Surgeon removed one of Adam's ribs and fashioned a woman. I can imagine how Adam's eyes must have bulged when he first saw this beautiful person. Every curve molded and designed for him. A good fit for the marriage puzzle. Love at first sight.

So without wasting time with a long engagement, Adam and Eve got ready for the first wedding ceremony—a garden wedding. God brought the woman to him, and Adam spoke the first vows:

> "This is now bone of my bones
> and flesh of my flesh;
> she shall be called 'woman,'
> for she was taken out of man."

"For this reason a man will leave his father and mother and be united to his wife, and they will become one flesh" (Gen. 2:23–24).

This is an incredible thing God did—to bring a man and woman together and give them the joys of married love and the power to recreate their own kind. Such a way of life! A husband and wife learning to live together, to give and take, to laugh and cry. Two separate lives, yet one. Each possessing a mind, a personality, and a potential to love (or hate). What a picture—an earthly picture—of the spiritual gift God offers to every person who is born into the human family.

The apostle Paul writes about marriage in Ephesians 5, especially verse 23: "For the husband is the head of the wife as Christ is the head of the church, his body, of which he is the Savior."

From this passage of Scripture we learn that marriage is a picture of the union between Jesus Christ and his "forgiven ones."

Can you visualize your marriage as a color slide projected on a screen? Does it portray the love Jesus Christ has for his church? I have to confess that my picture is a little blurry and out of focus much of the time, but I will keep adjusting it until it becomes sharp and clear. I believe that each day as Les and I seek to live our lives together, we are showing the world the union that can exist between God and man.

We are separate, yet one, both in marriage and in our relationship with Christ. The human family. God's family. What a mystery! I really don't understand all I know about this teaching, but the pieces fit.

God.

Plans.

Patterns.

"I do."

Lord, when I'm hurting and find it impossible to live up to my "I do," I ask you to do it for me as you promised in John 14:13: "I will do whatever you ask in my name, so that the Son may bring glory to the Father."

———————————————

♥ ADDITIONAL IDEAS FOR DEVELOPING INTIMACY ♥

The following ideas are adapted from Shirley Cook's *The Marriage Puzzle*, pages 18 and 19.

1. Discuss together and then write down your goals for your marriage. Remember that marriage is a partnership and, if you want to succeed, you need a unified plan and purpose.

2. Take time to list, individually and separately, five things that give each of you pleasure. A husband might write:

"I'd like to be left alone for the first fifteen minutes of each day."

"I'd like to be left alone for the first fifteen minutes after I get home from fighting the freeway."

"I'd like to see my wife in a skimpy nightgown rather than a flannel robe."

A wife might write:

"I'd like to be surprised with flowers for no special reason."

"I'd like to be invited out to breakfast."

"I'd like to be relieved of caring for the kids occasionally and given the day off to shop or do whatever I want."

After studying your spouse's list, ask God to help you set some new goals for putting pleasure and intimacy into your marriage.

Intimacy is discovering that . . .

> . . . marriage is a mixture of good days and bad, victory and defeat, give and take.
>
> . . . it doesn't pay to be supersensitive. You can let some things go over your head. (Remember Larry Crabb's diagram on the cliff of safety, the abyss of rejection and God's rope of love.)
>
> . . . a warm kiss and an "I love you," even when you don't feel like it, can change your spouse dramatically.
>
> . . . if you keep saying "I do," your lips will already be puckered up for a kiss. With God all things are possible— even a lasting, intimate marriage.

♥ REVIEWING HOW TO HAVE ONENESS ♥

The material in Part I, "Intimacy: It Takes Two To Have Oneness," has focused on these powerful ideas for growing a good marriage:

> ♥ The foundation of intimacy and oneness is an understanding of Genesis 2:24—a man (or woman) will leave

home and cleave to a spouse, becoming one flesh—one person.

♥ Your husband (or wife) has personal needs that must be met, but instead of depending on each other, you must depend on God, who will empower you both to meet the needs of your mate.

♥ Ministering to your spouse is the final act of true intimacy. Because your own needs are met in Christ, you can reach out, unafraid of rejection or indifference.

♥ Keeping your "I do's" from becoming undone means making a constant effort to set and pursue goals for your marriage that are based on the biblical pattern. The key to making "I do" last is saying "I will," even when you don't want to.

THE MATHEMATICS OF MARRIAGE:

Christians tend to view the mathematics of marriage as 1 + 1 = 1. They feel that becoming "one flesh" means being totally absorbed by each other. (But) the proper mathematics of marriage is 1 + 1 = 3. We are two individuals and a couple. As healthy individuals, we each bring to the marriage something different and unique.[11]

Fay Bustanoby

PART II

LOVE:
THE GLUE THAT HOLDS A MARRIAGE TOGETHER

Which description best fits your marriage?

Fifty/Fifty—each partner trying to give fifty percent to the marriage and taking (receiving) fifty percent in return. This is a favorite formula used in many articles on marriage appearing in today's popular magazines. The fifty/fifty arrangement is considered "ideal" and many wives, in particular, would be happy to achieve it.

Giver/Taker—one partner clearly giving more than fifty percent to the relationship, with the other taking all the giving partner has to offer and giving less in return. Some psychologists and counselors believe that, because people are born givers or takers and generally marry their opposite, the inevitable result is a Giver/Taker relationship.

Authors Cris Evatt and Bruce Feld (*The Givers and the Takers*, Macmillan, 1983) developed a questionnaire that they used in over one thousand personal interviews to demonstrate their thesis: The tendency toward giving or taking is an inborn characteristic. (You may think you both give and take, and most of us do, but one trait or the other is usually dominant.)

Undaunted by claims that this categorization is too simplistic or superficial, Evatt and Feld have established numerous axioms, principles, and tests to reveal the giver or taker in all of us. For example, the authors believe a romantic relationship, particularly marriage, uncovers the dominant characteristic in the partners.

Givers are sexually attracted to takers, and vice versa. Takers are more assertive than their mates, givers less assertive. This has nothing to do with "coming on strong," or being loud or soft. The point is, takers are good at manipulation and can usually get what they want from others, while givers give in, saying, "Oh, I'll get it, I'll take care of it, I'll be glad to do it."

Givers choose service-oriented careers—teaching, social services, nursing—while takers are attracted to more glamorous fields—medicine, law, acting, modeling, professional sports.

Takers don't want to be changed. Givers not only try to change people, especially their taker mates, but are themselves willing to change in order to please.

Givers communicate better than takers. The giver loves to talk; the taker is more action-oriented. In conversation, takers tend to concentrate on tangibles—what happened at work, a recent trip, plans for next summer. Givers prefer more emotional topics— people's problems, perceptions, feelings. Givers want to communicate about the relationship; takers don't see the need.

Takers have polygamous tendencies stemming from inner-directedness, while givers jealously guard their monogamous relationship. Takers are charming and seductive and often flirt without knowing it; at these times giver mates often suffer in silence, keeping their discomfort to themselves because they fear rejection. Takers take from wherever they can and are more likely to have affairs, usually with givers who are much like their giving spouses. Givers, on the other hand, wouldn't think of betraying their mates because they are busy pouring all their energy into one relationship.[1]

Authors Evatt and Feld believe "Christians are brainwashed with the aphorism, 'It is better to give than to receive.' "[2] In their opinion, this leaves the givers open to exploitation and manipulation. They believe that it is best to give and receive equally and abundantly, and their book makes a valiant effort to show givers and takers how to modify their behavior to achieve that goal.

But what about this "Christian aphorism" uttered by Jesus himself: "Is it not more blessed to give than receive"? Is there a third kind of marriage that could employ the biblical model successfully? Many Christian marriage counselors and specialists believe there is.

The Giver/Giver marriage is the ideal goal—each partner giving not fifty percent or even seventy-five percent to the relationship, but one hundred percent. Furthermore, neither partner keeps score on how much is received in return.

Does this make "natural-born" givers more vulnerable to "natural-born" takers? Of course, but biblical Christianity has never shied away from being vulnerable. God is the Ultimate Vulnerable Giver. He gave his only Son to a taking world, so it could learn to give.

Much of the world believes a one hundred percent/one hundred percent marriage is idealistic and naïve. But the Bible clearly teaches that such a marriage is the norm. Love means giving, not taking. Love means being open and vulnerable, not closed, protective, and shrewd.

As Dr. Ed Wheat observes, the word *love* is vastly overworked and grossly misused. We have as many as twenty-five different meanings for love that we might use on a daily basis: We love God, our spouse, and our children. We also "love" apple pie, our new car, and the Cosby Show.[3]

In the precise language of the New Testament, writes Dr. Wheat, there are at least five words that distinguish and describe the various aspects of love in marriage. These include:

Epithumia is a strong desire of any kind. In marriage, this is often expressed by sexual love-making.

Eros is the Greek word that gives us our concept of romance. It strongly includes the idea of yearning for another and wanting to possess the beloved. *Eros* love is romantic, passionate, and sentimental, but it cannot last by itself.

Storge is the comfortable, old-shoe kind of love you find in the family. It is shared by parents and children, brothers and sisters. *Storge* love gives security in which the other loves of marriage can flourish.

Phileo is the love of friends who are close companions. *Phileo* love cherishes the beloved but looks for response from the other— a fifty-fifty type of relationship where both parties are comrades who share and communicate their innermost feelings, attitudes, plans, and dreams.

Agape is the word for love used most often in the New Testament. It is the unconditional love that prompted Christ to come to earth as a Man on our behalf. *Agape* love is exercised by a choice of the will and does not depend on feelings. It is a love of action, not emotion. It focuses on what you do and say rather than on how you feel.[4]

Agape love keeps *eros* alive and growing. As Dr. Wheat writes: "*Agape* love is plugged into an eternal power source, and it can go on operating when every other kind of love fails. Not only that! It loves, no matter what. No matter how unlovable the other person is, *agape* can keep on flowing. *Agape* is as unconditional as God's love for us. It is a mental attitude based on a deliberate choice of the will, and so you can choose right now to begin to love your mate with an *agape* love, no matter how much indifference or rejection you must face."[5]

So much for Greek lessons. The point is, all five kinds of love described above should be present in a marriage if the marriage is to grow into a complete, lasting, and fulfilling relationship for both partners. Each kind of love has its own place, builds on the others, and all must be put into practice in a marriage.

The following chapters take a close look at *eros* (romance) and *agape* (unconditional, never-give-up) love:

In chapter 6, Anne Kristin Carroll (*Together Forever*) argues that *agape* love can save a marriage even when it's given by only one of the partners. In fact, most troubled marriages are saved by one partner who refuses to give up.

In chapter 7, William McRae offers a ten-question quiz to help you evaluate whether you are ready for marriage. (If you are already married, take the quiz anyway. Being married and being ready for marriage are very different things.) See also the chart "Is It Love or Is It Infatuation?" following the test. Infatuation is self-centered, more the state of the Taker. Authentic love is other-centered, more the state of the Giver.

In chapter 8, Dr. Ed Wheat describes the delicate condition called romantic love and how a couple can constantly tend and stoke the fires of *eros.*

In chapter 9, Dr. Wheat compares romantic love to unconditional love. Without the constant support of *agape, eros* will waver and wane.

In chapter 10, Cecil Osborne (*The Art of Understanding Your Mate)* recognizes that, while unconditional love is impossible to achieve one hundred percent of the time, it is still the goal of the mature marriage partner who is more interested in making the marriage work than in his or her own needs or desires.

In chapter 11, Shirley Cook (*The Marriage Puzzle)* draws some practical sketches of how *agape* love has worked in her marriage. She will show you how to say "I love you anyway" in even the most awkward, unromantic, and mundane circumstances.

These selections are some of the most important you can ever read. Whether you are a natural Giver or Taker is not the point. The question is, what does the Bible teach about married love and is it possible to have a one hundred percent/one hundred percent relationship? The Giver/Giver marriage *is* possible if both spouses commit themselves to the proposition that it is more blessed to give than to receive. And as they seek to give, they will find themselves receiving far more than they ever dreamed possible.

When the satisfaction or security of another person becomes as significant to one as one's own, then a state of love exists. So far as I know, under no other circumstances is a state of love present, regardless of popular usage.[6]

Harry Stack Sullivan

Chapter 6

HOW ONE GIVER CAN MAKE THE DIFFERENCE

BY ANNE KRISTIN CARROLL
Together Forever

Is it really possible to have *unconditional* love for your mate? A lot of husbands and wives would like to think so, but the pressures and stresses of marriage are so overwhelming, the hurts and slights are so painful. As one wife of five years and mother of three said: "The spirit is willing, but my flesh runs out of energy by five o'clock, and some days even sooner. I'm bound to put conditions on how I respond to my husband, especially when he comes home and flops in front of the TV and doesn't want to help with the kids. I just don't think *unconditional* love is humanly possible."

And she's right. Left to their own resources, human beings always put conditions on their love for each other. However, as the wife of a confirmed alcoholic, Virginia discovered there is another way. Your marriage may not be in the desperate plight Virginia's was, but this chapter is especially designed to speak to a husband or wife who isn't getting a lot of support or cooperation from his or her spouse. As you read, ask yourself one question: "Can I trust God enough to apply the truths of his Word to my marriage?"

ALONE, YOU CAN MAKE THE DIFFERENCE

If you think there's no hope because you are the only one in your relationship who wants or cares enough to try to save your marriage, you are wrong! In my experience, most torn marriages are brought to new life, new vitality, by the interest, basically, of only *one* party. Some of the people discussed in this book were once in exactly the same situation you are in now.

One woman shared the following story of how one person, applying God's concepts, can make a dramatic change in a bad situation.

> After fifteen years, our marriage had deteriorated until there was little left. I tried talking, nagging, manipulation, but to no avail. I tried new hairstyles, lost weight, bought sexy nightgowns, everything I could think of. While I was trying the world's solutions to our crumbling situation, Eldon was becoming more and more involved with a woman in his office. Then one weekend, without my knowledge, he left the country to secure a "quickie divorce"! As soon as he returned, he married the "other woman"! He returned to St. Louis, picked up his clothes, told me what he had done, and left.
>
> I was devastated. I didn't know what to do, who to turn to. I was a Christian, but I had been running my life my way, not God's, for a very long time. Like many others, when a tragedy befalls us, I fell to my knees and beseeched the Lord to do something to save our relationship. He beautifully supplied me with two answers.
>
> First, I had the opportunity to learn God's concepts of marriage. Secondly, I called our family lawyer, and he told me that the divorce my husband had obtained was not valid in the States, and his new marriage was therefore illegal.
>
> Of course, Eldon wasn't too pleased about the failure of his divorce, but he went forward with plans for a conventional one. As he proceeded, I studied God's Word, and began to apply his concepts to our relationship. Eldon noticed the change in me, the peace he found when he visited the children, but still he proceeded. Finally, our day in court came. As we sat outside the courtroom waiting for the court to convene, we talked. I shared with him some of what I had learned. I told him I had learned that I had often been the cause of our unhappiness, and no matter what happened in the future, I wanted him to forgive me. He sat quietly for a time, no response came from his lips, but silent tears began to stream down his face.
>
> As the bailiff announced the start of court, Eldon turned to me and said: "Melinda, I don't understand all that has happened to you, but I have seen actions which speak louder than the words you say. If you are willing to try and forgive me, I would like to walk out of this building and come home. I'm not sure we can make it, but there is a quality about you which seems to be giving me the strength to believe it is worth another try."
>
> Starting over certainly wasn't easy, but as I daily studied God's Word (Col 2:7) and moment by moment applied his answers to our problems, our lives took a miraculous change. God's answers weren't temporary patches. I know from experience,

because it was eight years ago that God moved in and divorce moved out. From the bottom of my heart, I can testify to the fact that "with God anything is possible, and nothing is impossible" (Luke 18:27).

BUT MY SITUATION IS DIFFERENT!

Many people I've talked to have expressed a common thought. They've said: "Anne, I'll understand if you can't help me. You see, our situation is quite different." In our loneliness and fear, most of us feel that way. I certainly did. In fact, I would risk saying that the statement "our situation is different" is the most used introduction that a counselor hears. I wish you could read the thousands of letters I have received. You'd soon discover that the same basic problems are shared time after time.

The Scriptures speak to this point in 1 Corinthians 10:13: "No trial ... has overtaken you and laid hold on you that is not common to man ... belonging to human experience." As human beings, we all want to be a little special, a bit unique, and God created each of us with unique talents and abilities, but when it comes to our basic desires, basic problems, we find there are many passengers in our boat. What makes a difference between you and them is not the problems, but your willingness to grow and become a victor through them.

HOW CAN I MAKE A DIFFERENCE?

To share with you how the changes you alone make can affect your entire marital relationship, let's first look at the following situation.

Virginia was married to a confirmed alcoholic. She had cried, screamed, hollered, and clearly let Ben know what a worthless, rotten person she thought he was.

He knew he wasn't the kind of man he should be. He didn't need Virginia to tell him. What he did need were excuses for his behavior, and unknowingly Virginia had been providing many of them. Her constant nagging about his drinking only gave him the excuse to drown her voice in liquor. Her criticism only gave him the excuse to justify his indulgence by thinking, "Any man who had to live with a wife like her would drink, too."

When Virginia realized she was contributing to his indulgence, she began to change her responses. The next time Ben came home roaring drunk, Virginia greeted him with a smile, offered to make him dinner, or run him a warm bath. The initial shock almost sobered him up. At first Ben responded to Virginia with more hostility than before. He resented her not fulfilling her old role. He fought hard trying to get her to fight, to help him justify his actions.

But Virginia continued to respond to him in love. By changing her behavior, a vacuum was created, and Ben couldn't respond in his normal way, because the circumstances were different. Of course, none of us likes our status quo changed; Ben didn't either. But in time, with love and patience, he began to see himself for what he really was. He began to clearly understand his real problems instead of the rationalizations he'd contrived over the years. Ben was then ready for help and change.

Certainly this is a drastic illustration, and I don't propose that every alcoholic wife or husband is transformed overnight by simply changing your reaction to him or her. There are many other basic factors involved, which we will discuss later. What I hope you will see in Ben and Virginia's story is that action creates reaction. When you change the action, or the reaction, you require your mate to make changes also.

Often a mate will test to see if the change is real. Perhaps, like me, you have tried so many personality changes or forms of manipulating before, that your mate feels you are just on a new kick, and it probably won't last long. Remember, an act is just that, an act, and sooner or later, if there is no truth in it, your mate will see through the façade.

A clear-cut shift in your reaction and relationship to your mate may initially be disturbing and confusing. It is rather like learning a new set of action and reaction patterns. In time, the mere circumstances will demand change. Your wife can't scream about never having money of her own if you sit down, make a budget together, and allot her a certain amount a month, plus extra for her. If your husband has refused to talk to you because he says you don't have anything in common, learn about his interests, learn about his work, learn to be a good listener. His reasoning and excuses are destroyed and a warm, new situation is created.

Some of the above suggestions only represent superficial changes in a relationship and do not deal with the root problems, but they are examples of how change occurs. Voids create vacuums which have to be filled. It only takes one person to make changes that will ultimately change a whole relationship.

BUT I CAN'T CHANGE

You say you have tried to change your actions and reactions in the past and failed. The idea of forcing yourself into a different life pattern, constantly thinking positively, pumping yourself up as you face the next crisis, only to find you don't have the inner strength, doesn't excite you. Well, I don't blame you.

When I said you alone can make dramatic and lasting changes in your marriage, I meant *without human support and help.* The only way to make true, honest transformations, ones that don't crumble with the first assault, can only be found when you are plugged into the ultimate power source. Human effort alone will result in failure. You may present a great first night, but the show will never have a long engagement. *Only with the power that is available through a personal relationship with Jesus Christ can this miracle be accomplished.*

Some of you are saying, "But I prayed. I went to church."

That isn't what I'm talking about. I am speaking of a personal, daily, moment-by-moment dependency on Jesus Christ to make changes in and through you. As a Christian, you can't say "can't," because as you recall, in 1 Corinthians 10:13, God says you can!

For now, remember Philippians 4:13: "I have strength for all things in Christ who empowers me—I am ready for anything and equal to anything through him who infuses inner strength into me, that is, I am self-sufficient in Christ's sufficiency." And you will be!

SMALL PROBLEM OR LARGE THREAT?

Too many people live in a state of fear and insecurity because they view every problem that arises in their marital relationship as a threat to its very foundation. Many of us become very unrealistic when we think of our own marriages. If we were at work and the typewriter ceased to function, we forgot to mail out the monthly statements, and the boss screamed at us for forgetting that important client's call, we would realize it had just been a bad day. On the other hand, if the oven overheats, dinner is ruined, we forget to pick up that favorite suit from the cleaner's and our husbands rant, rave, and say they wish they had married someone else, we panic. The situations are the same; only our reasoning has changed. Less pressure is put on our marriages when we learn to recognize problems for exactly what they are and nothing more. Utopia doesn't exist, and every relationship has disturbances.

Problems are just that and nothing more, unless we make them so. For instance, a bad cold can be very unpleasant, uncomfortable, temporarily debilitating, but you wouldn't assume for one minute that it was a terminal disease. Certainly, you wouldn't call all your friends, relate every symptom, then say your eternal good-byes. We do that in a marriage. A problem arises, we panic, certain that divorce is right around the corner. Most of us share, with anybody who will listen, all the pain and heartbreak we are experiencing, and then relate how hopeless our situation is. Beyond making molehills into mountains, we often plant a corrupting seed in our mate's mind. Did you ever realize that what you see as a threat may be viewed differently by your mate? Maybe he or she didn't see the issue as important at all, but when you mentioned that it could lead to divorce, you actually set the thought in motion!

You can't proceed with any real effectiveness in problem-solving until you stop using divorce as a scapegoat. The word itself must be stricken from your vocabulary.

Perhaps you view divorce as "the way out." The word itself suggests freedom, elimination of pressure and pain. You are convinced that next time it will be different. If you want out to marry that "right person," divorce appears to be a sweet release. Unfortunately, in our desire to find the ideal situation, we face not only the unsolved conflicts of the first marriage, but the new problems which will ultimately arise. For example, the problem in your first marriage may have been a critical spirit. Mate number one stunk up the house with his smoking, he drank too much, he was undependable. You complained, nagged, but to no avail. Now mate number two doesn't have the social graces to which you are accustomed, and try as you might, you can't change him. Certainly, the situation is different, but the critical spirit which wasn't resolved in marriage one is now affecting marriage two. Or in the first marriage your mate kept you in a constant state of jealousy. Of course, partner number two never flirts, and never starts drooling when an attractive girl comes on the TV, but the other day you met him for lunch, and were surprised at the beautiful blonde he'd just hired. Jealousy began to swell in your soul, and you became suspicious and miserable. Here again the circumstances are changed, but the basic unresolved conflict still exists.

Don't delude yourself into thinking that divorce is the panacea for a sick marriage. Isolate your problems *right now*, face and solve them; then you can experience true happiness and fulfillment right where you are planted!

If you know your mate is involved with someone else, you are hurting terribly. I know sometimes the pain gets so great that it actually becomes physical. I know—I have gone through exactly the same kind of hurt time and again. Only then I didn't realize how much my words and actions were the root cause of it. If you feel that running to a lawyer and getting a piece of paper will cure the pain, believe me you can't imagine what "finalized" pain can be like.

WHAT ABOUT GOD'S HELP?

I'm not telling you that if you truly want to save your marriage, if you sincerely trust and rely on Christ and apply the concepts for a happy marriage, that you will be too busy to hurt. I can't tell you that there won't be setbacks. But, remember, your marriage didn't get where it now is overnight; it didn't get there all by itself, and the return process is like growing—sometimes it's slow, sometimes it hurts, but the end results are worth so much. You must take the correcting of your problems one day at a time, remembering that you are not alone in your desire to save your marriage. The help of God almighty is available to you. Psalm 34:17–18a: "When the righteous cry for help, the Lord hears, and delivers them out of all their distress and troubles. The Lord is close to those who are of a broken heart." Isn't that fantastic! God loves you more than you love yourself, and he even loves your mate more than you do. Since he established the institution of marriage (Gen. 2:18), he wants more than anything in the world to have your relationship reconciled. You can relax, knowing his promises: (1) Hebrews 13:5: "He [God] himself has said, I will not in any way fail you nor give you up nor leave you without support. I will not in any degree leave you helpless, nor forsake, nor let you down. Assuredly not!" (2) 1 Corinthians 10:13: "But God is faithful and he can be trusted not to let you be tempted and tried and assayed beyond your ability and strength of resistance and power to endure, but with temptation he will always also provide the way out—the means of escape to a landing place—that you may be capable and strong and powerful patiently to bear up under it." (3) In 2 Corinthians 12:9 he promises us that he will be sufficient to see us through anything. (4) In 2 Corinthians 9:8 he promises that he will support us, bless us, so we may be strong enough for whatever problems we face.

Perhaps you may feel that these concepts won't work. You may think that God's directives are totally opposite to all human feelings and ideas. God clearly speaks to this feeling in Isaiah 55:8–9: "For my thoughts are not your thoughts, neither are your ways my ways, says the Lord. For as the heavens are higher than the earth, so are my ways higher than your ways, and my thoughts than your thoughts." You might think of the concepts this way: If you are familiar with skiing, you know when you began to ski, your first instinct was to lean back into the slope. It was natural, it seemed right. But what happened? You fell flat. When you were willing to do the opposite, to defy human logic, to risk and lean away from the hill, then your skis became firmly implanted and you were off on a lovely adventure. The same is true in life. God's concepts are often totally contrary to our nature. Remember Proverbs 14:12: "There is a way which seems right to a man and appears straight before him, but at the end of it are the ways of death." When we are willing to lean away from the hill, to depend on him to know what is best for us, only then do our lives and marriages become the wonderful adventure he has promised and planned for us.

Isn't it wonderful how *you* can change directions and move forward? *You* can actually begin correcting the problems that are destroying your marriage!

Do you realize how far you have progressed in your thinking patterns in just the last few minutes? You are on the brink of discovery; *hope* is now yours. Those answers that have eluded you for so long are now in your hands. You aren't alone any more, you are traveling a well-worn path, and at the end you'll find the most beautiful reward of all, love renewed.

Your goal at this moment is to realize that divorce *isn't* the answer that God would have you seek, nor is it the cure-all that the world has made it out to be. Your goal is to recognize that you are not alone in your problems, that thousands of others have walked this same way, and through the application of God's concepts have changed hell into happiness. You have to understand moment by moment, that the power of God almighty is always with you, always ready to support you, all that he asks is your availability. You are ready to become a survivor.

♥ WE ALL STRUGGLE TO LOVE UNCONDITIONALLY ♥

You may not be ready for divorce, but all of the insights in this chapter apply to every marriage in any state of growth. Remember, all marriages have problems; the difference is in how you perceive what can be done about it. Try making a list of six instances of loving behavior that you've shown your mate in the last month. Is the list rather blank? Then begin to change that. In two weeks, check on yourself to see what God has accomplished through you.

If your own needs seem overwhelming and just aren't being met, go back and review chapter 3 by Larry Crabb, which discusses how to step off the cliff of safety into the abyss of rejection by trusting in God's rope of love. And when things go slowly and nothing much seems to be happening, take time to make a list of all God's blessings in your life. You will soon see how much you have to be thankful for and, when depression and attacks of the blues hit hard, pull out that list and spend time thanking God for those blessings.

Of course, there is the possibility that you may doubt your love for your spouse. In the next chapter, William McRae shares insights on how to tell if you're "still in love."

Chapter 7

HOW CAN YOU KNOW
YOU'RE (STILL) IN LOVE?

BY WILLIAM McRAE
Preparing for Your Marriage

We have nothing in common any more," the despondent husband tells the counselor. "We seem to be growing in opposite directions. I guess we just fell out of love."

Is this husband right? Were he and his wife ever really in love in the first place? What does it mean to "fall in love"? And can you fall out of love just as easily? If someone asked you to define or evaluate the depth of your love for your mate, how would you go about it? William McRae shares ten ways you can test—and prove—your love for one another. While these tests were designed primarily for couples thinking about getting married, they are also helpful to people who have been married—for a few years or for many.

Married couples can take these tests in two ways: Look back on your courtship and consider how you would have answered the questions then; take a long hard look at the present state of your marriage and answer the questions accordingly. Where have you grown and in which direction?

TESTS OF LOVE

Several months ago a young couple with severe marital problems sought help. After the husband had told his tale of woe, he sighed and said, "I guess we just weren't ready to get married."

Many aren't, but realize it too late.

When is a couple ready for marriage?

"When we are sure we are in love!" This is the standard answer today. For most, love is the sole criterion for marriage. Yet many couples can hardly identify it, let alone define it.

To be told, "Oh, you'll know when it hits you; it hits you right between the eyes; you'll know when it is the real thing," leaves you a helpless slave to a master you can't even identify. There are, however, some time-proven tests of true, genuine love, the kind of love that builds great marriages.

In his book, *I Married You*, Walter Trobisch has suggested six tests for love:[7]

1. *The Sharing Test.* Are you able to share? Do you want to make your partner happy or do you want to become happy?

2. *The Strength Test.* Does your love give you new strength and fill you with creative energy? Or does it take away your strength and energy?

3. *The Respect Test.* Do you really have respect for each other? Are you proud of your partner?

4. *The Habit Test.* Do you only love each other or do you also like each other and accept each other with your habits and shortcomings?

5. *The Quarrel Test.* Are you able to forgive each other and give in to each other? The ability to be reconciled after a real quarrel must be tested before marriage.

6. *The Time Test.* "Never get married until you have summered and wintered with your partner." Has your love summered and wintered? Have you known each other long enough to know each other well enough?

To these six tests, four others may be added:

7. *The Separation Test.* Do you feel an unusual joy while in the company of each other? Is there pain in separation?

8. *The Giving Test.* Love and marriage are giving, not getting. Are you in love to give? Are you capable of self-giving? Is this quality of self-giving constantly evident?

9. *The Growth Test.* Is your love dynamic in its growth? Is it progressively maturing? Are the characteristics of Christian love developing?

10. *The Sex Test.* Is there a mutual enjoyment of each other without the constant need of physical expression? If you can't be together without petting, you don't have the maturity and love essential for marriage.

Walter Trobisch offers this profound insight:

> Sex is no test of love for it is precisely the very thing that one wants to test which is destroyed by the testing.[8]

Mutual respect becomes damaged, and emptiness creeps into the relationship. The couple becomes less and less sure of their love. So they intensify their intimacies in the hope of intensifying their love, but in so doing they become less sure of their love.

Consider for a moment Paul's description of the manifestations of true love.

> Love is patient, love is kind, and is not jealous; love does not brag and is not arrogant, does not act unbecomingly; it does not seek its own, is not provoked, does not take into account a wrong suffered, does not rejoice in unrighteousness, but rejoices with the truth; bears all things, believes all things, hopes all things, endures all things (1 Cor. 13:4–7).

Love is the unconditional acceptance of a person, flaws and all. It therefore demands a thorough knowledge of that person, a recognition of strengths and weaknesses, and acceptance.

Put it to the test. Examine it carefully. You are not ready for marriage until it is evident that your relationship is based on a genuine love for each other.

♥ TO TEST YOUR LOVE IN SPECIFIC WAYS ♥

This chapter turns to a well-known passage of Scripture in 1 Corinthians 13:4–8 to describe love in concrete and specific terms. Plan ways you can apply these attitudes of love to your marriage this coming week:

I will be patient with my spouse by: _____

I will be kind to my spouse by: _____

I will resist being jealous when: _____

I will resist being boastful or proud when: _____

I will be polite and courteous by: _____

I will resist being selfish (the Taker mentality), particularly in regard to: _____

When my spouse makes me angry, I will admit it and forgive. I will not keep score. _____

I will trust my mate to: _____

IS IT LOVE OR IS IT INFATUATION?

Stephen Grunlan *(Marriage and the Family)* examines the difference between love and infatuation. Infatuation is like a huge ice cream cone; it soon melts. Real love is enduring; it lasts.[9]

Infatuation	Authentic Love
1. Infatuation is born at first sight and will conquer all.	1. Authentic love is a developing relationship and deepens with realistically shared experiences.
2. Infatuation demands exclusive attention and devotion and is jealous of outsiders.	2. Authentic love is built on self-acceptance and is shared unselfishly with others.
3. Infatuation is characterized by exploitation and direct need gratification.	3. Authentic love seeks to aid and strengthen the loved one without striving for recompense.
4. Infatuation is built on physical attraction and sexual gratification. Sex often dominates the relationship.	4. Authentic love includes sexual satisfaction, but not to the exclusion of sharing in other areas of life.
5. Infatuation is static and egocentric. Change is sought in the partner in order to satisfy one's own needs and desires.	5. Authentic love is growing and developing reality. Love expands to include the growth and creativity of the loved one.
6. Infatuation is romanticized. The couple does not face reality or is frightened by it.	6. Authentic love enhances reality and makes the partners more complete and adequate persons.
7. Infatuation is irresponsible and fails to consider the future consequences of today's action.	7. Authentic love is responsible and gladly accepts the consequences of mutual involvement.

1 Corinthians 13 is a blueprint for keeping romance burning brightly in your marriage. In the next chapter, Dr. Ed Wheat and his co-author, Gloria Okes Perkins, give additional ideas for keeping romance alive.

Chapter 8

HOW TO FALL IN LOVE AND STAY IN LOVE

BY DR. ED WHEAT AND GLORIA OKES PERKINS
Love Life for Every Married Couple

One of the standard complaints about marriage is that the fires of romance and passion that burned so brightly during courtship and the honeymoon all too quickly fade as life together becomes plain, ordinary, too busy, or boring.

From being on their "best behavior," and looking their best, spouses slowly, sometimes quickly, are transformed into someone else. Warmth and attentiveness are replaced by lukewarm, or cool, preoccupation. Sensitivity turns to indifference. Having time "just for each other" is swallowed up by work schedules, diapers, crying children, and the seemingly thousand and one things that need doing every day. How does romance survive—or can it? Is romance a viable state, or is it fantasy invented by Hollywood and no more real than the images portrayed on the silver screen?

In this chapter, Dr. Wheat tells how to keep romantic love burning brightly, not by simply counting on luck or "chemistry," but by *choosing* to do so. As you read, think about one basic question:

♥ Is romantic love something we still try to nurture in our marriage? If so, how?

ROMANTIC LOVE—THE THRILL FACTOR

At first glance romantic love seems to be a controversial subject. For instance . . .

Some cynics scoff at romantic love as a myth.

Some sincere Christians consider romantic love the whipped cream on the sundae of marriage—decorative, but unnecessary. They see this as a lower form of love that husbands and wives should disregard in their search for higher ground.

Some individuals feel uncertain about the value of romantic love because they confuse the genuine article with that frothy substitute known as temporary infatuation.

Some try to suppress all thought of romantic love because they are not experiencing it. Some rationalize, "I don't have it; it must not exist." Others think, "It's not possible in *my* marriage."

In spite of all this, just about everyone inwardly longs for a thrilling love relationship involving oneness, a deep intimacy with another person, joy and optimism, spice and excitement, and that wonderful, euphoric, almost indescribable sensation known as "being in love." Some people say they are "on cloud nine." They mean that they feel energized, motivated, confident to conquer because they know they are loved by their beloved. There is a sense of awe in feeling *chosen* for this blessed state. With it goes a thrill of anticipation in being together. Most important, a fresh sense of purpose sweetens life because the two have found each other and have, as the expression goes, "fallen in love."

This is not overstating the case. As a physician, I have seen that the emotions of romantic love give people a new outlook on life and a sense of well-being. Romantic love is good medicine for fears and anxieties and a low self-image. Psychologists point out that real romantic love has an organizing and constructive effect on our personalities. It brings out the best in us, giving us the will to improve ourselves and to reach for a greater maturity and responsibility. This love enables us to begin to function at our highest level.

Quite honestly, if you are not in love with your marriage partner in this way, you are missing something wonderful, no matter how sincere your commitment to that person may be. Even contentment can be dull and drab in comparison with the joy God planned for you with your marriage partner.

In this chapter we will suggest ways in which you can revitalize your relationship by adding *eros* love to your marriage and learning how to enhance your present love so that it will become more exciting, not less so, as the years go by.

What if you are having serious problems in your marriage? This chapter is for you too. A film advertisement caught my eye recently. I'm not that interested in what Hollywood is producing, but the headline asked a relevant question: *What Do You Do When Everything Between the Two of You Seems Wrong?* The answer: *Fall in Love!*

This may sound far-fetched, but, in reality, it is good counsel for the couple with a troubled marriage. I have seen couples resolve their problems by falling in love. Other biblical counselors report similar results. Anne Kristin Carroll's book, *From the Brink of Divorce*, includes a number of case histories where marriages hung by a thread. In each of these cases the couple preserved their marriage by falling in love. Counselor Jay Adams tells of the many couples who come into his office claiming that their situation is hopeless because they don't love each other anymore. His answer is, "I am sorry to hear that. I guess you will have to learn how to love each other." He says that six or eight weeks later, if they really mean business, they are likely to go out of his office hand in hand.[10]

In all of these cases, the couples have applied specific biblical counsel such as that given in this book. But you may be wondering how it is possible, even under the best of circumstances, to evoke that dramatic happening we call *falling in love*. It seems to be mysteriously compounded of moonbeams and magic. It involves physiological reactions such as quickened breathing and a fast-beating heart. It is one of the most vivid personal experiences a human being will ever have. So how can it be developed— particularly within marriage where two people are caught in the realistic grind of daily life?

The answer is that romantic love can be *learned* emotionally. This brings it into the realm of possibility for all who want to experience it in their marriage.

TWO WAYS TO LEARN TO LOVE

There are two ways to set up the conditions under which this love can be learned. First, by utilizing your own God-given faculty of imaginative thought; second, by providing the right emotional climate for your mate.

Although you will be using mental, imaginative processes, this does not mean you are to force your emotions. Emotions cannot be commanded to appear, but they will come freely when the conditions are right. Begin by choosing to be willing to fall in love with the person you are married to. Falling in love begins in your mind with the choice to *surrender* to the compelling feelings of love. (This is in contrast to *agape*, where the choice must be made to give love consistently.) Surrender means vulnerability and the chance of being hurt; but in marriage it also offers the possibility of great happiness.

Men may find it more difficult to make this deliberate choice to fall in love than women do. Researchers claim that although men have the reputation for being matter-of-fact and practical, they are unlikely to let practical considerations guide their love life. Once their romantic feelings have been strongly awakened, they are more apt to be controlled by the emotions of love than their feminine counterparts and less apt to make decisions based on personal advantage. For instance, the king of England could and did abdicate his throne for the woman he loved. But would the lady have given up her crown, had the situation been reversed? A quarter of a century later, Princess Margaret of England, faced with a similar choice, chose her position and gave up the man.

Researchers have found that women are less compulsive and more sensible when it comes to love. They know how to fall in love instinctively and are more willing to try when they see that it is advantageous for them. As one young woman said, "If I wasn't in love with a man, but he had all the qualities I wanted—well, I could talk myself into falling in love!"

In a Christian marriage, the advantages of being in love with each other are so obvious that I hope both husband and wife will make this decision. Begin with the willingness to surrender and to let your emotions take you on together. Roadblocks such as anger and unforgiveness will, of course, get in the way of this surrender and must be removed. Then you are ready to set up the conditions for romantic love.

Romantic love is a pleasurable learned response to the way your partner looks and feels, to the things your partner says and does, and to the emotional experiences you share. As you consistently think on these favorable things, your response to them becomes ever more strongly imprinted in your mind. You are learning the emotion of love through your thought processes, and it becomes easier to thrill to the sight, sound, and touch of your partner.

Women's Bible teacher, Shirley Rice, tells her students that she would like to inspire in them the same eager anticipation for growth in their love life with their husbands that they have toward their growth in Christ. Then she shows them how to use their thought life—the faculties of memory and imagination—to build romantic love in their relationships. She says,

> Are you in love with your husband? Not, Do you love him? I know you do. He has been around a long time, and you're used to him. He is the father of your children. But are you in love with him? How long has it been since your heart really squeezed when you looked at him? Look at him through another woman's eyes—he still looks pretty good, doesn't he? Why is it you have forgotten the things that attracted you to him at first? This is an attitude we drift into—we take our men for granted. We complain bitterly about this ourselves because we hate to be taken for granted. But we do this to them. Men are sentimental, more so than women. We weep and express ourselves audibly. Because they don't do it openly does not mean they are not emotional. Your husband needs to be told that you love him, that he is attractive to you. By the grace of

God, I want you to start changing your thought pattern. Tomorrow morning, get your eyes off the toaster or the baby bottles long enough to LOOK at him. Don't you see the way his coat fits his shoulders? Look at his hands. Do you remember when just to look at his strong hands made your heart lift? Well, LOOK at him and remember. Then loose your tongue and tell him you love him. Will you ask the Lord to give you a sentimental, romantic, physical, in-love kind of love for your husband? He will do this. His love can change the actual physical quality of our love for our husbands.[11]

Husbands need to stop and remember how they felt when they fell in love. One described it this way: "To hold her in my arms against the twilight and be her comrade forever—this was all I wanted so long as my life should last."[12]

"When a man loves with all his heart he experiences an intensely thrilling sensation," a writer explains. "It has been described as a feeling almost like pain. . . . He feels exuberant and light, like walking on clouds. At times he feels fascinated and enchanted with the girl. Along with all of these thrilling and consuming sensations there is tenderness, a desire to protect and shelter his woman from all harm, danger and difficulty."[13]

How was it with you when you first fell in love with the woman you married? Or (if you feel that you were never in love) look at her now through another man's eyes. Think about those things that are attractive in her. Love her with a sensitive appreciation and watch her become beautiful as she reflects and radiates the love you have poured out to her.

USE THE POWER OF YOUR IMAGINATION

I am suggesting that both husband and wife must use their imagination to fall in love, renew romantic love, or keep alive the *eros* love they now have. Remember that love must grow or die. Imagination is perhaps the strongest natural power we possess. It furthers the emotions in the same way that illustrations enlarge the impact of a book. It's as if we have movie screens in our minds, and we own the ability to throw pictures on the screen—whatever sort of pictures we choose. We can visualize thrilling, beautiful situations with our mates whenever we want to.

Try it. Select a moment of romantic feeling with your partner from the past, present, or hoped-for future. As you begin to think about that feeling, your imagination goes to work with visual pictures. Your imagination feeds your thoughts, strengthening them immeasurably; then your thoughts intensify your feelings. This is how it works. Imagination is a gift from the Creator to be used for good, to help accomplish his will in a hundred different ways. So build romantic love on your side of the marriage by thinking about your partner, concentrating on positive experiences and pleasures out of the past and then daydreaming, anticipating future pleasure with your mate. The frequency and intensity of these positive, warm, erotic, tender thoughts about your partner, strengthened by the imagination factor, will govern your success in falling in love.

Of course, this means that you may have to give up outside attachments and daydreams about someone else if you have substituted another as the object of your affections. Many people who are not in love with their partner begin dreaming about someone else in an attempt to fill the emotional vacuum. Even if it is only in the fantasy stage, you need to forsake it and focus your thoughts on the one you married.

In a book on how to fall *out* of love, a psychologist counsels her patients to practice silent ridicule, microscopically concentrating on the flaws of the other party, even picturing that person in absurd, ridiculous ways, until all respect for that one is gone. This should indicate how important it is, if you want to fall in love, to give up mental criticism of your mate and practice appreciation instead.

To maintain respect for your partner, never allow another person to tear him or her down in your presence. One of Abigail Van Buren's ten commandments for wives says, "Permit no one to tell thee that thou art having a hard time; neither thy mother, thy sister, nor thy neighbor, for the Judge will not hold her guiltless who letteth another disparage her husband." Practice saying good things about your partner to other people. Think about how much your mate means to you and dwell always on the positive side of your partner's character and personality.

PROVIDE THE RIGHT CLIMATE

While you are doing all that we have just described, you need to provide your mate with the right emotional climate for love to grow in. What do we mean by this? Here's how one man won his bride, as she described to me later. As you read, remember that these same love-producing practices will work even better in marriage.

> From the night we met, somehow we knew God had a special purpose for us. We could hardly stay apart the ten months before we married. We saw to it that we spent a part of every day or evening together. He wrote love letters and sent cards, phoned during the day, and brought special little items to me. He always hugged me when we met. He kissed me passionately and because he spent so much time just talking and listening to me, I fell head over heels in love with him. He was

so proud of me he showed me off to everyone. I felt like I had been brought back from the dead.

Observe all the ways in which this man established a romantic climate and then ask yourself when you last gave your partner this kind of romantic attention.

In *The Fascinating Girl*, Helen Andelin tells how to create romantic situations. These suggestions can be put to good use by a wife seeking to provide a romantic climate for her husband. The best atmospheres include: dim lights; a cozy winter evening before an open fire; sitting out on a porch or patio in spring or summer moonlight; times spent on or near the water, especially at night; strolls through a beautiful garden; walks on mountain trails or in the woods; drives in the hills; a peaceful, homey setting; a romantic, intimate restaurant; picnic lunches in a quiet park. Whatever you do, keep it just for the two of you. Men seldom become romantic when other people are around.

Either husband or wife can suggest short trips (even just overnight) that become very special. Shared moments can take on significance. Researchers have found that shared emotional arousal is a catalyst in the development of romantic, passionate love. The emotions do not have to be positive ones, but they must be felt in common. For instance, you may experience an exciting moment together or share the glow of success; but you may also be drawn together as you react to the outside threat of danger. This may explain the noticeable increase in romance during the war years. The key factors are these: There must be a shared emotional experience involving intense feeling, resulting in a physiological response, and the receiving of a label approximating love in the minds of both.

A husband described such an experience to me. He and his wife had been contemplating a separation. He said,

> The other night we had a deep talk about our future. We both felt hopeless and didn't know what to do. She began crying and I cried some. It was strange because we ended up hugging each other. I felt like hugging her and she felt like being hugged. All of a sudden there was an exchange of something important. I felt as if she needed me, and I knew I needed her. It was a rare experience that has given us something to build on.

In providing the right emotional climate, do all that you can to avoid boredom even though your life must of necessity consist of routine. Think of your relationship as a continuing love affair and look at every tender, generous, romantic word or act that you bestow on your partner as an investment in pleasurable memories and emotional experiences that can grow and multiply into romantic love.

There are two additional things you can do to provide the right stimulus for the response of romantic love. The first is physical touching—and lots of it. I am not referring to sexual advances, but to the kind of physical closeness that draws very young people into romantic infatuations. This is how young teens fall in love so quickly and intensely. Married couples with monotonous relationships certainly can learn something from this about building the emotion of love. We all have a need to be held, fondled, caressed, and tenderly touched. As we experience this from our marriage partner and give it in return, love itself is exchanged and the resulting sparks kindle a romantic blaze.

AND DON'T FORGET EYE CONTACT

Equally important is eye contact. Psychologists have found by controlled experiments that people who are deeply in love with each other do engage in much more eye contact than other couples. As the old song goes, "I only have eyes for you." This is true of lovers.

Eye contact shows its significance early in life when an infant's eyes begin focusing at about two to four weeks of age. From then on a baby is always searching for another set of eyes to lock on to, and this becomes a necessity. The child's emotions are fed by eye contact. We never outgrow this need, and when a loved one avoids eye contact with us because of disinterest or anger, it can be devastating.

If you practice warm, affectionate, meaningful eye contact with your partner, you will see how enjoyable this is. When your eyes signal romantic interest and emotional arousal, a spiraling response from your partner is likely.

As everyone knows, *eros* love is visually oriented. This indicates that both husband and wife should be as attractive and well-groomed as possible, whenever possible.

You cannot demand that someone else fall in love with you or expect it as a matter of course, not even from your husband or wife. But you *can* set up the conditions whereby your partner will find it easy to love you. Always be mindful of the kind of emotional response you are establishing in your partner's thought patterns by the way you act, by what you do and say, and how you look at love. Remember to send out signals that are pleasant and pleasurable rather than painful or distasteful, for in a sense you are teaching your partner to respond to you all of the time, either positively or negatively. This is yet another reason why you must never even seem judgmental of your mate—not if you want to spark romantic love and keep it aflame.

One of the greatest hindrances to romantic love is the habit (easily fallen into) of nagging. In a Christian family seminar, J. Allan Petersen analyzed the syndrome of nagging in this manner.

> Nagging is basically a woman's weapon used against the man in her marriage. The recurrent irritation of nagging is designed to get the wife what she wants. When her husband surrenders out of exasperation, he secretly hates himself for doing it and then sets his feet a little more so that the next time around she has to nag more than she did before to accomplish the same purpose. This state of affairs continues until finally the woman has formed a habit of nagging, nagging to get what she wants. She really is achieving her selfish purpose at the expense of her marriage. While she obtains personal and immediate satisfaction of her "want," she sacrifices something very valuable in the relationship. The wife who has to obtain by nagging is a self-confessed failure as a wife. She is admitting, "I don't know how to make my husband so pleased with me, so grateful for me, and so proud of me that he will be happy to do something that pleases me." The nagging wife should ask herself, "How much do I really love? What do I know about real love?" Nagging basically is an expression of a selfish independence.

It should be observed that in some marriages where the wife dominates, a husband may resort to habitual nagging. No matter who does it, it effectively stamps out any spark of romantic love and should be avoided!

ROMANTIC LOVE IS MORE THAN A MYTH

At the beginning of this chapter we mentioned some controversies surrounding romantic love. Perhaps we can clarify the facts in these cases. If any reader still thinks of romantic love as a myth invented by the film industry, it can be pointed out that, based on biblical, literary, and historical evidence, romantic love has always existed. Researchers conclude, "Despite the assertions of some anthropologists, the phenomenon is neither of recent origin nor restricted to our culture. Although not always thought of as a necessary prelude to marriage, romantic and passionate love has appeared at all times and places."[14] In a cross-cultural study of seventy-five societies made in 1967, romantic love was found to be surprisingly predominant in other societies.[15]

As Christians we can be sure that romantic love is as old as Time itself, for it came into being in the Garden when the first man and woman gazed on each other. We must recognize that it was our Creator who gifted us with the capacity for the intense and passionate emotions required to fall in love. Clearly, God intended for our emotional potential to be fully developed in marriage and to find its fulfillment in oneness with our beloved.

We spoke earlier of some who feel that romantic love in marriage should be downgraded because it is selfish in origin. They judge it to be selfish because it desires a response. These people have overlooked the fact that romantic love is biblical. One entire book of the Bible, the Song of Solomon, has been devoted to the topic of romantic love in marriage, giving us an ideal pattern to follow in our own marriage.

Every facet of human love between husband and wife cries out for a response and there is nothing wrong with this. *Agape* may be the most selfless of the loves, but it does not hold exclusive rights to a life of giving. Natural loves also involve giving, even sacrificing, for the loved one. Researchers have observed that a significant component of romantic love is the keen desire to work for the beloved's happiness, no matter how much effort is required.

This brings Jacob of the Old Testament to mind—Jacob, the selfish young man, who, nonetheless, fell so deeply in love with Rachel that he worked seven years for a disagreeable father-in-law, then another seven in order to marry her. The Book of Genesis says that these years of labor "seemed unto him but a few days, for the love he had for her."

"To be in love," wrote the author of *A Severe Mercy*, "is a kind of adoring that turns the lover away from self."[16] He was describing his own experience in marriage, and lovers will agree with him. In another sense these words can be applied to the compelling emotional love that the believer feels for the Lord Jesus Christ—a love that parallels in many respects the feelings and responses of a husband and wife in love. Theologian Charles Williams wrote that he was "startled to find romantic love an exact correlation and parallel of Christianity."[17] This reminds us that true romantic love, undergirded by *agape*,and enjoyed in the permanent context of Christian marriage, beautifully portrays the love relationship of Jesus Christ and his church. Thus, the goal of building romantic love in marriage can be a matter of confident prayer, for this is pleasing to the Lord.

Some people may be confused about infatuation vs. true romantic love. Infatuation is based on fantasy; true romantic love has a foundation of strong but tender realism. Infatuation is occupied with externals; real love is a response to the whole person. Infatuation fades with time; love keeps on growing like a living thing. Infatuation demands and takes; love delights in giving.

An important guideline for Christians to follow is that of emotions vs. the standard of the Word of God. If you are infatuated, your emotions will clamor to take complete charge and they probably will do so. In real love, your reason, instructed by biblical concepts, guides your emotions and shapes your relationship according to God's wisdom. Deeper channels are carved for the expression of this love than could ever exist in an infatuation.

Within the depths of this relationship, thrills and strong emotions can add a sweet savor to the marriage daily.

If you have felt hopeless concerning the possibility of romantic love in your marriage, you can take heart. Romantic love does exist, and not just for others. I challenge you to put these suggestions to the test.

♥ HOW TO "WORK" AT ROMANTIC LOVE ♥

The idea of "working" to make romantic love happen may sound contradictory and even repugnant, especially if you are the romantic type. Nonetheless, choosing to romance your mate is something that still requires effort or it will not happen. You have to work at staying in love, but as you do so, you will find that it isn't work at all! Here are just a few ideas:

- ♥ Use the power of your imagination, which is a gift from God, to think romantically about your mate. What memories can you look back on? What pleasures can you anticipate?
- ♥ Create a romantic situation for you and your mate to enjoy this week—perhaps tonight. Keep it simple, just the two of you.
- ♥ Try candles and low lights for dinner instead of the usual meal gulped in glaring lights while watching TV news.
- ♥ Get a baby-sitter—even for just an hour—to be alone. Take a walk or perhaps a drive to see the sunset from a special spot.
- ♥ While on that drive, stop for a cup of coffee, a dish of yogurt, or even a candy bar to share—whatever both of you enjoy.
- ♥ Surprise your mate with a picnic—perhaps during lunch hour.
- ♥ Try giving each other back rubs.
- ♥ Share with each other on "how I am doing on the inside."

The possibilities are endless, though your romantic love may have cooled to the point where you are not sure you can find the energy and motivation to follow through. In the next chapter, Dr. Wheat tells how and why *eros* (romance) must be reinforced with *agape* (unconditional) love.

Chapter 9

THE *AGAPE* WAY TO LOVE YOUR MATE

BY DR. ED WHEAT AND GLORIA OKES PERKINS
Love Life for Every Married Couple

While romantic love is vital to a lasting marriage, it is delicate, fragile, and not always stable. Romantic loves depends on a reciprocal process: "You love me, be attentive, adoring, sensitive, and caring—and I'll do the same for you." When one feels neglected or "unloved" by a spouse who is tired, preoccupied or too busy, romance wavers and wanes.

Like any fire, romantic love needs constant tending and stoking. Romantic love needs the constant support of *agape*— unconditional love that is interested only in the needs of the other. *Eros* and *agape* go together like a hand in a glove. *Agape* is the hand; *eros* is the glove. Without *agape*, *eros* lies limp and helpless. In the following chapter, Dr. Wheat defines *agape* love as a choice you must make to ensure the growth of your marriage. As you read, ask yourself:

♥ How committed am I to showing my mate unconditional love, no matter how my mate treats me? How, specifically, do I love my mate the *agape* way?

BUT WHAT IF YOU GET NO RESPONSE?

"Dr. Wheat, what do you do about a marriage that isn't *emotionally real?*" The wife posing that question had good reason to ask. Barbara, who at age thirty is as lovely as any model, spends her days at home with two young children while her husband, a high-living executive, crisscrosses the continent on business (and pleasure), often accompanied by his mistress.

I think of many others committed to emotionally barren marriages that are devoid of the wonderful feelings of love we have been describing. Not much friendship or affectionate belonging or physical, romantic love in these marriages! Not presently.

I am reminded of Eric, whose wife, caught up in the sophisticated trappings of a new job, thinks she no longer wants what he can offer her and demands a divorce. . . .

Of Fran, whose husband pours all his affection and attention on his thoroughbred horses and tells her to "go find a hobby. . . ."

Of Quentin, whose wife has exhibited a sudden personality change and after an episode leading to her arrest refuses to come home. . . .

Of Iris, who has to stand alone in rearing the children, maintaining the home, and coping with finances, "all without a word of approval, encouragement, or even a love pat" from her husband, a brilliant but self-centered scientist. . . .

Of John, whose wife coldly rejects him as friend and lover. . . .

And of Una, whose husband has been spending most of his free time at home in an alcoholic stupor. . . .

What is the answer for these people and for others who have no reason to *feel* love for their marriage partners?

God has provided a remarkable solution: a love directed and fueled, not by the emotions, but by the will. Out of his own mighty nature, God supplies the resources for this love, and they are available to any life connected with his by faith in Jesus Christ: "God's love has been poured out in our hearts through the Holy Spirit who has been given to us" (Rom. 5:5 AMPLIFIED). This is the *agape* love of the New Testament—unconditional, unchanging, inexhaustible, generous beyond measure, and most wonderfully kind!

No book on the love life of husband and wife can be complete without a consideration of *agape*. Even in the best of marriages, unlovable traits show up in both partners. And in every marriage, sooner or later, a need arises that can be met only by unconditional love. *Agape* is the answer for all the woundings of marriage. This love has the capacity to persist in the face of rejection and continue on when there is no response at all. It can leap over walls that would stop any human love cold. It is never deflected by unlovable behavior and gives gladly to the undeserving without totaling the cost. It heals and blesses in unpretentious, practical ways, for it is always realistically involved in the details of ordinary life. To the relationship of husband and wife, which would otherwise lie at the mercy of fluctuating emotions and human upheavals, *agape* imparts stability and a permanence that is rooted in the Eternal.

Agape is the divine solution for marriages populated by imperfect human beings!

Two verses among hundreds in the New Testament will suffice to illustrate the nature of *agape* love:

"God so loved the world, that he gave his only begotten Son, that whosoever believeth in him should not perish, but have everlasting life" (John 3:16).

"God commendeth his love toward us, in that, while we were yet sinners, Christ died for us" (Rom. 5:8).

SEVEN WAYS TO LOVE WITH *AGAPE*

We can make these observations concerning *agape:*

1. *Agape* love means action, not just a benign attitude.

2. *Agape* love means involvement, not a comfortable detachment from the needs of others.

3. *Agape* love means unconditionally loving the unlovable, the undeserving, and the unresponsive.

4. *Agape* love means permanent commitment to the object of one's love.

5. *Agape* love means constructive, purposeful giving based not on blind sentimentality but on knowledge—the knowledge of what is best for the beloved.

6. *Agape* love means consistency of behavior showing an ever-present concern for the beloved's highest good.

7. *Agape* love is the chief means and the best way of blessing your partner and your marriage.

Let me illustrate with a case history—the most beautiful example of *agape* love that I have observed personally.

In this case a man loved his wife tenderly and steadfastly for a total of fifteen years without any responding love on her part. There could be no response, for she had developed cerebral arteriosclerosis, the chronic brain syndrome.

At the onset of the disease she was a pretty, vivacious lady of sixty who looked at least ten years younger. In the beginning she experienced intermittent times of confusion. For instance, she would drive to Little Rock, then find herself at an intersection without knowing where she was, or why, or how to get back home. A former schoolteacher, she had enjoyed driving her own car for many years. But finally her husband had to take away her car keys for her safety.

As the disease progressed, she gradually lost all her mental faculties and did not even recognize her husband. He took care of her at home by himself for the first five years. During that time he often took her for visits, she looking her prettiest although she had no idea of where she was, and he proudly displaying her as his wife, introducing her to everyone, even though her remarks were apt to be inappropriate to the conversation. He never made an apology for her; he never indicated that there was anything wrong with what she had just said. He always treated her with the utmost courtesy. He showered her with love and attention, no matter what she said or did.

The time came when the doctors said she had to go into a nursing home for intensive care. She lived there for ten years (part of that time bedfast with arthritis) and he was with her daily. As long as she was able to sit up, he took her for a drive each afternoon—out to their farm, or downtown, or to visit the family— never in any way embarrassed that she was so far out of touch. He never made a negative comment about her. He did not begrudge the large amount of money required to keep her in the home all those years, never even hinted that it might be a problem. In fact, he never complained about any detail of her care throughout the long illness. He always obtained the best for her and did the best for her.

This man was loyal, always true to his wife, even though his love had no response for fifteen years. This is *agape*, not in theory, but in practice!

I can speak of this case with intimate knowledge, for these people were my own wonderful parents. What my father taught me about *agape* love through his example I can never forget.

THERE IS NO SUBSTITUTE

Now I would like for you to apply the principles of *agape* love to your own marital situation. Remember that *agape* gives the very best to the one you love. In your own marriage, your partner needs one thing from you above all else: *unconditional love!* Christian therapists speak of "the almost unbelievable need for *agape*." Psychiatrist Ross Campbell points out that there is no substitute for the incomparable emotional well-being that comes from feeling loved and accepted, completely and unconditionally.

You will both experience tremendous benefits when unconditional love becomes a part of your marriage. First, your partner's self-image will be greatly enhanced. The better a person feels about himself, the better he is able to function in a marriage relationship. One who feels loved all of the time, knowing it is not based on his performance but on his unique value as a person, is going to be able to relax and love generously in return. The person who *feels* lovable can express all the loves of marriage. The person who feels he has something to give will gladly give it. Your partner will feel at ease with himself and, as a result, will become a more enjoyable companion.

Second, this habit of unconditional love can carry your partner safely through periods of severe stress. At times when our mates are most vulnerable to hurt because of stress, they are apt to behave in unattractive ways. That is the signal that we need to give more love than ever. Unconditional love will meet your mate's needs during the troubled periods that come to almost everyone at some time. Designed by the wisdom of God, *agape* is the best medicine for mental health.

Third, in an atmosphere of unchanging love, the two of you can find the security and stability that will help you to grow and become the individuals you want to be. The writer of Psalm 52 illustrates this when he begins by affirming that "the goodness of God endures continually" and concludes by describing himself as a green olive tree in the house of God, trusting in the mercy of God forever—planted, rooted, living, and growing. Unconditional love does this for us.

Fourth, unconditional love makes every day a smoother experience, even the most trying of days. Because you have established the habit of expressing *agape,* you do not behave disagreeably just because you are feeling depressed, worried, ill, or fatigued. You continue to treat your mate with courtesy and kindness, and you avoid those uncontrolled outbursts that can be devastating to the love life of marriage. Because you are practiced, you know how to draw on the divine supply of patience. Therefore, your partner does not become your emotional football because you consistently behave with love, no matter how you feel.

Fifth, unconditional love removes the spirit of defensiveness on both sides. Thus, you do not feel the need to defend yourself from attack or to cut the other down by criticism. The syndrome of incessant complaining and explaining is happily absent from your home.

Unconditional love means that we can love our mates even in the face of extremely unlovable behavior. It means, for instance, that a husband can go out looking for his wife when she has run away from him to become a prostitute. He can find her in the gutter (literally) and take her home to love her back to health and restore her to a place of honor. Does that sound too drastic? Too improbable? A husband named Hosea loved his wife with unconditional love, and their story had a happy ending. You can read it in the Old Testament, but it still happens today. In my counseling I have encountered several Hoseas—both men and women—who exhibited this pursuing, unconditional love for their mates.

HOW DO I LOVE THEE?

It is important for you to stop and evaluate your own approach to love. Do you presently love with conditional love? Or unconditional love? Try to answer these questions honestly:

- Is my treatment of other people usually based on their behavior?
- Does my partner's performance determine the degree of love I give him or her?
- Do I think that love should be shown only as a reward for good behavior?
- Do I feel that my partner has to change before I can love him or her *more?*
- Do I think I can improve my partner's behavior by withholding love?
- Am I reacting to other people most of the time?

As you may be aware, people who constantly react are never really free. Someone else is always in control, determining how they will feel and behave.

Your attitude toward unconditional love may well determine the ultimate happiness of your marriage. Remember, *agape* can begin with just one person. It can start with you, no matter what your partner is doing. That is the genius of this love.

By giving your mate acceptance through *agape,* you will find it immeasurably easier to work out whatever problems you have. But acceptance must be given in the framework of permanent commitment. To feel that you are accepted today but just might be rejected tomorrow is of little value. The total commitment of *agape* becomes the bedrock foundation of your marriage. As you express *agape* habitually, you will have a new serenity of heart because now you are not reacting like a rubber ball to everything that happens. You are behaving consistently with a giving love that flows right from the heart of God into your heart and on to bless the life of your marriage partner.

Here is how to make *agape* the central force of your marriage:

1. Choose with your will to love your mate unconditionally and permanently through attitude, word, and action.

When God created us, he gave us a wonderful faculty in addition to minds that think and emotions that feel. He gave us a free will. With our will we want and choose, and our will becomes the most influential part of our personality. When our will exercises its power of choice, it acts for our total person and the rest of our being falls into line with what we have chosen.

Thus, we choose to apply God's scriptural principles concerning love, and choose to give this love to our mate without limits or conditions.

2. Develop the knowledge you need in order to do the very best for the object of your love.

Knowledge is indispensable in the exercise of *agape* love. If the loving actions of agape are not guided by precise knowledge of your partner, they will miss the mark.

Two kinds of knowledge are involved. The first is biblical. When I became a Christian and discovered that I could and must love my wife with *agape,* I had to study the Scriptures to learn how a husband is to love his wife and what a wife needs from her husband. As our Creator, God knows how we can best relate to each other, and he has not hidden these facts from us.

Through simple Bible study a man finds that the best thing he can do for his wife is to become the kind of husband described in Ephesians 5. A woman learns that the best thing she can do for her husband is to become the kind of wife described in 1 Peter 3. A number of good books have been written on the husband/wife roles in Scripture, and you will want to read some of them as you make your own study. In brief, the husband will find as he studies the New Testament and the Song of Solomon that God has designed him to be a protective, competent leader who will take care of his wife, and a tender, kind, and courteous lover who initiates love for her. This is what his wife needs from him. The wife who studies these Scriptures will find that God has designed her to be a responder to her husband's love; one prepared to help, who can gracefully adapt to her husband's calling in life; who possesses the beauty of a gentle, quiet spirit as she respects and affirms her husband; and who continues to delight him all through his life. This is what he needs from her.

This basic design, established by God in his loving wisdom, reflects the inmost natures of husband and wife and cannot be altered by those who would try. It lies deep within the plan of God, dating from the dawn of Creation, and no matter what cultural changes people attempt to bring about in the name of unisex, the fact remains that God created us male and female with distinctive privileges and responsibilities. Men and women are *different,* thank God, and so we can enrich each other and bring the full measure of joy into our marriage.

To love your mate meaningfully, you must add personal knowledge to biblical knowledge. This must be an intelligent, intimate, perceptive knowledge of the unique individual you are married to. If you do not understand your mate's highly special-ized needs and desires, you will be unable to meet them with *agape* love.

Husband, you are told in 1 Peter 3 to dwell with your wife according to knowledge. You are to be totally relaxed and at home with her because you understand her so well. Because you understand her, you will know what she desires and needs; how to meet her needs; what will make her *feel* loved; and how 1o do the very best for her on a consistent basis.

The wife should study her husband in the same way to

discover what makes him feel loved and to find out what he desires and needs and how she can best meet those needs. This is the creative project of a lifetime for both partners. Remember that *agape* is always an appropriate love, not given to suit your own hang-ups, but to ensure and enhance your partner's well-being. One of the thrills of marriage is knowing that you are providing what your beloved desires!

Strangely enough, one can be loved and accepted unconditionally and still not *feel* genuinely loved. What feels like love will vary with the individual—this is why you must know your mate so well. One person may measure love by the way his material needs are met, or by tangible items such as expensive gifts. Another may feel loved when her husband helps her with the dishes. One will measure love by the amount of time spent together, or by the quality of openness and sharing of thoughts between the two. Another desperately needs to hear often the words: *I love you.* Still another measures love by physical affection—hugs and kisses. One person puts a heavy emphasis on the loyalty shown by the mate, especially in public. Another values sensitivity shown to feelings. Some will measure love by the support given to their personal growth and development. There are so many languages of love! While all I have mentioned are important, some of them will have special, and even critical, significance for your mate on an emotional level. Learn what speaks love to your own partner; then express your love in ways that cannot be doubted.

If the two of you are reading this book together, set aside some time to talk about each other's feelings. Share with your mate exactly what it is that makes you *feel* loved. Always keep the discussion on a positive basis without hint of reproach for past mistakes your partner may have made. Remember, you can never enhance or rekindle the emotions of love by heaping a sense of failure on your partner. I cannot overemphasize this. *Never* in the slightest way put a feeling of guilt upon your mate.

If you are more concerned about building love in your marriage than your partner is, and you are unable to discuss your feelings together, then begin to concentrate on a deeper understanding of your mate so that you, to begin with, can learn his or her special language of love by observation and discernment.

3. Apply everything that you know in giving agape *love.* Pour your life into it.

Never forget that *agape* is action, not just attitude. Make a specific effort to *do* loving things for your partner daily in addition to what you *are.* The wise husband or wife listens with the heart to consider and understand what the partner needs and desires, then acts to meet those longings.

Here is how one wife met her husband's deepest needs through the knowledgeable expression of *agape:*

"This began as a bleak time for us," Sue explained. "Because of my husband's change of job we left our pleasant life in a small town and moved to the big city where nothing seemed right. The house we rented was like a prison to me. I felt as if I had lost contact with the outside world! The neighborhood was unsafe, and I had no women friends, not even one good neighbor. Our church was so far away—clear across the city. Rob worked the evening shift so I was all alone with plenty of time to feel sorry for myself. I turned to the Bible during those long, lonely evenings.

"Rob and I had been Christians for years, but we had never enjoyed the oneness in the Lord that I had hoped for. Now, as I turned to Bible study and prayer—struggling with my fears and unmet needs—the Lord directed my attention to Rob and *his* unhappiness and *his* needs. I love my husband, and I could not bear to have him living such a joyless, sterile life.

"I began asking the Lord to teach me the right way to love my husband. I searched the Scriptures to find out how to meet Rob's needs. Do you know, the Lord took me to 1 Peter 3 and kept me there for months! I used to think of verse 1 as speaking of the lost husband: 'In the same way, you wives, be submissive to your own husbands so that even if any of them are disobedient to the Word, they may be won without a word by the behavior of their wives.' Now I realized that saved husbands are not always obedient to the Word either. Many of them don't know what it says. My husband was in that category, and he needed to be 'won without a word.' *Without a word* was something new for me! I had always tried to push my husband along in the Christian life. Now I made the choice to love Rob by obeying 1 Peter 3:1–6 in daily behavior and attitudes. Those were conditions that had to be met if I was to obtain this promise.

"I also determined to turn all my thoughts and my heart to God and to my husband. Every day I claimed Philippians 1:6, for I knew that a good work was begun in Rob long ago. I was confident that the Lord would complete it—now that I wasn't standing in his way. I also read Psalm 112 daily as an affirmation of God's purpose for Rob, putting his name in there. What a beautiful portrait of the righteous man. This is what Rob is becoming.

"It's been six months now, and I can tell you there is a transformation going on here that Rob and I can hardly believe. God's Word is absolutely true if we just do what it says in faith! We are developing such a beautiful relationship with each other, with God at the center of our marriage. Rob and I have a wonderful time together now. It is as grand as I always believed it could be. Fifty years old, and I am so in love with my husband! Such a beautiful life! Rob now wants to do things for me and with me. He seems to really enjoy talking with me, reading Scripture to me, and sharing insights about spiritual matters. Now the Lord has miraculously answered Rob's prayer that he would be able to work days and be home with me in the evenings.

"Rob told me recently that for a long time he had had one great desire—that the joy of his salvation would be restored. And now, Rob says, that desire has been fulfilled! The Lord allowed me to have a part in giving my husband what he wanted most when I chose to love him with *agape* love."

This wife has given us a concrete example of the way *agape* can transform the love life of marriage when even one partner chooses to do the very best for her beloved—the best, scripturally, and the best, personally. (The two always seem to go together.) *Agape* love often clashes head-on with our old learned habits of conditional loving, so when you choose the *agape* way as Sue did, you have an adventure before you.

I must caution you on one important point. Please don't start loving with *agape* just because you want to reform your mate. This is not *agape* at all, but another form of conditional love. Change comes only from inner motivation. So accept your partner exactly the way he or she is now and seek to change your own behavior in accord with biblical standards to lovingly meet your mate's needs. The rest is accomplished by the Holy Spirit working through the Word of God.

You may be interested to know that almost all of the individuals mentioned at the beginning of this chapter did set their feet on the *agape* way. Faced with "no response" in their marriage, they had only two options: give up or learn to love a new way. Quentin quickly became discouraged and gave up. Tragic disintegration of home and family resulted. Una, on the other hand, has already seen her marriage totally transformed. The others are faithfully continuing to love their mates with *agape*, some with dramatic personal results. Barbara, for instance, has become a radiant Christian in the process, and the change in Eric has been remarkable. He is a new man in Christ.

As a counselor for many years I can promise this: No one who has ever really tried the *agape* way has regretted it. After all, it is commanded by God, and he always has surprises of love for those who obey him!

♥ *AGAPE:* ACTION, NOT ATTITUDE ♥

As the song says, "Love Is A Many-Splendored Thing." The foregoing chapters have touched on love's most important components:

- ♥ Giving instead of taking.
- ♥ Working tirelessly to *show* your mate your love with actions as well as meaningful, believable words.
- ♥ Loving your mate unconditionally, an impossible task outside of the spiritual resources available in Christ. (You may want to review Chapter 3 by Larry Crabb.)

The important thing, however, is to put these suggestions into practice. Select ideas that apply to you, set goals, and actually *do* something on a *regular* basis.

For example, one good way to put *agape* into practical application is to practice Abigail Van Buren's commandment to wives: "Permit no one to tell thee that thou art having a hard time; either thy mother, thy sister, nor thy neighbor, for the Judge will not hold her guiltless who leadeth another to disparage her husband."

Husbands can practice this commandment, too, particularly when friends or colleagues at work make the same tired remarks about marriage and "the old lady." Dwell on the positives about your mate. In fact, try writing some of them down right now.

Agape love isn't something you master quickly. In fact, learning to love unconditionally is like growing up—it takes a long time, for some of us, all our lives. In the next chapter, Dr. Cecil Osborne candidly confronts the reality that loving unconditionally is impossible to achieve one hundred percent of the time. That doesn't mean, however, it shouldn't be the ultimate goal. For those who want to grow up and commit themselves to one hundred percent *agape,* Dr. Osborne spells out specifics about how to be a mature marriage partner.

Chapter 10

MARRIAGE IS FOR ADULTS ONLY

BY CECIL OSBORNE
The Art of Understanding Your Mate

In 1984, two psychologists, Connell Cowan and Melvyn Kinder, wrote a best-selling book, *Smart Women/Foolish Choices*, to help women discover why they are often magnetically drawn to the wrong kind of men for subtle but powerful reasons, and how to break that destructive cycle. In their work with married couples, Cowan and Kinder have discovered two kinds of marriages. In one, the partners tend to give up too quickly if early efforts don't yield good results. They decide marriage is too difficult—"too much work." In the other kind of marriage, the partners see things differently. They grow into happiness by working patiently at their relationship, accepting responsibility to develop constructive attitudes and behaviors. "Happy couples," say Cowan and Kinder, "know how to be smart about matters of the heart."[18]

Although Cowan and Kinder work in a secular practice and setting, many of the "secrets of success" they have learned are based on biblical truth and values. Some of these secrets include: "love is acceptance," "infidelity poisons love," "love doesn't blame," "love is unselfish," and "love forgives." Not surprisingly, happy marriages inevitably result from an attitude that stresses giving over taking, loving your partner unconditionally and unselfishly.

Cecil Osborne wrote his best-selling book, *The Art of Understanding Your Mate*, fifteen years before Cowan and Kinder came on the scene, but his ideas sound very similar. In the following chapter, Osborne shares from his many years of counseling experience to explain why "being smart in marriage" means never demanding unconditional love from your partner, but always giving it in the belief that "love begets love." As you read, ask yourself:

- ♥ How emotionally and spiritually mature am I in my marriage?
- ♥ On a scale of 1 to 10 (10 meaning always), how often do I try to meet my partner's needs?
- ♥ Do I work on trying to change myself, or do I continue to try to change my partner?
- ♥ Do I demand or even expect unconditional love, do I constantly try to give it?

WILL YOU STILL LOVE ME IF . . . ?

Someone tells of a wealthy husband, considerably older than his wife, who asked her if she would still love him if he lost all his money. She assured him that she would.

"Would you love me if I became an invalid?" he asked.

"Yes, of course."

"But would you still love me if I became blind and deaf?"

"Yes," she said, "I'd still love you."

"But what if I lost all my money, was a blind and deaf invalid, and lost my mind?"

"Don't be ridiculous!" she said. "Who could love an old, penniless, blind, deaf imbecile! But I'd take care of you."

The story, probably apocryphal, illustrates two basic factors: the need which everyone feels for unconditional love, and the innate practicality of the female. Everyone, consciously or unconsciously, is seeking unconditional love, despite the fact that no one is capable of giving unconditional love constantly. The desire is perhaps a holdover from the time when the infant does receive unconditional love. He is loved because he is his mother's child. He need not do anything to merit love. His needs are all met and he has no responsibility to do anything whatever other than to be just what he is, a helpless infant.

The infant always resident within us goes on wanting some of this unconditional love and acceptance. The reasonably mature adult learns in time that he must give love as well as receive it. Marriage is a reciprocal arrangement in which, ideally, we each seek to meet the needs of the other. If we meet the needs of the marriage partner in order that our needs shall be met, a kind of barter takes place: I'll do this for you if you'll do that for me. One who loves in a mature sense seeks to meet the needs of another, not in a manipulative sense, but simply because loving expresses itself in a concern for the welfare of the other.

FROM BASIC NEEDS TO MATURITY

There are three basic, elemental needs, holdovers from childhood, which all of us experience.

1. We want, consciously or unconsciously, to have all of our needs met.
2. We want to control or change those about us so that they will meet these needs.
3. We all yearn for unconditional love.

These three basic inner drives are almost universal. A marriage can be successful to the extent that both husband and wife mature emotionally and spiritually to the point where these early childhood longings are replaced by more mature concepts. Ideally one must achieve sufficient emotional maturity to be able to change these to read:

1. Instead of demanding that all of my needs be met, I will seek to meet the valid needs of my marriage partner.
2. Rather than trying to change others, I will recognize that I cannot change anyone else. I can change only myself, and when I change, others tend—in time—to change in relation to me.
3. Instead of expecting unconditional love, I will face the fact that no one can give this kind of limitless love consistently. I will give love rather than demanding or expecting it, believing that love begets love.

LOVE IS OUR WAY OUT OF PRISON

Love is a supreme effort to escape from the prison of our aloneness, to seek completeness for our incompleteness, to trade our isolation for companionship. We need expect no perfect marriage, since there are no perfect people. Nor can we even hope for an ideal marriage, since none of us is an ideal person. We cannot demand that another person gratify all of our needs, for no one person can ever be expected to satisfy all of our variable needs.

One's ability to give and receive love depends upon whether he was loved as a child, and the manner in which he was loved. Quite often a child is given love, but in a manner he is incapable of accepting. Consequently he may be showered with affection but feel quite unloved and alienated. Dr. William Menninger points out that we learn how to love only when we were loved in infancy. Parents may shower a child with evidence of their love but at the same time set standards which he is unable to meet. As a consequence the child may go through life feeling a sense of all-pervasive guilt.

Someone in a semi-facetious vein has delineated the ages of woman as the following:

> In her infancy she needs love and care.
> In her childhood she wants fun.
> In her twenties she wants romance.
> In her thirties she wants admiration.
> In her forties she wants sympathy.
> In her fifties she wants cash.

A woman usually needs to be needed more than a man. It appears to be one of her spiritual and emotional necessities. If she does not feel needed, she feels deprived, unloved, alienated from herself and others. She must be needed in order to be fulfilled. A woman likes to be *told* that she is loved, admired, needed. While a man has the same basic need to be loved and admired, often for different reasons, he may be embarrassed to express it verbally. A woman needs more constant reassurance that she is loved, chiefly because of her somewhat greater insecurity and more fluid emotional nature.

Freud thought that happiness is found in the fulfillment of our childhood wishes, which is one reason that money alone does not bring happiness, since the possession of money was not one of our basic childhood wishes. Theodore Reik, a disciple of Freud, modifies the assertion by saying that happiness ensues when the wishes of our childhood *seem* to come true. For most humans, happiness is a fleeting or momentary emotion. Usually we must be satisfied with contentment, that half-sister of happiness; the achieving of an enduring contentment is no little accomplishment.

A woman said to me once, "Everyone knows that the way to a man's heart is through his stomach, so I go to great pains to prepare the best possible meals for my husband."

I said, "Your actions are commendable, but your basic assumption is rubbish. The way to a man's heart is not through his alimentary canal. A man's basic need is for love and affection. A woman's fundamental need is for security."

She said, "I think it's just the other way around. Men work hard in order to be economically secure, while women are the ones so desperately in need of love."

"Wrong again," I said. "Consult your emotions, not your book of aphorisms or your intellect. Your basic need as a woman includes love, but this involves a whole spectrum of needs. Security for a woman means to feel loved, to find fulfillment in her husband, children, home, and to have economic security so she can enjoy them without anxiety. She wants to be taken care of and cherished while she fulfills a basic emotional and biological need, which is to bear and rear children. To achieve this she requires the security of her husband's love."

A typical male, on the other hand, is not emotionally insecure in the same way. He works, not basically to be financially secure, but because he is a doer, an achiever, a creator of things and circumstances. The financial rewards are symbols of his success in achieving his goal. The male functions better in reaching his goal if he has the emotional support and affection of his wife. A woman would bite her tongue rather than admit that security is her fundamental need, while a man will usually go to any lengths rather than admit that love and affection are his basic needs.

IT'S HARD TO BE CONSISTENT

Not only is it impossible for one to give unconditional love all the time, but it is even difficult to be consistent in our expressions of love. Few of us feel like being tender, thoughtful, considerate, or helpful day in and day out. When the physical, mental, and emotional selves are all in harmony with each other and with the outside world, one may reveal the utmost in consideration for another. But when we are out of focus emotionally, or rushed or exasperated, another side of our nature may manifest itself.

A husband related an experience which illustrates this. "I had been working long hours, six and seven days a week, for months. I was really holding down two jobs, and one morning my thoughtful wife said, 'Honey, you've been working too hard. Let me bring you breakfast in bed.' I demurred, but finally consented. As she served breakfast she said, 'Now any time you want breakfast in bed, just let me know. Anytime, understand? Just let me know.'

"A few weeks later," he said, "I was feeling pretty well dragged out. I sat up in bed wondering if I was going to make it. I finally managed to do something I find quite difficult. I am fiercely independent and find it hard to ask or permit people to do things for me. But remembering her fervent offer of some weeks before, I said, 'Dear, how about breakfast in bed this morning? I'm really bushed.'

"My wife said, with some irritation, 'Nothing doing. I'm tired too.'

"That did it," he related. "I had been booby-trapped again. I have seldom asked her to do anything for me since. I'm not interested even when she volunteers. If she insists, I may accept the gesture because I feel I owe it to her to let her feel needed, but I'd rather she didn't bother. I suppose I'd prefer to have my old, total independence than to be even partially dependent on someone who blows hot and cold."

Men and women are both sensitive, but about different things. Men often are irritated that women can be so easily upset about things which, to a male, seem insignificant. Women are equally puzzled over the seeming overreaction of their husbands to issues which would never disturb a woman.

A man is generally sensitive in the area of his capacity to earn a living and to succeed in his work. If he is compared to other husbands to his disadvantage, he feels emasculated. Any criticism of his performance or achievement which touches on some vulnerable point can affect him deeply. He may either explode in a rage, and attack, or he may become defensive and mildly hostile, or retreat into silence. Each individual man has his own sensitive areas, and a wise wife will make it her business not to push those particular "red buttons."

Women have their own areas of sensitivity which are usually quite different from those of the male. Criticism of her housekeeping, cooking, appearance, her performance as mother, or any depreciation of her femininity can leave a woman crushed. Anything which strikes at her self-image is devastating.

An insensitive husband may walk into his home after a hard day's work and ask, "Good grief, what have you been doing all day?" The house may look cluttered, especially if there are children. Even if she has been washing, ironing, shopping, driving the children thither and yon, doing a bit of gardening, running errands, and planning a dinner party for the next day, there may be no visible signs of activity to validate her frenzied and hectic day. She may be physically and emotionally drained by the incessant demands of children, telephone, and doorbell, but to her husband it may appear that she has been watching television all day. On the other hand, a husband who puts in a full day at his job may well have some grounds for complaint if his wife, with only a small house or apartment and possibly a child or two fails to keep up with her work. "My wife has a small house to take care of," said a husband, "and it's usually a mess. We have one child who never has any clean clothes to wear. Ironing is stacked up all over the house. She watches television hours every day and complains of being tired at night. So far as I'm concerned she isn't earning her keep."

In one of our small sharing groups a man told us that his wife had just filed suit for divorce. It was his first night with the group.

"She's been after me for years to do something about our marriage," he said. "I guess I was too preoccupied with earning a living to heed the warning signals. Now she's moved out.

"I grew up in poverty," he went on, "and I've kept my nose to the grindstone ever since I was a kid. I have put in long hours on the job ever since we were married. I guess she felt neglected; in fact, she often complained that we never went anywhere together, but I only half heard her. My whole concern was to keep the business going. I went broke twice, and that didn't add to my self-esteem. My wife wanted all the niceties of life, and I kept on working to provide these for her, but I neglected her as a person. I thought she wanted to be well taken care of financially, but she wanted some of me. I didn't get her signals. Now I suppose it's too late."

After she divorced him he left his highly competitive business venture and took an eight-hour-a-day job. "Perhaps," he said, "she'd have been satisfied with less money and more husband. Maybe it was not so much her demands on me financially, as my own neurotic expectations which were self-imposed demands."

THE REAL SOURCE OF MARITAL PROBLEMS

Actually there are few marital problems. There are chiefly personal problems which are compounded by marriage. In a group, or with a competent third person, charges and counter-charges eventually give way to an inner search for one's own emotional barriers.

We can seldom understand the basic problem in an impaired marriage unless we can understand the two persons involved. This is made the more difficult because no one fully understands himself. Men are admonished not to try to understand women, but to empathize with them, feel with them. Yet most women would die rather than have their innermost motives revealed to a man. They want to be understood, but do not wish to have their intimate feelings exposed.

On the other hand, men wish to be understood, but are usually reluctant to "go probing around on the inside," as one husband said. Most men have made a big investment of time and psychic energy in hiding their inner feelings, and they feel threatened at the thought of having someone discovering what they are like at a feeling level. They prefer to operate on an intellectual level and reject introspection or anything to do with emotions.

But until we are honest enough to look within and discover what we are really like, and learn to communicate true feelings, there is little hope of improving the marriage.

If the truth were known, most of us are somewhat reluctant to admit the degree to which we want to be loved and understood. It is almost as though to admit this would be a confession of weakness, a blow to our self-esteem. We surround ourselves with various layers of insulation. We pretend a self-confidence we do not feel, or over-compensate in some way that is perfectly obvious to everyone but ourselves.

The need to love and be loved varies enormously with individuals, of course. At one end of the scale is the neurotic personality caught in a paradox: such a person is incapable of loving, but desperately needs to be loved. At the other end is the self-reliant individual who needs affection but cannot accept it. The neurotic personality needs endless quantities of love and reassurance. In fact, reassurance is the chief aspect of love that such a person requires. However, these are "bottomless pits" which can never be filled. No amount of love is ever enough. The neurotic person will push, prod, manipulate, threaten, or become ill in an effort to secure the monumental quantity of love which he requires. There is no end.

Such persons are usually masochistic in some degree; that is, they have an inner self-punishing mechanism. Their unconscious goal is victory through defeat. They will *unconsciously* go to any lengths to achieve their goal. Unable to accept love normally, they may become physically or emotionally ill, or alcoholic. Some are accident-prone, an unconscious effort to secure attention, first cousin to love. Others are disaster-prone. Inwardly feeling unworthy of love, they settle for attention, or as a last resort, pity. This type of person can seldom achieve a satisfactory marriage relationship without intensive therapy.

In a group session involving about ten persons I said, in a facetious vein, "Maybe the trouble is that men are playing around, and women are playing for keeps." One young divorcée erupted with instant hostility and wanted to argue the point. I asked, "Why are you so hostile?"

She thought a moment, then laughed: "Because I know it's true."

The core of truth in my statement lies in the fact that marriage usually—though not always—means more to a woman than to a man. A man's basic drive is usually to fulfill himself through achieving some goal in the outer world. A woman's basic drive is to fulfill herself through achieving a successful marriage, with all of its implications: children, security, and inner contentment. For a typical male, marriage and the home may be of great importance, but because his work takes him into the outer world of facts, things, and events, the home tends to become a refuge rather than a primary goal.

For this reason the woman is the keeper of the home, and she must assume the primary responsibility for initiating changes and improvements. This is because she is usually more intuitive, more in touch with her emotions, better equipped emotionally to deal with such things as personal relationships. Most of the persons who seek counselors for any reason are women, not because they are emotionally less stable, but because they are more realistic. Often, though not always, when a wife is able to effect some changes in her attitudes and personality, even a reluctant husband will agree to undertake some form of therapy or marriage counseling. When she demonstrates to him by her improved performance that she is deriving some benefit from counseling or group therapy, he will often be more open to the suggestion that they seek help together.

LOVE—A SET OF RESPONSES

Love, far from being just an emotion, is a whole set of responses. It can involve, in a typical marriage, any or all of the following actions:

1. *Listening.* What the marriage partner has to say may not seem important to you, but it is important to the one relating it. Love implies caring enough to listen attentively. Usually, if a problem is being discussed, there is no need to offer solutions. Just listening with interest is an act of love. If one is tired or bored, it is not always easy. But love goes the second mile and listens; at that moment, listening is an act of love.

2. *Thoughtfulness and consideration.* To love means to be concerned for the welfare of another. "Give and it shall be given unto you," said Jesus. If you have needs which are unmet, instead of making demands or accusations, try to meet the needs of your marriage partner. Love begets love; resentment begets hostility; rejection begets rejection.

Many men are not as thoughtful as they might be concerning things which are important to their wives. Wedding anniversaries, birthdays, and special occasions need attention. I was aware of this fact, but bungled it badly early in my marriage, to my consternation. I had put in my date book a reminder to purchase a birthday gift for my wife. But fearful that I might forget, I asked my secretary to put it on her calendar and remind me a day or so in advance. My wife happened to be in the outer office one day, and as it would have to be, she happened to glance at my secretary's open desk reminder, on which was written: "Remind Dr. O to get birthday gift for wife." Understandably my wife reacted with some indignation later. "If you can't remember by yourself, you can forget it." She was right.

3. *Compromise.* Since any two persons have incompatible goals, it is obvious that in the intimate relationship of marriage there will have to be a lifetime of cheerful compromises. If one wants to spend a vacation camping, and the other prefers visiting relatives, it doesn't mean that either is unreasonable. You can visit relatives one summer and go camping the following year, or spend half the vacation with relatives and the other half camping. Any compromise must be made with no thought of "giving in." Only the immature or infantile expect to have all of their needs met all of the time. If we can achieve our goals half the time in the marriage relationship, that isn't too bad. And, one's displeasure over visiting relatives should not be taken out on the relatives or in futile

recriminations later. Similarly, one who hates camping must not make the experience miserable for the other by constant complaints.

4. *Avoidance of attack and accusation.* When we are attacked or criticized, we instinctively defend ourselves, or counterattack. This is a poor basis for communication. However, we each have a perfect right—in fact, a duty—to let the other know how we feel about matters that are important to us. Instead of the accusation, which puts the other immediately in the wrong, one can begin by saying, "When you do that it makes me feel angry." One's anger may be infantile or reasonable, as the case may be. We are responsible for our own reaction, but the feeling is valid, and we have a right to express it. We are not making any demand that the other shall change, just communicating our feelings.

Instead of saying, "I have no intention of spending my vacation visiting your neurotic relatives, and it's selfish of you to expect me to do so," one might better phrase it, "Visiting relatives, either yours or mine, is not my idea of how to spend a restful vacation; but perhaps we can work out some kind of a compromise so we will both be satisfied."

"You never take me anyplace!" is likely to produce a defensive reaction. Abandoning the martyr stance or the accusatory tone, one might better say, "Honey, we've both been knocking ourselves out lately. How about dinner out this week or next?" Perhaps more important than the actual wording is the feeling that accompanies it. Abandon the judgmental, critical, attacking method, and use a loving approach. If you don't feel loved, expressing this fact with hostility is not likely to make you more lovable.

5. *Meeting valid needs.* Instead of insisting that your needs be met, try to meet all of the valid needs of the other. We are all selfish to some degree. Love is unselfish and seeks to discover and satisfy the needs of others. Often, because humans are egocentric, neither husband nor wife goes to the trouble to discover the basic needs of the other. Displaying a fourth of the tender solicitude shown during courtship would go a long way toward creating a happier marriage. Instead of brooding silently or talking angrily about one's unmet needs, a far better solution would be to sit down for an hour-long discussion.

A husband might well ask his wife, "Will you tell me the ways in which I could make you happier?"

She, in turn, could appropriately say, "I'll make out a list, but I'd feel better about it if you'd make a list of the ways in which I could make you happier." A discussion based on their lists can be the starting point for a new relationship.

6. *Forgiveness.* Learn to forgive and refuse to dig up the past. "To err is human, to forgive is divine." We tap our inner divinity when we can forgive. No one says it is easy to forgive hurts, but it is

the price we must pay for inner peace and for a harmonious relationship. Again it needs to be emphasized that love is not just a feeling, but also an action; to forgive is a loving act. A husband confessed his infidelity to his wife in my presence. At first she could not forgive or accept him back. Eventually, however, she forgave him and they established a better marriage than ever, due in part to a year or two in a sharing group. Her ability to forgive rendered her a more mature person.

A husband said, "My wife has been playing around for some years. She is secretive and furtive. It shows in her personality and actions. She isn't nearly as good an actress as she thinks. I don't know whether I have forgiven her or not, because she has never admitted anything. How do you forgive someone who admits no wrongdoing?" They have what outwardly appears to be a good marriage. Both do all of the appropriate things. She, however, is not forgiven because she has confessed nothing; he feels guilty over his inability to accept her fully. "I go through all the motions of being a good husband," he said. "I'm 'faking' it, and don't feel too good about it. Something dropped out of our marriage so far as I'm concerned."

7. *Avoidance of competition.* Make sure you are not competing with each other. Everyone knows of instances in which a wife has little or nothing to say in a group, but who, when her husband is not present, opens up and becomes a real person in her own right. The converse is also common, with a wife doing all the talking for both.

Sometimes this can be attributed to the fact that one or the other is naturally timid, but when a capable and otherwise responsive person permits the marriage partner to take over the conversation and answer for both of them, there is a power struggle going on.

I recall a dinner party during which a highly successful man of great ability was constantly interrupted by his wife. She corrected him on minor details and challenged most of his quiet observations. He eventually subsided and permitted her to carry on her loud-voiced monologue.

Just as often, an overly aggressive husband is determined to dominate his wife in public and at home. I recall a thoroughly competent man with a deep sense of insecurity who made every effort to ridicule his wife in public. One sensed that he was expressing the buried hostility he could not express at home.

The power struggle goes on in millions of homes. Each has a point to prove or a position to defend or some subtle punishment to mete out. A mature and lasting love has in it elements of deep concern for others. It does not seek to control or to change another person. It is not defensive or easily upset. It looks for ways to meet the needs of others.

Love is gentle, but not weak. One who loves deeply also loves himself properly and respects himself, mingling elements of both humility and strength.

One who is capable of loving fully is also capable of accepting love, feeling worthy of love. Loving God and truth, one loves himself and others in equal amounts. Love is the ultimate in living and expresses itself best by giving, without thought of return. Love is, in the final analysis, the ultimate in human growth and maturity.

♥ **SET GOALS, THEN DO SOME** ♥
UNCONDITIONAL LOVING

Review the set of responses discussed by Dr. Osborne at the end of this chapter. Ask yourself:

- ♥ How well do I listen, even when I'm tired or bored?
- ♥ How often do I actually perform acts of thoughtfulness and consideration? What are they?
- ♥ How well do I compromise, or must I always have my own way?
- ♥ How often do I criticize or accuse my mate? How can I stop this?
- ♥ Am I meeting valid needs for my spouse? Have I ever asked my spouse for a list of his or her valid needs?
- ♥ How good am I at forgiving my spouse? Do I carry grudges and keep scores?
- ♥ Do I compete with my spouse in any way? Are the two of us in some kind of power struggle? If so, what part am I playing in it?

The questions above only become valuable if you get very specific with your answers and then actually make changes in your behavior based on those answers.

With a final thought on loving your mate unconditionally, Shirley Cook shares four words that can make all the difference during those inevitable moments when nothing else will.

Chapter 11

I LOVE YOU ANYWAY

BY SHIRLEY COOK
The Marriage Puzzle

All this theory about keeping romance in your marriage is good, but every now and then it helps to get the practical, life-in-the-trenches-view from a practicing wife like Shirley Cook. In this chapter, she invites you to visit her and husband Les in a less than romantic moment, when only *agape* love will survive.

There are no questions to think about as you read this chapter; just thank the Lord (and your spouse) for loving you anyway.

♥ HOW IN THE WORLD CAN YOU LOVE ME? ♥

"How can you?" I sniffed and wiped the tears away with the back of my hand.

"I just do." Les's tone was final, and his warm brown eyes and gentle hug assured me more than a detailed list would have. In fact, if he had been a list-maker, I could have been in trouble. There were too many reasons in my mind for him not to love me:

1. I had just found out for certain that I was pregnant with our *fifth* child! (And I thought my symptoms were the result of the anesthesia I had had recently for oral surgery.)

2. I was tired and cross and didn't want to be pregnant. Our youngest was only seven months old and the others eight years and under.

3. Les was finishing graduate school and trying to write his thesis in our small duplex amidst dump trucks, dolls, and diapers.

4. I felt ugly with my Bugs Bunny smile (I had to wait two months for my partial plate) and . . .

. . . his words, like a soothing ointment poured over my aching heart: "I love you anyway."

Through the years his love has remained steadfast. He admits he hasn't always "liked" me and that sometimes he has been exasperated to the point of abandoning ship.

Who hasn't?

I haven't always liked him, either. It scares me when I realize how closely love and hate are related.

I don't like him when he snaps at me when I need "gentling." I don't want to see his face after we argue about money. I've played "Simon doesn't say" by giving him the silent treatment when I didn't get my way. (He played it well, too.)

But even through those times when my heart was hard as steel or broken in shreds, I've loved him—anyway.

THE FUTURE WAS SHAKY UNTIL . . .

As I thought about the subject of love and acceptance over my second cup of morning coffee, I stretched my mind back to those first two years of our marriage before we knew Christ. I can remember the explosive bursts of temper, the punishing curses, the bitter quarrels.

Even with our great intentions and goals for a lasting marriage, the future looked shaky. Five years together loomed ahead of us like a sheer, unclimbable cliff.

Then Jesus Christ came into our lives. We found a new center for being. A new foundation for growing. A new life. A new love.

"Unless the LORD builds the house, its builders labor in vain. Unless the LORD watches over the city, the watchmen stand guard in vain" (Ps. 127:1).

I'm convinced that making Jesus Christ the Lord of our personal lives and marriages is the first and most important piece in the marriage puzzle. No matter how hard we work or how diligently we try to plan for success, without him in the center of the picture there will always be an empty space, and the puzzle will fall apart whenever it is moved or jostled in the process of growth.

It is never too late to give Jesus control of a marriage.

One couple we know had been married almost forty years when they split up. They had been churchgoers, claimed to be "born-again" Christians, but still their marriage seemed unable to survive. So they divorced. Recently, after two years apart, they began dating again, and now they have remarried. I asked, "Have you two resolved the problems that caused your marriage to break up?"

The "groom" smiled and with a tone of confidence replied, "Our problem was that Jesus Christ was not in the center of our marriage. We grew—but in opposite directions."

I believe marriage is going to work for them this time. Because God is love and the Lord of their home, this couple will now be able to forgive and say from their hearts, "I love you anyway."

> Some pray to marry the man they love,
> My prayer will somewhat vary:
> I humbly pray to heaven above
> That I love the man I marry.
>
> —Rose Pastor Stokes
> "My Prayer"

Love doesn't depend on feeling or sight or even being loved in return. Real love, God's love, *agape* love, comes as an act of the will from the lover.

WHAT IF HE'S UNLOVABLE?

If I don't love my husband anymore—like the bride who said, "I'll love you as long as I love you"—then the problem is mine, not his. He may be unlovable. He may be despicable and totally unworthy of love.

So?

I'm not exactly a lovable, righteous, holy person who deserves God's love either. A bargain, I'm not.

"But God demonstrates his own love for us in this: While we were still sinners, Christ died for us" (Rom. 5:8).

God loves us in our unregenerate, selfish, hateful state. Why? Because there is a spark of goodness in everyone? I doubt that. He loves us because he *is* love. It is his will to love. To serve. To be rejected. To sacrifice.

But what does that have to do with me or with my marriage? I'm not God. I can't love like that.

True. But as Christians, you and I have the God-life within. Over and over the Scriptures proclaim this truth: "Christ is in you!" That same Christ will minister to your strife-torn home as he did to the lame, blind, leprous multitudes.

Jesus calmed wild and raging storms (teen-agers trying to find the car keys). He fed cross and ugly travelers (husbands after an hour on the freeway). He strengthened a woman with "an issue of blood" (premenstrual depression).

How did he do it? In the same way you and I must do it. He made his Father the center of his life by choosing his will.

"Don't you believe that I am in the Father, and that the Father is in me? The words I say to you are not just my own. Rather, it is the Father, living in me, who is doing his work" (John 14:10).

"I love you anyway."

Just think. God chose to love me and send his only Son to bear my punishment for sin. Jesus chose to depend on the Father as he loved and healed pushing, shoving men and women. In the same way, Les can choose to love me when I've been lazy and neglectful about ironing his shirts; when I've put my interest and work ahead of him; and when my hair is turning gray. Someone has said, "It's easy to understand love at first sight, but how do you explain love after two people have been looking at each other for years?"

I can choose to love, too—on days when Les is more interested in sharing a darkroom with his photography hobby than with me; when he leaves dishes in the sink instead of stacking them in the dishwasher; and when his usual slim shape is a little on the paunchy side.

"We love because he first loved us." (1 John 4:19).

THE WORLD NEEDS A RAY OF HOPE

I suppose the one thing that depresses me more than any other is the rising divorce rate among Christians. If the object lesson, marriage, chosen by God to represent Christ and the church fails, what hope does a fearful and desperate neighbor have for the future?

The world—and by that term I mean the people in your office, the people at the plant, the young couple upstairs, and the teens who sit in the back of the sanctuary—that world of real people is searching for stability and security in the Christian community.

The kids know that stability and security are not found in drink and drugs. They've tried that. The unmarried couple wonder from day to day when they'll fall out of love. Is marriage the answer? And the people who work beside us leave the house every morning with the hope that somehow, someday, there will be peace and acceptance in their homes.

They want answers.

They don't want platitudes or pat answers.

They don't even want perfection.

Just a ray of hope will do.

Forgiveness. Acceptance. Security.

You want that. So do I. In Christ, we have the answer. A successful, long-lasting marriage is possible. We can choose to love. Regardless of circumstances, no matter how great and awful the problems, we can say, "I love you anyway."

Love is the security blanket we never outgrow.

"Above all, love each other deeply, because love covers over a multitude of sins" (1 Peter 4:8).

"Thank you, Lord, for loving me anyway!"

♥ ACT NOW, FEEL LATER ♥

♥ Be sure Jesus is Lord of your life. *Numero uno.* Ask him to supply his love for your mate. To love is God's will. "This is the confidence we have in approaching God: that if we ask anything according to his will, he hears us. And if we know that he hears us—whatever we ask—we know that we have what we asked of him" (1 John 5:14–15).

♥ Say aloud, using your spouse's name, "I will love _____ now." Repeat it five times, emphasizing each word: "*I* will love . . ." "I *will* love . . ." and so on. As you do this, you put your will, connected with God's will, into word power.

♥ Tell your spouse at least once a day that you love him (or her). Say it even if you don't feel it. Remember, love begins in the will. The feeling will come later.

♥ If you are holding any grudges or gripes against your mate, write them down, pray about them and forgive your mate, vowing not to let these things matter.

Grudges are too heavy for any marriage to carry. As Edna St. Vincent Millay wrote:

> It's not love's going hurts my days
> But that it went in little ways.[19]

Now take a long, hard look at your list, then say aloud, "I forgive him (or her) and I now forget."

Throw away the list.

Never mention these things again.

One of my friends bore a baby out of wedlock. A couple of years later she met and married a truly loving man. He adopted her son and accepted him as his own. One day she shared how this wonderful, forgiving man has forgotten her past. "Even when we get into our biggest fights and throw all the ammunition we have at each other, he has never once reminded me of my past or alluded to it in any way."

That's love.

Forgiveness.

Acceptance.

"I love you anyway."

UNDERSTANDING:
YOUR NEEDS, MY NEEDS, OUR NEEDS

In Parts I and II you have considered the very foundation for the growth of your marriage:

> To realize the importance of oneness in Christ
> To define a much misunderstood term—love—and describe the kind of love that keeps a marriage together and growing

Part III covers three more foundational concepts that are crucial in a growing relationship:

> Understanding the difference between men and women
> Recognizing the needs of your spouse
> Understanding and accepting your spouse's needs, strengths, and weaknesses

The following chapters build on the principle developed by Dr. Larry Crabb in Part II: fully trusting God for your own feelings of security and significance and then committing yourself to ministering to your spouse's needs with no strings attached. No matter how your spouse responds (or does not respond), you trust God for your feelings of worth and self-acceptance.

To recap Crabb's analogy, a partner in a marriage stands on the edge of a "cliff of safety" (the pride and defense mechanisms that keep one safe from rejection). Below is the "abyss of rejection" (the possibility of being hurt by a mate's lack of response or disinterest, disapproval or disdain). The only way to make the leap from the cliff is to trust the "rope of safety" (faith in God's provision of feelings of significance and security). But once you make that leap, where will you land in relationship to what your mate needs to grow and relate to you? That's where knowledge of the differences between men and women and the willingness to understand and accept your mate come into play.

Are there real and fundamental differences between men and women? Some say yes, and others emphatically claim the opposite, particularly certain vocal voices in the feminist movement. There is evidence for both opinions, but Zondervan author Gary Smalley flatly states, "I would venture to say that most marital difficulties center around one fact—men and women are TOTALLY different. The differences (emotional, mental, and physical) are so extreme that without a *concentrated effort* to understand them, it is nearly impossible to have a happy marriage."[1]

Examining these differences and the needs they create is what the next several chapters seek to do. Most importantly, the following selections give insights into understanding and accepting your mate. Every marriage has *his needs* and *her needs* but, to grow, a couple must finally deal with *our needs*—what it takes to make their oneness work on a daily basis.

In chapter 12, Gary Smalley (*The Joy of Committed Love*) spells out the differences in men and women and why men tend to be less able to build an intimate relationship.

In chapter 13, Anne Kristin Carroll (*Together Forever*) shares the story of Pam and Howard and how Pam saved her marriage by accepting her husband when there seemed to be no hope.

In chapter 14, Dean Merrill (*How To Really Love Your Wife*) describes the marriage made up of a master, a mistress, and two slaves: How are the chores and responsibilities parceled out in your home? A lot depends on each partner's awareness of the other's needs and abilities.

In chapter 15, André Bustanoby (*Just Talk To Me*) digs into the much-touted but seldom achieved area called "unconditional acceptance." Included is a sixteen-question tool for rating just how accepting your spouse is of you (and vice versa).

I would venture to say that most marital difficulties center around one fact—men and women are *TOTALLY* different. The differences are so extreme that without a *concentrated effort* to understand them, it is nearly impossible to have a happy marriage.[2]

Gary Smalley

Chapter 12

WHEN THE BUFFALO MARRIES THE BUTTERFLY ...

BY GARY SMALLEY
The Joy of Committed Love

Just how different are men from women and vice versa? This chapter opens with George and Barbara teetering on the brink of divorce. Barbara is ready to leave George because he has managed to drive her away without half trying. What's the problem? George has failed to realize that his wife is a special person—a "butterfly" who needs gentle care. But George is a typical "buffalo" and his butterfly is tired of being trampled.

Can their marriage be saved? Yes, if they will honestly face and deal with the very fundamental differences in their make-up, the way they think, and the way they feel.

As you read, make a list of the differences Gary Smalley discusses. How many of these have you been aware of all along? How many are new discoveries, and what do you plan to do about them?

CAN THIS MARRIAGE BE SAVED?

At the other end of the phone a quivering voice said, "You've got to help me. She has a court order against me." George was coming to me for help after his relationship with his wife Barbara was already in shreds. "We've been married over twenty years, and she won't even let me back in the house. I can't believe she would treat me this way after all I've done for her. Can you help us get back together?"

Before I answered his question, I wanted to talk to his wife.

"There's no way you can talk to Barbara," he said. "She wouldn't talk to you. The moment you say you're representing me in any way, she'll hang up on you."

"I've never been turned down by a wife yet," I assured him, "so we might as well see if this will be the first time. Would you give me her phone number?"

To be honest, as grim as things sounded, I did wonder if she would be the first wife unwilling to talk to me about her marital strife. But my doubts were unfounded—she was more than anxious to discuss their problems.

"What would it take for you to be willing to let your husband back into your life? What would have to happen before you would try to rebuild a marriage relationship with him?" Those were the same questions I had asked many wives who claimed they didn't want their husbands back.

Her response was typical. "I can't possibly answer that question. He's the worst husband in the world, so I wouldn't think of taking him back. I can't stand his personality or his offensive habits any more." The court order would take care of him, she told me. "Just keep him away!"

I gently asked her if she could tell me the things he had done to offend her. When I heard her response, I said, "It sounds like he hasn't been a very sensitive and gentle husband, has he?"

Once again I asked her to stretch her imagination and think about what changes would be necessary before she would take him back.

There was plenty of room for improvement, she told me. First, he was too domineering and critical of her. Second, he tried to control her every move with a possessive grip. Third, he trampled her sense of self-worth with constant ridicule. And fourth, although he always had time for business and other interests, he seldom took time to listen to her. On top of all that, he spied on her and didn't give her any freedom.

"Don't get any ideas, though," she told me at the end of our conversation. "Because no matter what, I won't stop the divorce."

When I relayed these complaints to George, I knew I had touched some sensitive spots. He defended himself and accused her. I let him rant for a while before asking, "Do you want your wife back?"

"Yes, I'd do anything to get her back," he said.

"Good. I'm always willing to work with someone ready to readjust his life. But if you're not totally serious, let me know now. I don't like to play games." Again he committed himself to change, but his commitment didn't last beyond my next statement, "We're going to have to work on your domineering and possessive nature. It shows you don't genuinely love your wife."

He fumed and spouted, defended and fought so much I

began to wonder if he really would commit himself to the necessary changes.

"I've never met a more belligerent, stubborn man in my entire life!" I exclaimed.

Suddenly subdued, he responded, "That's not my nature. I'm usually rather submissive inside. Maybe I'm putting up a front because I'm really not a pushy person. I feel like people run all over me."

"I don't think you and I are talking about the same person," I responded. "If I were your wife, I'm not sure I could bear up emotionally under your domineering personality."

That stopped him long enough for him to give our conversation some serious thought. After talking to his friends and even praying that God would help him understand, he returned to my office, able to confess his faults and ready to change.

"If you really want to love your wife, then you need to begin right now, at the divorce trial," I said. Now that we were on the subject, he mentioned that he needed to get a lawyer because she had one.

"No," I cautioned him. "If you want to win her back, you need to forget about a lawyer at this time." (I don't always recommend this, but based on their personal background, I felt he would stand a better chance of regaining her love without legal counsel.)

"You're crazy," he said. "They'll take me to the cleaners."

Feeling somewhat defenseless, he reluctantly agreed to forfeit legal counsel.

Two of his friends and I waited in the courthouse for the closed-room session to end. He came running out of the courtroom bellowing, "She wants twenty percent of my retirement . . . twenty percent! No way I'm gonna do that!"

Once again I asked him, "Do you want your wife back?" Again, he nodded yes! "Then give her twenty-five percent." I reminded him that *now* was the time to respect her and treat her sensitively. Later he emerged from the courtroom a divorced man, but not for long. . . .

Several months later I ran into him at the grocery store. "My wife and I remarried," he said triumphantly. "I thought you were crazy when you first told me the things I should do for my wife . . . there was no way I would ever be able to do them," he continued. "It took sheer will power at first. I only did them because you said that God rewards those who seek him and follow his ways. But you know, it's really amazing. After doing them for three months, I actually enjoy them."

He continued to give examples of the new ways he was treating his wife. Like the time she took a business trip and he wrote her a note telling her how much he wished he could be with her. Inserted in the note were extra money and directions on how to reach her destination.

George has finally realized that his wife is a special person who needs tender treatment, almost as if her forehead were stamped "Very Important—Handle With Care"!

He has discovered the secret to renewing any strained relationship—honor. Before we discuss rebuilding a failing marriage, let's examine two major reasons marriages fail.

TWO REASONS MARRIAGES FAIL

Men and women enter marriage with "storybook" expectations and limited training.

I once asked a college girl what kind of man she would like to marry. "I'd like for him to be able to tell jokes, sing and dance, and stay home at night."

"You don't want a husband," I told her. "You want a television set."

Her visions of a husband reveal one of the most common reasons marriages fail. We marry with unrealistic expectations and few, if any, caring skills. In fact, most of us are rather fuzzy when it comes to our mates' real needs.

Isn't it ironic that a plumber's license requires four years of training, but a marriage license requires nothing but two willing bodies and sometimes a blood test. Since most of us bounce through the educational corridors without any basic communication courses, many men marry with absolutely no knowledge of how to build a meaningful relationship. In short, most men have no idea how to love their wives in a way that makes both of them happy.

Recently I asked five divorced women, individually, "If your husband began treating you in a consistently loving manner, would you take him back?"

"Of course I would," each replied. But, unfortunately, none had hope that her husband would ever be like that.

Because I knew one of the men personally, I had to concur with his wife's hopelessness. If he were willing to try, he could win her back. Unfortunately, he wasn't interested in learning.

"What he doesn't realize is that a lot of women are as responsive as puppies," one woman explained to me. "If he'd come back and treat me with tenderness, gentleness, and understanding, I'd take him back tomorrow."

How sad that we men don't know how to win our wives back or even how to keep from losing them. How can we win their affection, their respect, their love and cooperation when *we don't even know where to begin?* Instead of trying to learn what it takes to mend a cracked marriage, most of us would rather jump on the divorce bandwagon.

We violate the relationship laws inherent in marriage, and then we wonder why it all goes sour. But we wouldn't wonder if the law of aerodynamics sent a one-winged airplane plummeting to the earth.

Imagine yourself an aerospace engineer working for NASA. Your job is to put several men on the moon, but something goes wrong halfway through their flight. You wouldn't dream of walking out on the entire project because something went wrong. Instead, you and the other engineers would put your heads together, insert data into the computer and ... *voilà!* You would discover the problem and make all the vital adjustments to get that spacecraft back on course. If the project had failed altogether, you still wouldn't forsake it. You would simply modify it to avoid similar problems in the future.

> Like the spacecraft, your marriage is subject to laws that determine its success or failure. If any of these laws are violated, you and your wife are locked into orbits, destined to crash. However, if during the marriage you recognize which law or principle you are violating and make the necessary adjustments, your marriage will stay on the right course.

Men and women lack understanding about the general differences between men and women.

I would venture to say that most marital difficulties center around one fact—men and women are TOTALLY different. The differences (emotional, mental, and physical) are so extreme that without a *concentrated effort* to understand them, it is nearly impossible to have a happy marriage. A famous psychiatrist once said, "After thirty years of studying women, I ask myself, 'What is it that they really want?' " If this were his conclusion, just imagine how little we know about our wives.

You may already be aware of some of the differences. Many, however, will come as a complete surprise. Did you know, for instance, that virtually every cell in a man's body has a chromosome make-up entirely different from those in a woman's body? How about this next one? Dr. James Dobson says there is strong evidence indicating that the "seat" of the emotions in a man's brain is wired differently from a woman's. By virtue of these two differences, men and women are miles apart emotionally and physically.

A WARNING TO ALL BUTTERFLIES

How can a man say something to his wife that cuts her to the core and an hour later expect her to respond romantically to his advances? Why does a man feel obligated to lecture his wife when he sees that her feelings are hurt? How can a man lie next to his crying wife, giving her the silent treatment, when she needs so desperately his compassion and concern.

These situations are not the exception; they are the norm in American marriages. When couples come to my office for help, they are usually surprised that I don't fall out of my chair in total shock as they tell me their feelings. They can't believe their experiences are common. Every marriage and every person is unique, yet the problems people experience are practically universal.

The purpose of this chapter is to help you understand some differences between you and your husband that are responsible for many of the problems within your relationship. This chapter should be encouraging to you because it will enable you to see *why* he does many of the things that hurt you. Chances are, you have always assumed he didn't care about the fact that he hurts you.

The fact is, he is a man, and many of the hurtful and calloused actions you have witnessed are simply the result of his basic nature as a man. This does not mean you have to resign to living with a calloused or insensitive man—quite the contrary. Once you understand some of the basic differences we will discuss, you will be able to help him balance his natural qualities.

Before we look at precise physiological and psychological differences, let me first draw your attention to the general differences and how they affect your relationship. The best example I can think of to illustrate these differences is to compare the butterfly with the buffalo. The butterfly has a keen sensitivity. It is sensitive even to the slightest breeze. It flutters above the ground where it can get a panoramic awareness of its surroundings. It notices the beauty of even the tiniest of flowers. Because of its sensitivity, it is constantly aware of all of the changes going on around it and is able to react to the slightest variation in its environment. Thus, the butterfly reacts with swiftness toward anything that might hurt it. (Try to catch one without a net sometime.) If a tiny pebble were taped to its wing, the butterfly would be severely injured and eventually die.

The buffalo is another story. It is rough and calloused. It doesn't react to a breeze. It's not even affected by a thirty-mile-an-hour wind. It just goes right on doing whatever it was doing. It's not aware of the smallest of flowers, nor does it appear to be sensitive to slight changes in its environment. Tape a pebble to the buffalo's back and he probably won't even feel it.

The buffalo isn't "rotten to the core" just because he goes around stepping on pretty flowers. In fact, the buffalo's toughness is a tremendous asset. His strength, when harnessed, can pull a plow that four grown men can't pull.

The analogy should be obvious. Your husband is the buffalo

(Don't say amen too loudly!) and you're the butterfly. He may tend to "plow" through circumstances, while you "feel" life and your surroundings with much more sensitivity. The "pebble on the butterfly's wing" may take the form of a sarcastic remark, a sharp criticism, or even an indifferent attitude. Whatever it is, it can hurt and even crush you, while he may not even notice what he's done.

The analogy ends in that the buffalo can never take on any of the butterfly's sensitivities, and the butterfly will never benefit from the buffalo's strength.

Such is not the case with your marriage. Your husband can learn how to be gentle, sensitive, and romantic, but he probably won't learn by himself; that's why I've written this book—to show you how you can help him. You must realize that your husband doesn't understand how much his cutting words or indifferent attitudes actually affect your feelings. He can learn, but you'll need to help him.

Now, let's take a look at some of the differences between men and women. We will discuss mental, emotional, physical, sexual, and intuitive differences. Each section is by no means exhaustive but will at least give you a better understanding of the differences we tend to overlook.

SOME ADVICE TO ALL BUFFALOS

Women tend to be more *personal* than men. Women have a deeper interest in people and feelings—building relationships—while men tend to be more preoccupied with practicalities that can be understood through logical deduction. Men tend to be more challenge-and-conquer oriented—competing for dominance—hence, their strong interest in sports such as football and boxing.

Why would a woman be less interested in a boxing match? Because close, loving relationships are usually not developed in the ring! Also, watch what happens during many family vacations. He is challenged by the goal of driving four hundred miles a day, while she wants to stop now and then to drink coffee and relax and relate. He thinks that's a waste of time because it would interfere with his goal.

Men tend to be less desirous of and knowledgeable in building intimate relationships, both with God and with others. For example, women are usually the ones who buy marriage books. They are usually the ones who develop the initial interest in knowing God and attending church. When a man realizes that his wife is more naturally motivated to nurture relationships, he can relax and accept these tendencies and *choose* to develop a better marriage and better relationships with his children.

Do you realize that your wife's natural ability for developing relationships can *help* you fulfill the two greatest commandments taught by Christ—loving God and loving others (Matt. 22:36–40)? Jesus said that if we obey these two commandments, we are fulfilling *all* the commandments. Think of it! Your wife has the God-given drive and ability to help you build meaningful relationships in both these areas. God knew you needed special help because he stated, "It is not good for the man to be alone; I will make him a helper [and completer] suitable for him" (Gen. 2:18). If you let her, your wife can open up a whole new and complete world of communication and deeper relationships.

Dr. Cecil Osborne says that women tend to become "an intimate part" of the people they know and the things that surround them; they enter into a kind of "oneness" with their surroundings. A man relates to people and situations, but he usually doesn't allow his identity to become entwined with them. He somehow remains apart. That's why a woman, viewing her house as an extension of herself, can become easily hurt when it is criticized by others. (One woman in her mid-fifties said she enjoys a card or flowers from her husband because they separate her from her identity with her home and family. The gift singles her out as an individual, with an individual's identity and self-worth.)

Because of a woman's emotional identification with people and places around her, she needs more time to adjust to change than a man does. A man can logically deduce the benefits of a change and get "psyched up" for it in a matter of minutes. Not so with a woman. She focuses on the immediate consequences of the change and the difficulties it may involve for her and her family. She needs time to get over the initial adjustment before she can begin to warm up to the advantages of the change.

Steve and Bonney had been struggling to make just enough money to put food on the table. His small business was requiring eighteen hours a day on his part, and she was putting in at least eight hours a day (and was seven months pregnant). Steve flew east to show his business ideas to a multi-millionaire. The man was impressed and made Steve a generous offer. Steve could hardly wait to call Bonney and tell her the great news.

It took Steve less than five minutes to accept the offer. It was the only "reasonable" course of action. He called Bonney and told her the news in "logical" order so she could get as excited as he was. He told her, "First, you won't have to work any more. Second, he's giving me twenty percent of the profits (he says I'll be a millionaire in a year). Third, you won't believe how beautiful it is back here, and he's going to pay all of the moving expenses."

Steve was shocked when Bonney began to weep uncontroll-ably. At first he thought she was crying for joy (I know it's hard to believe that he actually thought that, but remember, men can be like buffalos).

As soon as Bonney caught a breath between sobs, she had a chance to ask some questions which Steve considered totally ridiculous (in fact, he thought her mind had snapped). She asked questions like, "What about our parents?" and "What about our apartment? I just finished the room for the baby!" With her third question, Steve, with all of his masculine "sensitivity," abruptly terminated the phone call. She had the nerve to ask if he'd forgotten she was seven months pregnant!

After giving her an hour or two to pull herself together, he called her back. She had gained her composure and agreed to move east and leave her parents, her friends, her doctor and childbirth classes, and the nursery she had spent so much time preparing for her first child.

It took Bonney almost eight months to adjust to a change that Steve had adjusted to in minutes. Steve never made his million. The business failed eight days before their baby was born, and they moved again to another place, still three thousand miles from home. Steve eventually learned his lesson, and today he doesn't make any major change unless Bonney is in total agreement. He tries to give her ample time to adjust to other changes as soon as he can foresee them. However, Steve will never forget the loving sacrifices his wife made so many times. He even realizes that questions like "What about our parents?" or "What about the nursery?" can be more meaningful than money.

PHYSICAL DIFFERENCES

Dr. Paul Popenoe, founder of the American Institute of Family Relations in Los Angeles, dedicated his most productive years to the research of biological differences between the sexes. Some of his findings are listed below.

- Woman has greater constitutional vitality, perhaps because of her unique chromosome makeup. Normally, females outlive males by three or four years in the U.S.
- Woman's metabolism is normally lower than man's.
- Man and woman differ in skeletal structure; woman having a shorter head, broader face, less protruding chin, shorter legs, and longer trunk.
- Woman has larger kidneys, liver, stomach, and appendix than man, but smaller lungs.
- Woman has several unique and important functions: menstruation, pregnancy, lactation. Woman's hormones are of a different type and more numerous than man's.
- Woman's thyroid is larger and more active. It enlarges during pregnancy and menstruation; makes woman more prone to goiter; provides resistance to cold; is associated

with her smooth-skinned, relatively hairless body and thick layer of subcutaneous fat.

■ Woman's blood contains more water and twenty percent fewer red cells. Since the red cells supply oxygen to the body cells, woman tires more easily and is more prone to faint. Her constitutional vitality is, therefore, limited to "life span." (When the working day in British factories was increased from ten to twelve hours under wartime conditions, accidents increased 150 percent among women but not at all among men.)

■ On the average, man possesses fifty percent more brute strength than woman (forty percent of a man's body weight is muscle; twenty-three percent of a woman's).

■ Woman's heart beats more rapidly (average eighty beats per minute vs. seventy-two for man). Woman's blood pressure (ten points lower than man's) varies from minute to minute, but she has less tendency toward high blood pressure—at least until after menopause.

■ Woman's vital capacity or breathing power is significantly lower than man's.

■ Woman withstands high temperatures better than man because her metabolism slows down less.

SEXUAL DIFFERENCES

A woman's sexual drive tends to be related to her menstrual cycle, while a man's drive is fairly constant. The hormone testosterone is a major factor in stimulating a man's sexual desire.

A woman is stimulated more by touch and romantic words. She is far more attracted by a man's personality, while a man is stimulated by sight. A man is usually less discriminating about those to whom he is physically attracted.

While a man needs little or no preparation for sex, a woman often needs hours of emotional and mental preparation. Harsh or abusive treatment can easily remove her desire for sexual intimacy for days at a time. When a woman's emotions have been trampled by her husband, she is often repulsed by his advances. Many women have told me they feel like prostitutes when they're forced to make love while feeling resentment toward their husbands. However, a man may have NO idea what he is putting his wife through when he forces sex upon her.

These basic differences, which usually surface soon after the wedding, are the source of many conflicts in marriage. From the start, the woman has a greater intuitive awareness of how to develop a loving relationship. Because of her sensitivity, she is initially more considerate of his feelings and enthusiastic about developing a meaningful, multi-level relationship: that is, she knows how to build something more than a sexual marathon; she wants to be a lover, a best friend, a fan, a homemaker, and an appreciated partner. The man, on the other hand, does not generally have her instinctive awareness of what the relationship should be. He doesn't know how to encourage and love his wife or treat her in a way that meets her deepest needs.

Since he doesn't have an understanding of these vital areas through intuition, he must rely *solely* upon the knowledge and skills he has acquired *prior* to marriage. Unfortunately, our educational system does not require a training program for a husband-to-be. His only education may be the example he observed in his home. For many of us, that example might have been insufficient. We enter marriage knowing everything about sex and very little about genuine, unselfish love.

I am not saying men are more selfish than women. I'm simply saying that at the outset of a marriage a man is not as equipped to express unselfish love or as desirous of nurturing marriage into a loving and lasting relationship as a woman is.

INTUITIVE DIFFERENCES

Norman was planning to invest more than $50,000 in a business opportunity that was a "sure thing." He had scrutinized it from every angle and had logically deduced that it couldn't miss. After signing a contract and delivering a check to the other party, he decided to tell his wife about the investment.

Upon hearing a few of the details, she immediately felt uneasy about the deal. Norman sensed her uneasiness and became angry, asking why she felt that way. She couldn't give a logical reason because she didn't have one. All she knew was that it just didn't "sit right." Norman gave in, went back to the other party, and asked for a refund. "You're crazy!" the man told him as he returned Norman's money. A short time later, *all* of the organizers and investors were indicted by the federal government. His wife's intuition had not only saved him $50,000, but it may have kept Norman out of jail.

What exactly is this "woman's intuition"? It's not something mystical. According to a Stanford University research team led by neuropsychologists McGuinness and Tribran, women do catch subliminal messages faster and more accurately than men. Since this intuition is based on an unconscious mental process, many women aren't able to give specific explanations for the way they feel. They simply perceive or "feel" something about a situation or person, while men tend to follow a logical analysis of circumstances or people.

Now that you know WHY men and women cannot understand their respective differences without great effort, I hope you will have more hope, patience, and tolerance as you endeavor to strengthen and deepen your relationship with your spouse. With this in mind, let's look at some of the serious consequences of allowing a poor marriage to continue in its downhill slide.

SERIOUS CONSEQUENCES OF A POOR MARRIAGE

First, a woman who is not properly loved by her husband can develop any number of serious physical ailments needing thousands of dollars worth of treatment, according to Dr. Ed Wheat.

Second, every aspect of a woman's emotional and physical existence is dependent on the romantic love she receives from her husband, says Dr. James Dobson. So, husbands, if *you* feel locked out of your bedroom, listen closely. According to Dr. Dobson, when a man learns to love his wife in the way she needs to be loved, she will respond to him physically in a way he never dreamed possible.

Third, a husband's lack of love for his wife can drastically affect their children's emotional development, according to John Drescher in his book, *Seven Things Children Need.*

Fourth, a rebellious wife and children are more likely to be found in the home of a man who does not know how to lovingly support his family.

Fifth, when a man settles for a poor marriage, he is forfeiting his reputation before all the world. He is saying, "I don't care what I promised at the marriage altar; I'm not going to try any longer." By refusing to love his wife as he should, he is telling those around him that he is self-centered and unreliable.

Sixth, the son of an unloving husband will probably learn many of the wrong ways to treat his future wife by modeling after his father. Unloving parents simply can't keep their problems to themselves. They are bound to affect their children's future relationships.

And seventh, improper love increases the possibility of mental illness requiring psychiatric treatment of family members. According to an article in *Family Weekly*, 16 July 1978, Dr. Nathan Ackerman said mental illness is passed on within a family, transmitted from generation to generation. In that same article, Dr. Salvador Minuchin, a psychiatrist, said family members often get caught in a groove of mental illness by putting undue stress on each other.

AN ENCOURAGING WORD FOR HUSBANDS

I am not trying to force you into the "perfect husband" mold. I don't know *any* perfect husbands. However, I do know some who are learning how to respond to their wives' special needs.

What I do want to do is to help you learn how to love your

wife more effectively and consistently. At first you may feel like you're learning to walk all over again. Weeks, months, or even a year may pass before you reach your goal of consistent loving behavior. After you learn to slowly make progress, you will gain confidence. Soon you will be right in the midst of the kind of marriage you never thought possible.

Remember—you may feel it's impossible to change lifelong habits, but it's not. It usually takes from thirty to sixty days to change a habit. So I hope you will decide to try to change yours. I know from experience that the rewards are well worth the effort.

The secret to a fulfilling marriage is persistence! Sometimes in the middle of a conflict with Norma, I really want to give up. But that's only how I feel. Often I'm tired, run down, under too much stress—consequently, the future looks bleak. That's when I rely upon knowledge not feelings. I act upon what *will* strengthen our relationship, and in a few days I see the results. In fact, I usually feel better the next day and have renewed desire to work on our marriage. So *I never give up.* I keep acting on what I've learned from the Bible are the secrets of lasting relationships.

Remember, *you* are the one who gains when you strive to have a loving relationship with your wife. My wife has told me dozens of times that when I treat her right I'm the one who wins. My loving care motivates her to do extra things for me, to respond gladly to my needs and desires, but this has never been my main motivation. The strongest motivation for me has been the *challenge* and *rewards* of living my life as outlined in Scripture. For me, it's following the two greatest teachings of Christ—to know and love God and to know and love people (Matt. 22:36–40). All the joy and fulfillment I have desired in this life have come from these two relationships—with God and with others (Eph. 3:19–20; John 15:11–13). These relationships are so important that I have added to my own life another motivation—perhaps the best motivation for me. I allow a few other couples to hold me accountable for loving my wife and children. They have the freedom to ask me how we're doing, as a couple and as a family and I know they love me enough to lift me up when I fall. And I always try to remember that love is a *choice.* I choose to care about my relationships. That same choice leading to great rewards can be yours.

My wife and I have committed the remaining years of our lives to the study of skills needed to rebuild meaningful relationships. I have personally interviewed hundreds of women about what actions of their husbands tear down or build up their marriages. Basically, this book is a summary of my findings.

Your wife may be a career woman without children or a busy homemaker and mother of three. Whatever the case, I believe you can *customize* the general principles in this book to build a more fulfilling relationship with her.

♥ THIRTY WAYS TO BE MORE AWARE ♥

Husbands and wives are different, but they can do many things to strengthen their relationship. While the questions are directed toward husbands, many of them could apply equally well to wives. To use this checklist effectively:

♥ The husband should fill it out first.
♥ Husband and wife can talk together about the husband's answers.
♥ The wife can share her answers to the questions that apply to her.

Answer YES or NO to each question, then check your score below:

1. Do you make your wife feel good about herself? (yes____ no____)

2. Do you value the same things in your wife that you value in yourself? (yes____ no____)

3. Does your face spontaneously break into a smile when you see your wife? (yes____ no____)

4. When you leave the house, does your wife have a sense of well-being, having been nourished by your company? (yes____ no____)

5. Can you and your wife tell each other honestly what you really want instead of using manipulation or games? (yes____ no____)

6. Can your wife get angry at you without your thinking less of her? (yes____ no____)

7. Can you accept your wife as she is instead of having several plans to redo her? (yes____ no____)

8. Is your behavior consistent with your words? (yes____ no____)

9. Do your actions show you really care for your wife? (yes____ no____)

10. Can you feel comfortable with your wife when she's wearing old clothes? (yes____ no____)

11. Do you enjoy introducing your wife to your friends and acquaintances? (yes____ no____)

12. Are you able to share with your wife your moments of weakness, failure, disappointment? (yes____ no____)

13. Would your wife say you are a good listener? (yes____ no____)

14. Do you trust your wife to solve her own problems? (yes____ no____)

15. Do you admit to your wife you have problems and need her comfort? (yes____ no____)

16. Do you believe you could live a full and happy life without your wife? (yes___ no___)

17. Do you encourage your wife to develop her full potential as a woman? (yes___ no___)

18. Are you able to learn from your wife and value what she says? (yes___ no___)

19. If your wife were to die tomorrow, would you be very happy you had had a chance to meet her and to marry her? (yes___ no___)

20. Does your wife feel she's more important than anyone or anything else in your life? (yes___ no___)

21. Do you believe you know at least five of your wife's major needs and how to meet those needs in a skillful way? (yes___ no___)

22. Do you know what your wife needs when she's under stress or when she's discouraged? (yes___ no___)

23. When you offend your wife, do you usually admit you were wrong and seek her forgiveness? (yes___ no___)

24. Would your wife say you praise her at least once a day? (yes___ no___)

25. Would your wife say you are open to her correction? (yes___ no___)

26. Would your wife say you are a protector, that you know what her limitations are as a woman? (yes___ no___)

27. Would your wife say you usually consider her feelings and ideas whenever making a major decision that affects the family or her? (yes___ no___)

28. Would your wife say you enjoy being with her and sharing many of life's experiences with her? (yes___ no___)

29. Would your wife say you are a good example of what you would like her to be? (yes___ no___)

30. Would you say you create interest in her when you share things you consider important? (yes___ no___)

If you answered yes to *ten or fewer* questions, then your relationship is in major need of overhaul.

If you answered yes to *eleven to nineteen* of the questions, your relationship needs improvement.

If you answered yes to *twenty or more*, you show an awareness of the basic differences between men and women and are building a strong relationship.

Some couples are aware of their differences but one or both spouses can't accept those differences. The favorite line is, "He (or she) needs to change!" In the next chapter, Anne Kristin Carroll shares the story of Pamela and Howard and what happened when *he* wouldn't change and *she* had had enough.

Chapter **13**

GOD ACCEPTS YOUR MATE—WHY CAN'T YOU?

BY ANNE KRISTIN CARROLL
Together Forever

You can talk about differences forever, but sooner or later you have to start accepting those differences and living with them in a constructive way. Of course, each spouse has the best plan for doing that: "My mate needs to change and then everything will be fine." Changing your mate, however, is really quite impossible. Accepting your mate is another matter, but in order to do that, *you* may need to change. In the following chapter, Anne Kristin Carroll tells how Pamela finally accepted Howard, although it was clear he was the one who had to change. And when she accepted him, change he did! As you read, think about these questions:

♥ Do I accept my mate or do I keep pressuring him/her (even in subtle ways) to change?
♥ What is the significance of Pam's Nightblooming Cereus? What does it have to do with accepting someone?
♥ What is Anne Carroll's secret of acceptance? Can it work in your marriage?

HEART TO HEART

Do you accept your mate as he or she is? Following is a checklist of symptoms that are usually present when you fail to accept your mate, along with what happens when you try to force your spouse to conform to your idea of the ideal, your social standards, religious beliefs, etc.

Critical attitudes of mate and/or others

Rebellion

Constantly comparing one's mate to someone else

Alcoholism or use of legal or illegal drugs

Withdrawn personality of unaccepted mate

Sexual failure

Communication breakdown

Superior or self-righteous attitude

Beyond God's concept of coming to know Jesus Christ as your personal Savior, acceptance of your mate as he or she is is one of the most important concepts you can master. Failure to do so causes more marital breakups than any other.

Lois Weiss did a beautiful job of explaining the concept of acceptance in her poem, "Heart to Heart."

HEART TO HEART

There is a cord
Unseen
That binds us heart-to-heart.
The surest way
For me to shorten the cord
Is to let you choose the length.
For if I choose to tighten
That unseen cord
By poking,
Prying,
Wondering,
Why?ing,
You will dissolve the cord
And create
An unseen wall
For both of us to see.

And that, my beloved,
Would be the tragedy
Of this
Or any
Marriage.[3]

Those words really sum up this concept. Have you ever thought about the many ways you tell your mate that you do not approve of him/her, or you wish he or she would change? Sometimes you do it by making comparisons to someone else's husband or wife; sometimes through constant criticism, or by trying to make him/her fit into your unfulfilled expectations of a marriage partner. Whatever your personal mode of destruction, *you are killing your mate. Killing love and destroying your marriage.* Strong words, yes, but true.

Let's review how some of these symptoms occur when you

aren't accepting your mate as he or she is. If your marriage is suffering because of a lack of communication, remember that no one is very inclined to have depth-level talks, to really have a soul communication with a mate who has a disapproving spirit. I *sincerely believe that more adultery occurs because of nonacceptance in the home than for any other one reason.* I have talked to the hurt wives, the crushed husbands, and yes, to the other women and men in their lives, too. You'd be amazed that at least eighty percent of the time the cause is the same. The other woman, or the other man, gave the wandering mate the love, attention, and praise that was missing at home. Particularly men who have been involved in adultery have said to me: "Anne, it wasn't so much that I didn't love my wife, but there was never any peace at home. She was always pushing, always trying to change me, put me into a mold. I didn't intend to get involved in an affair, it just happened. You see the woman I'm involved with makes no demands, she takes me like I am, and although I know it is wrong, *I feel free* for the first time in years, *I feel accepted, I feel loved for me.*" Most wandering wives say the same!

If your mate doesn't know Christ, or is a carnal Christian, and is at a period in life where for some reason—business, home, children, whatever—he or she is having to face failure or disappointment, believe me, your spouse is all too aware of the failure. He or she doesn't need you to point it out. Sometimes your criticism is the final push that sends your mate to the bottle or to pills in an attempt to escape the reality that he or she feels unable to deal with.

You may not have realized what an influence you have in the life of your mate. Take a minute and turn to the third chapter of Genesis. As you begin reading, you will see that it took Satan almost six verses to persuade Eve to disobey God. In the closing sentence of verse 6 it says: "and she gave some also to her husband and he ate." What influence! Ever think about it that way?

THE DIFFERENCES HELP YOU GROW

When you walked down the aisle, you were probably full of dreams, Hollywood ideas, but few solid concepts of the reality of day-to-day married life. After you stepped through the door of that vine-covered cottage, you discovered that the white knight snores, doesn't put his clothes away, never gets to the table on time, and obviously was born in a barn. Likewise, your fairy princess wears cold cream, curlers, has gained weight, and often prefers soap operas or talking on the phone to cleaning the house or conversation with you.

You both brought many different ideas and attitudes, actions, likes, thoughts, and manners into the marriage. Constantly discovering and enjoying these differences, these interests, and exploring them together is what continues to make marriage a growing, exciting experience.

Did you ever realize that God can use just those traits you find so offensive to mold and conform you more to his image? You know, if we married someone just like ourselves, instead of fitting and complementing each other, like a lock and key, we would be like two keys or two locks—unworkable.

If your mate is irritable, perhaps the Lord would have you learn patience; if demanding, he would teach you to give, and give again; if depressed or withdrawn, perhaps through your example your mate will learn his or her true worth, that of one who is so important that the Son of God died especially for that person. If your mate is unaffectionate and unloving, you can demonstrate through your life what "real" love is. (See examples in 1 Corinthians.)

Ephesians 3:20 tells us that God has something wonderful, more than we could ever hope for or desire, planned for us, so begin learning his concepts, begin allowing him to conform *you* to his image, and the reward will be beyond your wildest dreams.

Marriage in God's eyes isn't just a piece of paper, a civil contract; it is a sacred vow made between you and your mate before God almighty. Remember John 10:10: "I came that they may have and enjoy life, and have it in abundance to the full, till it overflows." You say that doesn't sound much like the life that you are experiencing with your mate. You don't see how that is possible. Well, get out your Bible and reread Romans 8:28.

FREE LOVE HAS NO CONDITIONS

After we become God's children he continues to love and care for us, when we're in fellowship or when we fail. This is free love, love without conditions. Just as Christ loved us and died for us when we were sinners, so are we to respond to our mates!

"Impossible. No one could love someone like I'm married to," you say.

Impossible isn't in the Christian dictionary. Most of us get so wrapped up in our own desires, our own selfishness, that we begin to erect barriers around our mates—maybe not actual ones, but unspoken lists of do's and don'ts. They know, and if you are honest with yourself, you'll admit that when they transgress these barriers all hell breaks loose.

Slowly but surely you are binding them, limb by limb, like a prisoner. You are saying, I don't trust you, I don't approve of you, I want you to change. The harder you try to possess, the more rebellious they become. Proverbs 25:23–25 expresses the disgust and rebellion this brings out in the heart of man.

Remember Proverbs 16:25: "There is a way that seems right to a man and appears straight before him, but at the end of it are the ways of death." This is exactly what happens when you refuse to accept your mate as he or she is. When you have erected fences, set the standards, it is as if you have confined a beautiful tree. You want it to grow tall and straight, but it needs room, freedom, space to branch out and to reach up. When we allow our mates true freedom to be the persons God created them to be, the miracles that begin to happen are amazing.

Think about it this way: As long as you have barriers, fences, standards, you, in essence, have a robot responding to you. Just as God created you with a free volition, to be and do as you choose, you must give your mate the same right. Do you really want actions, presents, forced endearments that are produced because your mate has no other choice? Or would you prefer the freedom, the spontaneity of love as it was when you met, love that wasn't demanded, love that was given freely because of who you are? The choice is yours.

BUT MY MATE NEEDS TO CHANGE

"Anne, you don't understand. My mate needs to change for his/her own good." I have heard these words often enough, and ofttimes the complaining partner is right. Perhaps the mate is degenerating with drugs or alcohol. But all the good intentions of the marriage partner—and direct action trying to effect a change—won't work. No matter how a person may be destroying his/her life or hurting you, when you start communicating your desire for change, the message is: "I don't approve of you. I don't love you. I want you to be different."

The Proverbs are full of wonderful words of wisdom on keeping your critical thoughts to yourself, such as Proverbs 21:23: "He who guards his mouth and his tongue keeps himself from troubles." And Proverbs 21:9: "It is better to dwell in a corner of the housetop (on the flat oriental roof, exposed to all kinds of weather) than in a house shared with a nagging, quarrelsome and fault-finding woman!"

"Well, if I'm not supposed to change my mate, who is?" God! God is the life changer, and *only God*. We only slow down the process of his work in the lives of our mates by our nagging. God did not put you here on earth to do the work of the Holy Spirit. You can talk until you are blue in the face, but John 6:44 reminds you: "No one is able to come to me unless the Father who sent me attracts and draws him and gives him the desire to come to me." Read 1 Thessalonians 5:19, and don't be guilty of quenching the Spirit's work in the life of your mate.

WHAT DO I DO IN THE MEANTIME?

Take inventory of your life! Ask God to show you areas that are antagonizing your mate, causing him/her to rebel, or possibly supporting problems in your relationship. When you become what God wants you to be, when you get out of the way long enough for God to go into action, then change will occur.

It might be well to stop here to reread Matthew 7:1–5 (LB): "Don't criticize, and then you won't be criticized! For others will treat you as you treat them. And why worry about a speck in the eye of a brother when you have a board in your own? Should you say, 'Friend, let me help you get that speck out of your eye,' when you can't even see because of the board in your own? Hypocrite! First get rid of the board. Then you can see to help your brother."

Before we discuss God's formula for letting go and loving freely, let me share the following story with you, and perhaps you can better see how disastrous our attempts at changing our mates can be, but how beautiful God's ways always are.

"Anne, you know when God starts his chain of events, it is like the Night-blooming Cereus," said the friend who was sharing her experience with me. "That flower begins unnoticed, but unfolds in full view for us to see."

This is Pamela and Howard Phillips' story:

PAMELA

Howard and I had been married nineteen years. There was something missing in our lives. Although I had been brought up in a Christian home, I never came to know Jesus Christ personally. Howard and I looked like we had it made. Howard had a good job with Lockheed in Burbank. We had a lovely home, a boat, a beach house, healthy children, plenty of money, everything. Yet, like the song, I felt, "Is That All There Is?" Howard and I would talk about trivial things, but our souls never seemed to communicate on a deep spiritual level.

Howard seemed to be happy. He told me on numerous occasions that if he died tomorrow he wouldn't have felt that he'd missed a thing. Howard had been raised in quite a different atmosphere from me. His parents didn't go to church. His mother had to work because his stepfather was an alcoholic; his real father deserted them when Howard was three months old. He was brought up with nothing. He had to work all through high school and college to pay for his own clothes, books and tuition. So his main desire was to have material things, and he told me once that he hoped to have his first million by the time he was forty.

The nagging fear that something was missing in our lives turned into a real problem during the next year.

Howard began staying after work and going to a nearby bar

with some of the men from the office. Sometimes he'd get too drunk to come home and would stay over at a friend's apartment. (And sometimes, he said later, he could have made it home but didn't want to listen to my sermons or face the condemnation in my eyes.)

He quit his well-paying position with Lockheed and began selling real estate in California. With no one to account to for his time or his whereabouts, and with all forms of discipline gone, he gradually went from bad to worse.

Real estate wasn't the gold mine he'd thought it would be, and between the lack of income and the bills piling up, he turned more and more to the bottle.

I hated him for what I felt he was doing to me, to the family. I even hated him because he wouldn't fight back. He usually ignored me.

HOWARD

I don't know when I crossed that invisible line from a social drinker to an alcoholic, but it didn't happen overnight.

My heavy drinking began two years before I left Lockheed. Time was passing and I wasn't reaching the financial goals I had set—and Pamela was always home keeping an eye on everything I did.

PAMELA

As things got worse, I had a friend who kept telling me about Al-Anon meetings, but at this time I felt I could handle the situation myself. The whole idea was too embarrassing. Dear God, I learned what real embarrassment was like as Howard continued to slip deeper and deeper into the bottle.

I was desperate, but I kept my desperation to myself. I tried praying. Even though I didn't know Christ, I prayed that God would put a stop to Howard's drinking. I felt if Howard would stop drinking, all our problems would be solved.

Why, I asked myself, was I having to live like this? I didn't have any idea that I could possibly be a contributing factor, not then. I felt so alone, so depressed. I felt I was being put in a situation I didn't deserve.

I continued to try to get through to Howard. I constantly reminded him of what he used to be, and what a "sorry no good" he was becoming. "You could quit if you really wanted to . . . it is just that you are so weak. Howard, are you listening to me? I said, If you cared anything about me or the children, you would quit."

Silence. The more I fussed and nagged, the more he retreated. On one occasion when I was going through my speech, he responded.

"Pamela, my dear, I don't give a damn about you or the kids!"

I had forced an answer, hadn't I? Now, could I live with it? Was that actually how Howard felt, or was it the liquor talking?

I pressed Howard hard, stayed on his back night and day. In my mind I rationalized that *I* had to straighten him up for the children's sakes! I realize now that most of the problems with the children occurred because, when he wasn't home on time, I'd fuss and say, "I guess he's out drinking, that no-good." Occasionally I'd even put the kids in the car and go out and look for him, no matter what time of night it was.

Our oldest child, Betsy, finally couldn't take the nightmarish situation at home any longer, and when she graduated from high school she moved out. I thought it was a good thing because she said to me, "Momma, if I keep staying here I'm going to begin to hate him. I hate seeing what he's becoming and I'm going to get to where I hate my daddy." So she left. Occasionally she'd drop by, but only when she was sure that he wasn't home.

The boys felt the same way, but they weren't old enough to leave, so they had their own ways of avoiding him. When he came home on time, they'd leave the house. If he came in drunk, they'd retreat to their rooms, or to a friend's house.

I didn't know what to do when I realized that Howard had a problem bigger than either of us could handle. We made the rounds of psychiatrists and counselors, but the drinking continued.

One psychiatrist believed that Howard was deeply depressed, had a low opinion of himself, and recommended tranquilizers three times a day! Tranquilizers—just exchanging one problem for another. Besides, the mixture could have been deadly! *This is why I feel all physicians should have a real working knowledge of alcoholism.*

When Howard came home with the pills, he threw them across the room. "I have one problem already," he said. "I'm not going to get hung up on another." I didn't know anything then, so I tried to get him to take them. Here again, I was trying to run his life for him, thinking, Anything is better than alcohol. I realize now that isn't true.

Then a friend told us about a "Christian psychiatrist" who was supposed to be very good, so reluctantly we went. Of course, Howard only went because I pushed him. At the first meeting, Howard sat there like a knot on a log. I knew he was resentful, and he let me know that he wasn't going to tell her anything. She suggested we come back to group therapy sessions. Howard was to go to one, and I to another. *I think that was one of the biggest mistakes we ever made.* They were a collection of mixed-up people trying to analyze each other's problems. "I wouldn't put up with that . . . I'd leave him," was their answer for my particular problem.

They were mainly "group pity sessions," which could easily have led me down the road to depression.

HOWARD

I went to three of those meetings and then decided that I wasn't going to any more. I told Pamela, "My problem right now is that we're in debt, and you're just adding to my problems with all of these extra doctor bills. That woman is charging us too much money."

PAMELA

I called the doctor and told her what Howard had said, and also what I thought of the group sessions. Her reply was huffy to say the least: "You don't love him as much as you say you do because you are letting him kill himself. It is my advice that you leave him." Some Christian advice!

It left me feeling mighty low.

Then, one July night, God's plan began to unfold. I have this old Night-blooming Cereus, an ugly plant that you keep hidden all year until the one night when it blooms. The bloom is the most beautiful thing you have ever seen. Its flower resembles the Christ child in the manger, and the five-pronged tassles look like a star. It is breathtaking in detail and the fragrance is so sweet, you can smell it all over the neighborhood. It opens at midnight, and when the morning sun hits it, it closes, turns brown and drops off.

This night, while I was waiting for my Cereus to come out, had started like many others. Howard had come in that night drunk as usual.

Around midnight, my Cereus had opened fully, and it was so exciting to see this miracle once more that I wanted to share it with someone. I remembered that my neighbor had said that she had never seen one, so I called her and offered to bring it over for her family to see.

Kay and I kept each other's boys on occasions, but we were not what you would call close friends. I don't know why we began to talk that night. I know I was terribly depressed, and I really didn't want to go back home and see Howard passed out on the couch.

Kay mentioned a Bible study class she was going to, and asked if I'd like to join her.

"I'm not going anywhere," I said. "Those Bible studies aren't for me. I've tried them and they haven't worked." Then I blurted out, "Kay, I guess you know about Howard and his drinking problem."

She said, "Well, I sort of thought he drank." Her quiet manner brought out my need to confide in somebody. "Well, Kay, I have had it," I said. "I am seriously considering divorcing him."

Her answer wasn't what I had expected. "Pamela," she said, "I know you will think this is crazy, but do me a favor and don't do anything until I get a book to you tomorrow morning." Then she suggested that *I might have a problem,* too, or at least I might be contributing to Howard's problem! The only problem I had was a problem living with the problem named Howard.

Bright and early the next morning she brought me a copy of *We Became Wives of Happy Husbands.* It was a lovely summer day, so I got my tea and went out on the patio and read the whole book that day. It was like one woman sat down on that patio, and another one got up. What I learned were God's concepts, my responsibilities as a wife.

I saw myself for the first time in my life. Here I was judging Howard, when God said a wife's role was to be submissive, to pray to God *not* to try to change my mate, but to let God change *me!* The more I read, the more I realized I'd been trying to do it myself. I wasn't accepting Howard as he was, as Christ accepts us; I was trying to manipulate him, change him. I realized the many things I did that provoked him, especially trying to get him to quit drinking. You can't change another human being; all you can do is pray for that person and ask God to do the changing, and get out of the way.

I realized that I had not fulfilled my responsibilities as a wife; I had just been living for my children. I put a meal on the table for Howard and that was it. He wasn't first in my life as the Scriptures said he should be (1 Cor. 7:34). My children came first.

The next morning I had an interview for a job. I was going back to work to make my own money and leave Howard. When I got there the man I was supposed to talk with was out, so I told his secretary that I'd just wait in the car until he got back from lunch.

When I went back to the car, I began reading Tim LaHaye's book, *How to Be Happy Though Married.* I'd never known how simple it was to accept Christ and what he'd done. I didn't realize his forgiveness and love were available if only I'd ask. Sitting in the car, I prayed and asked Christ to come into my life. I read Colossians 2:9–10 over and over: "For in him the whole fullness of Deity (the Godhead) continues to dwell in bodily form—giving complete expression of the divine nature. And you are in him, made full and have come to fullness of life—in Christ you too are filled with the Godhead: Father, Son and Holy Spirit, and reach full spiritual stature." I thanked him for filling me with his Spirit, which would provide the power to live the Christian life, my life, even the one I had with Howard.

In the past, when I had prayed that God would make Howard quit drinking, I'd say, "If you are as loving a God as they say you are, all you have to do is take the desire away from him, and he won't even want another drink, and all our problems will be solved." Of course, that isn't the way God works, and it wasn't his plan for us. But at that time, when nothing changed, I simply got fatalistic about it and decided, "What will be will be." I hate to say this now, but sometimes we would be lying in bed, and I would look over at him drunk and wish that he would die and get out of my life. At the same time, I'd say to the Lord, "Why are you leaving him here to torment me this way? I haven't done anything to deserve this."

I began to regularly attend Al-Anon meetings, and I was learning and beginning to understand the problem of living and helping an alcoholic. Funny, their answers were the same messages I read in God's concepts and his Word. The first thing I learned was that the alcoholic must face up to the fact that without self-discipline, without being honest about his problem, he cannot survive. They told me that all my threats, tantrums, and tears would do nothing but add to the guilt he already carried, and send him even faster back to the bottle. I learned that I must accept him just as he was.

Howard noticed a change in me. I wasn't acting the same, and just like Anne says, a vacuum was created, and it demanded a change from him. To begin with, he resented me. I became a threat because he saw that I was getting help, that I was coping, and it quietly condemned him.

When he'd call and say he'd be home in a few minutes, and hours passed, and bedtime came, I just put Howard in the Lord's hands, and the children and I would go to bed. If he came in, I thanked the Lord that he was all right. If he didn't, I knew that the Lord was quite capable of caring for him wherever he was. I relied constantly on Philippians 4:6–9.

Sometime in November 1972, Howard called and said he was going to election headquarters. About 2 A.M. he called from jail; he was drunk and had been driving on the wrong side of the street. The police had picked him up and put him in jail. I went and got him, and he was crying like a baby. He said, "I've got to do something about this problem." I took his hand, and said, "Yes, I know you do. I think if you really want help A.A. is the place. But, Howard, this is something you will have to do yourself, if you want it bad enough." He just sat quietly and thought. He wasn't quite ready yet.

God continued to give me strength to deal with our daily lives (2 Cor. 2:9). Now, I prayed for Howard. I felt for him. I realized that it was his problem. I still loved him, and I helped him all I could, but I had to stop being a crutch for him. So when he would come in drinking, I would have his supper ready, no matter what time it was. Or, if he didn't want to eat and wanted to go to bed, I would let him. I didn't say anything to him about the problem. I could see that he was having a struggle within himself.

I encouraged the children to pray for him. We discussed ways in which we could help him. The boys did their best to acknowledge his presence in the house, and tried not to avoid him as much.

The night of December 23, I was busy cooking our Christmas dinner. It was an awful night, pouring rain and foggy. Howard called at 10:30 P.M., so drunk he didn't even know where he was. All he said was, "I'm on my way home," and hung up.

I went to my room and got down on my knees by the bed. I prayed harder than I had ever prayed in my life that God's will be done where Howard was concerned. "Please, God, if it's your will, please don't let him get killed or kill or hurt anyone else. I know you love him more than I do. Thank you, Lord, for loving me, saving me, teaching me your concepts. Now, Lord, I will commit Howard to your care." In my prayer I was claiming the promise of John 14:13–14: "And I will do—I myself will grant—whatever you ask in my name so that the Father may be glorified and extolled in (through) the Son. (Yes) I will grant—will do for you—whatever you shall ask in my name."

Then I relaxed in his peace (John 14:27).

At 4 A.M. on Christmas Eve, Howard called and said he was in jail. He had gotten in touch with a lawyer friend who was sending someone down to pay his bail and he would be straight home. I called the jail and they said no one had come to get Howard out. I called the lawyer and he said he couldn't find anyone with the money but that he was still working on it. It was noon before Howard came home. The rest of the day was spent getting his car, which had been impounded. He was so ashamed. He couldn't look me in the face. He said, "I know you won't believe me, but I've made up my mind. I am going to A.A."

HOWARD

Boy, that first A.A. meeting was something. I was scared, embarrassed—all sorts of mixed feelings were running around inside of me. But a little after eight o'clock the chairman called the meeting to order. The group, which had been mingling and talking, took their seats. They ranged in age from the very young to grandfathers. The chairman began by stating the purpose of A.A., which he said was a group of people who shared their strength, hope, and experience with each other so that they could solve their common problems and help others to overcome alcoholism.

A speaker then introduced himself. He said, "I'm Roger D. and I'm an alcoholic. It's good to be here tonight, and it's great to be sober!"

Another member then rose and gave his name, then shared the tormented story of his downhill fight with the bottle. Every word was my story!

When the meeting was over, I realized here were people who actually knew what I was going through; they'd experienced it all, yet they stood tonight, sober, happy, with families reunited. *Dear God, maybe there is hope for me*, I thought.

I realized I had to take the first step. I had to admit I was an alcoholic. At my second meeting, with trembling knees I stood up and said, "I'm Howard and I'm an alcoholic!" Tears started running down my face as everyone applauded. They knew how hard those words were for me. I felt strength pouring into me from these people, and with God's help and their human support, for the first time I believed I could make it.

PAMELA

Not long after the first A.A. meeting, Howard started going to church with us. Oh, what a wonderful feeling it was to be in the house of the Lord together, to be a family again. As I continued to be the wife God created me to be, Howard continued to change. Then one Sunday he, too, came to know Jesus Christ as his personal Savior! The Lord had performed the miracle I'd prayed for all these years. He just did it his way instead of mine.

Money was still a problem, but Howard realized that the material things which had been so important in the past weren't the fulfillment that he desired any longer; he had learned the truth of Matthew 6:21: "For where your treasure is, there will your heart be also." I noticed one evening that he was reading and rereading Matthew 6:19–34. Not long after that, Howard left real estate and returned to Lockheed. It took some time to straighten up our finances, but the Lord was gracious and blessed, and today we are happily debt-free.

HOWARD

The Lord didn't just restore our family. He renewed our love, both emotional and physical. He gave me the ability and the desire to be the head of my home. He also gave me the desire to be the spiritual leader of my home, which was a switch for us. It is so beautiful, so natural for Pam and me to commune with Jesus together.

PAMELA

God works in mysterious ways to bring us to him. It has been four years since that dark night I took the Night-blooming Cereus over to Kay's. Four years—and Howard hasn't had a drink in the last three! God may be waiting right now to be the answer in your life to your problems, to your broken marriage. All you have to be is willing. He may not work through a flower as he did in my life, but I will always call my flower the miracle flower.

This story, as told by Pamela and Howard, illustrates a point that I would like to make clear.

If the problem in your home is alcohol, remember that all your problems won't disappear when the bottle does. Your problems weren't born in that bottle. Take a deep inventory of all the areas of your life compared to God's concept, because herein lies the root from which the bottle grew.

I know right now some of you are thinking, "That's a great story, but if I really let out all the reins and turned my mate free, no telling what he or she would do." Most of us feel that way. I know I certainly did. I held on to Jim, watched him, kept the leash short. But the shorter the leash, the more rebellious he became. Change only began when I was willing to use God's formula, which is given in Philippians 4:4, 6–9: "Rejoice in the Lord always—delight, gladden yourselves in him; again I say, Rejoice! Do not fret or have any anxiety about anything, but in every circumstance and in everything by prayer and petition (definite requests) with thanksgiving continue to make your wants known to God. And God's peace (that tranquil state of a soul assured of its salvation through Christ, and so, fearing nothing from God and content with its earthly lot of whatever sort that is, that peace) which transcends all understanding, shall garrison and mount guard over your hearts and minds in Christ Jesus. For the rest, brethren, whatever is true, whatever is worthy of reverence and is honorable and seemly, whatever is just, whatever is pure, whatever is lovely and lovable, whatever is kind and winsome and gracious, if there is any virtue and excellence, if there is anything worthy of praise, think on and weigh and take account of these things—fix your minds on them. Practice what you have learned and received and heard and seen in me, and model your way of living on it, and the God of peace— of untroubled, undisturbed well-being—will be with you."

God says, "To get with my plan, the first thing you are to do is just dump the whole mess in my hands." You may say, "I'm not sure I understand, Anne. How do I give Christ my burdens?" You commit your every burden, your every care, to Jesus through prayer, simply talking with God. God understands your situation. He knows every pain, mental and emotional, that you are feeling. He is capable of carrying the load. The question is, Will you let him?

We humans have a habit of thinking we need to let the Lord know how to handle our lives. Someone once gave the illustration, and it is a good one, that our lives are like a beautiful needlework picture; the problem is we are only seeing the underneath side and it always looks like a mess, but our heavenly Father sees the finished picture, from the top side, and he knows where each finishing thread should go.

LOOKING ON THE TOP SIDE

After you have given God your cares, problems, worries, then begin to look at the picture as if you could already see the top side of it. Remember in Philippians 4:8 it says to set your mind on whatever is kind, lovely, winsome, virtuous, etc. Well, that is the beginning.

I'll tell you a little secret, and *believe me it works.* The Scriptures share it in Proverbs 16:24: "Pleasant words are as a honeycomb, sweet to the mind and healing to the body!" Begin to look for areas in your mate that you can praise. For instance, instead of looking at your mate's negative traits, reverse them in your mind, and share that reversal with him. For instance, if he is stubborn, realize that stubbornness can also be considered perseverance, and compliment him. If his conversation is inconsiderate, or too direct, consider the fact that he is open and frank. Look for the good.

Tolstoy, in *The Kingdom of God Is Within You,* makes this approach very clear when he says: "It seems to me that love, if it is fine, is essentially a discipline. . . . In wise love each divines the high secret self of the other, and refusing to believe in the mere daily self creates a mirror where the lover or the beloved sees an image to copy in daily life."[4]

If your goal is to turn your mate over to the Lord, and learn to accept him/her exactly as the Lord accepted you—unconditionally—you might apologize for your past mistakes in this area, mistakes which included not trusting him/her, being his/her Holy Spirit, making unrealistic demands, and not being the loving mate God intended you to be. Begin to apply Philippians 4:4, 6–9. Caution: Do not confess past immoralities in your life; it may make you feel better, but it may plant deep seeds of hurt and mistrust that may take years to correct. If you have made morality mistakes yourself, confess these to your Father in Heaven, claim 1 John 1:9 and get going. Your main goal is to learn that true love can only grow and develop in an atmosphere of acceptance and freedom, and that if you want to save that marriage on the brink, you are going to have to risk enough, trust God enough to let go, and let God!

♥ FIVE STEPS TOWARD ACCEPTANCE ♥

Your marriage may not be plagued by an alcohol problem, but there may be other tensions due to non-acceptance of one another. Here are steps you can take to turn your mate over to the Lord and learn to accept him/her exactly as the Lord has accepted you, unconditionally.

- ♥ Memorize Philippians 4:6–9 and use it daily, especially in those moments when your mate irritates or disappoints you—again.
- ♥ Pray daily about the situation. Each day try to take your problems and anxieties to the Lord and leave them with him. If you keep carrying the day's problems, you are failing to trust God to do his work.
- ♥ Instead of praying, "Lord, please change my mate," say, "Lord, please change me." Ask God to make you the kind of marriage partner that will honor him and motivate your mate to decide to do some changing on his/her own.
- ♥ Begin to look for positive traits in your mate. Start praising instead of criticizing and tearing down.
- ♥ What do you appreciate about your mate? Start today to compliment him or her on these qualities.

A major part of "unconditionally accepting" each other is being willing to share the work and recognize who needs help and when. In the next chapter, Dean Merrill talks about sorting out roles in marriage.

Chapter 14

A MASTER, A MISTRESS, AND TWO SLAVES

DEAN MERRILL
How to Really Love Your Wife

Who does the "dirty work" at your house? That is, who winds up with the dull routine and drudgery that are part of keeping the place from sinking into a chaos of clutter and confusion? In years past, these duties usually fell to the wife, who was automatically in charge of the home while the husband went off to "earn the living." Today, with millions of wives in the work force, many couples try to divide the dirty work equitably. Some husbands and wives work this out nicely with clearly marked roles and responsibilities; others struggle, one spouse taking more than his or her share and usually feeling resentful and "taken advantage of."

In this chapter, Dean Merrill describes the synergistic approach he and his wife follow—pitching in together to do what needs to be done, lightening each other's load, and mutually making life together much more fulfilling and enjoyable. As you read, dwell on this question: Just who *really* does the dirty work in your marriage? Is it fairly distributed, or is one spouse carrying most of the load?

WHO'S CARRYING THE LOAD?

Time and energy are gifts from God just as money is. Especially *discretionary* time and energy—the leftovers after we've finished working, sleeping, and eating. The question may again be posed:

What shall *we* (husband and wife) do with *our* time and energy?

Sounds pretty wide-open, doesn't it? But the fact is that society and tradition have rather thoroughly programed us with a set of answers. Husbands do certain things around the house. Wives do certain things around the house. Each has his/her "place."

How valid are the traditions we've been handed? Before you read on, find a pencil and mark this checklist according to the actual nature of each task, not according to what usually happens at your house.

	Basically a husband's job	Basically a wife's job	Doesn't really matter
1. Opening pickle jars	☐	☐	☐
2. Having babies	☐	☐	☐
3. Changing the car's oil	☐	☐	☐
4. Changing the baby's diapers	☐	☐	☐
5. Mowing the yard	☐	☐	☐
6. Vacuuming the carpet	☐	☐	☐
7. Waxing the car	☐	☐	☐
8. Waxing the kitchen floor	☐	☐	☐
9. Painting a ceiling	☐	☐	☐
10. Getting kids to bed	☐	☐	☐

Women's Liberation, of course, has forced all of us to think twice about these things, with the net effect of moving more and more items into the "doesn't really matter" column.

Tasks related to basic anatomy, of course (such as numbers 1 and 2 on the list), are not going to get bumped around. In terms of brute physical strength, men are estimated to be fifty percent stronger than women, and that's simply not going to change. Women, on the other hand, have been found to have a somewhat greater tolerance for extreme heat.

But when it comes to the overwhelming majority of tasks that really have nothing to do with anatomy, a lot of things are up for grabs. Some of us are cheering the current reassessment. Others of us are disturbed by it. Some of us are worried that the ultimate goal is to completely obliterate *la différence*, to create a unisex world. Many of us are confused about the new definitions of masculinity and femininity and whether they're improvements or setbacks.

And while we're philosophizing about the state of the culture at large, we're overlooking the nearest and most relevant situation: our own households. It's much easier to critique Barbara Walters as a TV news anchorperson or to expound the merits and flaws of the Equal Rights Amendment than it is to look at what's happening under our own roof.

We might as well face it: It takes a fair chunk of work to run a house. Work on the outside that brings in a paycheck, yes, but also work right there on the premises. And it's not all fun work. A certain percentage of it is outright drudgery. Servant-type work.

Who's going to do it?

Tradition says, "If it's anything to do with the kitchen, laundry room, bathroom, bedroom, or living areas—the wife. If it's anything to do with the garage, basement, or yard—the husband."

Now you may have altered that tradition to a greater or lesser degree. You and your wife may not have come to the marriage in the first place with identical traditions. Grace's father, a minister and former denominational executive, happens also to be a rather happy vacuumer as well as grocery shopper. I don't remember my dad doing either, unless it was a special occasion. So I naturally don't think about volunteering to vacuum or go to the supermarket—which sometimes, even after eleven years, Grace still finds herself expecting more or less from habit.

But these are minor wrinkles in the overall pattern of traditional husband and wife roles. None of us are free from them. And if someone were to follow any of our wives around with a stopwatch, chances are she'd pile up a greater number of drudgery minutes than we could any week of the year.

HOW ONE HUSBAND GOT THE MESSAGE

Mike McGrady, a newspaperman, traded places with his wife for a year. One night as he ironed clothes while his kids watched TV, he came to a sober realization:

> I have known little in life more depressing than that experience, standing there ironing my daughter's massive wardrobe, listening to Bob Hope and actor Burt Reynolds trading tacky little jokes about the actor's affair with an older woman.

> On second thought, it might have seemed as depressing without the television set on. Any job requiring the constant repetition of a simple act is going to seem dumb. No assembly-line worker in Detroit, no person tightening the same bolt on the same door of every sedan coming out of a factory, ever put in more dummy time than a normal housewife.[5]

Granted, life at McGrady's old newspaper office had not always been a lark. There had been cranky people and unreliable machinery and all of the normal irritants of any job. But there had also been some significant and applaudable goals in spite of the obstacles. It had its rewards.

Mike's wife Corinne was a person of considerable talent. Nevertheless, from almost the beginning of the marriage, Corinne had

> played Female. That is to say, she stayed home with the children and did the cleaning and cooking. It is, in retrospect, incredible that she did all this routinely and without complaint. . . .
>
> And since she was an artist, since she was gifted and creative, she not unnaturally attempted to apply her skills to her new life as housewife. It was a little like asking a nuclear physicist to apply his talents to sweeping public streets. She did well at the most mundane tasks, very well indeed, but who can measure the toll? Not just the toll in years—for these could have been her most productive years—but a toll in spirit. There were rough times, times when in the middle of the night she would flee family and house, get in the car and drive for hours along shore roads. There were other times when her patience would be worn thin as gauze and that normally well-modulated voice turned into something out of a low-budget horror movie.[6]

It was out of a desire to change some of that that the McGrady experiment was born.

The question for us husbands is not whether our wives are willing to be the servants of the household. The question is, *are we? Do we really want to be servants in our own homes on a day-to-day basis?* There is a certain irreducible amount of work to a household, requiring a certain amount of human time and human energy, modern conveniences notwithstanding. Whose time and energy shall be expended to do the work?

If you are committed to the idea of one common life, and if you are determined before God to be the leader/servant of that common life, then you face the practical need to take your place along with your wife (and your children, as they're able) in doing the work. The fun work. The drudgery. The so-so kind of work. You also share in the enjoyment of leisure time when the work's done. Whatever's happening, whatever is to be endured or enjoyed, you're in it together.

Here are some specifics to remember:

SHE'S NOT DUMB.

Your wife has a brain. She spent a number of years in school cultivating her mind. She's lived approximately as long as you have—maybe longer. She's no dumb kid.

And her mind is probably as flexible and as capable of

adapting to various challenges as yours. It is never very smart to assume that she couldn't understand or comprehend this or that.

Harold and Jeanette Myra are close friends of ours; he and I worked together for several years at *Campus Life* magazine. One January night the four of us were at their place. The temperature hadn't gotten above zero all day. I can't remember the details, but for some reason one of the cars had been left sitting outdoors in a parking lot since the day before, and Jeanette said, "Would you two mind dropping me off on your way home so I can pick up the car and bring it back here?"

"Fine," I said. Then I made a terrible mistake. I temporarily forgot that Jeanette was a farmer's daughter from Wisconsin. "But don't you want Harold to come along to get it started?" I asked.

She looked at me as if I'd just questioned her ability to make a decent pot of coffee.

"Why do I need Harold?" she shot back. "If I can't start it, he sure can't start it!"

Harold duly agreed with that, I duly apologized, and we drove her to the dark, icy parking lot. She hopped in the car, turned the key, kicked the accelerator the way it needed to be kicked, and started the engine on the first try just like it was her father's old John Deere.

There's no biological reason why women shouldn't be allowed to touch the mechanical side of life. There's no reason of any kind to shield wives from the higher disciplines of the mind: politics, economics, law, theology, mass communications, international affairs, and the other supposedly masculine domains. Indeed, to do so is criminal. It is a denial of divine gifts and aptitudes.

ARE THE GRUNGY JOBS BENEATH YOU?

So long as there are certain understandings, spoken or unspoken, that you are "above" having to do certain grungy jobs, you are not a servant. It's sometimes hard to realize where the pockets of privilege still lie. The traditions are so strong. They may never come out into the open unless you get up the courage to ask your wife directly, "Are there some things that you 'just know' not to ask me to do? In what ways am I still playing the role of the big cheese without realizing it?" She'll tell you!

I think every father who's ever changed a diaper can remember his first clumsy attempt. I recall thinking that somebody sure botched the engineering design along the way; how was that big, square piece of cloth supposed to fit this little, tiny, rounded bottom?

And, of course, the smell and the mess are not exactly

pleasant. Especially at the beginning, when you're getting used to it.

But since when is a grown man afraid to get his hands dirty? That's the first thing you learn on your first after-school job as a teen-ager—sometimes you just have to get in there and do the job and clean up later. I will always remember a particular chicken coop on a certain widow's farm four miles north of Whitewater, Kansas, where I as a high school sophomore learned that lesson. We'd just moved into the community, and this woman offered me half a Saturday's work using a pitchfork and shovel on about a ten-inch layer of manure. Well, I survived. You can probably tell a similar tale yourself.

So what's so bad about diapers?

After the twins arrived (180 diapers a week to start), I even did something about the engineering problem. Grace was gone for several hours, and I said to myself, *There's got to be a better way.* So I put my masculine mind to work and figured out a tighter way to fold and pin.

I realize that not all my readers have kids, and many of you who do are past the diaper stage. I'm just using this as an illustration of the servanthood motif in a very practical area for husbands.

FIND A NEED AND FILL IT

The more we reexamine our male and female roles in Western society and the more we question the old stereotypes, the more we have to face the necessity for a new order. Some couples engage in writing marriage contracts, in which they spell out precisely who shall pay for what and who shall be responsible for the less exciting parts of running a household. It's all there in black and white. The contracts are rewritten from time to time as needs and feelings change.

Such an approach is probably an improvement over the old silent assumptions—but I think we Christians can do even better. We can, if we really want to, create a miniature of God's kingdom of love right here and now in our own homes. Instead of worrying about the protection of egos, instead of searching for the perfectly just and equitable division of labor, instead of safeguarding against infringement of rights—we can surrender our rights and our lives to each other. This results in a *flow* of service unhindered by union rules; both husband and wife jump in and do whatever needs to be done at the moment. If a child's nose needs to be wiped or a flower patch needs to be weeded, either spouse responds without reference to a contracted list of duties.

There are times—not as many as I would like—when I sense Grace and myself flowing as a work team in an effective and strangely rewarding way. Walking in from an evening church service with three cranky children who need to get to bed, we both sort of spring into action. There's almost no conversation between us; we know the fifty-nine things that need to be done, and in what order, and we go at it. About twenty minutes later, when all three are down and the lights have been turned off, we meet each other in the hall, sigh, and usually say something inane like, "Hello— how are you?" Our work is done—notice, *our* work—and now we're ready to enjoy some adult time together.

I don't mean to imply that all things can be handled by instinct. Some parts of household life are complicated enough— menu-planning, for example—that an administrator is needed. Somebody has to accept it as a responsibility and follow through more or less by himself or herself. But there are probably not as many of these as we think. The sensitive husband and wife can in most areas develop a synergistic approach that lightens the load and deepens the love of both.

As Ambrose Bierce, an American journalist of three generations ago, said, "Marriage is a community consisting of a master, a mistress, and two slaves, making in all, two."

♥ TIME TO REASSIGN THE DIRTY WORK? ♥

Make a list of all the routine and unglamorous jobs that have to be done every day in your home, and then decide if they are basically the husband's job, the wife's job, or if they can be done by either spouse. Then total up to see who is doing the most dirty work. Is it time to reassign some of the tasks?

In the chapter you've just read, Dean Merrill and his wife demonstrate a nitty gritty example of "unconditional love" for each other. But does acceptance mean always agreeing with one another? Does it mean letting your spouse walk all over you as you "accept" whatever treatment is handed out? In the next chapter André Bustanoby explains how to be acceptant while preserving self-worth and self-respect.

Is Your Spouse Your Best Friend?
Adapted from André Bustanoby,
Can Men and Women Be Just Friends?

To take the following "Couples Friendship Inventory," score each question from 1 to 5. A definite yes is a 5, a definite no is a 1. A "can't decide" is a 3. A 4 or a 2 means a lesser degree of yes or no. Both partners should take the test and then discuss the answers. Total scoring: very good friendship, 73–85; good friendship, 60–72; needs work, 47–59; poor friendship, 34–46; very poor friendship, 17–33.

	No				Yes
1. I respect him/her.	1	2	3	4	5
2. I like him/her as he/she is.	1	2	3	4	5
3. I could live without him, but my life would be poorer for it.	1	2	3	4	5
4. I enjoy sharing what we have in common with others of like mind.	1	2	3	4	5
5. If we were not married, we would still share a lot of the same ideas, ideals, and activities.	1	2	3	4	5
6. I respect him/her even when he/she does things that upset or annoy me.	1	2	3	4	5
7. I know him/her well enough that I can anticipate what his/her words or behavior will be in most circumstances.	1	2	3	4	5
8. It's easy to turn a blind eye to his/her faults.	1	2	3	4	5
9. I want what is best for him/her.	1	2	3	4	5
10. I care enough to let him/her go or even give him/her up.	1	2	3	4	5
11. My respect for him/her is *not* based on his/her accomplishments.	1	2	3	4	5
12. I know he/she is a kindred spirit even though I may not be assured frequently that he/she is.	1	2	3	4	5

	No				Yes
13. He/she seems to bring out the best in me.	1	2	3	4	5
14. I feel that we stand together against the views of outsiders.	1	2	3	4	5
15. I can be both strong and weak with him/her.	1	2	3	4	5
16. My giving to him/her is characterized by freedom and willingness and not grudging sacrifice.	1	2	3	4	5
17. My relationship with him/her is characterized by trust.	1	2	3	4	5

Chapter 15

ACCEPTANCE: HOW TO GET IT, HOW TO GIVE IT

BY ANDRÉ AND FAY BUSTANOBY
Just Talk to Me

Sometimes the best way to define something is to describe what it does *not* mean: Acceptance does not mean being a doormat or a punching bag. Acceptance does not mean agreeing with everything your spouse says in order to keep peace at any price. Acceptance does not mean being dishonest when you share your opinions.

Unfortunately, thousands if not millions of women find themselves locked into marriages where being acceptant means "taking it" from a husband who is neglectful, disrespectful, or even abusive. One of the most lucrative kinds of publishing during the 1980s has involved books that give advice to women who are being manipulated and even abused by men.

In 1985 Robin Norwood, Santa Barbara, California-based marriage, family, and child therapist, wrote *Women Who Love Too Much: When You Keep Wishing and Hoping He'll Change* (St. Martins Press). Based on her extensive counseling experience, the book seeks to help women deal with partners who are unkind, uncaring, or emotionally unavailable. According to Norwood, many women simply can't give up these kinds of partners. They are obsessed with them, an obsession that is not based on love but fear—"fear of being unlovable and unworthy, fear of being ignored or abandoned or destroyed."

Women Who Love Too Much was written for the women who inevitably seem to find unhealthy, unloving partners. The book sold nearly 300,000 copies in hardcover and over two million in paperback. Hundreds of support groups based on Robin Norwood's Ten-Point Recovery Program sprang up all over the country.

In 1986 Dr. Susan Forward, with the help of writer, Joan

Torres, wrote *Men Who Hate Women and the Women Who Love Them* (Bantam Books, 1986), a book based on her wide experience as a group therapist, instructor, consultant, and daily radio talk show hostess. Designed to help women married to emotionally or physically abusive men, the book describes the thinking and actions of the *misogynist*, the "woman hater" who paradoxically loves his wife but must cause tremendous pain and suffering for her. In simple step-by-step fashion, she tells this kind of woman how to change her behavior to gain self-respect, renew confidence, and find courage to love a truly loving man.

The bottom line in the Norwood and Forward books, and others like them, is to teach women not to accept bad treatment from a man, but develop a relationship based on mutual self-respect and nurturing of self-worth. Many women may not find themselves in the extreme situations described in the books by Norwood and Forward, but almost all married people—husbands and wives—know something about "lack of acceptance." Every marriage is an arena in which acceptance or a lack of acceptance is played out each day. How well a husband or a wife learns to be acceptant of a spouse is a crucial key to a growing and comfortable relationship.

In the following chapter, André Bustanoby confesses how he had to deal with his own lack of acceptance of others. He describes some typically non-accepting spouses, including the Lawyer, the Bible Thumper, the Fact-Finder, and King James, the purveyor of the "authorized version," which is always his or her personal opinion.

Later in the chapter, André's wife, Fay, introduces a sixteen-question quiz to help you rate how acceptant you and your spouse are of each other. As you read, dwell on the real issue: Just what *is* acceptance? As Bustanoby says, acceptance doesn't mean you never question the other person's behavior, opinions, or ideas. *Acceptance means you do not question the other person's worth as a person.* To do *that* is a priceless skill, an invaluable part of a growing marriage.

IN THE IMAGE OF GOD

As a highly opinionated person, I have had a great deal of difficulty accepting a person who holds a different point of view from mine. And worse, as a Bible-believing Christian, I have used the Bible not only to support my view but also to club the other person into submission. For many years my attitude was, "If God's Word says it, you believe it and do it whether or not you like it!"

Someone may ask, "What's wrong with that?" The thing

wrong was my attitude. I could not separate the person from his opinion. I could not accept the person if his opinions differed from mine.

God has come down hard on me for my lack of acceptance. Twelve years ago when I was a pastor I gradually was made aware of my unloving dogmatism, which made me a very unaccepting person. Even Fay suffered from it. I remember being shaken by something I read while preaching through the Book of First Peter. In 2:17 the Greek text reads literally, "Honor all men! Keep loving the brotherhood, keep fearing God, keep honoring the king." Evidently the Christians to whom Peter writes were loving the brotherhood (other Christians). They were fearing God and honoring the king. Peter says, "Keep it up, but do one more thing. Honor *all* men."

The word *honor* (timaō) means "to recognize the worth of something." Peter is asking us to recognize the worth of all human beings. According to Genesis 9:6, human beings are of great worth because they are made in the image of God—yes, even unregenerate men are made in the image of God. The fall did not efface the image.

Opinionated, dogmatic people are the world's worst at accepting other people as creatures worthy of honor. Christ and the Pharisees illustrate this difference. When Christ ate with publicans and sinners he was not approving of their sinfulness, but he did make them feel accepted as people. Feeling accepted, they were ready to listen to what Jesus said. The Pharisees withdrew from the sinners.

THE IMPORTANCE OF ACCEPTANCE

One of the skills essential to counseling is "non-possessive warmth." This is an attitude of acceptance that says, "You don't have to agree with me in order for me to accept your worth as a human being and to share my warmth with you." This skill must be learned not only by counselors but by all who would communicate effectively.[7]

This does not mean that you surrender your own point of view. It means that you care enough about the other person not to bludgeon him into accepting your point of view. This is why it's called *nonpossessive* warmth. Your warmth toward that person is not conditioned on his agreeing with you. This is why some psychologists call the attitude "unconditional positive regard."

God's Acceptance. The finest example of this is God's attitude of acceptance toward us. The Bible declares that while we were yet *sinners* God reached out in love and sent his Son to die for our sins

(Rom. 5:8). He didn't wait for us to agree with him before he showed his care for us.

Acceptance doesn't mean you never question the other person's behavior. It means that his *worth* is not questioned.

George and Ella. George is a devout Christian and a serious student of the Bible. He sought marriage counseling because, according to him, his wife, Ella, was not being a submissive Christian wife. He made it clear that he expected me as a Christian counselor to convince her of her disobedience.

George was rigid and unloving. He was giving Ella the clear message that she was a bad person because she was not submissive to him.

When I pointed out to George how harsh and unloving he was, he became indignant. The very idea that I should find anything wrong with *him!* He wasn't the disobedient one. It was his wife. How dare I suggest that there might be a problem with him?

What was happening here? George did not understand unconditional positive regard. His regard for his wife was indeed conditional. The only way she would find any positive regard or acceptance from him would be to see things exactly as he did and do exactly as he said.

Needless to say, Ella's self-worth took a beating at George's hands. And by this attitude George guaranteed Ella's resistance. She wasn't going to let him completely destroy her self-worth. She just dug in her heels and resisted him with all she had.

If George had accepted Ella, he would have boosted her feeling of self-worth. And out of those good feelings of self-worth she would have been more willing to consider George's point of view. By not forcing Ella, George would have found her more willing to give. We often give freely what we do not permit a person to take by force.

ACCEPTANCE OF FEELINGS

Acceptance is not just a philosophical or mental exercise, however. It sounds noble to say, "I accept this human being's worth." It goes deeper than that. It respects his *feelings.*

Feeling Versus Fact. Many couples make the mistake of trying to establish who's right and who's wrong. They attempt to establish what the *facts* are and the *right course of action* based on those facts. Now that is reasonable enough—if you are in a court of law with rules of evidence, a judge, jury, lawyers, and appeals procedure. But an adversary proceeding—which this is—is unworkable in marriage. We don't have the machinery in marriage to communicate and solve our problems this way. Strangely enough, in marital communication we really can't start with the facts!

How many times have you been frustrated in your attempt to communicate on the basis of fact? The wife says, "Now the facts are . . ." But the husband says, "No they're not! You have the facts all wrong. The facts are . . ."

The Real Issues. The real issues are these: (1) How do I *feel* about this? (2) Are you willing to respect my *feelings?* (3) How do you *feel* about this? (4) Am I willing respect your *feelings?* Here we get back to the cardinal rule of communication: *My position is not better than, but different from, yours.*

Now remember, I am applying this only to marital communication. In a court of law we can be interested in the facts. When we go to church, we are interested in an authoritative opinion from the preacher.

But the relationship between husband and wife is different. It is supposed to be a relationship of mutual acceptance and respect. We are not attempting to find out what the facts are. We are trying to discover how each feels. Once we understand where we are in relation to each other, we can decide what we want to do about our differences. We are in a position of compromising, or agreeing to disagree. If we can't do either, we can go to court and let someone else decide who's right and who has the facts. That's called divorce!

As a Christian marriage and family counselor I often find that facts do have a bearing on the cases I handle. And I often must address those facts in the light of Scripture because my authoritative point of view is being sought. But in my relationship with Fay, I cannot be the authority. If she wants to put me in that position, inadvisable as it might be, that's her choice. I don't force it on her. But our relationship is that of husband and wife and not preacher and parishioner, counselor and client.

Keep Off the Grass! I was having difficulty getting my boat trailer turned around in order to back into my driveway. So I decided I would pull up a few feet on the lot next to my neighbor's house to make my turn. Fay, who was riding with me, stiffened and asked, "What are you doing?"

"Turning around," I answered.

"On Bill's grass?"

I really didn't think Bill would mind, but I did know that Fay *felt* that Bill would mind, and she reacted accordingly. So I backed up and made my turn without driving on Bill's grass. It was more difficult, but I was willing to go the more difficult route out of respect for her feelings. Because I love her, her feelings were more important than right or wrong.

The next day I had the boat out again, but this time Fay wasn't with me. Still, I respected her feelings and stayed off Bill's grass when I brought the boat home. As I was getting out of my van, Bill came over and asked, "Why didn't you pull up on the grass to make your turn? It would be easier that way."

I must admit I felt smug. And it did cross my mind to tell Fay that *I was right!* But what would that accomplish, except to identify myself as her adversary and encourage her to start keeping score when she is right?

It cost me very little to respect her feelings—and to continue to respect her feelings. I want her to know that she doesn't have to think and feel as I do in order to be okay in my eyes.

Saying that I felt smug may come across as a put-down of Fay. Hadn't Bill said it was okay? Wouldn't Fay then feel it was okay? It's not a matter of who's right, but of the right thing to do, isn't it?

That would be true, except for a further complication. Over the years I had damaged our relationship by always trying to prove I was right. If I opened the issue again, it might have appeared to Fay that I was trying to prove I was right.

If *Bill* had told Fay it was all right to drive on his grass, there would have been no problem. She would have been free to decide what she wanted us to do in light of that new information. But if *I* told her what Bill had said, it might have sounded as if I couldn't let the matter drop. It would have sounded as if I had to be right.

Now I know that Bill volunteered the information and that I would only have been passing it on. But given the history of my bad behavior, it was far better to drop the matter and not appear as though I was trying to prove I was right.

Owning the Problem. I have been stressing the acceptance of the *person.* Quite apart from his behavior, this person has worth. But what happens when he behaves in a way that jeopardizes my sense of security and well-being?

For example, a husband may grant that his wife is a creature made in God's image and is worthwhile. But her flirtatiousness with other men may make him feel insecure. He has in marriage established a strong emotional bond with her, but now he feels that it is jeopardized by her *behavior.*

Rather than tell her what a bad person she is, he would do better to own the problem *as his.*

By "owning the problem" I mean this: He is to approach her with the idea that the problem between them is not due to the fact that she is a bad or morally defective person. He cannot establish himself as the authority in the relationship and sit as judge on her behavior.

But he can report *his feelings* about the problem. By reporting his feelings he "owns the problem." He accepts responsibility for finding a problem with what's going on. When he sees her act overly friendly *he feels insecure* and *fearful* for the marriage.

Ultimately, she may see her behavior as a problem and may accept the responsibility to change. But it cannot be forced on her. By calling attention to the problem without condemning the other person, we are able to address the problem without alienating that person.

I'll have more to say about this later. But I must point this out here so as not to leave the impression that I think all behavior is relative and that anything goes in marriage. Indeed, it does not.

When the woman caught in adultery was dragged before Jesus, his attitude was non-condemning toward her. But he did say, "Go and sin no more" (John 8:11).

WATCH OUT FOR THESE

Non-accepting spouses tend to fall into one of four categories. They are similar in that they ignore feelings and stress fact, but their emphasis differs.

Lawyers. Lawyers want to build a *case.* If necessary, they will call in *witnesses* to corroborate the *facts.* They are masters at *cross-examining* and discrediting the spouse's case.

Bible-Thumpers. Bible Thumpers are the religious counterpart of lawyers. They use the *authority of Scripture* to support their position and quote *chapter and verse.* Differences with the spouse are met with the *preaching of the truth.* Their byword is, "It doesn't matter how you feel. If God's Word says it, we are to do it."

Fact-Finders. Fact Finders may be religious or irreligious. They pride themselves in having a good *memory* and *recall* of the *facts.* They pride themselves in being *logical, unemotional* people who don't let feelings cloud the *issues.* Clerks, accountants, and others who have an eye for *detail* make good Fact-Finders.

King James. King James doesn't have to build a case like the lawyer. He may not quote the Bible. Logic and memory may not be his forte. King James always has *"The Authorized Version,"* and his version is to be accepted because he is king!

Summary. The all-important question I'm attempting to answer here is this: "Can we live together in a spirit of good will, respecting each other's feelings?" Others may be able to bring the facts to bear on our situation—doctors, lawyers, and marriage counselors. And sometimes we must resort to outside authority. But the day-to-day conflicts we must solve are too numerous and usually too insignificant to be solved by appeal to authority. They are most readily solved in a spirit of good will where we accept each other and respect each other's feelings.

RATING YOUR SPOUSE'S ACCEPTANCE FACTOR

How accepted does your spouse make you feel? Sixteen rating statements below are provided for your evaluation. You are to answer how *you* feel. For example, in response to number one, do you or don't you feel guilty when you ask for things or want your way? You need not defend or justify your answer. Just be honest about the way you feel.

HOW TO RATE YOUR SPOUSE

You will see that each statement has three choices: no, mid, and yes. If you cannot answer yes or no, you may use the mid. But use the yes and no responses as often as possible.

Take a sheet of paper and number it from one to sixteen. When you respond to each statement, use the number from the appropriate column. For example, if the answer is no, write down the number you see in the no column, even though it is sometimes three and sometimes one. Both husband and wife should fill out a rating sheet and evaluate each other without consultation. Be sure that you respond to each statement.

	NO	MID	YES
1. I feel guilty when I ask for things or sometimes want my way.	3	2	1
2. I am afraid of making mistakes around him/her.	3	2	1
3. I feel it necessary to defend my actions when I'm with him/her.	3	2	1
4. I am bothered by fears of feeling stupid or inadequate with him/her.	3	2	1
5. Criticism from him/her hurts my feelings of worth.	3	2	1
6. I feel free to show my weaknesses in front of him/her.	1	2	3
7. I can care for myself in spite of his/her feelings for me.	1	2	3
8. I am afraid to be myself with him/her.	3	2	1
9. I feel free to express my needs to him/her.	1	2	3
10. I find that I must give him/her reasons for my feelings.	3	2	1

	NO	MID	YES
11. I can be negative or positive with him/her.	1	2	3
12. My wants, likes, dislikes, and values are respected by him/her.	1	2	3
13. I sometimes ask for my needs to be met.	1	2	3
14. I can be inconsistent or illogical with him/her.	3	2	1
15. I am afraid to show my fears to him/her.	3	2	1
16. I am afraid to show tears in front of him/her.	3	2	1

Scoring. After you have responded to each statement, add up your score. The highest possible score is 48; the lowest score is 16.

Remember, you are rating your spouse by saying how accepted *you feel.* Let's rate as follows:

40–48	Strong feelings of acceptance
32–39	Lack some feelings of acceptance
24–31	Serious feelings of unacceptance
16–23	Your communication needs lots of work.

Evaluation of the Questions. After you have rated your spouse, go back to the rating statements and look at each response. Several of the statements are similar and probe the same area of self-worth. They are worded differently to approach it from many angles. Let's consider each statement separately, however, so you can locate the ones you are especially interested in talking about.

1. "I feel guilty when I ask for things or sometimes want my way." The ideal answer is no. If your spouse accepts you, it means that you should be able to ask for what you want, or ask for your way, without feeling guilty. Equality in marriage means give and take. Ephesians 5:28–29 and 1 Peter 3:7 teach equality of the spouses as "fellow-heirs of the grace of God."

If you do feel guilty, be sure it's not a lack of self-acceptance. Sometimes people are brought up with the idea that they should not ask anything for themselves. Here the problem is lack of self-acceptance, which may or may not be aggravated by the spouse.

2. "I am afraid of making mistakes around him/her." The ideal answer is no. In an accepting relationship your mistakes are not thrown in your face. This is the spirit of 1 Corinthians 13. Love is longsuffering and kind. So is acceptance.

A yes answer may indicate the likelihood of ridicule for mistakes, or it may indicate impatience. Sometimes it's verbal and other times nonverbal. A disgusted look, a sigh with eyes rolling is enough to give the message, "I can't accept you that way—you dummy."

There's always the possibility, on the other hand, of making "mistakes" on purpose so you can make the other person lose his cool.

3. "I feel it necessary to defend my actions when I'm with him/her." The ideal answer is no.

Gross or sinful behavior ought to be questioned. But when practically all of your actions are called into question, your spouse is giving the message that you can't do anything right. The message is that your entire approach to life is wrong. It is another way of saying, "Do it my way and you'll be right."

Usually your spouse's actions are not better or worse than yours. They are just different. Remember, *not better than, but different from.*

4. "I am bothered by fears of feeling stupid or inadequate with him/her." The ideal answer is no.

An accepting attitude builds the other person's confidence. It believes in the other person. Again, the spirit of 1 Corinthians 13: Love "bears all things, and believes all things, hopes all things, endures all things" (v. 7).

I'm not advocating naïve optimism. What I say here should be balanced by an understanding of people who don't want to communicate. What I'm saying here relates to normal, healthy people who want to communicate and make the relationship work.

5. "Criticism from him/her hurts my feelings of worth." The ideal answer is no.

This doesn't mean we never criticize. How we go about it is another matter. The criticism should be gentle, constructive, and indirect—in the form of an "I" message, which is discussed later in this book. Criticism is given in the spirit of Galatians 6:1.

A yes answer may not indicate the fault is entirely in a critical partner. A person who is overly sensitive to criticism may feel criticism when it's not really there. A fragile ego tends to see criticism everywhere.

6. "I feel free to show my weaknesses in front of him/her." The ideal answer is yes.

This is a variation on statements 2 and 4. Mistakes, stupidity, inadequacy, and weaknesses are all issues that come up in a relationship.

A no answer may not necessarily indicate unacceptance, however. Often, when I ask a husband this question, he will say, "Yes, I'm afraid to show my weakness to my wife. But it doesn't have anything to do with her. I can't show my weakness to anyone. A man ought to be strong and have his act together."

7. "I can care for myself in spite of his/her feelings for me." The ideal answer is yes.

It's unrealistic to expect the unflinching approval of your spouse at all times. But the spouse's lack of approval should not exceed your ability to like yourself anyway.

8. "I am afraid to be myself with him/her." The ideal answer is no.

One's self-identity is very important in marriage. Can I be me and still be accepted by you?

Again, we're not dealing with sinful or gross behavior here. I once heard a woman-chasing man tell his wife, "That's the way I am. I have to be true to my own needs." Her reply, "I have to be true to myself too, so I guess it's good-bye."

9. "I feel free to express my needs." The ideal answer is yes. This is a variation on statement 1. Refer to my comments there.

10. "I find that I must give reasons for my feelings." The ideal answer is no.

Whether or not we *should* feel as we do, a comfortable relationship depends on acceptance in spite of those feelings. Identifying and reporting those feelings is the first step to doing something about them. If I am unaccepted because of the way I feel, it's unlikely that my feelings will change. I will just create distance from you.

11. "I can be negative or positive with him/her." The ideal answer is yes.

Acceptance means that I can take a position different from you and still be okay. Some marriages suffer from a "chameleon syndrome." One spouse continually takes on the color of the other to avoid conflict. This kind of marriage is in danger because they never talk about their differences.

12. "My wants, likes, dislikes, and values are respected by him/her." The ideal answer is yes.

Here we have a variation on the chameleon syndrome mentioned in statement 11. Your wants, likes, dislikes, and values need not be colored the same as mine in order for you to be accepted by me.

Again, we're not dealing with sinful or gross behavior or with a value system. Generally, the value system of each spouse is the same. It's the particulars in that system we have problems with. We may be committed to going to church, but whether or not we miss a Sunday for a particular reason will reveal our differentness. For example, you may not feel like attending church when you're traveling. But I may think we should go to church whether we're at home or on the road.

13. "I sometimes ask for my needs to be met." The ideal answer is yes.

This is a variation on statement 1. See that statement for comment.

14. "I can be inconsistent or illogical with him/her." The ideal answer is yes.

This is a variation on statements 3 and 10. Remember, acceptance means that we avoid being a lawyer and building a case. Total consistency and logic are not essential to good communication. But at least some consistency or some logic is necessary.

Sometimes, to avoid being pinned down, people will continually change their position. Here we get into sick communication, which we deal with later in the book.

15. "I am afraid to show my fears to him/her." The ideal answer is no.

Fear is a special type of feeling. Can I feel the way I do and still be okay in your eyes?

Sometimes fears are not revealed for another reason. Often Andy avoids expressing his fears to me simply because he doesn't want to alarm me! He thinks that if he tells me his fears I'll become more fearful than necessary. It doesn't make for good communication, I know. But he sees me as a worrier, and he doesn't want to aggravate my tendency to worry.

16. "I am afraid to show my tears in front of him/her." The ideal answer is no.

This is a variation on statement 6 (weakness) and 15 (fears). See these statements for comment.

Summary. The purpose of this rating exercise is to give each spouse an idea of how accepted the other feels. After you have completed your rating sheets, sit down and go over the responses together. You may go through all the responses one sheet at a time or you may want to compare how you each responded, item by item. But be careful how you respond to the other's rating. If your spouse reports feelings of unacceptance, be careful of your response. Don't say, "You shouldn't feel that way." If you do say that, you will have missed the point and will reveal the basic flaw in your communication style. Whether or not *you* think your spouse's evaluation is correct, that's how your spouse feels. Don't fall into the role of being Lawyer, Bible-Thumper, Fact-Finder, or King James.

You must start with how your spouse feels, whether or not you like it. The harmony of the relationship must not depend on your spouse's agreeing with you. It must start with a respect for those feelings.

♥ ACCEPTANCE TAKES LOTS OF PRACTICE ♥

Ideally, both of you should take the sixteen-question quiz to rate each other on acceptance. Then talk about changes each of you could make to help the other person feel more accepted.

Acceptance and understanding do not become real until they are practiced. And your acceptance and understanding of your spouse does not become real until your spouse experiences it.

To put more understanding in your marriage:

♥ Regard your spouse as important. Ask his or her opinion frequently. Always value what he or she says.

♥ Let your spouse feel your approval and affection. Be gentle and tender and always make an effort to understand his or her feelings. Even if you can't understand why your spouse is feeling a certain way, acknowledge those feelings and give your spouse the right to have them.

♥ Avoid making sudden changes without discussing them with your spouse. If you have a new idea, give your spouse time to adjust to it. The worst practice in any relationship is *fait accompli*—going ahead and doing something and then letting a person find out about it later after it is too late to give input or suggestions. The literal meaning of *fait accompli* is "an irreversible fact." Be careful about doing things that are irreversible before discussing them with your spouse.

♥ If you must differ with or correct your spouse, do it gently, tenderly, and respectfully. And if you are being corrected or differed with, be teachable without being defensive.

♥ When your spouse fails, don't harp on what went wrong. First encourage and comfort and then, at a better time, discuss how to remedy the situation or avoid the same situation again.

♥ Be willing to admit your mistakes; don't be afraid to be humble.[8]

Little expressions of affection and approval mean more to a woman than a man imagines. She wants to be remembered, adored, cherished, complimented, listened to; she wants to have her feelings validated even when they seem childish or unreasonable to her husband. She needs to be made to feel feminine by being protected, cared for, looked after, to have affection often without sex, to be accepted especially when she feels unacceptable to herself.[9]

Cecil Osborne

PART IV

COMMUNICATION:
HOW EVERY MARRIAGE LIVES OR DIES

In Parts I through III, we have looked at the who, what, and why of marriage, seeking definitions and principles—the bedrock values that form the foundation for joining two lives in lifetime commitment. Now it's time to look at the how, where, and when, which deal with the basic skills, techniques, and habits needed to keep a marriage thriving, blossoming, and maturing. Parts IV through VIII will deal with:

- ♥ developing good communication
- ♥ processing conflict and anger
- ♥ achieving sexual happiness
- ♥ growing spiritually together
- ♥ maintaining steadfast love on a daily basis

This second half of the book begins with perhaps the most crucial area of any marriage: communication.

When a couple winds up in the divorce court, the "grounds" often cited for splitting up are incompatibility, mental cruelty, or adultery. In truth, as many marriage counselors will tell you, the real cause is poor communication.

Most women will put communication right at the top of their list of what they hope for in their marriage. And many women have to admit they aren't getting it. The complaints heard in pastors' and counselors' offices make up a familiar depressing litany:

"We don't talk ... we just don't talk."

"We don't communicate enough."

"All he does is sit and watch TV. I'm going crazy here with the kids but he doesn't seem to care!"

"We *can't* communicate."

In Part III we looked at the first step toward better communication, which is understanding and accepting your mate. In the following chapters, Zondervan authors will help you take the second step that centers around learning to listen to your mate and to share not only facts, but feelings.

In chapter 16, Dr. Ed Wheat and his co-author, Gloria Okes Perkins (*The First Years of Forever*) discuss building and maintaining a strong communication lifeline system in which both spouses feel free to express themselves because they are sure they are being understood and aren't being pulled into win/lose arguments.

In chapter 17, Anne Kristin Carroll (*Together Forever*) shares the story of Betty Jo and her husband R.D. and what happened when their communication lifeline was cut.

In chapter 18, André Bustanoby (*Just Talk To Me*) digs into the familiar but often misunderstood subject of listening and teaches you how to "actively listen" to the feelings of your partner as well as the information and facts that your partner is trying to convey.

In chapter 19, Fay Bustanoby (*Just Talk to Me*) helps you rate your spouse (and yourself) as a listener.

In chapter 20, Gary Smalley (*The Joy of Committed Love*) shares one of the most valuable techniques you can ever learn to gain better communication with your spouse. Smalley's principle simply stated is: "Never communicate your feelings or information you consider to be important without first creating a burning curiosity within the listener."

In chapter 21, Shirley Cook (*The Marriage Puzzle*) shares her secret for achieving intimacy with your husband: "Say what you mean."

In chapter 22, Anne Kristin Carroll (*Together Forever*) lists thirty-eight do's and don'ts of good communication.

In chapter 23, Dr. Ed Wheat and Gloria Okes Perkins (*The First Years of Forever*) share a poignant essay by Richie Wadsworth, who communicated lovingly and beautifully with her husband, John, until he drew his final breath.

André and Fay Bustanoby have spent over thirty-five years learning about communication, often by trial and error in their own marriage. They say: "Communication, like any other skill, can be learned. But it requires setting aside our fears, our prejudices, and our own way of doing things. . . . At the core of good communication is a respect for each other's differentness. My position is not *better than* yours; it is just *different from* yours. Once that concept is mastered, the techniques of good communication are easily mastered."[1]

WHERE COMMUNICATION BEGINS

The primary speech organ, the birthplace of our words, is the human heart.[2]

Ken Durham

Chapter 16

TENDING THE LIFELINE
OF YOUR MARRIAGE

BY DR. ED WHEAT AND GLORIA OKES PERKINS
The First Years of Forever

An unknown sage once said, "Sometimes we wake up to the startling discovery that many of our most important relationships are suffering from verbal malnutrition."[3] In no relationship are those words more true than in marriage. With good communication, a marriage grows—stronger, richer, more meaningful. When a couple has little or no communication, the marriage dies, much like a plant that gets no water.

In the following chapter, Dr. Ed Wheat helps you evaluate the communication system you are now using with your spouse. Perhaps you never thought about it as a system, but you are using some kind of system, nonetheless. Dr. Wheat calls that system the "lifeline of your marriage." As you read, ask yourself:

- ♥ Is our communication lifeline working effectively? How would I rate it?
- ♥ What four vital things does a good communication lifeline deliver to a marriage? Is our lifeline providing all four of these supplies?
- ♥ What are five characteristics of a communication system that is in good working order? Are all five of these present in our marriage?
- ♥ Which listening skills do I need to develop?

THE MARRIAGE LIFELINE

Communication is one of the extraordinary delights of marriage, when it's working. *Nothing,* not even sexual fulfillment, will bring as much enriching intimacy into your relationship.

But it's more than a luxurious pleasure. Call it the *lifeline* of a love-filled marriage—the means by which indispensable supplies are transported from husband to wife, and from wife to husband.

WHAT A GOOD LIFELINE SUPPLIES

If you have good communication in your marriage, the lifeline will provide these supplies:

- The knowledge and understanding of one another which you need for intimate closeness

- The interchange of information and ideas you need to work together as a husband-wife team

- The capability to work out your differences and resolve your conflicts

- The continuing "in touch" contact you must have to grow together in the same direction, and to be there to support each other during the changes and difficult times of life

Obviously, couples trying to operate without these supplies will encounter major problems. In the troubled marriages we counsel, communication lines are almost always clogged or severed. In fact, researchers believe that ninety percent of all marriage counseling involves the attempt to restore communication, or to teach the couple to communicate effectively for the very first time.

It's easy when you're dating and lulled by soft lights and romance to assume that you communicate well, but under the floodlight of marriage, any flaws or trouble spots in your communication system will quickly show up. Domeena C. Renshaw, M.D., an expert on communication in marriage, explains: "Soon after marriage, as daily routines evolve, there is less talk but many more (frequently inaccurate) assumptions about what the other thinks and wants."[4]

"Less talk and inaccurate assumptions" about one another, if not remedied, will lead eventually to one of these common complaints: "We *don't* communicate"; or "We *can't* communicate," which is most serious because it is perceived as marital failure. In fact, "no communication" has become the catch phrase of the 80s, replacing "mental cruelty" and "incompatibility" as the commonly voiced reason for couples to give up on their marriage.

WHY MARRIAGES FAIL

In a 1982 survey, when four hundred psychiatrists were asked why marriages fail, they gave poor communication as the most common cause.[5] And couples themselves perceive poor communication as the proof that "all is lost." Dr. Renshaw warns,

> Once a couple agrees, "we don't communicate," then they may give up, withdraw emotionally, and conjointly decide that nothing can, be done.[6]

Researchers report that most husbands express marital dissatisfaction through anger and *withdrawal*, while most wives show their dissatisfaction through depression and *withdrawal*. In all cases, the withdrawal into silence is devastating and should be regarded as a "red alert" for the marriage.

> The most urgent indicator of distress in a marriage may not be the uproar of discord, but rather the ominous sound of silence, the lack of any communication.[7]

ALL IS NOT LOST

No couple needs to get to that point, however. Any communication problem can be worked out because communication involves skills that can be learned and practiced. In preparation for your first years of forever, we want you to have some advance knowledge of the communication problems that often spring up in marriages and the skills couples need to develop to overcome them.

This may be a good time for you to pause and evaluate the communication system you're now using. Are you and your partner free to express yourselves spontaneously with each other? Are you able to confide in each other as best friends? Or are there difficulties? Do you hear what she's really saying? Do you understand what he's really feeling? Do you share your ideas, thoughts, and feelings? Or do you just talk about practical necessities? Is your communication on practical matters clear enough for things to go smoothly? When you hit a snag in communicating, do you keep on trying until you have overcome the barriers and the flow of meaning opens up between you again? Or do you give up and not try, get angry, yell, or retreat into silence? When you feel rejected, do you retaliate by rejecting your partner?

CHECKING OUT THE SYSTEM

How can you be sure that your communication system is working as it should? Judson Swihart, who also likens communication in marriage to a lifeline, has given five characteristics of a system in good working order:[8]

1. A sense of freedom to express yourself
2. A sense of being understood
3. An absence of win-lose arguments
4. A reduction of tension
5. A sense of being safe and secure in the relationship

On the other hand, a system that is shut down and critically impaired will manifest these two characteristics:[9]

1. One or both partners repeatedly assume negative intent on the part of the other.
2. There is increasing distance and silence.

Most people, however, fall somewhere in between with a partially flawed system, which may reflect some, but not all, of the five positive characteristics listed above. Here's how you can build them all into your relationship.

HOW TO BUILD YOUR LIFELINE SYSTEM

1. You will feel free to express yourself when both of you accept one another just as you are.

Acceptance is the key factor in good communication, for acceptance (or rejection) sends one of the most powerful messages known to human beings. We have an enormous need for unconditional acceptance from the person closest to us. Critical comments or attitudes will make us afraid to express ourselves for fear of being judged. A wife wrote us, "How can I communicate with my husband when he makes a value judgment on everything I say? If he decides it's not worthy of his attention, he quits listening, or he tells me, 'That's not important enough to discuss.' What he's really saying is that *I* am not worth his time and attention."

A critical attitude will also make us want to avoid "intimate talks." A husband said, "Intimate talk means I have to explain why I haven't gotten her vacuum cleaner fixed or why I seem to dislike her mother. My wife enjoys getting things out in the open because, once they're there, I usually have to apologize for them."

Replace a judgmental or fault-finding attitude with a positive response and a consistently accepting attitude, and you will have the ideal climate for a loving interchange of thoughts and feelings. This can lead to the deepening of your love relationship. A young husband, who had been admittedly impatient and somewhat critical, told us, "I have become sensitive to Katie's reaction when I criticize or even show impatience. It seems to be a function of the love God has given me for her that now it hurts me so badly when I see her hurt that I have to back off." He's learning the secret: Good communication *begins* with acceptance.

2. You will feel understood when both of you learn to listen with your ears and hearts to one another.

Listening is an important, but often flawed, part of the marital communication system. A specialist in interpersonal communication says,

> Even though couples spend over forty percent of their communication time listening, it is an underdeveloped skill in most families. Research indicates that we listen at about twenty-five percent efficiency, and that much misunderstanding is attributable to poor listening.[10]

♥ TO CHECK OUT YOUR OWN LIFELINE ♥

Sit down with your spouse and go over the five characteristics of a communication system that is in good working order. Each of you should rate each characteristic on a scale of 1 (poor) to 10 (excellent).

	Husband	Wife
1. I feel the freedom to express myself.	_____	_____
2. I always have a sense of being understood by my spouse.	_____	_____
3. Our marriage has few win/lose arguments.	_____	_____
4. Our communication system keeps tension at a minimum.	_____	_____
5. Our system gives me a sense of being safe and secure in our relationship.	_____	_____

Please note: As each of you rates the five characteristics above, certain problems or needs may come to light. Work at accepting each other's feelings, without defensiveness.

Next, go over the nine ways to develop listening skills and check off the ones you need to practice more often.

	Husband	Wife
1. I will give my partner my full attention instead of just half listening.	_____	_____
2. I will not interrupt my partner when he or she is trying to put thoughts and feelings into words.	_____	_____
3. I will work at repeating my partner's thoughts and feelings so I am sure I understand.	_____	_____
4. I will work on eye contact while trying to communicate.	_____	_____
5. I will turn off the TV (or any other distraction) to give full attention to my partner.	_____	_____
6. If I am silent, I will send positive nonverbal communication (a smile, loving look, a pat, etc.).	_____	_____
7. I will never demand more communication than my partner is ready to give.	_____	_____
8. I will keep confidences.	_____	_____
9. I will listen to my spouse because he or she is important to me.	_____	_____

Like any lifeline, your communication system needs constant maintenance if it is to work properly. The next chapter graphically pictures the tragedy of a marriage that began with a poor communication system, and was almost destroyed before both partners decided to do something about it.

Chapter 17

THE CAUSES AND CURE OF COMMUNICATION BLACKOUT

BY ANNE KRISTIN CARROLL
Together Forever

Most of the following chapter centers on a case study from the files of Counselor Anne Kristin Carroll that illustrates what happens when a communication lifeline is totally cut. You may ask, Did adultery cut the lifeline or did cutting off communication lead to the adultery? Chicken and egg questions are always hard to answer and maybe the best answer in most cases is "both." The important thing to see in this story is that when communication was restored, the adultery stopped. As you read, think about this principle:

> ♥ Good communication will protect your marriage from an affair.

ARE YOU LISTENING?

Communication is necessary in almost every area of life, but in the intimate state of marriage, it is vital. Unfortunately, you can sit in almost any public place and pick out the married from the unmarried. The unmarried girl is looking directly into her escort's eyes, obviously listening, clinging to every word. She is interested in his every thought and idea, and readily responds to them. On the other hand, the married woman is too often looking at what other women are wearing, who is with whom, wondering if she can make her beauty appointment and still keep that tennis date with her friends—all this, while her husband is trying to communicate. While the wife is talking, expressing her excitement in areas the husband is not interested in, or knowledgeable about, his mind wanders off to replay Sunday's football game, or to wonder why he missed that putt on the eighth hole. His disinterested responses let her know he isn't listening. It is sad how quickly some couples move from the attentive unmarrieds to the preoccupied marrieds. Marriage grows and blossoms, and withers and dies, almost in proportion to the kind of communication involved.

Before we get into the right and wrong ways to communicate, I'd like to share with you the story of a couple whose major marital problem lay in their inability and lack of development in the area of communication. This is R.D. and Betty Jo Taylor's story:

BETTY

It was a beautiful, sunny day in July when I left my home in Charlotte, North Carolina, to visit my cousin, Beth Ann.

Beth Ann is the perfect picture of a true southern hostess. I had hardly arrived when she told me that she had planned a get-together for me and some of her friends.

I danced with a number of the young men Beth Ann had invited, but as the evening progressed, an attractive young Marine approached our table and asked if I would like to dance. I was a bit hesitant, but Beth Ann said, "Oh, Betty Jo, go ahead." So I thanked him and walked out to the floor.

When I returned to the table, I told Beth Ann how impressed I was with R.D., and that he had asked me to drive down to West Onslow Beach with him the following day. "But you know, Beth Ann, I just got here, and it simply wouldn't be fitting for me to run out on you like that." I think deep down I was hoping that she'd give me an excuse to do just that.

"Don't be silly, Betty Jo, go right ahead."

"Oh, thanks, Beth Ann, I really hoped you'd feel that way."

I spent what was left of the evening dancing and talking with R.D. I was surprised to find that he was from Charlotte also. I was thoroughly impressed when he told me his parents lived in the Eastover area, one of Charlotte's best and definitely not the side of town on which I had been raised.

The next morning, R.D. drove up in this terrific little red Porsche convertible, and off we went. As we drove, we talked, laughed, and swapped high school stories. The day was perfect.

On the way back to Jacksonville we had long silences, listening to mood music on the radio, and I suppose reviewing the day in our own minds. I silently dreaded the thought of not seeing R.D. again.

When we pulled up in front of Beth Ann's, R.D. gently pulled me over to him, kissed me in the most tender way, then said, "Betty Jo, I want to see more of you."

He reached in his pocket and pulled out a pen and notepad

and wrote down his address and a phone number where he said I could leave messages for him.

The next morning Beth Ann and I took off for two weeks on the beach, but my mind stayed behind. Those weeks seemed like months. I felt like we were never going to get back to Jacksonville. As soon as I got in the house, I called the number R.D. had given me and left him a message saying that I had returned.

"I have a pass for this evening. Can you make it for dinner?"

Could I make it! I was half undressed as I ran up the stairs to bathe and dress.

R.D. kept asking me out, and I stayed on in Jacksonville. Mom and Dad were getting a bit concerned and asked me to come home, but each time I'd beg and plead and say it would be just a few more days. Finally, time caught up with us. I almost missed registering for my fall classes at the university because I continued to stall.

On our last night together, we returned to the supper club where we had met, and spent a lovely but rather sad evening. There were promises of writing, talk of love, but I'm not sure that either of us realized at that time that we were serious. I do recall we stayed until the last dance. The band was playing "More," and I felt so torn inside. I wanted R.D.'s arms around me always.

R.D.

Betty Jo was in college and I seldom got passes long enough to drive to Charlotte to visit her, so for nine months the U.S. Mail carried most of our messages.

My first extended leave was in June 1968, the same time Betty Jo was to graduate from college. My first impulse was to surprise her and just show up at the graduation ceremonies. But then I decided that two June ceremonies would make our lives complete, and I wrote Betty Jo asking her to marry me. We really didn't know each other, but I thought we did, and she agreed. You know you can put so many things in letters, but it is nothing like the day-in-day-out living and communicating with someone . . . nothing!

BETTY

I was thrilled that R.D. had planned for us to be married in a church near his home. I must admit I was impressed with the beauty and what I felt was "prestige" in having our wedding there.

Dad even suggested that Mom and I drive down to Atlanta to look for a dress, but we assured him that we could find just what I needed in Charlotte.

As I finished dressing in the bride's room at the church, I was almost moved to tears, because R.D. had remembered something special between us, something dear to me—the song we had last heard when we met. As Beth Ann handed me the penny for my shoe, I heard the strains of "More" being sung. It was going to be perfect, our whole life was going to be this way, I just knew it.

After the wedding, R.D. and I boarded a flight to Miami for a short but beautifully fulfilling honeymoon. I have often read how the honeymoon isn't all that a couple expects, but for R.D. and me it was more.

We only had a week in Miami before we had to return to Charlotte and look for an apartment prior to R.D.'s return to camp. We found a nice duplex and began our married life there.

A few months after R.D. left, I discovered that I was pregnant! I was thrilled and unhappy at the same time. I would have liked to have had more time with R.D. alone, time for us, time to get better acquainted, but babies don't wait.

R.D.

I was discharged six months after we were married and I returned to Charlotte. I was so happy to be home and really looked forward to the birth of our child.

I had been in the food brokerage business before I went into the service, so when I came home I returned to the only business I knew. For a time our marital life went smoothly. Naturally, there were adjustments to be made on both sides, but I felt that as soon as the baby was born, Betty Jo wouldn't be so moody and things would return to normal.

Return to normal. What was normal? We didn't know each other; we really didn't have any idea what to expect when we began living together. For a time our lives seemed to go well, but after a few months our strong independent personalities began to clash.

BETTY

It was an adjustment for me when R.D. did come home for good. I had been used to doing things my way, answering to no one, and the change was difficult. R.D. was rather chauvinistic in his ideas about family structure, whereas I believed in a fifty-fifty relationship; you have your money, I have mine, and no one accounts to anyone. We argued over everything, from who was going to pay the bills, to what kind of baby food to buy. I felt I was capable of earning as good a living as he was. My basic nature caused continual problems. I am innately jealous, suspicious, and I fell into the destructive trap of constantly questioning R.D. when he wasn't home at the exact moment I thought he should be. Dear God, where had all the love, the romance, the tender moments gone? In only a few weeks we were about to rip each other apart.

About eight months after our wedding, I sensed that we had serious problems, but I just discounted it. The duplex was too cramped for the forthcoming baby, so we decided that we needed our own home. In the process of moving I knocked off his tennis gear and out fell a bundle of notes that a girl at his office had written him! I sank to the floor, shocked, and weeping as I read through the descriptive, wanton language. My mind didn't want to believe it, not R.D! But the facts lay in a wadded heap in my lap.

"You rat, you rotten, no-good, cheating creep! Look at these notes, just look! R.D., how could you? How could you?" I screamed when he came in. He almost turned white, and for a moment I thought I saw a look of pain cross his face, like this discovery was hurting him as much as it was me. But I was so wrapped up in my own feelings I dismissed it. He became very humble. He knelt down beside where I sat crying and said, "Betty Jo, please, please don't leave me."

"Why shouldn't I? Just give me one good reason," I cried.

"It was a mistake, Betty Jo. I promise it will never happen again. Honey, it was just the pressure of adjusting to marriage, the realization that I would soon be responsible for a child, just settling down in general. Baby, she meant nothing to me, honestly. Please believe me, please forgive me."

The pleading and begging broke my heart. I couldn't stand to see R.D. so broken, so humble. Inside, I wanted to believe him. I didn't understand, but I wasn't willing to give up this soon.

We moved. Relations weren't easy. We were afraid to communicate, afraid of setting off an argument that would throw us over the brink. There became more and more "subjects" that were off limits, because when they were brought up, only hostility and fights followed. The words we'd said so easily in letters didn't seem to flow when we were actually together.

It seemed everything that I was interested in—good books, social causes and music—R.D. knew nothing about. Everything he thought was stimulating, such as politics, camping and sports, were either superficial or dull to me. There were few words shared and fewer listened to in our "home." I had a college degree; he didn't. Our interests were in opposite directions, and neither of us was willing to give an inch to change the situation.

R.D. was in a business that I didn't really understand. It irritated me when he came home complaining about customers, late shipments, bad product, or tried to use me as a verbal sounding board for his plans to get new customers. I figured that that stuff was his business and it belonged at the office, not at home, and certainly not where I had to be bored stiff listening to it.

After our baby, Matthew, was born, things seemed to improve for a while. I was teaching full time and found my work extremely stimulating. I was able to again interrelate with people who were interested in the same things as I. I imposed on my mother to take care of the baby and, to further fulfill myself, I began taking night courses at the university. R.D., his business, and interests didn't have the power to invade this artificial world I had created.

A year passed and I was pregnant again. I continued to teach until the baby was born. Isolated inside my cloistered world, I still felt things at home were fine. I was accomplishing what I had set out for myself in life, and I presumed R.D. was doing the same.

Oh, there were still fights over my lack of interest in R.D.'s business. By this time he had opened his own food-brokerage house, with financial backing from his father. Our main area of stress came because he was constantly pressing me to entertain more and more. I found many of the customers he wanted to court brash, boorish, uneducated, or downright "red necky." I saw no reason why I should have to spend time smiling, being polite, or playing up to these people. R.D. felt it was my responsibility as his wife to help him. I just felt his chauvinism was cropping up again, and I refused to cooperate. I told him, "Now, look, R.D., I don't ask you to teach my classes, to get me promotions or raises. I don't expect you to go to school to further my education, do my homework, or take my tests. I am capable of taking care of my job without your help. I should think a grown man could take care of his without his wife's help."

"I understand you, Betty Jo, but you are out in left field. There are few successful men who don't have a helpful, interested wife somewhere in the background. With all your education, you should know from history, if nothing else, that behind most successful men is a supportive, loving wife. My dear, if you haven't learned that you don't know anything about the real world, about life, about what makes for success."

The discussion ended in a draw. No one won, no one lost, we just remained in our normal "Mexican stand-off" position.

R.D.

There was no understanding, no support, no love or care at home, and again I began to look for an interest in me as a person, as a man, beyond my own doorstep.

BETTY

Eight weeks after our second child was born, R.D. came to me and said he was in love with someone else and wanted a divorce! I couldn't believe it. Before we could make any definite moves or decisions, I discovered I was already pregnant again! I couldn't stand the stress, the infidelity, plus another child. I totally broke down and had to quit work.

Every affair R.D. had was with someone he either worked with, or someone who was in a like business. Now I realize he'd told me verbally, over and over, but I never heard him. I wasn't listening. He was finding with other women the understanding, the interest in what he was doing, what he was, something he didn't find at home. I was always too busy advancing myself, considering my career.

R.D.

When Betty Jo told me she was pregnant again, I felt like a man caught between a rock and a hard place. Respectability deemed I couldn't forsake her while she was pregnant. I knew, since I had told her about Wanda, that I would have to break off that affair. Now what would I do? We were back to the same old games, faking out everyone with our "happy little family" while the fires of dissension and hostility grew and grew inside.

What I found beyond home and didn't find with Betty Jo was an acceptance of me, just plain ole R.D.; there weren't any pressures and there was an interest, a oneness of minds which I could never seem to create with Betty Jo.

It is one thing to "listen" to what one is sharing, but it is another thing to understand. Most of the time, when I honestly tried to communicate with Betty Jo, she would already have her mind made up, interrupt me before I finished, trying to state for me what I was saying. I felt I was continually being prejudged, that no matter what I said, she had her thoughts preset, and that would be it. Finally I just retreated and turned to someone who did seem to care, who did know how to listen, turned to someone who understood my pressures, my business, and could at least help me sound out all the problems and anxieties I faced.

BETTY

Here came R.D. saying that he loved me, and that he was sorry. I started to tell him that he should have just made a recording of that speech so he could have it on hand to play at the appropriate times. We could never seem to get beyond that point. The why's and wherefore's of the situation, the reasons for his wanderings, were *never* discussed. We had always had a perfect sexual relationship, and instead of talking out a problem we tried to dismiss it with a romp in the bed. Sex is beautiful in the context in which God created it, but when it is *used* as an escape for serious problems, sooner or later the bedroom door can't hold back the flood of undealt-with bitterness, anxiety, frustration, hostility, and jealousy.

R.D.

The communication brownout was turning into a blackout. I recall one day I came home so excited I was about to burst at the seams. I rushed in the door, threw my arms around Betty Jo, and said, "Baby, guess what happened today?" Without even raising her eyes from the book she was reading, she disinterestedly asked,

"What?" Her blank look, her detached response, made me feel like cold water had just been thrown in my face. Sharing the triumph of the day just drained out of me. It didn't seem to matter any more. I silently walked out of the room, went into the den and flopped down in front of the boob tube. You know, the whole evening passed and she never even asked what had happened. I got the message loud and clear: "I don't care what is happening in your life. If it is convenient I might give you the pleasure of my attention, but if it interferes with my interests, then forget it." She didn't say that, but that is what I heard from her actions and her silence.

BETTY

The communication breakdown was a two-way street. R.D. reacted to my accomplishments with about as much enthusiasm as I did his. I recall I came in from night school, right after finals, grinning from ear to ear. When I entered, R.D. was sitting at his desk working on some business papers. "Guess what I did on my finals?" I yelled excitedly.

"What?" he asked, hardly looking up to notice me.

"I made a ninety-three on my literature test, and a ninety-six on my grammar exam. Isn't that terrific?"

"Uh-huh, that's nice."

Some response!

Well, baby number three finally arrived, but baby didn't cure our marital strain, although with two under two, silence wasn't a problem! I became more bitter, more jealous, more possessive than before. My artificial world had been crushed, and now I was again facing and having to deal with the reality of our relationship. R.D. said he felt responsible for my horrible attitude, but that didn't change anything between us. I pouted much of the time. I felt trapped, and it wasn't fair, I thought. I continually checked up on him, followed him, searched through his wallet, all those things that a scared, insecure, jealous woman does. Of course, it accomplished nothing, only added to my angry feelings and drove us further apart.

There were two more affairs. I found out about the last one when I borrowed R.D.'s car one day and opened the glove compartment and discovered a charm bracelet that didn't belong to me. It was obvious that subconsciously R.D. was leaving things around all through the years; he seemingly wanted to get caught, either in an attempt to force me to leave, or as a silent plea for me to stop him. Neither of us has ever figured out which.

R.D.

I had become a Christian when I was a young teen-age boy, but through the years I had gotten away from God's teachings and was as carnal as a Christian could be. Betty Jo became a Christian right after we were married, but neither of us had any deep foundation in God's Word, we didn't rely on it, make decisions by it, or study anything it had to say about God's position on marriage or his concepts for family living.

BETTY

We always attended church, even through the heartbreak. We were right there, I suppose, because it was the "proper" thing to do. R.D. was even a Sunday school teacher, a dynamic one, but we never opened the Bible at home.

I thought, "If you are such a big Christian, how can you be doing all of this?" Of course, I realize now that a carnal Christian can be as rotten as the lowest thing that walks the earth, but I didn't understand that then. Because my sins were either verbal, or mental, neither of which I really knew or considered to be sin at the time, and since I had never been physically unfaithful to R.D., I held this up to him like a banner.

As this last affair progressed, R.D. finally came to me and said, "This time I am serious. I love this girl, and I want a divorce."

R.D.

I was serious this time. I had had it with Betty Jo, her lack of care and interest in me. I felt I had found a woman who really loved me, who understood me, and would be the wife I needed. So after I told Betty Jo I wanted a divorce, I made provisions for her to live *very* comfortably, and I moved out.

BETTY

R.D. hadn't been gone but a few weeks when Matthew became quite ill with an undiagnosed disease. R.D. realized the strain on me, and my need to be at the hospital with Matthew, so he returned home, with the understanding that as soon as school was out, he would leave again. In my mind, this was my "last chance," so to speak. I had to make whatever move, whatever power play I had while R.D. was still under our own roof. My mixed-up mind came up with one sure way to keep him. I deliberately got pregnant! This would save our marriage—I just knew it would. I was so desperate. I didn't want a divorce, yet I didn't want things to stay as they had been in the past. I don't know what I had planned if my scheme worked. I just thought getting pregnant would keep him home a while longer, and maybe we would have time to work things out.

R.D.

When Betty Jo told me she was pregnant again, I hit the roof. "If you think you are going to keep me trapped in this marriage because you deliberately got yourself pregnant again, you are sadly mistaken!" I yelled. Shock shot across her face; she couldn't believe her plan wasn't working. When we both calmed down a bit, we tried to talk it out. Both of us have blocked out the memory of that conversation, but we decided to abort the child!

BETTY

As soon as the abortion was over, R.D. left. That wasn't in my plan. Somewhere in my mind, I thought if I went through with the abortion, he'd stay. I finally filed for a divorce on the grounds of adultery. As soon as I filed, I let everyone in Charlotte know exactly what kind of a man R.D. Taylor really was. I told everyone and anyone who would listen what I had put up with for years.

R.D.

I was surprised when I was served with the divorce papers. I hadn't thought Betty Jo would rush to court so fast. I was in no hurry. It was my thought that perhaps after a time apart we might begin to see the basis of our problems, and perhaps work them out. Then Betty Jo started slandering my name all over town. That did it. I wasn't going to put up with that kind of defamation, so I countersued.

BETTY

I hadn't intended to go through with the divorce, but it was too late. I hadn't counted on R.D. taking any action. In reality, I had filed only intending to let the proceedings drag on and on, postpone them over and over, thinking that during this time he might get his head on straight. But when he countersued, that forced the case to court.

R.D.

When we got to court, we just looked at each other, almost like strangers. There was nothing left to say. Of course, that was the problem. We had never really learned how to talk, how to share; we only knew how to act and react according to our feelings and emotions, and that is what kept us in a constant turmoil.

BETTY

I used the children against R.D. as a punishment. I wouldn't let him see them. He loved them very much, and this tore him up. Finally, the court stepped in and said that he was to have the children on alternate weekends, and that he would be able to keep them from 6 P.M. on Friday to 6 P.M. on Sunday.

One Sunday when I got in from church, he was there early with the kids. I went to the kitchen, fixed lunch, and he sat down with us, like nothing had changed. I couldn't stand it, sitting there at the table, playing like a family. I got up and ran into the bathroom, with tears streaming down my cheeks. I still loved him, and the whole phony scene just broke my heart. R.D. followed me into the bathroom, grabbed me, kissed me, and said, "I still love you! I know you have been seeing other guys since we have been divorced, and I can't stand it."

We began to talk that afternoon, really talk for the first time in our lives. After that, we would occasionally see each other, although we both continued to date other people. R.D. was still seriously involved with the girl he had left us for, and I was enjoying the attention and stimulation of dating and being back in circulation.

R.D.

Divorce certainly did something for Betty Jo. She lost thirty pounds, restyled her hair, and changed her make-up and wardrobe. What a doll, and I wondered why she'd let herself go, why she hadn't cared enough to do that for me.

BETTY

By the end of the year, I had made application to teach at a private school in Colorado. I put the house up for sale. I believed that R.D. and I were never going to get our lives straightened out while we were living so close together. After R.D. found out about my decision and then discovered that I had a buyer for the house, he was around all the time. He said that he wanted us to try to work something out, to remarry!

I told him, "You have got to make up your mind one way or the other, because I have to let this buyer know about the house, and the school know if I am definitely going to teach in the fall."

"Betty Jo, I just want to come home, I want to try again."

"R.D., I think that I would, too. But what makes you presume anything will be different?"

"I don't know. There has to be a better way; maybe the Lord will show us how."

I couldn't believe those words. He had never before said anything about Christ leading our lives. I thought, *I don't know how things can be different. We are the same people, we have the same problems, but maybe he is right, maybe the Lord will honor our recommitment to each other and send us some insight, some help.*

We were remarried about a year after our divorce. It still isn't perfect, but I know that in this life nothing will ever be perfect. But just a few weeks after we remarried, the Lord let me meet a fantastic Christian woman. I shared with her how I felt, the problems we faced, and she suggested that I read a book entitled *We Became Wives of Happy Husbands.*

I sat down and cried when I saw, through God's Word, how out of line I had been. I realized I had been judging R.D., yet I personally had distorted and broken almost every concept God has for a wife. I saw myself for what I really was—a selfish woman who had belittled her husband, isolated him, failed to listen and respond to him, and certainly *never* followed his leading.

I realized that in my marriage I had *talked* too much and *listened* too little. I wanted so much to be the wife God created me to be. As I was willing and obedient, our relationship began growing and developing a communication not just verbal, but of the soul, too.

R.D.

Bless her heart, Betty Jo really had a hard time at first in learning to back off and let me lead in the home. She had been deeply affected by the doctrine of the Women's Liberation movement, but with Christ's help she is changing, not just for me, not just for herself, but for the woman she knows Christ would have her be.

Slowly we are learning to talk; but more important, we are actually learning how to listen, with our minds and our hearts. Now when there is a victory in either of our lives, there is excitement and sharing, and rejoicing in our home. No one is ignored any more.

I wish I could undo all the mistakes I made in our first marriage, particularly allowing Betty Jo to have the abortion. Of course, I know they can't be undone, the baby can't be brought back, but I just thank God that his grace is sufficient to forgive even tragic mistakes like that. Betty Jo and I are both back in church now, but this time a Bible-teaching church where we can learn the Word, a church where we are hearing God's viewpoint, not man's. We are doing our best through his strength to walk in his steps so that our relationship, our marriage, will be an example to others.

It is often easy to communicate on what you feel is a deep, meaningful level through letters. Many romances have begun that way, only to disintegrate when the couple has the opportunity to interact on a direct and personal level. Betty Jo and R.D. didn't take the time to make this vital discovery. Two strong personalities met head on, each desiring his or her own way and neither having the zeal, knowledge, or ability to change.

The beginning of love is based on the Greek word *eros*, which is a sexual, physically expressed love. In a healthy relationship, that love would progress to *philia*, a more mature love, where deep friendship, companionship and self-giving result. Of course, this type of love finds its roots in open, free, caring interchange between mates. Ultimately, marital love can evolve to *agape*, a love for one's mate which is similar to that which the Lord has for us.

During their first marriage, Betty Jo and R.D. never progressed beyond the *eros* stage.

Although R.D. and Betty Jo were both Christians, neither had ever intently studied the Scriptures, so they failed to learn and apply God's concepts to their lives or marriage.

It was a difficult struggle for them to openly face each other and begin to rebuild the shattered pieces of a shallow relationship. But they began by getting the ship on the right heading. Before remarriage, they came to the conclusion that they personally did not possess the capability to change themselves or salvage their marriage. As with so many couples, they didn't have the slightest idea of how to begin repairing the damage or break down the walls, but they finally realized that they knew One who did, and in prayer they asked God for guidance, for answers, and he led them (Prov. 3:5–6).

As they searched the Word, they became intimately acquainted with Jesus Christ, and recognized that he was the supreme example of love, and that the example which he set was in giving. As they allowed the Holy Spirit to control their lives, patience, care and kindness entered their relationship. The cold, forbidding walls of strife began to crumble (Gal. 5:16).

THE "OTHER WOMAN" SYNDROME

If you women think that knowing your man and being able to discuss his goals, desires, plans, and business aren't important, then I imagine some of you already have an "other woman" problem. Far from being the sexy blonde he met at last year's convention, the other woman is usually knowledgeable in his field of interest, either because she happens to work in the same field, or because she wanted your man enough to learn what he cared about, enough to discuss it intelligently; and beyond that, she has learned the secret of communication—*she has learned how to listen,* she's taken the time to *hear* what he says verbally and nonverbally.

There is one aspect of men few wives seem to realize, and that is the difference between the man he is and the one he wishes to be, or in some cases imagines himself to be. He likes to think of himself as the world's greatest lover, a success in business, a fascinating conversationalist, the light-hearted, unrestricted young man you probably met ten or twenty years ago. In most instances, we women fail to recognize this. We let him know exactly what he is, we ignore him instead of giving him the attention he so dearly needs and seeks; we fail to praise his love-making prowess. All he either wishes to be, or thinks he is, is crushed the moment he looks at us.

He may choose to have innocent relationships at the local

bars just to satisfy his ego; he may go there so he can again be the man he "thinks" or "wants" to be; or he may become seriously involved with someone who is wise enough to realize that he isn't exactly what he wants to be, but who doesn't remind him of that— a woman who is long on praise, and acts as though he is the most fascinating, irresistible man she has ever met.

The other day, a young girl called me about the marital problem she and her husband where having. She vividly shared with me his constant infidelity, but said their main problem was that they simply couldn't communicate. She asked me whether I would talk with her husband if she could get him to call. I told her I normally don't counsel men, but she was so persistent that I said if *he called* me, we'd discuss their problems. Surprisingly, the next day the phone rang, and a male voice said, "This is Joel Maxwell, Lana's husband."

I must admit, after hearing all about Joel and his indiscretions the day before, I had a hard time fighting my preconceived ideas of what type of man I was dealing with. But when we really got down to the nitty-gritty, he confirmed that communication was their major problem. I discussed his infidelity with him, but I felt that they both might be right, so I just let him talk for a while. During his complaints about Lana, he said: "You wouldn't believe how immature she is. All she talks about is movie stars. The other day, when Burt Reynolds was down here shooting a new picture, she was over near the set all the time, trying to get a look at him."

I laughed and jokingly replied: "The only personality I ever went to that much trouble to see close up was Bart Starr!" That did it. Joel opened up like a book. "Do you like football, Anne?" he asked excitedly.

"Love it, but I'll have to admit I didn't always. My husband, who is from Green Bay, brought me up on the Packers of the 1960s."

From the Packers, we discussed the stock market, international politics, economics, and more. All of a sudden I realized that we had been talking almost two hours about everything under the sun but their marital problems, and from long experience I could see that Joel was ripe pickings for any woman who could and would communicate with him about anything but her own feminine interests. Joel had been wrong in trying to find someone else to relate to, but Lana had opened the door and pushed him out because she was too self-centered to meet his verbal/mental needs and interests.

THE "OTHER MAN" SYNDROME

The "other man" syndrome occurs less frequently than the "other woman" does, but it occurs just the same, and from recent surveys and studies it seems to be on the increase. Women who once were willing to accept their lot in life, even some Christian women, have been tainted by the new mores introduced by Women's Lib and are becoming impatient with a life which they've been told doesn't give total personal expression and fulfillment.

Women look to other men for the same reasons that men are attracted to other women. But, husband, if your wife still stays home, takes care of the house and children, she will have *more* need for communication than the working wife. You see, while you have been out in the adult world all day, no matter how much pressure you have faced, you have had people of your own age and educational level to converse with. Meanwhile, your wife, in many instances, has interacted with "Puff, Spot, Dick, and Jane," vacuum cleaners, stopped-up toilets, and boiling-over dinner pots. After a few years of this same routine, she has probably begun to feel that "glamour" and "romance" have gone out of her life. When she has had time to stop and relax for a minute, she probably has picked up some woman's magazine, which tells her in essence that she doesn't have to live like this, that there is more to life, and that she should demand her rights, her own fulfillment. If you husbands don't step in before she buys the whole feminist program, you are going to have massive disruptive problems on your hands and in your home.

What she is looking for, what most women are looking for in the way of satisfaction, is appreciation, a reaffirmation of herself as a woman, not as the children's mother, but as your woman, personally, as a living, breathing female. If she isn't reassured *verbally, and nonverbally*, she will find that in time appreciative looks from other men become more and more appealing. She may try to shake the feeling off, but if she is continually ignored at home, if her feminine needs for appreciation, affection, romance, quiet talks, aren't met, she may in time secretly turn to that man who has noticed her *as a woman,* who has reminded her that she is attractive, who perhaps flirts with her, letting her forget for a time that her teen-age years are long past.

No, she may not go to the local bar to find the feminine reassurance she needs, although more and more "liberated" women do. Most starved housewives run into an appreciative man accidentally—perhaps the insurance agent who drops by with the new policy, the tennis or golf pro she is taking lessons from. But sooner or later, if she is hungry to feel feminine, and you aren't fulfilling your God-given position to "love, cherish, and make her happy," then some man is going to pick up the signals. It had better be you!

HAPPINESS IS "WORKING AT IT"

When the wedding bouquet has withered a bit, and the day-to-day routine has set in, you begin to learn the differences in the male and female needs for communication. You also begin to learn that years of conditioning have probably brought the male to the point that, because of his male ego, he won't converse or communicate on a subject with which he isn't acquainted. This is the reason that only about three or four men out of every hundred will seek counseling when their marriage "is on the rocks." Admitting that there are problems he can't solve, emotions he can't cope with, is a direct threat to a man's self-identity, his masculinity. It isn't that he doesn't want to share, to let it "all hang out," to take his mask off; it is a matter of conditioning. But a wise woman can learn to bring her man out, help him across the walls.

Just as men often build walls of defense, women usually go the other way, nagging and talking their men right out the door and into someone else's arms.

♥ TAKING STEPS TOWARD COMMUNICATION ♥

Communication is first an attitude, then an action. Read and reread James 3:1–18 two or three times a day for a week, with your spouse primarily in mind. Pray about how the two of you are communicating and ask the Lord to make your heart particularly sensitive to any area where you are sending or receiving messages incorrectly. Ask the Lord to open your heart to your mate, to create in you the ability to be available to truly listen to his or her needs, wants, plans, desires, gripes or whatever he or she needs and wants to share with you.[12]

Begin exploring your mate's areas of interest. Learn the basics of one thing your mate is interested in. When you can intelligently communicate about that area, pick another. You will be amazed at what this will do to your relationship.

Work at earning your mate's trust. Communication—the sharing of innermost thoughts, feelings—doesn't happen if there is lack of trust. Can your mate trust you: to be on time? to follow through? to be there when he or she needs you? Start working on simple things and trust, plus communication, will grow stronger between you.

For women: List different ways you can begin to sincerely show your husband respect and admiration. How can you help him succeed in his job or his business? Don't be content with asking him, "How did it go today at work?" and having him grunt, "Okay, I guess." Draw him out with questions that go beneath the surface. Let him know you really care and want to hear what he's feeling and thinking.

For men: Begin today to reaffirm verbally and overtly your wife's femininity as a living, feeling, breathing woman. Plan special dinners out, once or perhaps twice a month. Schedule special quiet times together—evening walks, drives in the country, or whatever the two of you really enjoy doing. Set aside special times each evening to be totally available to talk together.[13]

Ironically, a crucial part of talking is listening! How do you rate your own communication according to the following scale?

Always Talk		Always Listen
1	5	10

Ideally, you should be somewhere near the middle. In the next chapter, André Bustanoby describes the valuable tool called "active-listening."

Chapter 18

ARE YOU REALLY LISTENING?

ANDRÉ BUSTANOBY
Just Talk to Me

Ironically enough, the key to communication is not sending messages but receiving them. Communication always breaks down if one or both partners fails to listen. Most husbands and wives know they should listen, but lack motivation and skills to do so. As you read André Bustanoby's tips for learning how to listen better, think about these questions:

- ♥ How good a listener am I? How can I be a better one?
- ♥ How often do I consciously "active-listen" to my mate?
- ♥ How good am I at restating what my mate has just said? How often do I practice this skill?

CAN YOU HEAR ME?

Fay and I are getting better at listening to each other. In fact, I think we do a pretty good job.

It wasn't always so. We both have had problems listening. The expression on my face and my body language once were very clear signals that I wasn't listening. When Fay would say something I didn't like, I'd become fidgety and act as if I were ready to jump in at the first opportunity to give "The Authorized Version." I was thinking of what I wanted to say instead of being attentive to what she was saying.

Fay's style was different. She would withdraw when she didn't like what she heard. I could see the walls going up just by the expression on her face.

LEARN TO ACTIVE-LISTEN

Every effective communicator must learn the skill of "active-listening." It's called "active" because the listener has a responsibility. He works at grasping what the speaker is saying and attempts to help him express those feelings. This is extremely difficult to do, especially when we hear criticism, or something we disagree with. Our inclination is to tune out or correct what is said. It's foreign to self-preservation to help someone dump a load of painful verbiage on us! But when we do active-listen we convey a clear message of acceptance. Whether or not we agree with what is being said, we convey the message that this person is worth being heard.

How To Active-Listen. Just exactly what do we do when we active-listen? We must crawl inside the speaker's skin and see life as he sees it, hear it as he hears it, and feel it as he feels it. All effective counselors have this skill. It's called "accurate empathy."[14] Empathy is a caring attitude that enables us to perceive life the way the speaker perceives it. But it's called *accurate* empathy in that we perceive it *exactly* as that other person perceives it. We neither overshoot nor undershoot.

If someone tells you he's depressed, you need to assess the degree. Is this a passing symptom, does it border on suicidal urge, or is it a chronic problem that has been wearing on him for weeks?

When you accurately touch that person where he is hurting, that in itself is healing. Often, I have had clients brighten up at that moment of contact and say, "You're the first person who really has understood where I am!" A marvelous transaction takes place at that moment when the pain and hurt are shared by the accurately empathic listener.

Many times in marriage, solutions are not necessary. Often, a husband or wife only wants to be heard and understood. Satisfied with that, they may even drop the matter.

We must do several things in active-listening.

1. *Listen to both words and feelings.* Every message has two components: words and feelings. If we do not tune in to how the feelings qualify the words, we will not have heard accurately. Consider the following:

Husband to wife: "Be sure to have the oil in the car checked every time you get gas."

Now consider saying it this way:

Husband to wife: "If you keep driving the car without oil, you'll burn out the engine for sure!"

Both of these messages carry essentially the same words: The oil in the car should be checked regularly. But the second message definitely carries a *feeling* of hostility. To ignore the feelings and simply to agree to have the oil checked is to miss an important part of the message. The husband is telling his wife *more* than the words convey. He's telling her he is irritated at the way she treats the car. That message is as important as the message about checking the oil—perhaps *more* important. Cars are easier fixed than marriages!

2. *Respond to feelings.* The second thing we must do is *respond* to those feelings we hear. And we must do it without attack or defense.

Wife to husband: "I don't know what you're getting huffy about. I usually have the oil checked" (defense). "And anyway, who are you to talk about neglecting the car?" (attack).

The following response would be more constructive:

Wife to husband: "It sounds as if you're irritated over the way I take care of the car."

In the first case, the wife is responding to the feelings of her husband both defensively and offensively. Her response is saying in essence, "You have no right to feel the way you do." Whether or not he *should* feel that way, he *does*. And that's what she needs to deal with. The quickest way to deal constructively with negative feelings *is to make that person feel heard and understood.*

In the second case, the wife is saying, "I hear your irritation, and I want you to know that I'm open to hearing more about it." This may lead to the revelation of lots of other feelings that have been creating a breach between husband and wife.

3. *Look for nonverbal cues.* We must tune in to all the cues the speaker is giving. What emotion is being revealed by his behavior and the tone of his voice? Is it anger, nervousness, despair, or what? By tuning in to those cues you sometimes will put the speaker in touch with emotions he may not be aware of. For example you can say, "It sounds as if there's a lot of despair in what you say." It gives the speaker an opportunity to listen to what he's saying.

In looking for nonverbal cues, ask yourself what the eyes are saying. Are they downcast, darting about, glaring at you, or warm and friendly? The body—what is it saying? Is it tense or relaxed? The inflection of the voice—what mood does it convey? Is it optimism, anxiety, despair? Does the person mumble or speak up?

How we dress and the way we present ourselves when we speak carries a message of how we want people to hear us. The hostile person may be conveying the message, "You better treat me right. I can be mean." The docile person may be saying by that behavior, "Don't hurt me. I'm harmless." Trust your instinct. How does that person affect you? And don't be afraid to relate your experience back in a non-threatening way.

For many years I presented myself as a confident, hard-driving person who was quite immune to having his feelings hurt. The message was, "If you compete with me I'll blow you away. And it doesn't matter how you try to beat me. You can't hurt me." I was really protecting myself by discouraging competition and attack. But when I really did hurt and wanted comfort, no one could believe I really needed it. I made my nonverbal cues of confidence that believable!

4. *Give adequate feedback.* Active-listening requires adequate feedback. When we listen we are not to absorb passively. We are to respond in such a way as to let that person know we have accurately heard. Use various forms of feedback:

- "I see, you are saying . . ."
- "Let me see if I understand you correctly . . ."
- "Help me to understand; you mean . . ."
- "It sounds as if . . ."
- "You find it difficult . . ."
- "You are really . . ."
- "It's kind of like . . ."
- "So you are saying . . ."[15]

Your feedback should reveal empathy. It should match the mood of the speaker. A deadpan, mechanical response does not reveal empathy. Active listening is not a gimmick. You must be able to feel what the speaker feels, and let him know that you feel it in a believable way.

5. *Words are not the only vehicle for the communication of understanding.* The following nonverbal clues aid in creating an atmosphere of acceptance and an attitude of listening:

- Eye contact
- Nodding
- Body expression
- Facial expression

Listed below are appropriate and useful verbal expressions that are effective in facilitating active-listening:

- Simple acknowledgement—"Uh-huh"; "Oh, yeah"; and so on.
- Paraphrase—Restating main idea or feelings in your own words indicates your receptiveness and understanding of the message.
- Door openers—"I'd like to hear more about it"; "Would you like to talk about it?"
- Summarize—Briefly recap and synthesize what you thought you heard.
- Seek information—Without introducing new topics or going off on a tangent, ask for confirmation. Check perceptions: "From what I'm hearing, it seems you feel that. . . . Am I right?"

- Ask for elaboration, expansion—"Can you give me an example?"
- Ask for definition (of words introduced by sender)— "What's a ...?" "Who's ... ?"[16]

WHAT WE ACHIEVE BY ACTIVE-LISTENING

Active-listening is the practical application of acceptance. It makes the speaker feel accepted. You have cared enough to stop and hear what he has said, and you care that he feels as he does. It doesn't mean that you have forsaken your own convictions or that you look at things the way he does. But it does mean that you care about him and are able to put yourself in his shoes.

We Help Others Hear. When we active-listen, we help that person to hear himself. I remember once unburdening myself to a friend who was active-listening. I said in angry, bitter tones, "I don't care how they feel!" He replied, "You sound hurt and angry." That was true. I was so hurt that I couldn't even tune in to where the other people were. I couldn't believe that I actually said I didn't care about them. But that was the truth—hard as it was to face.

We Reduce the Threat of Criticism. When we active-listen we reduce the threat of criticism. It's always difficult to tell someone else what's going on inside you because he might criticize. If you want your spouse to talk, don't make him sorry he opened his mouth. By active-listening you will reduce that threat.

Listening Brings About Change. I mentioned earlier in the chapter the counseling skill of accurate empathy. This type of caring forms a bond between the speaker and the listener. When the listener touches the speaker where he hurts, an intimate bond of sharing is established. The listener has not judged the speaker, but rather has helped bear the burden.

When this kind of bond is established, the listener is in a much better position to be a positive, changing force in the speaker's life. He is no longer an adversary, but a friend and companion. As such, his life might be a worthwhile model to consider. Listening usually is met with listening in return.

Truax and Carkhuff, writing to counselors in training, speak of this phenomenon. Husbands and wives should have the same therapeutic impact on each other.

> It is in this sense that the therapist, through trial identification, becomes the "other self" or "alter ego" of the client; and through his example leads the patient into a deeper self-exploration and experiencing of feelings and emotional content. As the patient moves tentatively toward feelings and experiences that he experiences as shameful, fearful, or even

terrifying, the therapist steps into the patient's shoes and takes him one step further in self-exploration, doing so in a self-accepting and congruent manner that lessens the patient's own fears of coming to grips with the experiences or feelings. It is as if the therapist were providing a model for the patient to follow; as if he were saying by his example, "Even these fearful or terrifying experiences or feelings are not so terrible that they can't be touched and looked at." The therapist's example of self-acceptance and congruence is perhaps as crucial as his ability to sense or at least point to the next step in the patient's self-exploration.[17]

HOW TO KNOW WHEN YOU'VE LISTENED

Understanding what another person is saying is really more difficult than it seems. Here are two suggestions that may help you test your listening skills.

Restate What You Have Heard. The next time you're involved in a lively discussion that seems to be going nowhere, try this. Restate the other person's position *to his satisfaction* before you proceed to state your own. It must be more than a repetition of words. You should be able to catch the feeling of the words and rephrase them in your own words.[18]

Remember, active-listening requires your active participation in understanding. Nodding the head and saying, "Yes, I understand," lets the speaker know you're with him. Eye contact is important, too. He needs to know you're with him.

Revolving Discussion Sequence. When the discussion really is hot and heavy and you need to slow it down, try the Revolving Discussion Sequence. It has three elements: statement, restatement, and agreement. The statement must be a *feeling* statement, not an opinion.

One cue that lets you know you're going to state an opinion rather than a feeling is the word "that." If you say, "I feel that . . ." you're probably going to give an opinion rather than a feeling. For example, "I feel that you're neglecting me," is not a feeling—it's an opinion. The opinion is that *you* are doing something. And if I accuse you of doing something bad, you're going to defend yourself with an opinion of your own. On the other hand, "I feel neglected" is a statement of feeling that accuses you of nothing. I feel something. Because you are not accused, you will be less likely to challenge the statement.

The statement in the Revolving Discussion Sequence involves a feeling and the reason for the feeling. For example, a husband may say to his wife, "I feel neglected because the children seem to get more of your time than I do."

The wife is to restate his feelings and the reason for it. She will say, "I hear you saying that you feel neglected because it seems that the children get more of my time than you." Or she can put it in her own words. It is important that she restate the husband's statement until he is satisfied that she has heard him.

Then comes the agreement. *She must agree that he feels that way.* She may want to argue that she doesn't spend more time with the children and may want to advance proof of her position. She must not! If she does, she is not listening to his feelings.

The fact of the matter is that he does feel that way, and nothing short of being heard and understood will do. I'm not saying that she cannot have feelings of her own. She will, and her opportunity to express them will come. But this step of the sequence is essential to the whole. Whether or not she thinks her husband *should* feel as he does, the fact of the matter is, that's where he is!

Having completed that stage of the sequence, it's the wife's turn to speak. She may say, "I feel overloaded when I hear all the needs you and the children have."

The husband may be tempted to say, "You shouldn't feel that way. All you have to do is . . ." Suggestions for change are inappropriate at this point. He needs to hear all that she has to say on the subject, and she needs to hear all he has to say. Many times we offer solutions before we fully understand the problem.

After the wife makes her statement, the husband must restate what she has said. He must do it to her satisfaction. She needs to know he has heard her. He must not be impatient in trying to get it right. An attitude of impatience says, "You shouldn't feel that way."

Once the wife is satisfied with the husband's restatement, he then must agree with her. Yes, she does feel overloaded. Whether or not he thinks she should feel overloaded, that's where she is.

And she must know that she can feel that way and still be okay in her husband's eyes. He may want to see some changes in the household routine, but those changes have nothing to do with the okayness of his wife as a person. *Change comes quickest where there is mutual acceptance and respect!*

ERRORS IN ACTIVE-LISTENING

When you practice active-listening you will want to watch out for some common errors.[19]

Active-Listening When Other Help Is Needed. Active-listening is inappropriate when other help is needed. When a young mother is distraught trying to diaper a screaming baby and keep her two-year-old off the coffee table at the same time, she doesn't need to be listened to. She needs help!

Focusing Only on Feelings. It is important to listen to feelings. But we must not let the feelings get in the way of hearing *why* the person feels as he does.

Active-Listening When You Don't Have Time. You and your wife are having breakfast. She feels very blue. Life is uninteresting, and today looks as if it's going to be another dull day. Your car pool leaves in five minutes. Don't try to active-listen then. Call her when you get a chance or set a time to talk that evening.

Being Too Interpretive. There's a big difference between making a person feel heard and engaging in psychoanalysis. You may restate with accurate empathy *what* your spouse is feeling, but *why* he feels that way is really his to discover. When we try to focus on *why* people feel as they do, they often think that we're really not interested in *what* they are feeling.

Feeding Back With no Effect or Empathy. A truly caring person shows it in his attitude toward those who reveal their feelings. This is one of the distinguishing characteristics of Jesus Christ, who is "touched with the feeling of our infirmities" (Heb. 4:15 KJV).

Feeding Back Only Part of the Feeling. Often, the expression of many feelings adds up to a few general feelings. We must stay with the flow of feelings and try to put together an overview of what's happening. The speaker may ramble, but the listener should be able to hear an underlying theme.

Summary. Active-listening is a way to convey to the speaker your feeling of acceptance. You may not look at life as he does, and you will want to express your view, too. But for the moment, as an active-listener, you are making that person feel that he's worth being heard.

Remember, listening begets listening.

♥ BETWEEN THE LINES/UNDER THE SURFACE ♥

Active-listening doesn't sound too difficult as you read about it, but you may be surprised when you start actually trying to do it. Like any other skill, active-listening takes a great deal of practice, and the ideal situation is to practice with your mate.

If your communication is on a fairly decent basis right now, you can practice active-listening to each other. If communication is weak or almost non-existent, you may have to experiment as you talk with your mate and seek to improve as best you can on your own.

As you active-listen for feelings, you will start hearing things "between the lines" and under the surface. Review the author's illustration of a man who tells his wife, "If you keep driving the car without oil, you'll burn out the engine for sure!" This message carries a feeling of hostility and it would be easy to get defensive. Work on giving responses that let your mate know you hear his or her irritation, fear, anxiety, etc., and want to learn more about that and how you can help.

Practice looking for nonverbal cues in what your mate says. Watch the eyes and the body. Listen to the voice. Does your mate need comfort? understanding? Does your mate need patience or acceptance? Whatever you see or hear, your partner does not need your counter-attack, or statements that deny his or her feelings. Whatever you do, don't turn active-listening into a game where you think you can identify your mate's feelings and blandly assure your mate that he or she "shouldn't feel that way."

Practice giving feedback that shows empathy, putting yourself in your mate's shoes. There is a real difference between good feedback and "parroting" what is said. Remember the various forms of feedback and practice using them often.

If you try active-listening and it "doesn't seem to work," don't get discouraged. This form of communication is not simple, but it is well worth every effort you put into it. Every time you attempt active-listening, you are building better communication bridges with your mate.

As you gain skill in actively listening to one another, it's well worth your while to rate each other on how well you do. In the next chapter, Fay Bustanoby gives you a sixteen-question scale for doing that kind of rating.

Chapter 19

HOW TO RATE YOUR MATE (AND YOURSELF) AS A LISTENER

BY FAY BUSTANOBY
Just Talk to Me

If you and your spouse rated each other on your skills as active listeners, how would you come out? As you read the following suggestions by Fay Bustanoby, keep these questions in mind:

♥ Am I being honest and fair in my rating?
♥ Am I more interested in rating my spouse or hearing what he or she says about me?
♥ What do I intend to do with the results of this test after we share ratings with each other?

RATING YOUR MATE

How does your spouse rate as an active-listener? The rating scale below is provided for your evaluation. How you respond to the statements will help your spouse understand how well he rates in this skill. This rating is not intended to be a scientific instrument. It is an estimate of your spouse's listening skills and will give him an idea of the relative strength and weakness of his listening. Your spouse is to rate you also.

Do not consult each other as you are doing the rating. You will have an opportunity to discuss the answers when you are done.

Take a sheet of paper and number it from one to sixteen. When you respond to each statement, use the number from the appropriate column. If the answer is no, write down the number you see in the no column, even though it is sometimes one and sometimes three. Remember, rate your spouse on the basis of how *you feel*.

RATE YOUR SPOUSE AS A LISTENER

	NO	MID	YES
1. He/she understands the way I feel.	1	2	3
2. He/she values me as an individual or unique person.	1	2	3
3. He/she feels deeply my most painful feelings.	1	2	3
4. He/she can understand my weaknesses.	1	2	3
5. He/she tries to understand my point of view.	1	2	3
6. He/she has an appreciation for my value as a human being.	1	2	3
7. He/she cares enough to let me go, or even to give me up.	1	2	3
8. One of his/her feelings for me might be described as a love for mankind.	1	2	3
9. He/she demands my appreciation.	3	2	1
10. Being rejected by him/her changes my feelings for him/her.	3	2	1
11. His/her feeling for me has a quality of forgiveness.	1	2	3
12. His/her feeling for me has a quality of patience.	1	2	3
13. He/she can tell what I'm feeling even when I don't talk about it.	1	2	3
14. His/her feeling for me has a quality of compassion or sympathy.	1	2	3
15. He/she has a deep feeling of concern for my welfare as a human being.	1	2	3
16. He/she feels I have great worth and dignity.[20]	1	2	3

Scoring. Add up your responses. The highest possible score is 48; the lowest score is 16.

Let's rate as follows:

40—48	Your spouse really does listen.
32—39	You feel your spouse doesn't always listen.
24—31	You feel your spouse seldom listens.
16—23	The active-listening skill needs a lot of work.

Evaluation of the questions. After you have rated each other, go back to the rating statements and look at each response. These statements are adapted from Everett L. Shostrom's test called the "Caring Relationship Inventory." The statements are probing for empathy. Several statements are similar. I'll consider each separately, however.

1. "He/she understands the way I feel." The ideal answer is yes. A truly empathic spouse will focus on the feelings and understand them. He will not dismiss them and tell you, "You shouldn't feel that way."

2. "He/she values me as an individual or unique person." The ideal answer is yes. You should not be required to feel a particular way or feel as your spouse does in order to have value as an individual.

3. "He/she feels deeply my most painful feelings." The ideal answer is yes. Your spouse is to do more than give mere mental assent to your hurt. He should feel it himself.

4. "He/she can understand my weaknesses." The ideal answer is yes. We should be able to understand each other's weaknesses because we are in touch with our own. This is what put the Pharisees out of touch with the common man. They just didn't see any weaknesses in themselves and were, therefore, intolerant of weakness in others.

Often husbands and wives are not understanding of each other for the same reasons. They see themselves as so spiritual they cannot understand why others are not as they are. They sound much like the Pharisee Jesus spoke of in the parable of the Pharisee and the tax-gatherer. "The Pharisee stood and was praying thus to himself, 'God, I thank thee that I am not like other people: swindlers, unjust, adulterers, or even like this tax-gatherer'" (Luke 18:11).

5. "He/she tries to understand my point of view." The ideal answer is yes. We should be able to crawl inside each other's skin and look at life through each other's eyes. It does not mean that we have no opinions of our own. But it does mean that we can accurately perceive the other person's point of view.

6. "He/she had an appreciation for my value as a human being." The ideal answer is yes. You should not be required to see things as your spouse does in order to be valued as a human being.

7. "He/she cares enough to let me go, or even to give me up." The ideal answer is yes. Valuing a person's worth means a willingness to let go if that person feels that it is in his best interest. This is even true of a prodigal (Luke 15:11–32). When we respect another person's need to go his own way, we create a climate for his return, should he discover that his way wasn't so good after all. Often what we cannot accomplish by preaching and moralizing we can accomplish by lovingly letting go. This is one of the cardinal rules in the treatment of alcoholics.

8. "One of his/her feelings for me might be described as a love for mankind." The ideal answer is yes. Christians, above all, ought to be lovers of mankind, or, as Peter puts it, "Honor all men" (1 Peter 2:17). We are truly made in the image of God and are to be valued as such (Gen. 9:6).

9. "He/she demands my appreciation." The ideal answer is no. Appreciation is in order. But if you demand it, then it cannot be given willingly. You rob your spouse of a significant opportunity to show caring by demanding it. This is why possessiveness is so damaging to a relationship. You are robbed of the opportunity of *freely* loving. It is expected of you because your spouse owns you. This does not mean that you are free from your marital vows. It does mean that you are not clubbed over the head with demands.

10. "Being rejected by him/her changes my feelings for him/her." The ideal answer is no. In every marriage we experience a certain degree of rebuff or lack of empathy. But it should not be so severe or chronic that it changes our feelings for our spouse.

11. "His/her feeling for me has a quality of forgiveness." The ideal answer is yes. Forgiveness carries with it an understanding of how that person failed you. Even though Jesus Christ was sinless he still could understand how we can fail him. The denial of Peter was met with a great deal of compassion (John 21:15–23).

12. "His/her feeling for me has a quality of patience." This is similar to the previous statement. Our patience with others shows our ability truly to put ourselves in that person's place. Often when we are impatient or unforgiving, we place ourselves apart as being quite incapable of those failures. This is a Pharisaical attitude— and is the reason why the Pharisees were unforgiving. They lacked the human quality of empathy.

13. "He/she can tell what I'm feeling even when I don't talk about it." The ideal answer is yes. If your spouse is tuned in to all of your nonverbal cues, he ought to be able to have some idea of what you're feeling.

14. "His/her feeling for me has a quality of compassion or sympathy." The ideal answer is yes. Compassion and sympathy are closely related to empathy. It's another way of saying, "I care how you feel, and I feel it too."

15. "He/she has a deep feeling of concern for my welfare as a

human being." The ideal answer is yes. As with statement 8 this statement focuses on that element of caring that values man as a creature made in God's image.

16. "He/she feels I have great worth and dignity." The ideal answer is yes. As in statement 15 man has worth and dignity as a person. For your spouse to make your worth and dignity contingent upon your seeing things as he does denies this.

Summary. Listening is intimately linked to the act of love called "empathy." Carl R. Rogers, writing on the characteristics of a helping relationship, summarized the matter well when he said this:

> Can I let myself enter fully into the world of his feelings and personal meanings, and see these as he does? Can I step into his private world so completely that I lose all desire to evaluate or judge it? Can I enter it so sensitively that I can move about in it freely, without trampling on meanings which are precious to him? Can I sense it so accurately that I can catch not only the meanings of his experience which are obvious to him, but those meanings which are only implicit, which he sees only dimly or as confusion? Can I extend this understanding without limit?
>
> . . . I am impressed with the fact that even a minimal amount of empathetic understanding—a bumbling and faulty attempt to catch the confused complexity of the client's meaning—is helpful, though there is no doubt that it is most helpful when I can see and formulate clearly the meanings of his experiencing which for him have been unclear and tangled.[21]

The "bumbling and faulty" empathy of husbands and wives toward each other also is without a doubt helpful. You need not be a pro to show empathy and listen.

♥ A WORD TO THE WISE ACTIVE-LISTENER ♥

If your communication with your mate is poor or nonexistent, guard against having this quiz turn into a "pity party." For example, you might have to answer most of the questions no in regard to rating your spouse as a listener. But feeling sorry for yourself will not help. It would be better to use the quiz to rate yourself and perceive how your spouse might rate you. How can *you* improve in these sixteen areas? As you seek to improve your own listening skills, your spouse will detect the difference and communication between you will begin to build.

In the next chapter, Gary Smalley shares a useful technique for piquing your partner's interest, and ensuring better listening on his or her part.

Chapter 20

USE SALT AND LIGHT TO GAIN UNDIVIDED ATTENTION

BY GARY SMALLEY
The Joy of Committed Love

In his work with married couples, Gary Smalley constantly hears wives complaining that "I just can't get him to listen to me." Is there a way to motivate or teach your husband to be a better listener? Smalley has proven that there is. It is called the "salt principle" and the following chapter describes how it works. As you read, keep these questions in mind:

- ♥ How can I use the salt principle to motivate rather than manipulate my husband?
- ♥ What would be the best topic to initiate the conversation and when should I bring it up?
- ♥ What kind of attitude must I develop to use the salt principle successfully?
- ♥ How can I use the "light up principle" to make my husband feel more important and gain his attention at the same time?

CREATE A BURNING CURIOSITY

Lois had a pretty good marriage by today's standards. She considered her husband a good provider and an excellent father. However, the romance had faded from their marriage, and her feelings of affection toward Mark were very inconsistent. She decided she would do all she could to make her marriage what she wanted it to be. She began reading various books on what she could do to be a better wife and was gaining enthusiasm each day.

After several weeks, she stumbled across two books written for men, telling them what they could do to strengthen their marriages. She brought them home for Mark and decided to give them to him after dinner. The moment of truth finally came. She walked over to Mark with a sweet smile and said, "Honey, I've really been working hard lately to learn how to become a better wife so I can be what you deserve to have. I found two books that can help a husband better understand his wife. Would you read them for me?"

Mark gave her a condescending look and said, "We'll see."

Not giving up at that sure sign of defeat, she said, a little more defensively, "I've been reading a lot of books lately and really working hard to make our marriage better. This is the least you can do."

Mark gave excuse number four on man's "Ten Most Widely Used Excuses" list. He simply said, "Sweetie, you know how busy I am these days. I'll really try when my schedule slows down." She knew that could be a while, because in their nine years of marriage she had never seen his schedule "slow down."

But there was something Lois could have said that would have motivated Mark to read both books within three nights. In fact, he probably would have taken time off work to finish them the next day.

This principle is not given to be used as a manipulative tool. I share it because it can help you enter into a more loving, attentive conversation with your husband. As you do, you'll be able to search out his deepest needs and selflessly dedicate yourself to meeting those needs. It's called the "salt principle." Salt makes people thirsty, and the goal of this principle is to create a thirst for constructive conversation in which both you and your husband can learn about each other's needs.

Simply stated, the principle is this:

NEVER COMMUNICATE INFORMATION YOU CONSIDER TO BE IMPORTANT WITHOUT FIRST CREATING A BURNING CURIOSITY WITHIN THE LISTENER.

This principle is so easy to learn that even a child can master it. One day my seven-year-old daughter came running into the house, crying. I called her over and asked what was wrong. She told me that her little girlfriend never listened to her. Every time Kari would start to tell her something, the friend would interrupt and start talking. Kari told me she felt she didn't have anything important to say because her friend would never listen.

I asked Kari if she would like to learn a way that would make her friend want to listen to her. She was all ears as she hopped up into my lap, and I asked her, "What were some of the things you wanted to say to your friend?"

She replied, "I wanted to tell her what I did with my dollhouse, but she didn't want to hear."

I told Kari that first she had to get her friend's attention with a statement or two that would make her friend want to hear more. She would have to make these statements with *enthusiasm*. We decided she could say something like, "You won't believe *what I did* to my new dollhouse!" Then she would pause and come back with a second statement, "My *parents* couldn't even believe what I did with it."

When I came home from work the following evening, Kari was all smiles. She told me that our plan had worked so well that her friend not only listened to her, but came over and played with the dollhouse.

Obviously, for adults the situations are more complicated, although the principle remains the same. Arouse their curiosity and you've got their attention!

Faye was worried because Jack was too busy to spend time with their son Randy. Jack's work schedule kept him so busy that he spent very little time with Randy when he was home. Faye realized how much their son needed him, but Jack was usually too preoccupied to listen. Faye decided to give the salt principle a try, and here's how it went:

Faye: (salt) "I heard some very discouraging news from school today about Randy."

Jack: "Oh, no, what was it?"

Faye: (more salt) "I don't know what we're going to do about it . . . I'm really worried."

Jack: "Well, what is it?"

Faye: "Unless you can help out, it will probably end up costing us a lot of money."

Jack: "Faye, what are you talking about?"

Faye: (The words *special help* begin to resalt for the next thing she's going to say.) "Randy's teacher called and said Randy has a reading problem. Unless he gets *special help*, it could handicap him for the rest of his education."

Jack: "What do you mean 'special help'?"

Faye: "The teacher explained that if you or I didn't do something about it, we would probably have to pay a lot of money to have it corrected later. She said the longer it goes uncorrected, the worse it will become."

Jack: "What could we do now?"

Faye: (salt) "Well, there's not too much I can do, but she did say there was something *you* could do."

Jack: "What's that?"

Faye: (more salt) "In fact, she said if you would do it consistently, it would provide just what he needs to whip the problem. I told her you were very busy and I didn't know if you could find the time—"

Jack: "I'll make the time . . . what is it?"

Faye: "She said that the basis of the problem involves motor skills. If you could do something like beginning to throw the football with him consistently, his hand/eye coordination would increase and she would be able to help him get his reading up to par."

Today, four years later, Jack still plays football with Randy. Jack not only enjoys their time together, but he also has the satisfaction of knowing that he has done something to help Randy in school that no one else could have done. All of this was a result of Faye's taking the time to creatively communicate a genuine need using the salt principle.

Knowing that you need to arouse your mate's curiosity is one thing, but actually doing it is quite another, right? You're probably wondering, "So now what? How do I apply the salt principle to my circumstances?"

Let's examine the principle a little further to see what it really means.

CATCH YOUR HUSBAND'S INTEREST AND KEEP IT

1. *The first step is to clearly identify the need or concern you wish to communicate to your husband.*

In our first illustration, Lois wanted Mark to learn more about what a woman needs from a man, and, more precisely, she wanted him to read the two books she had just purchased for him on the subject. In the second illustration, Faye wanted Jack to begin spending more time with Randy.

2. *The second step is to identify related areas that are of high interest to your husband.*

This is where Lois failed and Faye succeeded. Lois simply communicated what she was interested in (a happier marriage) but failed to relate her interest to any of her husband's interests. He could not see that he needed any help in becoming a better husband, so becoming a better husband was not of particular interest to him.

Faye, on the other hand, succeeded at this point. She knew her husband's business schedule was of greater interest to him than spending time with Randy. However, she also knew from past discussions that he was extremely interested in their son's education. She identified that interest and remembered Randy's teacher's comments about his reading problem. Since a big part of Randy's problem was his hand/eye coordination, she figured anything Jack could do with Randy to increase his hand/eye coordination would help solve the problem. And then she thought of football. She saw how she could relate Jack's interest (Randy's education) to her interest (wanting to see Jack and Randy spend more time together and also wanting to help correct Randy's reading problem).

Lois didn't have to fail with Mark. Mark has told me that his sexual appetite is much greater than Lois's. That being the case, I am sure Lois was aware of Mark's interest in increasing her sexual appetite. This is the area of *high interest* she could have used to increase his interest in reading the two books. In the next steps I'll show you how she could have accomplished this.

3. *Using his area of high interest, share just enough information to stimulate his curiosity to hear more.*

Since Lois knew of Mark's strong sexual desire, she could have started with the statement, "I can't believe these two books! I began reading them while you were at work, and I started to get so turned-on I had to put them down. I was really wishing you were home so we could make love."

Knowing Mark, I guarantee that she would have had his undivided attention. Even the Super Bowl would have been turned off at this point.

4. *Add a little more salt. Don't answer his response to your first dose of salt; rather, pause and build his curiosity even more.*

Mark probably would have responded to the first dose of salt with the following:

> "You're kidding. What did it say?"
> "Really? Let me see it."
> "It's not too late! I'm home now!"

Now Lois applies her second dose of salt, *without* giving any relief to Mark's budding curiosity: "They really are unbelievable. They tell a man just what he needs to do to prepare his wife mentally and emotionally for sex. Those authors really understand what it takes to turn me on."

5. *Use a short question to gain a commitment to his pursuit of your interest or to teach him what you're trying to communicate.*

Lois, at this point, can gain a commitment from Mark to read this first book by asking him one of several short questions: "Have you ever read a book that tells you the five things women can't resist?" or "Would you like to know five things that turn me on?"

Lois's goal was not to turn her husband into a manipulator of her sexual desires, but to get him to read two books that would encourage him to do the things that would build up their emotional relationship. She knew the "five things" would motivate her husband to treat her with greater tenderness and respect which, in turn, would help her to become more sexually responsive.

6. *After you have taken these five steps, if he still doesn't show sufficient interest or commitment, keep adding salt.*

Lois could further salt with a statement like, "I'm glad you haven't learned any of these yet; my sexual drive would probably get so strong we'd never get any work done around here."

As I said at the beginning of this chapter, the salt principle is irresistible if used correctly. Every aspect of loving and communicating can be used either beneficially or detrimentally—the salt principle is no different. To use it effectively, there are a few things you definitely want to avoid.

WHAT NOT-TO-DO WHEN SALTING!

1. *Do not begin the conversation with a plea or request for his attention or time.*

When using the salt principle, never start the conversation with statements like the following:

> "Can I see you for a minute?"
> "I really need to talk to you!"
> "Can we talk about something really important
>   a little later?"
> "I've been waiting a long time to talk to you. Can we
>   *please* talk tonight?"

Introductory statements like these usually generate a negative response because some husbands can't visualize setting aside time "just to talk." Chances are, you'll only be hurt from his lack of interest. The following dialogue shows a typical example.

Alice: "I would really like to talk to you about a few things after dinner tonight. Okay, dear?"

Fred: "There's a game on tonight that I've really been counting on seeing. Besides, I've got some work to catch up on."

Alice: "Well, how about when you're done? This is really important."

Fred: "Look, I'd like to talk, but it's been a tough day and I'm really tired. Maybe tomorrow."

Alice: "There's always something else . . . you never want to spend time with me. . . ."

And from there the fight is on. Instead of using an introductory statement, start out with a statement that creates curiosity.

2. *Do not start your conversation with your main concern or your solution.*

For example, if Faye had opened her conversation with the statement below, she would have evoked a different response from Jack.

Faye: "Dear, Randy needs more of your time, and throwing a football would help his reading problem. Could you start playing football with him?"

Jack: "I'd love to play with my son, but I just don't have time. You know my schedule."

3. *Don't try to persuade him with your first few statements.*
Some women tend to think the only way they can get their insensitive husbands to do something is to try to shove them into action with a strong statement or threat. This may work for the short-range, but it has no lasting value.

Faye: "Dear, you have to start spending more time with Randy or else there are going to be real problems."

Jack: "Don't tell me what I have to do. I don't have time to play with him and do my job too. Why don't *you* go to work, and I'll stay home all day? Then *I'll* have lots of time to play with him."

DON'T GIVE UP! SALTING REALLY WORKS

If you don't succeed the first time you use the salt principle, don't give up. You may have to use it several times before you become skilled at it . . . but given time and practice, it will work! I've never met anyone who didn't succeed as long as they just kept trying. Surprisingly, it works even if the other person knows what you are doing.

Use the following exercise to help you tailor this principle to some of your immediate needs and concerns.

1. *List four of your current needs or concerns that you would like your husband to understand more fully.*

(For example: a material need, your feeling about someone, an activity you would like to do with him, or a "hurt" that you want him to understand.)

1) _____
2) _____
3) _____
4) _____

EXAMPLE:

1) *My feelings about his mother*
2) *My fear of moving again*
3) *My need for understanding instead of lectures*
4) *My need for more companionship with him*

2. *List five areas that are of very high interest to your husband.*
(For example: hobbies, business projects, career and related interests, religious concern, friends, sports, TV programs.)

1) _____
2) _____
3) _____
4) _____
5) _____

EXAMPLE:

1) *Success in business*
2) *Sexual fulfillment*
3) *Concern for the total welfare of the children*
4) *Acceptance among the men at his office*
5) *Relationship with God*

3. *Write down at least two statements or questions that would create curiosity about one of your four concerns or needs.*
Try to relate it to one of his five areas of high interest.

1) _____
2) _____

EXAMPLE:

1. *Do you know what psychologists say is the greater determining factor in the emotional stability of a child?*
2. *If you and I would decide to work on this together, not only would our children gain emotional stability, but I would probably develop a stronger sexual desire just by being around you.*

She is talking about her need for companionship *and* she is relating it to two important areas of her husband's life—his concern for their children's welfare and his desire for greater sexual fulfillment. In this example, the wife had remembered that she had read that children become better balanced when they see consistent affection and warmth between their parents. She tied all of this together and created two "salty" statements.

The salt principle is undoubtedly the most effective way to gain your husband's undivided attention. Although learning to use this technique does take some practice, once you've mastered it, you will invariably gain his full attention—even if he knows what you're doing. Remember to use this technique with a loving, gentle, kind attitude. If your attitude or tone of voice reflects pride or cockiness, your husband will only resent your attempt to arouse his curiosity. He will consider it a weapon, especially if you use it to create curiosity and then refuse to fulfill it with something like, "Well, I'll just tell you later when you have a better attitude!" I can't think of a better way to immunize your husband against the effectiveness of the salt principle.

With the right attitude, the salt principle is so powerful that it works even when the listener is in a hurry or under pressure. You don't have to wait until your husband is free from tension and deadlines to stimulate his curiosity. Just give it all you've got with salty questions, pleasant facial expressions, and a gentle tone of voice.

TEACH YOUR HUSBAND TO LISTEN TO YOU

By now I hope I've made one point clear: *Most* men do not understand women. Since you know your needs better than anyone else, you can be your husband's most effective teacher. He needs to learn from you *why* it's important to listen to you and *how* to listen.

First, explain why it's important to you that he spend time listening with his undivided attention. (The woman called "virtuous" [also, "excellent"] in Proverbs 31:10 was so called because she had convictions and influence. Convictions bring influence. When you're sold on something, like the importance of a better relationship, it will show through your facial expressions.) Let him know that when he doesn't listen to you attentively, it makes you feel unimportant and unappreciated. Explain that this, in turn, decreases your desire to meet his needs. Make it clear, however, that the opposite is also true. When he consistently listens to you with attentiveness, you feel more important and have a much stronger desire to meet his needs with greater creativity. You may have to tell him these things repeatedly before they sink in. But each time the opportunity arises, you have another chance to stimulate his curiosity.

In addition to explaining *why* you need his undivided attention, you must show him *how* to give it. Discuss the nonverbal means of communication with him. As he learns to understand your feelings by looking at your eyes and facial expressions, your communication and your relationship will deepen. Gently remind him that his partial listening doesn't do any good, that you don't want to compete with work, sports, and TV.

Be careful not to let your times of communication deteriorate into arguments. Use your sensitivity to learn how to side-step issues, words, or mannerisms that ignite an argument. Some women concede that the only way they get their husband's undivided attention is to start an argument. Unfortunately, that's not the type of undivided attention which builds a healthy relationship. Let your communication be as encouraging and delightful as possible.

Learning to gain your husband's undivided attention on a consistent basis will be a major undertaking. However, gaining his attention is not an end in itself. It is a means to develop several beautiful facets in your relationship.

On a recent flight to Los Angeles the pilot announced that a world-famous cheerleading squad was aboard and would be strolling the aisles singing "Happy Birthday" to anyone who had a birthday that month. When they finished singing, I asked if I could interview the married members of the group for a book I was writing. They graciously consented, and I had the opportunity to spend more than an hour with two of them. One had been married for a year; the other had been married for three years. Both were articulate, intelligent, and physically attractive.

I started our interview by asking them what was the greatest single disappointment in their marriages. The answers? Each young woman replied that it was nearly impossible to get her husband's undivided attention unless he had ulterior motives.

I wasn't surprised that they gave the same answer. I have heard it from hundreds of women, young and old, attractive and unattractive. The "inattentive husband" seems to be a universal complaint among women. Both of the cheerleaders said they had given up any hope of seeing a change in their marriages. They had simply resigned themselves to what society says is "only natural."

It *isn't* "only natural," and it *can* be changed! No matter what your situation is, there are ways to gain your husband's consistent, undivided attention. Both of the NFL cheerleaders were excited to learn how to make their husbands eager to listen, and you, too, can be encouraged by the changes possible through use of the next principle.

USING THE "LIGHT-UP" TECHNIQUE

Something about my father attracted me like a magnet. When school was out, many times I would rush to his hardware store instead of going out with my friends. What drew me to my father? Why did I prefer a visit with him over some of my favorite activities? As soon as I set foot in his store, it seemed as if his whole personality lit up. His eyes sparkled, his smile gleamed, and his facial expressions immediately conveyed how glad he was to see me. I almost expected him to announce, "Look, everybody, my son is here!" I loved it. Although I didn't realize it at the time, those tremendously powerful nonverbal expressions were the magnets that drew me to him.

Ninety-three percent of our communication is nonverbal. Your husband can be attracted or repelled most often, then, by your nonverbal behavior. If he comes home from work to a worn facial expression that says, "Oh, brother, look who's home—Mr. Gripe," or "It's only you," then of course he will be repulsed. Whenever you see him, you've got to "light up" with enthusiasm, especially in your facial expressions and tone of voice. That light comes from the inner knowledge that he's valuable.

Norma shows that sparkle whenever I walk in the door, and consequently, I want to spend time talking to her and listening to her. If she "lights up" when a particular subject is mentioned, she increases my desire to talk about that subject; as a result, I enjoy listening to her, her opinions, and her needs.

As a husband "sees" your sincere expressions of his worth, he will be drawn to you (1 Peter 3:1–2).

The students in a psychology class picked up on the powerful effect of "lighting up" when someone is talking. They met after class without the professor and decided to try an experiment. Every time the professor walked close to the room heater (a radiator) they agreed to appear more attentive—sit up straight, liven their facial expressions, take notes more diligently—to look as interested as possible without being too obvious. Each time their professor walked away from the radiator, their interest in his lectures would dwindle noticeably—they would look at each other with bored expressions, slouch in their chairs. Their experiment proved the "light-up" principle. Within a few weeks the professor was giving his entire lecture while seated on the radiator.

While I was in college, I decided to try a similar experiment of my own. I asked my ten-year-old niece, Debby, to make up one hundred sentences using any one of the following pronouns: he, she, we, they, it, or I. I had predetermined that every time she used the pronoun "he," I would make encouraging movements with my body or positive expressions with my face and tone of voice. Each time she used other pronouns, I would sit back in my chair, look bored, and mumble in an indifferent tone of voice.

By the time we reached the fiftieth sentence, Debby was using the pronoun "he" in every sentence and continued to do so until we finished. Unaware of what I had been doing, Debby said she thought I had been checking on her sentence structure. She was unaware of her frequent usage of "he." Since then I have used the "light-up" technique to demonstrate that I am genuinely interested in what others are saying. I've also found that my positive nonverbal communication increases others' interest in what I say.

I encourage you to use this technique to show your husband

how *important* he is. It's an invaluable way to build a more loving relationship.

♥ TO ADD SALT AND LIGHT TO YOUR ♥ COMMUNICATION

This chapter has covered examples of how a wife can use the salt principle to gain her husband's attention, but husbands can use it as well. Like any other good tool, the salt or light-up principle can be abused and used for the wrong motives and in the wrong way. If you use either one, be sure you are sincerely trying to improve communication and not to manipulate your spouse.

When using the salt or light-up principles, start small. All the right questions and phrases won't come naturally to mind without some practice. The key is not so much in what you're saying as in your attitude and goal while saying it. In one sense, the salt principle works best when you say less and don't spill everything that is on your mind. This is what piques the curiosity of your mate and has him or her saying, "Tell me more."

If you try the salt or light-up principles and they don't seem to work, don't give up. Keep at it. If your motivation is right, using either principle can't hurt and eventually you may make a real breakthrough.

Review the examples in this chapter of how to use the salt and light-up principles correctly, as well as "what not to do" when salting. Remember the key to success is to take your time; don't try to "say too much" too quickly. These principles can do wonders to improve your ability to gain your spouse's attention and interest if your goal is to communicate and not manipulate.

Be patient as you use these techniques. They are only tools, not panaceas. Some couples have always struggled to communicate and probably always will. In the next chapter, Shirley Cook shares her own struggle and explains why every bit of it is worthwhile.

Chapter 21

SAY WHAT YOU MEAN

BY SHIRLEY COOK
The Marriage Puzzle

According to some marriage counselors, "true intimacy" is the ability to communicate trustingly, openly, freely, and honestly. This kind of communication is hard to come by for many couples. Take Shirley Cook and her husband for example. In this chapter, Mrs. Cook shares what it's like to love a husband who doesn't talk easily about his private thoughts. As you read, ask yourself:

- ♥ How easy/hard is it for each of us to be open and honest about our deepest feelings?
- ♥ What differences in our backgrounds and temperaments hinder intimacy/real communication?
- ♥ How can I be more consistent in saying what I mean?
- ♥ How does Shirley Cook treat her less communicative spouse? Are there tips here for me?

STRAIGHT TALK

This is a difficult chapter for me to write because "straight talk" is still a weak area in our marriage puzzle. It is not so weak, though, that the entire puzzle falls apart; so let's find out how to strengthen it. Les and I are committed to a lasting marriage, and I say that without a till-death-us-do-part tone to my voice. It's fun. A joy. We love each other and think it worthwhile to make our puzzle pieces fit.

I recently read an article based on Dr. Zev Wanderer and Erika Fabian's book *Making Love Work* (Ballantine, 1982). The tagline over the article read: "True Intimacy Is the Key to Having a Happy Marriage."

I agree with that sentiment in part, but based on my own happy marriage, I would change that from *the* key to *a* key. There are many keys.

Many unique pieces.

Fitting together.

With hard work.

With patience.

With tears.

Marriage counselors report that lack of communication—real intimacy—is the major problem in today's dissolving marriages.

What is involved in intimacy? What does it mean?

Intimacy is *trust.*

It is openness without fear.

It is free expression of hopes, fears, feelings.

It is honesty.

ONENESS IS NOT SAMENESS

For some, openness and sharing come easily. For others, a do-it-yourself appendectomy would be less painful. The important thing we need to realize is that in marriage, just because we are *one,* we are not necessarily the *same.*

Two people come together from different family backgrounds and try to change each other to fit a preconceived idea of what is the "best way."

My way.

To that, add personality or temperament differences. He's the life of the party. She's a homebody. He was taught to bear pain without a word. She was encouraged to get her way by crying. Problems.

On top of both these major differences—background and temperament—is the greatest contradiction of all. He's a man. She's a woman. Marriage is not going to eliminate these differences, but illuminate them.

No matter how loudly "persons" claim to be alike, they are dissimilar. Inwardly. Outwardly.

Dr. Joyce Brothers says in her book *Woman* that if we go into marriage expecting our mates to be like us, we will miss "the companionship of opposites, the mutual enjoyment of natures unlike their own."

Since we are dissimilar in so many ways, how can we accept and grow from our differences?

As a child I was encouraged to talk about my fears, to share my innermost thoughts. I carried this kind of openness into my marriage with the desire to share *all* my thoughts, grievances, and dreams with my husband. I wanted him to know all about me, and I wanted to know all about him.

His background was different. His parents were quiet and refined (I admit mine were rather rowdy), and he spent much of his time alone with his thoughts. Sharing his innermost being was not part of his heritage. He was full of fun and energy. He had a quip and a joke for every occasion, but when it came to his feelings, his hopes and fears, they were kept inside. Private.

"Why don't you talk about your feelings? Say what you mean!"

"Why do you have to tell everything? Can't you keep some things to yourself?"

TWO DIFFERENT EGO SYSTEMS

Often a couple goes into a marriage expecting to find instant intimacy, but we need to realize that into our relationship we are bringing background, personality, and sex. And the greatest of these is sex. Men and women operate from different ego-systems. As a rule, men are not as talkative. When an event is in the past, he wants it to stay there. He isn't interested in discussing the tiny details that so interest a woman.

A man thinks nothing of wading through swamps in the middle of the night to wait for a stray duck to fly overhead, but he hates to wade through a laundry basket to search for a matching pair of socks.

A woman loves to barter and bargain for a reduced price at a garage sale, but she hates to give an account for every penny she spends when it is time to balance the checkbook.

These are general statements, of course, but a mutual appreciation of our likes and dislikes will help us to reach a more intimate relationship.

Time helps, too.

My husband is more open today than he was a year ago, and he will be more so next year. I am more selective in my sharing of thoughts and feelings; my mouth isn't in perpetual motion anymore. In fact, learning to speak less has encouraged me to write more.

I find that writing my thoughts is a terrific outlet. You may enjoy giving that a try, too. Even if you have no desire to publish your words, recording them in a journal can be healing and cathartic. At least when you write instead of speak, you can throw it away if you don't like what you said. Not so with spoken words.

> "I regret often that I have spoken; never that I have been silent."
>
> —Syrus

One couple I know decided after many years of marriage that because they hadn't learned to "communicate," their marriage was a failure. They broke up their home and family, and now both live alone, all hope of intimacy lost. Sad. They had fun together, went to church together, raised three children together. Surely that marriage puzzle was worth saving—even if one piece didn't fit quite right.

FULFILL YOUR MATE, NOT YOURSELF

The emphasis today seems to be on personal fulfillment. Is that really the proper emphasis when it comes to building a lasting marriage?

I don't think so.

Couples become discouraged when they discover they are not fulfilling each other, or if they find intimacy difficult or impossible. "It must have been a mistake," they argue. Or, "We've outgrown our marriage. It's time to move on."

Suppose we reverse this order, and instead of focusing on fulfillment as the major criterion for a lasting marriage, concentrate on commitment. When we determine to stay together our entire lives *regardless*, we will find creative ways to fulfill our mates. And in the process we will build a satisfying and rewarding relationship. A lifelong union.

Intimacy is a key to a happy marriage and well worth working toward, but if you haven't yet reached that kind of relationship, don't use that as an excuse for a failing marriage. Place the blame where it belongs—on a lack of commitment.

My prayer for Les and me is that we will grow closer and closer and one day be able to share freely with each other, but until then, I'll not climb his wall of reserve. Neither will I throw my dirty laundry over it. Dumping on him does not encourage intimacy.

Some days I write little notes to share a deep hurt or concern. This gives him time to think about how he will answer me—coolly and calmly.

Sometimes I see him make a manly swipe at his eyes and I know he hurts, too.

We're learning.

We're growing.

Our marriage puzzle is forming a picture.

Meanwhile, back at the ranch . . .

. . . I need a hearing heart, someone I *can* dump all my problems on, someone who will accept me no matter how stupid, vile, or ugly I may be. I need a friend who will never let me down, never misunderstand my motives, never tell my secrets. Someone never too busy to listen.

But where on earth can I find a person willing to meet me on such an intimate level?

My husband can't be that to me.

I can't be that kind of wife either.

My mother can't.

My daughters can't.

My best friend can't.

They're all too full of their own personalities, their own ideas. They're too human.

Like me.

God alone can supply our deep need for intimacy. He created us with a built-in longing to know and be known. He satisfies that longing with his own desire to be known to us.

King David had a glimpse into the intimacy between God and man and wrote about it in Psalm 139.

I hope you will take the time to read his words. Talk about fulfillment!

> "You perceive my thoughts from afar. . . . You are familiar with all my ways. Before a word is on my tongue you know it completely, O Lord."

God shares his thoughts, too.

> "How precious to me are your thoughts, O God! How vast is the sum of them!"

Intimacy.

> "Search me, O God, and know my heart; test me and know my anxious thoughts."

Do you want intimacy? Then work for it with your mate. Learn to trust and be trusted. Practice sharing your feelings with each other, but don't expect each other to satisfy the greatest need of intimacy. Only God can do that. It's not fair to put such a burden on our marriages.

The marriage puzzle—what makes it last?

A man and woman with nothing between them—but God.

"Lord," wrote David in Psalm 143, "I ask you to 'let the morning bring me word of your unfailing love, for I have put my trust in you. Show me the way I should go, for to you I lift up my soul.'"

♥ EVEN RUBIC'S CUBE CAN BE SOLVED ♥

Think often about Shirley Cook's wise words. Do you want intimacy—real communication—in your marriage? Then you must work for it—intently, tirelessly, patiently. And when the marriage puzzle seems to make a Rubic's Cube look simple, take time to be intimate with God. Tell him your hopes, fears, and hurts. Tell him your gripes; even your less-than-perfect thoughts filled with anger, jealousy, and self-pity. He won't shut you off or punish you, because his Son took all the punishment for sin a long time ago. Jesus not only intercedes for you and your spouse, he can help the two of you learn intimacy—and communication—as well.

Work at talking straight with your mate. Say what you mean rather than playing games or lying. For example:

Wives don't have to whine: "I bought this dress because it was on sale." Instead, simply tell the truth: "I like the way I look in this style, so I bought it."

Husbands don't have to bluster, "I don't have time to mow the lawn today." Instead, they can admit honestly, "I don't want to spend my day off working in the yard. Let's call the kid across the street to do it."

Most importantly, don't give up. On many days it will be two steps forward and five or six back. You will be tempted to get defensive if your mate says things that hurt or frustrate. As serious as your problems might be, they could be worse. When things get bad, think about this story, shared by Shirley Cook.

After a whirlwind courtship, a couple eloped. After a few days, the fact came out that the wife was a snake charmer. The shocked husband asked, "Why didn't you tell me you were a snake charmer?"

"You never asked."

That's lack of intimacy!

Chapter **22**

DO'S AND DON'TS OF GOOD COMMUNICATION

BY ANNE KRISTIN CARROLL
Together Forever

Becoming a better communicator is exemplified in the well-known story about a man who flagged down a taxi on a New York City street and asked, "Quick! How can I get to Carnegie Hall?"

The cabby leaned out of the window and said, "Practice, man, practice."

But skills and techniques are useless unless your heart is right. Master and apply God's principles and allow him to do the changing. Your heart will open to your mate's needs, and as your mate responds to your love by learning to share and listen also, communication will light up your life together. And remember to leave the changing of your mate's communication problems to the Lord. Whatever you do, don't shove this part of the book under his or her nose and say, "Here's something you ought to read." That's a perfect way to kill communication. Instead, try the salt principle.

Following is a list of do's and don'ts, developed by Anne Kristin Carroll, to help you work on verbal and nonverbal aspects of communication. Begin practicing these suggestions on a daily basis until they become a way of life. As you read, circle or check ideas that are especially pertinent to your marriage.

SOME BASIC DO'S OF COMMUNICATION

1. Speak only for yourself, and be direct, clear, and, if necessary, descriptive in your statements.

RIGHT

Husband: "I sure would like to go to a movie tonight."
Wife: "I would, too."

This situation was handled correctly. The husband stated clearly what he wanted to do that evening, and the wife clearly stated that she would also enjoy a movie.

WRONG

Husband: "I sure would like to go to a movie tonight."
Wife: "Whatever you say, dear."

This situation doesn't express the wife's real feelings, her preferences, and it leaves the conversation on a closed basis. The husband is probably confused as to whether she wants to go out, and is most likely irritated about the martyr-type answer she gave.

2. It is risky, but use the *first person* in speaking, because it is honest, reveals your true feelings, and is the best way to establish clear communication.

3. Make your statements and comments *concise*, and state your desires *clearly.*

Wife: "I am *tired of discussing* whether or not we are going to the beach, or going to the mountains. You are so busy pushing the beach idea that you probably haven't heard a word I've said!"
Husband: "I thought you were primarily interested in discussing this vacation until you got your way."
Wife: *"What I am really interested in is being with you.* Whether we are on top of a mountain, or lying in the sand isn't the issue with me."
Husband: "I didn't understand you felt that way. Honey, you're wonderful!"

In this exchange the wife first made a clear statement that she was tired of the discussion. She added that she thought she wasn't being listened to, probably from past experience, since they were new at this type of clear talk. Next the wife stated concisely what she truly cared about, which was being with her husband; the place wasn't the issue with her. The husband *openly admitted* that he hadn't understood, but because both had been clear and concise, the discussion turned out to be a sweet time of coming together, of knowing that being together mattered more than where they were.

4. Learn to listen carefully to your mate. Listening is as important in communication as talking (James 1:19 and Prov. 18:13).

5. If you have something important to discuss with your mate, certainly if the subject is a controversial one, *don't* just open your mouth and let the words begin to flow. Spend time thinking out exactly what you want to say, or ask. Consider the words you will want to use, words that will best express how you *feel,* what you *desire,* or what the *problem* or *situation* is as *you* see it. Run your side of the conversation through your mind to see how it sounds, to be sure it is *clear,* and certainly to eliminate any type of blame or abusive language. "Have you seen a man of hasty words? There is more hope for a fool than for him" (Prov. 29:20 BERKELEY).

6. Carefully select the correct time to open an important discussion. The moment a man walks in the house from work, tired, hungry, and bushed from the five o'clock traffic is not a smart time to begin any type of discussion. If your wife is in the middle of fixing dinner, or the children are crying and calling for her, or she is otherwise harried and tired, again wait. Get to know your mate well enough that you know when it is best to approach him/her. *Never* make the bedroom the place for problem-solving. Decisions, discussions, children, etc., are always to be left outside the bedroom door. Later you will learn about the table of harmony; it may be your solution to a time of sharing. But if it isn't a workable solution for your personal circumstances, then at least don't approach your mate in a negative form, or when he/she is tired, emotionally upset, hurried, hungry, or preoccupied with another problem. *Wait.*

You can share with your mate that you have something you need and would like to discuss with him/her, and ask when it would be convenient for the two of you to have a time of sharing. Be sure that you agree on a specific time; *don't* leave the subject with a vague "later." This leaves both of you uncertain as to when you may engage in the conversation and can cause conflict. Proverbs 15:23: "A man has joy in making an apt answer, and a word spoken at the *right* moment, how good it is!" Keep in mind, if at all possible, Paul's advice in Ephesians 4:26.

7. When you feel there is a problem in your relationship, remember that most problems are created by more than one person. And even if this problem is one you feel you have no direct part in, if it is upsetting you, then *you* are the one who needs to bring up the conversation. The best method to approach your mate at such a time is by saying, "I have a problem," since *you* are the party who is upset. Your mate may have no idea that you feel offended, so if you are disturbed, it is you who must take the initiative. The Scripture in Matthew says you are to go to him and correct the discontent (Matt. 18:15). When you use the right approach, your mate is not likely to feel you are blaming him for the situation.

8. There is a system which you might find very helpful. I like

to call it "statement-restatement." Many disagreements, arguments, and the like begin because what you are saying and what your mate is hearing are *two different things*. To begin the "what I hear you saying" approach may sound and feel a bit silly, but it will help clear up many misunderstandings. The statement-restatement is approached this way. John says, "I really am tired tonight."

WRONG

Carol: "Do I understand you to say that you are too tired to go to Nancy's party?"

John: "No, that isn't what I said. What I said was, I am tired. Period."

Carol: "Then, what I hear you saying is that you are tired, but you still plan to attend Nancy's party, right?"

John: "Right."

In trying statement-restatement for the first time, Carol and John forgot some of the rules and almost had a misunderstanding. Statement-restatement is used to make sure you are hearing exactly what the other person is communicating. On her first try, Carol was constantly *adding* to what John said. This is a *no-no*. So let's give them another chance to see if they have learned the system correctly.

RIGHT

John: "I really am tired tonight."

Carol: "Do I understand you to say that you are tired?"

John: "Yes."

Carol: "Does that mean that you would prefer not to go to Nancy's party?"

John: "No, that is not what I meant. I still intend for us to go to Nancy's party."

Now both John and Carol are completely clear on how John feels, and also on what their plans for the evening are.

9. Be aware of your mate. *Listen* to what he/she has to say. Check yourself out:

- Am I *really* interested in what he/she is saying?
- Do I honestly value his/her opinion, feelings, or wishes?
- Am I honestly encouraging him/her to be more open and free in his or her communication with me?
- Am I being self-centered or other-centered?
- Do my actions express love, giving of myself, or mere toleration of my mate?
- Who is in control of my life? If I am, before we proceed to

conversation, I should use 1 John 1:9 and get back into fellowship with the Lord.

SOME BASIC DON'TS OF COMMUNICATION

1. Don't approach communication, conversation, and discussion with the attitude that there has to be a winner and a loser every time. Communication *shouldn't* involve competition. You are trying to share, to get to know your mate—his feelings, desires, wants and interests—not beat him at a verbal game. When competition enters in, then normally self-centeredness enters with it.

2. Don't be a *blabbermouth*. In other words, don't try to dominate every conversation. Studies prove that more marriages fail where there is too much talk rather than too little. "Self-control means controlling the tongue! A quick retort can ruin everything" (Prov. 3:13 LB).

3. Don't drawl out your story, situation, problem, etc., so slowly that your mate loses interest before you get to the point. Nothing is so boring as listening to every minute detail of something as you anxiously await the "punch line." Be sure you have thought through your conversation and have eliminated the needless details. The longer you talk, the less intently your mate will be listening.

4. Don't speak so fast that your mate can't understand a word you are saying. Rapid-fire speech is an obvious sign of anxiety and insecurity. Not only that, but a negative atmosphere will be produced, and your whole conversation will probably be tuned out. Your nonverbal message is, "I must get through this real fast, because I know you aren't interested in what I am saying anyway, and you aren't going to listen to me very long because what I have to talk about isn't important to you." With this kind of negative reinforcement, you can most likely expect a negative response, even if your mate happens to have heard most of what you have said.

5. Don't try to communicate with the "silent treatment," whichever special form yours happens to take—pouting, sulking, or openly refusing to respond verbally. Obviously, silence precludes your solving *any* problems, sharing any feelings, and at times is a violently hostile weapon used to hurt one's mate. *Marriages can't be mended when you are stabbing with silence!* Silence certainly isn't the example Christ set for believers. We are told in Ephesians 5:2a: "And walk in love—esteeming and delighting in one another." This admonition precludes the "silent treatment."

6. Don't refuse to learn how to communicate correctly. Talking on an intimate basis is very difficult—for some people,

particularly men, because of cultural precondition; for others, because of the home situation in which they were reared. Some fear that they may accidentally reveal their real selves, and either be hurt or rejected. Love *requires* risk; marriage *requires* communication. Ask the Lord to give you the ability to express yourself, your desires, feelings, problems, and ask him to change your fear of intimate communication. You can trust him. He will never put you in a situation which, through his strength, you can't handle.

7. Don't let your emotions run away with you when you are conversing, either in tone of voice, facial expression, or through tears. These are not honest ways to try to make your wants and wishes known. These tactics cut communication short, because they either turn your listener off, or they require a response to your emotions instead of to what you are attempting to communicate. In other words, this means that the listener is no longer dealing with the message you desired to share but with your emotions. There are *rare* exceptions to this rule—for example, sharing the serious illness of a loved one, a serious problem outside your marital relationship, or the death of a dear one. When Christ is in control, your emotions will be also. If you need to cry, don't do it in the presence of your mate. You may have found that you often get your way when you start crying, but don't fool yourself; tears are confusing and frustrating to men; they don't know how to deal with them, and usually give in only to stop the flow. *The problem between you hasn't been solved; you have just postponed it until the next time.* And in time you won't have enough tears to cover the resentment you have created in your husband, because he will realize that he is being manipulated.

8. Don't generalize when you are trying to make a point. Generalizations are a hindrance to *clear* communication—for instance, "Everyone does it," or "Women are all alike." Such comments mean nothing, because everyone *doesn't* do whatever you are talking about, nor are *all* women alike. This type of approach makes your *real* point unclear and clouds your message. Your mate will either tune you out or miss your point when you fall into the trap of generalities. Making comparisons is spoken of in 2 Corinthians 10:12b: "However, when they measure themselves with themselves and compare themselves with one another, they are without understanding and behave unwisely."

9. Don't butt in—interrupting is rude. Important points may never be completed, and it is certainly a good way to wreck communication and build walls of hostility between you and your mate. "A fool hath no delight in understanding, but that his heart may discover itself" (Prov. 18:2 KJV).

10. Don't allow certain topics to be off limits in your discussion. There *can't* be any of "those subjects that we just can't discuss" in the intimate relationship of marriage. If you are both

maturing in Jesus Christ, and he is in control of your lives, he does not war against himself, and you *can* freely discuss anything. When a couple admits having "certain subjects" that they just can't discuss, what they are actually saying is that some areas of their life together are so weak that a discussion might break the whole relationship. If this is true, these areas should be turned over to the Lord. You won't always agree when you finally get around to discussing these "untouchable" areas, but first see what God has to say about whatever subject is the "silent" one between you and your mate. Let his Word guide you.

11. Don't speak negatively to your mate. Remember, you'll gain more ground with honest praise, love and adoration than with a critical spirit. If you are allowing the Holy Spirit to guide you, peace and joy will radiate from your face. *Please* remember your motivation is *most* important. You *don't* bestow praise, arrange a congenial atmosphere, etc., because you "feel" like it or to achieve a selfish end. *Every* action, plan, or outreach to or for your mate should be done "as unto the Lord." God speaks of a positive, happy mental attitude in Proverbs 15:15: "When a man is gloomy, everything seems to go wrong; when he is cheerful, everything seems to go right!" (LB). "Gentle words cause life and health; griping brings discouragement" (v. 4 LB).

12. Don't expect perfection, in yourself or in your mate. If you blow it, admit your mistakes; your mate never expected you to be perfect anyway.

13. Don't ride a horse to death. Once you have discussed a subject, once you both have contributed all that you currently know, and once you have checked the Scriptures to see how God would have you deal with it, then if you can't find a clear concept or principle in the Word, *wait*. Turn the subject or decision over to the Lord and seek his leading. Read 2 Peter 3:9: "Keep your tongue from evil and your lips from speaking deceit, turn away from evil and practice good: *seek peace* and *keep after it*." If you continue to discuss a dead-horse subject, most likely one or both of you are trying to get your own way, and you will fall into the sin of quarreling, from which bitterness and hostility grow.

14. *Don't bring in your past or your mate's past*, especially when you are dealing with a subject which could be controversial. Deal *only* with the two of you; leave the relatives, the dog, the neighbors, and everyone and everything else out, *period!* Clear-cut discussions are often drowned in a tank of other people, and a digging-up of old bones which should have been left buried. Proverbs has a multitude of things to say on this subject: "Do not contrive or *dig up* or cultivate evil against your neighbor, who dwells trustingly and confidently beside you" (3:29). "A worthless man devises and *digs up* mischief, and in his lips there is a scorching fire" (16:27). And last but certainly not least: "He who

covers and forgives an offense seeks love, but he who repeats or harps on a matter separates even close friends" (17:9).

15. Don't be underresponsive—you have *equal* responsibilities in communication. If, when you talk together, you are carrying on a monologue because your mate isn't shouldering his share of the load, be patient. In time, when you learn the happiness and enjoyment that intimate conversations can bring, you will begin to trust and respond, but remember, *let Christ* do the changing, *let Christ* do the motivating, and don't expect a Bob Hope overnight!

16. Don't be a judge; be an example, a Christian example. "Why do you criticize and pass judgment on your brother? Or you, why do you look down upon or despise your brother? For we shall all stand before the judgment seat of God" (Rom. 14:10). Read for yourself Luke 6:41–49. Philippians 2:5 also admonishes us to be a Christlike example: "Let this same attitude and purpose and (humble) mind be in you which was in Jesus Christ. Let him be your example in humility."

17. Don't expect to move from no conversation, idle conversation, and silence to deep intimacy in a matter of days. Don't quit after the first try. Just keep on trying and keep on praying that the Lord will open your mate's heart, help break down the barriers and walls that you both have erected over the years, and teach you the beauty of true verbal communion. As you begin, keep Ephesians 3:20 in mind. It is a powerful pledge, and one which should excite you by the promises it holds for you personally.

In your heart, between you and the Lord, you know where you have built walls instead of bridges. Just confess this to the Lord (1 John 1:9) and ask him to direct your path and make his will for you personally clear, claiming Proverbs 3:5–6. Don't wait till you "feel" differently. Do as God has commanded you to do; be the right kind of marital partner, and the "feelings" will follow the correct action. Become other-centered, become a listener as Christ was, become a giver, get to truly know your mate, and leave the wall-wrecking to God. Begin today to apply God's concepts; use Christ as the supreme example of a communicator and a listener, and watch as Christ moves in and begins to make the changes in *you* that, if at all possible, will ultimately draw your mate out and unite you as God intended the day you said, "I do."

IN THE OTHER'S SHOES

The beginning of true love is caring enough to listen deeply enough that self is eliminated and you can "walk in your mate's shoes." Paul talks about this in 1 Corinthians 9:19–27. Only openness can bring a couple to true understanding of the other. To commune on this level takes time and work, but most of all it takes love and care.

When you have developed your relationship to this point and a misunderstanding arises, you might try role-reversal-playing. Each of you verbally assumes the role of the other, and does his best to explain how and what the other feels and desires about a given situation.

For instance, a situation like this might arise in your home. Jim has been on the road all week. He comes in tired. The phone rings. It's Bill, who wants us to go with him and Barbara to their mountain cabin for the weekend. Jim readily responds to the invitation. The idea of the quiet solitude of the mountains, the cabin overlooking the lake, is appealing. When he gets off the phone, he excitedly shares the plan with me. Of course, since he has been gone, he has no idea that I planned to go to a conference for marital and family counselors the next morning. What to do? We switch roles and discuss how we think the other feels. I begin by saying what I think Jim feels: "I have had so much pressure on me this week, the idea of staying in town, having to talk with customers on the phone, is just more than I can take. The mountains relax and refresh me, and I hardly ever get a chance to fish and boat. Anyway, I really enjoy Bill's company, we have a lot in common, and the whole experience is like an escape into a slower, less complicated time."

Then Jim takes my position: "I had no idea that you would have plans for the weekend. You usually play golf on Saturday mornings and I thought that this would be an ideal time for me to take in the conference. More and more people are coming to me, questioning me, relying on my knowledge to help them with their family and marital problems. I feel very responsible to take in all the Christian counseling training I can. When I am at the cabin, you and Bill are usually out on the lake anyway, so I don't feel you'd miss me too much if I didn't go. Of course, I would really like to be with you, and I hate to disappoint Barbara and leave her with the total responsibility of taking care of both of you, but on the other hand, I feel I must attend the conference, since I have already committed myself to it. I guess you all can just make do without me."

Now each of us has tried on the other's shoes and walked a bit. We can now discuss what to do about the weekend. Jim finally comes up with a perfect solution. He suggests that he and Bill go ahead Friday night, and that Saturday noon, after the conference, Barbara and I drive up to the mountains in our car. He says, "You know, I'd like to have our own car up there anyway, because I'd like to drive over to Highpoint on the way home. I know how much you love the waterfalls. Sunday afternoon we can pack a lunch before we leave and just spend a quiet time together, picnicking."

SOME DO'S OF BODY LANGUAGE

Beyond what you say, the clarity of your statements and the time you pick to discuss your problems and desires, there are two other things which come into play in complete conversation and communication: the tone of your voice, and "body language."

1. Speak softly, clearly, and in love. "A soft answer turns away wrath" (Prov. 15:1). Studies show that in a one-to-one conversation, the softer the voice, the more attention the listener pays.

2. Your face should be as relaxed as possible, smiling if the occasion calls for it, certainly showing interest and attention to your mate.

3. If you are standing, face the person you are talking to. If you are sitting, sit in a relaxed position, with your body directed toward your mate. Face-to-face arrangements indicate that a couple is ready to talk on a one-to-one, intimate basis, whereas a side-by-side position reveals a cool neutrality.

4. Look into his or her eyes. If you have picked the correct time to talk about a problem, your feelings, any situation, then obviously your mate won't be watching TV, or have his nose stuck in a newspaper. The eyes are one of the most important modes of communication we have.

5. Sit close to your mate. Don't smother him, but perhaps pick up his or her hand and hold it gently as you share your thoughts, hopes, dreams, problems, and feelings.

6. Be sure you have privacy when you want to communicate on a personal level. Either send the children outside to play, or be sure they are fast asleep.

7. A relaxing setting is conducive to more intimate, open conversation. Soft background music might set just the right mood in which to begin.

SOME DON'TS OF BODY LANGUAGE

1. Don't raise your voice to make what you feel is a vital point. Don't speak in monotones, which give your mate the feeling of being neutralized. They are dull and death to interesting, stimulating communication.

2. Don't frown, fiddle with things, look at your watch, or wear a blank, disinterested look on your face. These nonverbal cues say, "I am not interested in what you have to say, and I want to get this conversation over with."

3. Don't sit on the couch beside but not facing your mate while he is talking. This lets him know that you are tense, and would like to escape the conversation and the situation.

4. Don't neutralize your mate's conversation by looking at everything in the room but him. *Your insecurity* is really showing

when you avoid eye contact, and it doesn't make for a healthy relationship or communication. The nonverbal giveaways are: "I'm scared" or "I'm not interested" or "I don't care." All are negative signals.

5. Sitting at a distance when involved in a serious or intimate conversation is simply telling your mate that you would prefer that there be distance in your relationship.

♥ CHOOSE A TIP AND WORK ON IT ♥

The foregoing pages contain some thirty-eight ideas for better communication. Don't try to use all of them at once. Do try to use one or two of them immediately. When you master those, move on to others. The result can be a marriage like John and Richie's, described briefly but beautifully in the final chapter of this section.

Chapter 23

"I LOVE YOU, JOHN"

BY RICHIE WADSWORTH
Excerpted from *The First Years of Forever*
by Dr. Ed Wheat and Gloria Okes Perkins

For forty years, the marriage of John and Richie Wadsworth grew rich in love and intimacy. Then the X-rays gave their grim verdict. Here is a short, short story of a long life of communication and the beauty of being able to communicate when it counts the most. Richie wrote about it afterward, and we asked if we could share it with our readers who are just beginning their journey together.

"I LOVE YOU, JOHN"

Basically we were the same persons who had, for forty years of marriage, been together, laughed, teased, made decisions, argued, agreed, and cried together. We had stubbornly said, "I love you," even when we didn't like each other much. We had said it passionately, contentedly, reassuringly, proudly, and "just because."

Communication was open when cancer invaded our lives, because communication had been kept open during our years of marriage.

Illness didn't change our ability to laugh and kid around. We reminisced lots. We cried unashamedly. Most of all, we communicated every thought we had. Fear was never present because Christ was at the center of our lives and he had removed fear on the cross for us. We marveled at that.

Sometimes the medicine gave John fantasies when he slept; usually they were not disturbing ones, but mostly he would be traveling. One day he said, "It is so strange, but I was on this trip and in this house that was mine, and yet not this one; and in this room that was mine, and yet not this one—"

I interrupted. "Well, you're going to be taking a trip and—" Together we said, "In my Father's house are many mansions . . . I go to prepare a place for you."

Communication made our last days together rich. If it hadn't been building through the years it wouldn't have been there for us to enjoy in the last days of our life together.

In the middle of the night, Friday, I came back in the room with fresh water. When John heard the ice tinkle in the glass, he turned his head and smiled. I said, "Hey, I love you."

He groped for my hand with his left hand, because by this time the bone in his right arm had disintegrated, pulled my hand to his lips and said, "I love you too. Oh my, yes!"

I had prayed so much that John would not lose his ability to speak and God had granted my desire. We had talked about the fact that if we hadn't been open and loving all these years, the last days of our life would have been too late to start.

Saturday and Sunday, the voice I loved became a whisper, but still I communicated and as I held his hand and his quiet breathing stopped, he stepped over the threshold and I was saying, "I love you, John."

♥ TO KEEP COMMUNICATION FLOWING ♥

The goal of this section of "The Marriage Collection" has been to make you aware of how vital communication is to your marriage and how to do it better. No matter where communication with your mate is at the moment, it can improve if you begin to practice what you have learned in the previous chapters. And don't get discouraged if it seems silly or awkward. One reason certain skills or principles may be difficult is that you are used to doing the wrong things and you need to start practicing the right ones. Instead of building walls, you want to build bridges to your mate and you can do this as you use the dozens of suggestions given.

One more thing: Don't try to master all these techniques at once, and don't be in a hurry. Undergird all your efforts with constant prayer. Allow Christ to change you, always keeping Philippians 2:3, 4 in mind: "Live together in harmony, live together in love, as though you had only one mind and one spirit between you. Never act for motives of rivalry or personal vanity, but in humility think more of each other than you do of yourselves. None of you should think only of his own affairs, but should learn to see things from [your spouse's] point of view" (PHILLIPS).

Mastering the art of communication is a lifetime job but, as you work to keep the lines open and flowing, your marriage gains strength, depth and intimacy. There is, however, one major stumbling block in your way: the feelings of anger and frustration that come when you face the inevitable times of disagreement and confrontation. Part V is devoted to how to use communication skills to work through these difficult times.

COMMUNICATORS ARE GROWN, NOT BORN

She is changing and growing and becoming. Time does not stop for her. Like a tiny computer, she is being programmed each moment of every day for what she will be the rest of her life. Bit by bit her daddy and I are filling her heart and soul with pieces of ourselves. And these pieces are being stored away in the depth of her little being.

Through affection
through love
through patience
through understanding
through belonging
through doing
through being—
    Thus a child learns

Day by day the child comes
to know a little bit of what you know,
to think a little bit of what you think,
to understand your understanding.

That which you dream
and believe
    and are
In truth—becomes the child.

How much can this small hand hold?
    Not much really.
But her heart?
    It can hold all of ourselves and more.[23]

PART V

ANGER:
TURNING A DEADLY ENEMY INTO A FRIEND

Do you agree or disagree?

The most important task for any married couple is to learn how to manage anger.

Perhaps you disagree because "The most important task is achieving intimacy and loving each other unconditionally."

Or you may be disagreeing along these lines: "That's not a problem for us. We never get angry with each other."

And a third possible protest could be: "Naming the most important task for all married couples is impossible. It depends on where they are in their relationship."

All of these are good answers, but the question remains: How important is managing anger in a marriage?

Dr. David Mace and his wife, Vera, who have been married for over fifty-five years rate their marriage a happy one and enjoy a close relationship. As marriage specialists, the Maces have always earnestly tried to "practice what they preach." But Dr. Mace admits that the early years of their marriage were not as close and intimate as they could have been. In fact, he says, "By comparison with what we now enjoy, our marriage in the earlier years was relatively superficial."[1]

In more than five decades of teaching about marriage and being married himself, Dr. Mace has gained significant insight in areas like relational growth, the communication process, the creative use of conflict, and especially the positive role that anger can play in close relationships. Unfortunately, anger seldom seems to help a relationship, but only erodes or destroys it. Dr. Mace believes that every married couple must learn how to handle anger if goals like intimacy and unconditional love are to be achieved. Dr. Mace's basic assertions, definitions and principles concerning anger include the following:

> Being married and in a family can make you angrier than any other kind of experience.
>
> When other situations (certain friendships or working relationships) continually make you angry, you can break them off, ask for a transfer, or avoid the problem in some way. And if none of that works, you can always develop a "skin of indifference" toward the other party to make the relationship tolerable. But in a marriage, you can't ask for a transfer; and indifference doesn't build love, it destroys it.
>
> When a marriage breaks down or ends in divorce, it always happens *from the inside.*
>
> "Problem areas" in marriage are generally thought to be sex, money, in-laws and child-rearing, to name a few. But these are not the real problem. All of these areas are only the arenas in which the inner failure of the marriage relationship is being played out.
>
> A close relationship fails from within always for the same reason: because the husband and wife are unable to achieve mutual love and intimacy.
>
> Their failure to achieve love and intimacy is almost always due to one thing: they are unable to deal creatively with anger. Everywhere husbands and wives, children and parents, become alienated from one another because they don't understand how to process their anger correctly.
>
> It is possible (not easy) to learn productive, creative ways to use anger so that it reinforces, instead of destroys, love and intimacy.
>
> Anger is not a sin. It is an emotion that serves as our basic survival kit, providing lifesaving resources when our very existence is threatened.
>
> A simple definition of anger is: "Any feeling of displeasure directed against the person (or object) accompanied by a desire to remove the cause."
>
> Anger is an automatic emotional response to any threat or negative stimulus. Your brain responds with a state of anxiety and your body mobilizes for action with changes in heart rate, blood pressure, etc. This process happens with tremendous speed and is well engaged before your conscious mind comes into play. The onset of anger, therefore, is not volitional—not your idea. You are not responsible for being in a state of anger; you are only responsible for what you do with your anger after your conscious mind has taken over. That is why anger cannot be sinful. Anger can be used to commit sin, but that is a different matter.

There are four possible responses to anger: fight, flight, freeze or relax. Any of these responses might be legitimate as long as they are under your control.

All marriages operate on a love/anger cycle that includes having differences and disagreements which can lead to conflict. As a couple seeks love and intimacy, they find many areas where they support and reinforce each other. If all their living patterns did this, they would have no conflict, but no two people ever want to do the same thing in the same way at the same time. Differences, therefore, are inevitable and disagreements are inevitable. Conflicts, however, are not inevitable. At least theoretically, because a disagreement can be resolved without anger.[2]

Because understanding anger and how to deal with it are so vital, the first two chapters of this section will feature several excerpts from Dr. Mace's book, *Love and Anger in Marriage.* You will not only learn how to deal with anger, but how to work through disagreements, confrontations, and conflicts in a positive, productive way.

In chapter 24, Dr. Mace recalls the problems he and his wife had with anger early in their marriage and steps they took toward a solution.

In chapter 25, Dr. Mace explains the typical nonproductive ways most people deal with anger: *venting* it or *suppressing* it. A much more productive way to deal with anger, however, is to *process* it and use it as a positive force to build more intimacy. Dr. Mace explains how to do this through a "Plan for Your Marriage" which he has introduced to thousands of people over the years.

In chapter 26, Dr. Ed Wheat and Gloria Okes Perkins (*The First Years of Forever*) tell you how to avoid WIN/LOSE arguments and replace them with real communication when resolving disagreements and conflicts. Included are six ways a discussion goes wrong, eight ways to replace arguments with communication, and tips on how to fight the biblical way.

In chapter 27, André Bustanoby (*Just Talk To Me*) gives additional tips on how to process anger and disagreement by using "I" messages as well as active-listening.

In chapter 28, Dean Merrill (*How To Really Love Your Wife*) deals with one of the most dangerous communication killers in any marriage—money. Making a budget work is not primarily a matter of putting the right numbers in the right columns. A budget is often a challenge to communicate that will call for the use of plenty of active-listening and "I" messages.

There are no easy answers or sure-fire formulas for handling conflict and disagreement, but there are ways to do it more productively. At the risk of repetition, the key is keeping anger in check and processing it in a positive way. Seneca, the Roman philosopher, once said, "The greatest cure for anger is delay." In other words, "Count to ten." But Seneca was wrong. Counting to ten is useful, but then you must take the next step and deal with why you had to count to ten in the first place. That's what these next chapters are all about.

It is the intermittent fever which bespeaks unintermittent disease within; the occasional bubble escaping to the surface which betrays some rottenness underneath; a sample of the most hidden products of the soul dropped involuntarily when off one's guard; in a word, the lightning form of a hundred hideous and unchristian sins. For a want of patience, a want of kindness, a want of generosity, a want of courtesy, a want of unselfishness, are all instantaneously symbolized in one flash of Temper.

Hence it is not enough to deal with the Tempter. We must go to the source, and change the inmost nature, and the angry humors will die away of themselves. Souls are made sweet not by taking the acid fluids out, but by putting something in—a great Love, a new Spirit, the Spirit of Christ.[3]

Henry Drummond

Chapter 24

IT'S OKAY TO BE ANGRY IF ...

BY DR. DAVID MACE
Love and Anger in Marriage

It won't happen to us," the engaged couple says. "We'll never fight because we love each other too much." But as David Mace points out, couples fight for exactly that reason—they love each other very much. In the following excerpt, he shares the early encounters he and his wife had with anger and how they moved quickly to find a solution. As you read this chapter, keep these questions in mind:

♥ Do either you or your spouse deal with anger by withdrawing? Why does this give only temporary relief?
♥ Do either you or your spouse deal with anger by venting—"letting it all hang out"? Why is this seldom productive in the long run?
♥ What is the key principle in the three-step plan that the Maces put into action to develop better communication while dealing with anger?
♥ Have you ever thought about dealing with anger by "processing" it? Does it sound like a worthwhile concept? Why or why not?

GETTING ANGRY MAKES ME SICK

I was aware of a rapidly developing state of tension. Somewhere in my chest, or down in the pit of my stomach, I felt a tangled knot that was giving me pain. There seemed to be a rapidly accumulating mass of hot, poisonous material somewhere inside me. I was not conscious of any urge to attack Vera physically, but I was certainly clenching my fists and trying to keep myself under control. At the same time I was aware of a devastating sense of alienation and disillusionment because I was actually feeling hate toward the person I wanted, of all people in the world, to love.

My overwhelming urge was to disengage, to get away—out of Vera's presence—so that I could somehow deal with these frightening emotions which she seemed to be generating in me. My whole world seemed to be collapsing, and my impelling urge was to escape, to hide somewhere until I could begin to cope with the tumult within me.

This desire to escape dictated the policy I adopted at that time. Without explanation, I would make a hasty exit. Then, in isolation, I would try to calm my confused and heated emotions, striving to see the incident in clearer perspective and to balance it out with more positive feelings. As time passed, I would slowly calm down, get myself tidied up, and then return in the hope that our original good relationship could be restored.

Vera remembers that I was often gone for long periods of time. She had, of course, been made aware that something was wrong. Sometimes she could guess what it was, but often she had no idea what had happened to me. She concluded that I was a very "moody" person, and she had no idea how to respond to me. She wanted to talk with me about the situation, then or afterward, but she sensed that if she tried to do so, she would "rock the boat."

Her judgment was certainly correct. If she had tried to probe into the cause of my withdrawal, I would have responded negatively. Why? Because I feared that if we reactivated the issue that had caused my anger, the anger itself would also be reactivated, and I would be back where I had started. So, on the basis of an unspoken agreement, we put the situation behind us and proceeded as if it had never happened. Thus, we were reconciled—but only until the next anger situation erupted.

I am reporting only my side of the picture. Vera is "slower to anger" than I am, but she *can* become very angry, too. When she did, the "silent treatment" was her usual response.

We were not, however, willing to accept this situation. Although at that time we were unable to communicate directly about it, we were both unhappy and wanted to find a solution. This led me to a study of the psychological literature about hostility and aggression, which I'm afraid didn't prove very helpful. However, I did become convinced on one point. I learned that psychologically it is healthier to vent anger than to suppress it. (I still believe that to be true, though it can have dangerous implications.)

Anxious to find a solution, I decided to put this "venting" concept to the test. At first it was hard for me to stay with Vera and confront her, but I learned to do it. The inevitable result, of course, was that when I attacked Vera, she defended herself. And since the best form of defense can often be counterattack, we were soon getting into fights. As Vera puts it, "I waited till he was out of breath and then launched my offensive."

These were entirely verbal fights, but they were very painful to us both. One distinct advantage was that the issue was now out in the open, and we both knew exactly what was going on. Otherwise our arguments and hassles produced little in the way of positive results. Then Vera sometimes cried, and that made me quite miserable and prevented any further communication about the issue. In the end we made up, and that was a pleasant relief, but little or nothing was accomplished in the way of improving our relationship.

Now we faced a crisis. It was clear that we would go on getting angry with each other from time to time; and it was equally clear that we had found no effective or constructive way to deal with our anger. This just didn't satisfy us. We believed there must be a better way.

Fortunately, by this time we were in the process of trying to improve our communication system. This made possible some calm, serious discussions about our inability to deal with our anger. And by way of further exploration, I had begun to study the *physiology* of anger—the bodily changes it brought about, and how these could be modified in certain circumstances.

MOVING TOWARD A SOLUTION

We now began to see anger in a more positive light. We recognized that it was a normal, healthy emotion which was evoked in certain circumstances and, when rightly responded to, could serve useful purposes. I realized that most of the psychological literature I had read was concerned with anger as a response to attack from a hostile source, a way of dealing with an enemy. But Vera and I were not enemies, and didn't want to be. We were friends and lovers, and anger between us seemed alien and out of place.

After much thought and discussion, we began to move toward a solution. Finally, after a good deal of experimentation, we devised an arrangement which, over the years, has proved highly effective.

Step One was an agreement that we would *communicate* our states of anger to each other as soon as possible, and hopefully before they could lead to unpleasant consequences. This was based on our conviction that anger was a healthy emotion which was trying to tell us something about ourselves and our relationship. We accepted as perfectly normal the fact that, in a close relationship, we would from time to time get angry with each other, and we gave each other full and free permission to do so. That really cleared the air and freed us from guilt.

We were greatly helped at this point by our understanding of the psychological dimension of anger, which I will discuss in detail later. We saw that it should be as natural to say to each other, "I'm angry," as to say, "I'm hungry," "I'm tired," or "I'm depressed." All are physical states.

Step Two was a pledge we made to each other that while it was okay to be angry, it was definitely *not* okay to attack the other in response to that anger. We saw that no gain of any kind could come from launching an attack. In fact, we used a vivid analogy which dramatized the situation for us: we made a contract that we would stop spitting at each other! We saw the venting of anger as a psychological equivalent of spitting, and we saw no justification for this between people trying to develop a loving relationship.

This agreement provided a valuable safeguard. If I knew that Vera was angry with me, but knew also that she would not attack (however much she felt the urge to do so), I had no need to develop retaliatory anger and launch a counterattack. This provided a reasonable hope that we would not both be angry at the same time, so that normally one of us would remain calmly objective and in control of the situation.

While these two steps could be counted upon to keep us in communication and to prevent the possibility of fights, they were not of themselves, enough. The anger, though now acknowledged and safeguarded from being vented, was still there. It was real and painful, and demanded action. So something further was needed.

Step Three met this need. We made a contract that every anger situation that threatened our relationship would be *worked through by both of us* and *owned by both of us*, not as a personal weakness in the one who was angry, but *as a function of our total relationship*. In Step Three, the angry person requested help, and the one toward whom the anger was being directed gave assurance of a response.

The concept behind this was new to us, but of vital importance. It was a way of looking at anger which made our process work. I had often heard people say, "Your anger is yours, and you must own it and take responsibility for it." I had even heard it said that, "You make yourself angry—nothing and nobody else is responsible." This concept, of course, led me to withdraw from Vera, taking myself and my anger away and trying to deal with it alone. But that didn't work—because it was based on a misconception. While I alone have to deal with my anger against the motorist who drove me off the road, or the teacher who gave me the low grade, or the coach who dropped me from the team, in a *close* relationship, the anger of either against the other is a function of the total relationship and *can be processed positively only by both acting together.*

So we adopted a policy that every anger situation between us was, in fact, an opportunity for growth in our relationship and must be dealt with accordingly; otherwise, we were missing a valuable chance to achieve a deeper understanding of ourselves and of each other. In other words, anger is not something evil to be avoided or suppressed. It is not even something inconvenient to be disposed of so that we can get back to the business of living. It is, properly understood, *raw material to be used* in the positive development of a better and more secure relationship.

Anger is a secondary emotion—triggered by another emotion, deeper down. By getting back to the underlying primary emotion and dealing with it, that particular source of anger can be cleared up and removed.

When we sat down together after an anger situation and processed our anger, Vera and I discovered that this was always the case. And always we found either one of two situations. In the first, it turned out that I was angry with Vera for something I *thought* she had said or done to me; but when we really examined the situation, it became clear that I had misunderstood or misinterpreted the message I thought I received from her. In the second situation, Vera was angry with me for provoking her; and I had indeed, accidentally or intentionally, pushed her beyond the limits of her tolerance. By working through the situation, I began to understand how much tolerance Vera really had, and she learned what kinds of pressure pushed her over the edge.

ADVANTAGES OF PROCESSING ANGER

Most importantly, we were steadily gaining confidence that we were now able to deal constructively with anger when it inevitably developed in our relationship. As time passed, we found that we had examined the major causes often enough to be familiar with them, so that if and when they recurred, we knew we would deal with them. And, of course, many of them stopped occurring, because we adjusted our behavior, and our interpretation of each other's behavior, so that the causes were finally removed.

We didn't expect that we would stop getting angry with each other. But since occasions for anger were being reduced and we were more confident now that we could cope constructively with anger when it *did* develop, our relationship was freed from any fear that anger could do us harm. This enabled us to take down defenses against each other that were no longer needed. Thus we became able to make ourselves vulnerable to each other without any fear of exploitation.

We have now come to understand that such vulnerability

makes intimacy possible and removes the major hindrance to the growth of love in a close relationship.

This way of processing anger has made a marked and very welcome difference in the quality of our marriage. We don't say it is easy to do—it takes times and involves, at first, a good deal of work. But the rewards are tremendous.

Although we have not attempted to collect data of this kind on any systematic scale, we have evidence from other married couples that they have put these principles into practice and found them to be effective. And, of course, there may be other approaches that work equally well, or better, for some couples. All we claim is what we have personally experienced.

The primary test for us has been in our marriage, but we have also made ventures in using these procedures in other relationships. In any social relationship, if those concerned understand what is involved and are ready to make the necessary commitments to each other, the same good results should be possible.

♥ ATTACK THE ANGER, NOT EACH OTHER ♥

If you and your spouse are at a place where you can work productively together on dealing with conflict and anger, sit down and talk about how to implement the three-step plan described by Dr. Mace. Keep these principles in mind:

- ♥ It's okay to be angry—in fact, it's perfectly normal to be angry, especially in a close relationship like marriage. Don't wallow in guilt over your anger.
- ♥ While it's okay to be angry, it's not okay to attack each other. The key to this plan is to agree not to attack each other, but to work on the anger instead.

Make the same kind of contract that David and Vera Mace made: Agree to work through every anger situation, with both of you *owning the anger* as a function of your total relationship. (In other words, banish the phrase, "That's your problem," from your vocabularies.)

The following chapter describes a plan the Maces have used and taught successfully for many years. It explains how to process anger creatively.

Chapter 25

A WIN/WIN PLAN FOR PROCESSING ANGER

BY DR. DAVID MACE
Love and Anger in Marriage

Do happily married couples ever fight? In their study of three hundred marriages that have lasted fifteen years or longer, Jeanette and Robert Lauer (*'Til Death Do Us Part*, Hayworth Press, 1986), discovered that all of the couples they interviewed had times when they irritated one another, fought, and even considered divorce. Their secret to staying happily married was not avoiding conflict, but dealing with it through the art of "good fighting."[4]

According to the Lauers, destructive conflict is the typical WIN/LOSE battle. One spouse outtalks, outshouts, or outhits the other. Another destructive type of fighting is LOSE/LOSE, when both partners emerge from an argument feeling defeated and depressed.

But there is a third kind of "conflict" that sees the partners fighting *for* their relationship and not *against* each other. It's called WIN/WIN and the goal is to make both spouses feel they have gained ground, made their point, were heard by the other person, and remain friends and lovers at the same time.

Studies show that husbands and wives may use as many as five different fighting styles when settling disagreements: competition, avoidance, compromise, collaboration, and accommodation.

When you use the competitive style, you have a high concern for yourself and a low concern for your mate. This is the classic WIN/LOSE approach, pure and simple.

If you prefer the avoidance style, you don't have much concern for yourself or your mate. You prefer "not to talk about it." Nothing gets settled and in many ways this style is more damaging than competition. Avoidance is the LOSE/LOSE approach and can destroy a marriage quickly.

The other three fighting styles are all examples of a WIN/WIN approach to disagreement. When you compromise, you have concern for yourself and your mate. You stand up for your rights, but you are always ready and willing to give a little to achieve harmony.

When you collaborate, you operate 180 degrees from avoidance. With an even higher degree of concern about yourself and your mate, you negotiate to find creative solutions to problems.

And if you are a believer in accommodation, you tend to neglect your own interests and give in to your mate. You aren't an avoider—that is, you still engage in "combat," but in the end you always go along with what your partner wants.[5]

All of these approaches and fighting styles are ways of dealing with anger. In the following chapter, Dr. David Mace finds three typical ways people deal with anger and outlines a plan for WIN/WIN "fighting" that focuses on processing anger rather than allowing it to pickle your marriage in the brine of malice, ill-will and hostility. As you read, ask yourself:

♥ What is my approach to disagreement or conflict? WIN/LOSE, LOSE/LOSE or WIN/WIN? Would my spouse agree?

♥ What is my favorite fighting style? Am I out to protect our relationship, or just defend my own ego?

ANGER ISN'T A SIN

If anger in itself is not sinful, but offers raw material for growth and change, how do we go about using it for this purpose? Any two people angrily confronting each other as adversaries have, theoretically, four choices. In practice, however, this may not always be true, because by the time they get into a conflict, the way in which they will behave is almost certainly predetermined by the pattern of interaction they have already established between them. Also, only three of those choices are available to a married couple, because they have taken the step of involving themselves in a shared life. I will, however, refer briefly at the end of this chapter to the fourth choice—the process of *dissolving* anger by detaching yourself from the other person and deciding that the relationship is simply not worth being angry about!

Let's take a look at a couple, John and Mary, caught in a distressing situation, and consider some options for dealing with their anger.

THREE WAYS TO DEAL WITH ANGER

Venting Anger. As we have seen, the condition of being angry is a state of readiness to commit an act of aggression. In marriage this is likely to be motivated either by fear or by frustration, or by a mixture of both.

John may fear that Mary will use the occasion of her parents' proposed visit to make him change by giving up his easygoing, untidy pattern of behavior; or he may fear that her indignation will goad her into telling other people, particularly her parents, that he is a sloppy, irresponsible individual. However, it is much more likely that he is frustrated and irritated because this present situation is disturbing the normal easygoing pace of his life. He is probably annoyed because Mary has so far been reasonably tolerant of his pattern, but now she is suddenly taking a very critical view of it. Certainly he is blaming her parents as the cause of this disturbance, even if innocently so. He is wishing they would cancel their proposed visit, and he is tempted to punish Mary by being really mean to them if and when they do come. He is stubbornly determined not to let Mary use this situation to gain control over him, and he has resolved not to act submissively in response to the dominant role she has assumed. He is ready to fight her on that issue.

Mary, for her part, is anxious to prove to her parents that she has made a good marriage and chosen a good partner, but she is afraid that if John doesn't put on a better performance they may conclude that she hasn't done so well, after all, or that she has been unable to improve John's behavior in an area where they know that she herself has high standards. She is frustrated because John isn't willing to change his behavior, at least while her parents are with them, and thus support her. She fears that his unwillingness to do this may reveal that he doesn't love her as devotedly as she hoped he would, and this makes her feel that maybe after all she isn't as great a prize to him as she had imagined. Mary is, therefore, feeling somewhat insecure, but doesn't want to show this in case John interprets it as weakness and despises her for it. She has doubts as to whether she is going to win him over, but she is determined not to give in easily. So she also is prepared to put up a fight, though not at all sure that she is going to win.

If they do have a fight, what is likely to happen? Mary may keep up the battle for a time but then cry with vexation, which is a good way of shutting off all further discussion and making the other person feel like a heel. John may fall for this and make a few concessions, unwillingly, but in order to end an unpleasant experience. The issue will then be set aside, but is likely to recur at a later time. They will both be hurt, and not much will have been achieved.

Suppressing Anger. This is the policy of avoiding the issue—"Peace at any price," or "Just forget it." All difficult or painful situations are swept under the rug, and nothing ever gets openly and honestly settled.

If John follows this course, he may suggest to Mary that they should avoid getting into an unpleasant situation that will only make them both mad. He may suggest that they talk no more about it now, because doing so is only making them upset. He may say in a half-hearted way that he'll try to be a bit less untidy, and then do nothing about it, or make such small improvements that they are just about back where they were before. He may suggest that they forget about the whole thing and offer to take her out to dinner to cheer her up. In one way or another, he will probably act evasively.

If Mary takes this line, she may stop pressing John to change and seem to drop the whole question, but inside she will feel martyred and decide to take up her cross and bear her burden with fortitude. Though she really feels mad at John, she will swallow her indignation, give him the silent treatment, and become more obsessed than ever about tidiness in order to demonstrate that, although *he* won't cooperate, *she* intends nobly to keep the flag flying. She will probably have a splitting headache and ask John to bring her an aspirin.

Processing Anger. If they are fortunate enough to adopt this course, John and Mary will agree to sit down together, now or later, and look at the whole situation as objectively as possible. Each in turn will share with the other just what is going on in his or her inner thoughts and feelings. They will ask for feedback from each other to make sure that their messages are getting through. They will avoid any accusations of each other, sharing only what they are personally feeling and what they would like to have happen. When they are sure that all their feelings are out in the open, they will try to list all possible options and then narrow down their choices to the one on which they can reach the highest level of agreement.

Consider some possibilities: John might agree to be exemplary while the parents' visit lasts, in return for a fair exchange in the form of something Mary is willing to do for his benefit. Mary could agree to examine her rigid attitude to tidiness, which might be unreasonably compulsive and could be a source of real trouble later when there are children scattering playthings in the home. Along the same line, they might agree on defining a "halfway house" policy, with John tightening up his standards somewhat and Mary relaxing hers. Whatever they decide, it would be an experimental solution to be watched and evaluated again from time to time.

What processing anger does is to say in effect—"We got angry with each other, and we need to find out exactly why. Anger is a secondary emotion, usually triggered off by one or more underlying primary emotions. Let's try to explore our anger to get back to the primary emotions—fear, frustration, lowered self-esteem, hurt feelings, etc.—that produced the anger in the first place. Then let's see how we can help each other work through those deeper feelings. And let's follow through on this from time to time and check to see if we're making headway."

In other words, anger will never be sinful if we learn to make it the servant of our love and use it creatively to promote the growth and enrichment of our relationship.

Two analogies may be helpful:

1. Anger is like the smoke-alarm signal in your house. It warns you when there is danger and enables you to take appropriate action.

2. Anger is like the squeak in the motor of your car, which tells you something needs to be fixed. Attend to it, and the car will run better than ever. Ignore or avoid it, and you may end up with a breakdown on a lonely road on some dark and stormy night.

We may not assume that John and Mary have, in one of the three ways open to them, dealt with the crisis with which they were confronted. But we must not conclude that the issue that caused the crisis has therefore been settled. Moreover, this is only one issue. There are plenty of other areas in their relationship which are capable of creating new anger situations. So unless they understand the process of working through and adjusting their differences, and unless they use wisely the skills they will need for identifying and dealing with the areas where close contact with each other is sure to produce aggressive impulses, they are going to be denied the opportunity to achieve the loving, warm, and intimate relationship which both of them, in their hearts, earnestly desire.

In that critical process of growing together, anger should be their most reliable guide. It will identify accurately for them each new area of adjustment on which they need to work, and this will enable them to carry out together the growth process that will make their relationship more and more rewarding as the years go by.

But if they believe that anger is an enemy, and not a friend, how will they fare? If they choose to deal with their anger either by venting or suppressing it, what chance will they have of processing their feelings, identifying their unmet needs, and together developing a cooperative approach to their growth as individuals and as a couple?

The answer, alas, is that if John and Mary lack these insights and the skills they make possible, their chances of achieving a really good relationship, in which they develop their full potential for love and intimacy, will be poor indeed. In this they will not be at all exceptional. Perhaps ninety percent of all married couples are living well below the level of their relational potential. If present rates continue, about forty percent of all couples presently married (in the U.S.) will ultimately divorce. If we assume that ten percent will achieve their full potential, with or without help or guidance, that leaves fifty percent unaccounted for. A good many of these marriages, although they will not break up, will achieve mediocre relationships, and some of these will be deplorably poor. We need to remember that the alarming figures about battered wives refer to marriages that are still intact—it isn't easy to go on battering a wife from whom you are already separated.

Obviously the root cause of family violence lies in accumulated anger which piles up to explosive proportions. Once we understand how much anger the marriage relationship generates, and how little guidance and help couples receive about dealing with it constructively, family violence is not at all surprising. The tragic fact is that most of it could be prevented by training couples to understand and use the resources I am trying to make available in this book.

DIFFERENCE AND DISAGREEMENT

Because of its vital importance, let us review, in more detail, what John and Mary need to know and to act upon.

First, they need to accept the fact that *there are differences between them which are capable of bringing about a clash of wills.* There is nothing wrong or unfortunate about that. It occurs in *all* marriages—even when husband and wife come from very similar backgrounds. No two people are entirely alike; and if such people existed and married each other, the marriage might turn out to be rather dull.

It would make sense for any couple, as they move into marriage, to identify the differences between them that are sure to cause them trouble, to make a list of them, and to take time to explore thoroughly their potential for troublemaking. For example, I am a person who likes to live at a pretty fast tempo—moving ahead and getting things done; while Vera is a much more contemplative person who just cannot be hurried. This difference has given us endless trouble, but we have worked on it steadily through the years. I have learned to be much more relaxed, while Vera is now a usually punctual person in managing time and keeping appointments.

Second, John and Mary need to understand how, *under certain conditions, differences will become disagreements.* When they want to do things together, to get close and share their lives more deeply, they must reduce their living space and become more confined. It is exasperating that becoming more intimate should increase and intensify our areas of disagreement, but it is a fact of life that has to be faced. Intimacy is not a free gift—it has a price.

Third, John and Mary should recognize that disagreements are really hard to settle in ways which respect the freedom and personhood of both parties. *As a disagreement is confronted, it can very easily heat up and become a conflict.* The heat, of course, is generated by anger—all the bodily changes we have already described. Once anger has taken over, the relationship is really in danger, and no effective solution can be reached until the aggressive impulses have abated. To aid in this cooling-down process, it may be advisable to give each other more space temporarily and return later to address the issue. As a marriage counselor I have often advised that as soon as one member of a couple is aware of unmanageable emotional tension, he or she should raise the right hand as a silent signal to disengage; both should then, without any spoken word, go to different rooms and not resume communication until the angry partner is calm again. Of course that is not a resolution of the conflict—it simply takes the heat out and avoids exchanges that would be damaging and unprofitable.

An issue can seldom be helpfully handled while it remains hot. The first rule in dealing with a conflict is to take the anger out. In a state of hot anger it is impossible to be loving, caring, and understanding because you don't really hear your partner, you only see your own point of view, and you want your own way. Hot anger and objective thinking just don't go together.

FINDING SOME ANSWERS

The concept of growth in relationships appeals to many couples. In their heart of hearts, these couples know that their relationship has not turned out as they had hoped, and the idea that it could still do so reawakens for them a dream they had given up. However, when they realize that their goals in marriage, as in anything else, can be attained only by learning a set of new concepts and then working hard to put them into practice, discouragement often returns. Yet some are ready to make the commitment to ongoing growth when they see clearly the areas they must work on and the precise nature of the task. These areas, of course, differ from one marriage to the next, and each couple must find out for themselves just what their agenda is. Over and over again, we have found that they cannot do this until effective communication has been opened up between them. So, after they have made a commitment to growth, the couple should get training in couple communication.

Although effective communication is a major milestone on the road to better marriage, it is not the final destination. We used to think that if a couple could communicate effectively, they were ready to get on with the job of enriching their marriage. Now we know that this is not necessarily so.

Many couples, faced with the need to communicate in greater depth, find themselves blocked. Why? Because when they begin to open up to each other, they reactivate old, unresolved conflicts, and this becomes very painful to them. As they try to grapple with these issues, they find themselves in disagreement, and then anger develops and heats it all up. At that point they are in danger of giving up and sinking back into lethargy. The field of marriage in our culture is, regrettably, littered with shattered dreams and abandoned hopes. The roadblock that is preventing millions of couples from realizing their legitimate expectations for a happy and successful marriage is their inability to process their anger in any effective manner.

A PLAN FOR YOUR MARRIAGE

In this chapter, therefore, I want to suggest a specific course of action that Mary and John might follow in order to develop a really successful marriage. I will talk to them directly, and to any other couple willing to listen.

A good way to begin would be to find out about the marriage enrichment movement. There are books to read. But books can only give you *ideas;* it is *action* that will really bring growth. So after some basic reading and discussions, it would be very helpful to participate together in a marriage enrichment event. Quite a number of national organizations are now offering programs in this field. The value of an experience of this kind is that it puts you in touch with other couples who are also working together on their marital growth; it also gives you an *experiential* rather than an informational introduction to the field of marriage enrichment.

Beware, however, of those who suggest that the marriage enrichment weekend will perform some miracle that will change your life. It won't. Nobody's life ever changed in a weekend. You may get the mountaintop vision of the way you want to go, but you have to follow through by taking the long road, a step at a time.

To make it as clear as possible, let me suggest that you give yourselves at least a year to get well started on a new course. By the end of that time, if you have really taken it seriously, you should see enough difference in your relationship to prove to you that it works. Accept this as a challenge if you like. You have nothing to lose.

HOW WE LEARNED TO PROCESS ANGER

The program I offer you is what Vera and I have already carried out and are continuing to follow. It involves more than just processing anger; but we have found that the processing of anger is the key that really turns the lock and opens the door.

In the year ahead, I would suggest that you make your utmost effort to do three things; pledge to each other now that you will do them faithfully together:

1. *Get together every day for a "sharing time."* I can hear you say, "How can we ever, with the pressures now upon us, squeeze out more time for something like this?" My answer is that Vera and I, often with very heavy schedules, can't afford *not* to have our sharing period. The time it *saves*, by not later having to clear up misunderstandings and get back in touch with each other, alone makes it worthwhile, quite apart from the positive gains it brings.

Actually, it needn't take a lot of time. Indeed, it shouldn't. It is *not* a time for general conversation, catching up with each other's news. It is *not* a time to report to each other on projects. It is *not* a time to work together on issues in your relationship. It is *not* a time to exchange ideas you may want to discuss.

What, then, is it? *It is a time to tell each other just what you are feeling right now.* No more, and no less, than that.

What good will that do? Try it and see. You'll be surprised. Most married couples just don't report their feelings to each other. They report where they went, what they did, who they met, how they interpret their latest news, what needs to be done, and so on. But their hopes and fears, their excitement and anxiety, their joy and sorrow, their pride and embarrassment, their apprehension, their feelings of inadequacy, and their *anger*—these, in most marriages, are seldom really shared, and then only casually. But these are the really important things about us, and certainly these are the things that need to be known and understood and shared by people who love each other.

Let me be quite specific. Twenty minutes in a day will be enough if you get right on with it. Each should take a turn—about ten minutes will do. Just relax and listen to the voices coming up from your inner self, the voices that are telling you where you are right now, which is what you and your partner need to know. Without self-awareness, you are not in charge of your own life—it's as simple as that. And without other-awareness you don't know where your partner is, and in consequence you don't know when to comfort, when to support, when to praise, when to help—the very things loving people do for each other.

Try this experiment. Each of you, separately, take a sheet of paper. In ten minutes write down every feeling you can identify— positive or negative, strong or weak, physical, emotional, aesthetic, spiritual. If you're in touch with your inner self, you should in that time identify eight or ten feelings. Put them all down. If there is one you *can't* write down, ask yourself why. (It's particularly important to share "pinches" you have had in the last twenty-four hours. I'll explain this in detail later. It's the way to catch anger situations before they can get out of hand.)

Now get together and share all the feelings you have recorded. Don't discuss them or analyze them. *Just report them.* Then go over each other's list and find out how many of these feelings you would have known if your partner had not shared them. Then you'll begin to see why you need a daily sharing time.

Just *when* you have your sharing time doesn't matter, but it should be an *uninterrupted* time. We have ours first thing in the morning. Some couples have it last thing at night, or any time in between. Make it *pleasant*—over a cup of coffee, relaxed. But keep on doing it until it becomes a habit. Vera and I are now agreed that we would soon be out of touch with each other if we didn't do this *every day.* After a year, my guess is that you'll feel the same way about it.

2. *Make time to work through every issue that brings any kind of tension into your relationship.* This should *never be done in your sharing time,* though issues do come up then. Schedule a specific time for a major decision, a serious misunderstanding, an anger situation. It's a matter of keeping your relationship clear of clogging, disturbing, confusing, painful situations. The golden rule is: "Keep nothing on the back burner."

I am referring, of course, to issues in your relationship that could alienate you if they are not cleared up. Face the fact that *you just can't afford to be alienated.* It costs too much in time, effort, hurt feelings, foolish actions, bad decisions, and misunderstandings.

Clearing up an issue is top priority. It justifies skipping a meal, losing some sleep, revising your schedule, canceling an engagement. The warmth and closeness of your love relationship is the powerhouse in both your lives, and if the power gets cut off, everything else is soon out of action. If you need to be really alone together, the cost of a night in a motel is a very worthwhile investment. If you find you can't cope alone together, bring in another trusted couple, or see a marriage counselor. But *don't drift apart and get alienated.* That can be the beginning of the end.

3. *Join a growth group with other couples, or start one of your own.* One of the most exciting discoveries I've made in recent years is that couples are really good for each other. I'm not referring to those dull, formal social get-togethers where everything is elegant and lavish and the conversation is utterly trivial. I mean a group of couples who are committed to sharing their experiences of

marriage in order to help and support each other in growing closer together and enriching their relationships.

I have already referred to a myth which I call the "inter-marital taboo." It says, "When married couples get together, they must never, never, never tell each other what's going on in their relationships." It goes back to the time when people lived in small villages and had to safeguard their privacy. Today, it's a tragic barrier which prevents couples from sharing with other couples the most important things in their lives. We can testify that when couples relax the taboo and share honestly where they are, it can bring a marvelous sense of closeness and mutual support. So get into a couples' group if you can. We call it a support group, and the couples normally meet regularly (usually once a month) in each other's homes.

Don't fall into the trap of making it a "discussion group" or a "study group" based on a book (even this book!). That's all head stuff and won't get you very far. When a real support group meets, we each report just where we are in our relationships right now, and we share our joys and sorrows, our hopes and fears, our growing edges. Soon couples are identifying with each other, learning from each other, helping each other, caring deeply about each other.

Well, that's the program for a year. And when the year is over, plan for the next year. If you've used the time right, my guess is that it will be more of the same.

ACT ON THE PINCH!

In conclusion, let me satisfy your curiosity about something I said earlier—about "acting on the pinch." Psychologists have now realized the importance of catching anger as early as possible, before it piles up. How does it start, and can we stop it there?

Consider John and Mary again. They are talking together. Suddenly John says something that gives Mary a twinge of pain. John may have done it intentionally, or he may not. Anyway, Mary feels hurt, put-down, demeaned.

What John did to Mary was a pinch. If he had pinched her physically, she would have recoiled and moved away out of reach. In just the same way, she now shrinks back, though not visibly. A tiny wave of resentment, annoyance, indignation pulses through her. This is a pinch—the first faint stirring of anger and alienation.

What should Mary do? She may say to herself, "After all, it's a very small twinge, and really not important. Is it worth mention-ing?" She decides that it isn't. The conversation flows on, and the pinch is ignored.

Next day, Mary does something that annoys John. Again, it's

only a mild annoyance, but it's a pinch. He says nothing since it hardly seems worth mentioning.

But evidence shows that pinches *are* worth mentioning. Each tiny experience of alienation is in itself of little importance. However, add them all up, day after day, week after week, and they can cause a couple gradually, almost imperceptibly, to drift apart. Their love cools.

Now suppose these pinches are acted on. Mary shares with John her reaction to what he said. He shares with her his disapproval of what she did. These responses must not be made harshly or critically, but gently, with an honest desire to understand. They talk it over quietly together. That may be enough. Or they delve deeper and discover something they hadn't previously been aware of. They decide to do something about it, and both feel comfortable and reassured. Instead of a small alienation, there is a small reconciliation. Both feel a new confidence because these small irritations can be openly shared, examined, and cleared up. Over time, dealing with pinches gradually brings a couple closer together. And there is no chance for small angers to accumulate and become big angers.

So learn to be free to say "I feel pinched." It may not be necessary, or convenient, to say it right away. Here is the value of the daily sharing time. Often it is easier to say, "I felt pinched yesterday, and I'd like to share it with you." Then describe what happened. No further discussion may be needed, unless it raises an issue to be investigated and cleared, and that should, of course, be done at another time. What is important, though, is that *all pinches have to be shared within twenty-four hours*, so there can be no buried resentment festering and poisoning the relationship, ending up with a major crisis.

We sometimes talk about an "intentional" marriage. We mean simply that the couple is working for the improvement of their relationship, with a specific, agreed plan and goals clearly stated for, say, a year ahead. They are not drifting, rudderless, like ships at sea with no clearly defined destination. As the years pass they check off goals that have been achieved, and then set new goals.

It's a good way to live. But you can't make it happen by wishing it would, or by dreaming about it, or even by talking about it together, though that's a good way to start. Even having the *intention* isn't enough in itself—the road to hell, somebody once said, is paved with good intentions!

There has to come a time when, being convinced, you *act* and act *together*. If in reading this book you have been convinced that you see new possibilities for your marriage relationship, you should understand very clearly that this will make little difference unless conviction is followed by appropriate action.

♥ FIGHT FOR YOUR MARRIAGE, NOT AGAINST IT ♥

As Dr. Mace says, books like this one can only give you ideas. But it is action that will really bring growth to your relationship. If possible, try his suggestion to attend a marriage enrichment weekend of some kind.*

Also be sure to try the plan for relational growth that the Maces use. Get together every day for a sharing time, even if it's only for a few minutes. Go over the steps and see how it goes. The key is to work through any issue that brings tension to your marriage. Don't wait until you are "really angry" to do your fighting. Instead, engage in the "good" kind of fighting that works for your marriage and not against one another.

You can't get enough training in the WIN/WIN approach to marriage. In the following chapter, Dr. Ed Wheat and Gloria Okes Perkins give you over twenty ideas for the kind of communication that leads to compromise, collaboration, and accommodation—all WIN/WIN approaches to working out differences and disagreements.

---

*To obtain information on marriage enrichment activities in your area, write to: Association of Couples for Marriage Enrichment (ACME), P.O. Box 10596, 459 South Church St., Winston-Salem, NC 27108.

Chapter 26

COMMUNICATION INSTEAD OF WIN/LOSE ARGUMENTS

DR. ED WHEAT AND GLORIA OKES PERKINS
The First Years of Forever

Whenever you and your spouse wind up in a WIN/LOSE combat, communication goes down to defeat. As one marriage researcher observes, simply to "talk" is not enough.[6] "Let's talk" can quickly turn into "Let's fight."

Couples in long-lasting happy marriages emphasize two important tips for communicating when disagreements or conflicts start to arise: *reciprocity* and *self-control*.[7] Reciprocity calls for talking *and* listening, a skill already discussed in detail in Part V. Self-control means keeping your cool.

"Experts" may get on talk shows like Donahue or Oprah Winfrey and confidently advocate "venting" as a good way to deal with anger, but they don't always tell the whole story. "Letting it all hang out" may do you some temporary good, but it does little to strengthen your relationship with your spouse. A student once said to his professor, "I lose my temper, but it's all over in a minute." His professor answered, "So is the hydrogen bomb!"[8]

But there is a better way. In this chapter, Dr. Ed Wheat and Gloria Perkins show you how to stop win/lose arguments before they can start by knowing what causes them and replacing conflict with positive, productive communication. As you read, ask yourself:

♥ How many of these tips apply directly to *me?*
♥ How can I change my communication style to avoid arguing and do more communicating?
♥ If it does turn into an argument or a fight, do I know how to fight the biblical way? Am I willing to keep it clean?

SIX WAYS A DISCUSSION GOES WRONG

Why is it that differences of opinion between husband and wife so often lead to arguments and a breakdown in communication? Usually the differences are not life and death matters. They aren't even right and wrong matters. Just different ways of seeing things or handling a situation. At such times the couple's communication skills are tested. Here are some of the ways the conversation may go wrong.

A War to Be Won. The disagreement becomes a war to be won—a power struggle. But the fact is that no one wins in an argument. Your goal should be to win by reaching an agreement or an understanding, while maintaining your good feelings for one another.

A Personal Rejection. The disagreement is taken as a personal rejection. Unfortunately, people often confuse rejection of their ideas with rejection of themselves. You can benefit in marriage from bringing your varying viewpoints together and discussing them, finding a solution, and gaining a deeper appreciation for one another at the same time.

A Change of Weapons. People change the subject and drag in other issues to use as weapons against their partners, instead of limiting the discussion to the original disagreement. As soon as one feels attacked and reacts with defensiveness, communication and loving intimacy are on the way out the door. If you want to avoid this and resolve the issue, agree ahead of time to discuss only the matter at hand. Let the law of kindness be on your tongue. The Bible says that words can pierce like a sword, but the wise tongue brings health and well-being.

Sweeping Generalizations. People, frustrated by their inability to make their point, resort to sweeping generalizations characterized by the use of these expressions: "You *always* . . ." and "You *never.* . . ." These are "fighting words" and there is almost no adequate response to them. The temptation is to stoop to the same tactic and argue, "I do not!"

Shouting or Siberia. People sometimes respond to disagreements in even more inappropriate and childish ways. One wife wrote us, "I wish my husband could discuss a matter without shouting. He seems to think that talking loud and fast is the only way to communicate." A husband told us, "My only option is to agree with my wife on every point. Otherwise, she sends me to Siberia for weeks at a time."

Yes, But. . . . People often pull out this prize communication-stopper: "Yes, *but* . . . ," which simply escalates the argument. Once we recognize how thoroughly annoying and disheartening this reaction is, we can choose to learn other ways of responding when we disagree. Here's how: Refuse to use those two words in combination again. Learn to make your point differently, beginning with a favorable response, such as "That's an interesting way of looking at it. I hadn't thought of it that way." Or, "I see what you mean." Move right on smoothly into your point, presented as a question, "Do you think that . . . ?"

In other words, present your original reaction in the framework of a measured and respectful response to the other person's idea by taking it seriously. Then tactfully offer your question in such a way that it is not regarded as an attack or a put-down. The discussion begins without ever using a "but," and your partner will feel more like rethinking the issue because you have recognized the validity of his or her position.

All these childish attempts to "win" the disagreement can be changed, if there is a genuine desire to learn to communicate. Excitable people can learn to talk more slowly and calmly, to take deep breaths while they are talking, and to stop to listen. People who pout, who use the deep freeze to express their displeasure, can learn that open, honest discussion has its rewards. Most importantly, marriage partners can learn to appreciate the peace (the restfulness), which comes when they respect one another's right to hold different views and to express those views in a calm discussion.

When a disagreement occurs, it's important to defuse its explosive potential by reducing what's at stake. When your attitude changes from a win/lose, I'm right/you're wrong position to a "Let's talk this over, but it doesn't affect our love and respect for one another" perspective, you've won the real battle. Here are some principles to follow.

EIGHT WAYS TO REPLACE ARGUMENTS WITH COMMUNICATION

Response, Not Reaction. Don't interrupt. Listen carefully before you respond. Don't react. Respond. Keep the discussion squarely on the issue at hand. You need to agree, long before disagreements arise, that you will limit any discussion to the present, leaving the past out of it, and limit the discussion to the one issue, refusing to allow side issues to enter in.

Disagreement, Not Disapproval. Acknowledge that you understand what your partner is saying, even though you disagree. Show him or her respect. Don't let your disagreement of this issue sound like *disapproval* of your partner.

The Gift of Empathy. Make it a point to share your feelings, but not in such a way that your partner feels criticized. Encourage your partner to share his feelings and respond to them lovingly. Give him or her the gift of sympathy and empathy. This is one way to teach each other to give what you both are longing for.

Carefully Clarify. Carefully clarify what you are both saying so there can be no misunderstanding. Take turns doing this, with no interruptions.

Truthing in Love. Speak the truth in love. The original expression in the New Testament (Eph. 4:15) is literally *truthing in love*— maintaining truth in love, both with your speech and with your behavior. Honesty and love are needed, so speak the truth but speak it gently.

Say "I need you." Be willing to show your vulnerable, needy side to your partner. Don't be afraid to say "I need you." Sometimes we want to conceal our feelings to protect ourselves, but when you begin communicating, you learn the value of being honest, even about your own weaknesses. Real communication means revealing yourself even at the risk of rejection. When both are willing to do this, you are well on your way to building loving intimacy in your relationship.

Surprise and Disarm. Stop being defensive when the issue is a personal one. Surprise and disarm your partner by agreeing there is wrong on your side, since there always is (even if you don't wish to admit it). Be specific. "I was wrong" can stop a fight and demonstrate to your partner how to admit wrong, too.

Apply the B-E-S-T. Apply the B-E-S-T principles in your communication. As you talk with each other, *bless* with your words; *edify* (or build up) your partner by what you say and by your interest in what your partner has to say; *share* openly and honestly; and *touch* affectionately while you talk. *Bless, edify, share, and touch*— communicate the BEST to your mate.

You can reduce tensions by recognizing and correcting the communication practices that cause frustration and by learning to fight the biblical way—a way that deals constructively with anger, resentment, and hurt feelings.

RECOGNIZING THE FRUSTRATIONS

We have already mentioned many of the communication practices that cause frustration. Here are five "deadly sins" in communication, which can blight any relationship:

SHUTTING DOWN: Not listening.

SILENT TREATMENT: Not talking.

STABBING: Using the other's words against him/her.

SCOLDING: Putting guilt, blame on the other.

SHALLOW LIMITS: Surface talk only.

WHEN SILENCE IS A SIN AGAINST LOVE

We need to take another look at one of these sins against love, for that is what they all are. The "silent treatment" as a punitive measure may be the most hurtful of all. It makes us feel unloved, even despised, and it taps into old childhood fears of being abandoned and helpless. To be shunned by the person we love severs the links of trust, which are so necessary for an intimate relationship. In short, it is one of the most destructive things a person can do to a marriage.

> Silence is often used . . . in a power struggle. . . . The with-holder often feels powerful for he can manipulate both the feelings and behavior of the other. This is a favorite ploy in the "something-is-wrong-but-I-will-NEVER-tell-you" game. Some-times a fierce competition takes place and the goal is to see who can hurt whom the most. If the competition is in the form of who can be the coldest and most uncommunicative, breaking the silence becomes a sign of weakness. . . .
>
> Silence can be passive-aggressive behavior, which is indirect, covert, and camouflaged hostility. The hostility is never dealt with openly and, therefore, often feeds on itself and becomes greater. Because the silence prevents hostility from being overtly recognized and dealt with, alienation may result, which is more destructive than fighting.[9]

THE MESSAGES WE MISS

Alienation leads to more alienation. The more distance you've placed, the more likely you are to miss or distort messages transmitted between you. Considering the delicate and complex nature of the hundreds of messages sent and received in a day's time between husband and wife, with words comprising only seven percent of what is communicated (the rest coming through tone of voice, body language, and even more subtle factors), is it any wonder that misunderstood messages can seriously damage an already shaky relationship?

The Five-Second Pause. Take this example: The wife asks her husband, "Do you really love me?" The husband waits five seconds and answers, "Of course I do." Every woman knows the important part of that message: the five-second pause. It changes the husband's answer from reassuring to ambiguous and unsatisfying.

The Silence of a Closed Door. There is another sort of painful silence when a partner will not go beyond shallow conversation. It is the silence of a closed door. When this silence refuses the other's entrance to his heart, the relationship becomes empty, seemingly dead in the water.

> To be silent about one's deepest feelings in a marriage often leads to a dead space in which there is nothing to communicate.[10]

This problem will require loving persistence, patience, and prayer, but unconditional love does have power to open doors. The reward for both partners will be a growing and deepening love as they allow themselves to become known without self-imposed barriers.

OTHER FRUSTRATIONS

Here are some other frustrating communication practices:

1. *Pretending you are communicating, when you're merely attacking your spouse.*

2. *Not knowing how to express your feelings without putting each other down.*

3. *Stating your views as though they are the absolute truth.* (There's the old proverb, "One who is too insistent on his own views finds few to agree with him.")

4. *Not hearing the message from your partner because you're too busy figuring out what to say next.* You can take it as a general rule that you will never be able to send messages successfully unless you are also paying attention to receiving them.

5. *Faking attention, but not really listening.* This is dangerous business. Faking attention with a glassy-eyed stare while you're thinking of something else will trip you up, and your partner will be understandably insulted. Researchers say that good listening is accompanied by a slight rise in temperature, a faster heartbeat, and a quicker circulation of blood. In other words, listening is not a passive activity! You should establish eye contact, think while listening, and not only concentrate on the words, but observe the nonverbal behavior of the speaker. All of this must be integrated into the meaning of the message.

6. *Trying to communicate when you have two different goals for the conversation.* For example, when a wife pours out her

problem to her husband, she may not be looking for an instant solution. Her husband, who views himself as a problem-solver, gives her a quick way to handle the problem, and then becomes frustrated when she does not appreciate his brilliant solution. She's equally frustrated because she needed just to talk with him about it and to feel his support and understanding. But he says, "Okay, if you don't want my help and don't want to take my advice, then don't talk to me about it." So they are both disappointed. She wants to be listened to and empathized with. He wants to be respected for his ability and smart thinking. Neither is getting what he or she wants!

It's best to know the initial purpose of the conversation. The one who is being approached should be sensitive to the other's needs and goals for the conversation. If necessary, ask in a tactful way. Body language, tone of voice, and facial expressions will tell you a great deal.

Usually, the wife will be more relationally oriented, and the husband more data-oriented. He doesn't realize how short he sounds when he asks where the tax file is. He just wants to get the job done. She is more concerned about relating to her lover and feels surprised and wounded by the curt, businesslike edge to his voice. The result may be a minor crisis in which fence-mending, for that night at least, becomes more urgent than filing the tax form.

This illustrates one of the most frustrating areas of communication in marriage—the difference between men and women.

7. *Husband and wife communicate differently, and this can lead to misunderstandings and mutual exasperation.* At a national seminar session on communication, the speaker suggested that men are outclassed when it comes to verbal facility. Women talk better. They develop the language earlier and are more skillful in its use.

He also said men are more linear in their thinking, moving from a to b to c, while a woman can surround the subject from nine directions. And she is usually more concerned with "people" issues.

The speaker said he had discovered firsthand from his wife that women will repeat the same thing several times to their husbands because to share it you have to say it several times. He added that men do the same thing, but they say it to three different people!

One significant difference to keep in mind is the way men and women use the words *want* and *need.* Women don't mind saying, "I need," and may say it often. Men do not. To express need makes many men uncomfortable. When they say anything, it's usually "I want." Wives need to remember that men have needs, whether or not they are willing to express them.

8. *Cultural differences and personality differences also take*

their toll on patience. In the pressure cooker of marriage, the cool Swede from Rockford, Illinois, may seem too cold for comfort to his Italian wife from south St. Louis. And the girl he loved because she was so vivacious and delightfully unpredictable becomes "noisy and undependable" instead.

Even if you came from similar backgrounds, you will be surprised at the differences that emerge and the adaptations that are necessary. Strong clashes are inevitable between two people who love each other, but the Bible shows husbands and wives how to deal with their anger, resentments, and hurt feelings constructively.

LEARNING TO FIGHT THE BIBLICAL WAY

In *Strike the Original Match,* Charles R. (Chuck) Swindoll says that Ephesians 4:25–32 "offers seven rules for having a good fight. These rules will allow you to carry on normal, natural, disagreeable times without breaking with Scripture." Here are Chuck Swindoll's *Rules on How to Keep It Clean* from the Ephesians passage.

1. **Keep it honest (v. 25).** Be committed to honesty and mutual respect.
2. **Keep it under control (v. 26).** Make sure your weapons are not deadly.
3. **Keep it timed right (vv. 26–27).** Agree together that the time is right to talk.
4. **Keep it positive (v. 28).** Be ready with a positive solution right after taking a swing.
5. **Keep it tactful (v. 29).** Watch your words and guard your tongue.
6. **Keep it private (v. 31).** Don't swing at your mate in public. When you swing in public, your malice is showing.
7. **Keep it cleaned up (v. 32).** When it's all over, help clean up the mess.[11]

We encourage you to study these "rules" and make them a part of your new life together. They are practical; they are wise; they work! They can guide you through your conflicts in a controlled, constructive way that hurts neither of you and actually causes you to love each other more, after "the fight" is over.

You will feel safe and secure in your relationship if you get to know one another through good communication and remain closely in touch for a lifetime.

Think about this rather melancholy statement spoken by the Duke of Wellington at the end of his life in 1852:

> It's a strange thing that two people can live together for half a lifetime and only understand one another at the very end.

Does it have to be that way? Definitely not. It is possible to build a lifeline system of loving, unhindered communication that will enable you to become:

- Intimate lovers
- Best friends who always enjoy being together
- A team that can accomplish anything because you work together rather than fighting for control
- Two people who understand one another as unique individuals, not as extensions of yourselves, and accept each other just as you are
- A couple who stay in touch during the changes of a lifetime, who "grow up together" and "grow old together" and remain "at home" with each other no matter what else changes
- Compassionate partners who can help one another adjust to the difficult times of life and endure them together

GUARDING YOUR LIFELINE

Security takes a bit of guarding. In your case, you will know more than anyone else about the sensitive points in your relationship, which need special watchfulness. Here are six warnings for lovers:

1. *Be alert to unusual tension.* Be sensitive to the danger when an uncomfortable tension is felt concerning some topic. Nothing does more harm to a good marriage than the rising of invisible walls because of something that cannot be talked about together. The caring may remain, but the intimacy and trust depart.

Therapists name *loss of effective communication* as the most common cause of distress in a previously stable marriage.[12] When some kind of distress cuts the lines that unite you, you must take quick action to resolve the situation.

2. *Never betray your best friend.* Be on guard against taking something shared with you in a vulnerable moment and turning it against your mate as a weapon. This is easy to do when you're angry, feeling condemned, and fighting back. But as one husband said, "If you get into a revenge mode of thinking, it's like trying to stop a moving train." NEVER give way to the temptation. Remember, this is the person you want for your best friend.

3. *Beware of the heat of the moment.* This is another "heat of the moment" danger. When you have a confrontation (and you will) about something so significant that you both become overwrought, you may say too much—something you'd give anything to take back later. But it's too late then. So have the good sense to stop and cool it when you recognize you're getting to that point. Go in separate rooms for a short time, and write down your feelings just

as they are. Then come back together with the intensity of the moment dissipated, remembering that, no matter what, this is your intimate lover whom you don't want to wound, or lose.

It's good to make Psalm 141:3 your prayer and to pray it together before talking: "Set a watch, O Lord, before my mouth; keep the door of my lips."

4. *Never look at your mate without compassion.* Never close your heart to your loved one, even in the heat of the moment. To see your *one flesh* partner without feeling compassion is unthinkable. To see your partner in need and not pity him or her is to be without love. The principle—one of the most important you can learn for your marriage—is: "We know love by this, that he laid down his life for us; and we ought to lay down our lives for the brethren. But whoever has the world's goods, and beholds his brother in need and closes his heart against him, how does the love of God abide in him? Little children, let us not love with word or with tongue, but in deed and truth" (John 3:16–18 NASB).

First, we are to be willing to lay down our lives for one of our own. To "lay down" means to divest ourselves of something that is part of us, for instance, our selfish desires. We are to love as he loved us. His love is to pour through us and touch others, especially the one closest to us, our own marriage partner. We are to give definite form to the love of Jesus Christ and show it by example. This kind of love reveals itself in details, in acts of behavior, attitude, small words, little smiles, as well as enormous acts of self-giving, done in such a way that there is no hint of martyrdom. If your partner feels you are sacrificing, something is wrong with the way you are showing your love.

Second, we are not to close our heart against a loved one's need. To look at our mate without *splanchna* (pity) is not love. That pity is a deep-seated emotional concern and affectionate sympathy. We must *feel.* Jesus was moved with compassion. He was torn up. He wept. He felt compassion. We need to emerge from our self-centeredness and affirm our solidarity with our partner. We need to open our inner life and feel deeply for and with our mate.

The award-winning movie *Ordinary People* portrays an outwardly charming woman who is unwilling to open herself inwardly to her husband and son at the time of their deepest needs. They desperately want her compassion, some outward sign of her caring, but she cannot or will not give it. Defeated in his efforts to reach her, her husband says sadly, "I don't know you. I don't know what we've been playing at all this time." He adds, "We could have done all right if there had been no mess in our life." But all lives have "messes." We all need compassion from our partner.

So, thirdly, we must act. Not just love with our words—with our tongue that says pleasant things when we're in the right mood—but in *deed* (action) and truth. That should be our response to the compassion we feel.

5. *Remember the power of words.* Remember what power your words have to affect your partner's life. Sometimes we discount their potent influence. Emily Dickinson put it this way,

> A word is dead
> When it is said,
> Some say.
>
> I say it just
> Begins to live
> That day.[12]

YOUR MARRIAGE DOESN'T NEED A THIRD PARTNER

One psychiatrist has observed that "the TV *itself*, that noisy box in the corner of the living room, has become an equal—an essential—partner in many marriages. Even when it's turned off, there's that blank screen waiting to rejoin the conversation or to monopolize one's—or worse, one's spouse's—attentions."[13]

Couples are realizing what a thief television can be—robbing them of their prime time together. One bride said, "We decided not to get a TV, and it's been wonderful. There's nothing else to do but spend time paying attention to each other!"[14]

♥ START USING THESE IDEAS—NOW ♥

Unless you have reached perfection in the art of communication, there are many do's and don'ts in this chapter that you can start using now.

Do you make any of the six mistakes that can make a discussion go wrong? For example, do you need to stop using the words, "You *always* . . ." and "You *never* . . ."? And what about the prize stopper of them all—"Yes, *but*. . . ."

Which of the eight tips for replacing arguments with communication could you start using today? For example, do you need to work on not interrupting and waiting for the proper time to respond when talking together? Can you disagree with your partner without having a tone of disapproval in your voice? Can you speak the truth gently and in love? And if you want to really pull out all the stops, try disarming your partner by simply saying, "I was wrong."

Which of the five deadly sins of communication do you need to confess and turn away from? Many other tips are in this chapter. If you start using just one or two of them, it can make a tremendous difference in your communication with your mate.

Above all, remember Emily Dickinson's poem about the power of words: A word isn't dead after it is said—in fact, it just begins to live in the heart and mind of the one who hears it.

One of the most valuable communication tools you can ever use is the "I" message. In the next chapter, André Bustanoby tells how to "own the problem" and send an "I" message in a noncondemning way.

Chapter 27

"HONEY, I HAVE A PROBLEM ..."

BY ANDRÉ BUSTANOBY
Just Talk to Me

Part III, "Understanding: Your Needs, My Needs, Our Needs," strongly emphasized being acceptant of your mate but never settling for being a doormat. What happens, however, when the conversation heats up and you start feeling you're being stepped on in one way or another? As André Bustanoby says, "Respect and acceptance of the other person does not mean that you have no self-respect or convictions of your own or that anything goes. You are to have self-respect, too. In fact, if both the husband and wife do not have a high degree of self-respect and limits to what they will accept, the relationship will be sick."[15]

But how you convey your need for self-respect and the limits you will accept is all-important. You want to do it without sounding defensive or as if you are simply justifying your own position. In the following chapter, Bustanoby gives specific instructions for using the "I" message, instead of attacking your mate with "you" messages. As you master the use of the "I" message, you will not only keep your own self-respect but preserve your mate's as well. As Bustanoby says, "People who *care about each other* need not defend or justify themselves."

As you read, ask yourself:

- ♥ When my spouse and I disagree, do I own my share of the problem?
- ♥ As a rule, do I send "you" messages or "I" messages?
- ♥ When my spouse sends me an "I" message, do I actively listen, or do I get defensive?

WHEN A STORM BREWS

The summer day dawned bright and sunny. A light breeze was blowing from the Pacific, but the water was calm—a perfect day for sailing.

Fay and I had agreed that I needed time out of doors by myself. Being alone on the ocean was a tonic for me. So I decided I'd trailer my little Coronado 18 down to Seal Beach and spend a day on the water.

I didn't set a time to be home. I knew I wanted to be in by sunset, which would put me home about 9 P.M. But, as I later found out, Fay had other ideas.

The day was fabulous. The wind kicked up a little more than I had anticipated, so it was quite a challenge to keep myself from getting dumped in the water.

I was pooped when I got home. Bedtime would be early that night—I thought. I hadn't planned on a major confrontation with Fay!

As I ate a snack I noticed Fay giving me the freeze. I can always tell when she's unhappy with me. Her face is expressionless. She doesn't look at me and has nothing to say.

Finally, I raked up the courage to ask what was wrong. Fay was angry. But she wanted me to know that the anger wasn't just over the events of that day. She felt angry every time I went sailing.

My usual pattern was to sail all day, come home late, and flop into bed exhausted, leaving no part of the day for companionship with her. Sailing was like everything else I did—all or nothing.

What had happened here? Though Fay wanted to be accepting of me, my behavior stood in the way of her having her own needs fulfilled—her need for companionship. By staying out all day and then going to bed exhausted when I came home, I was creating a situation that had become a problem to her.

OWNING THE PROBLEM

"Owning the problem" means that I approach the problem with the attitude that the problem exists because of the way *I* feel and not because the other person is bad or defective. I accept the responsibility for finding a problem in my relationship with my spouse.

Owning the problem is a non-condemning way of expressing your inability to accept your spouse's behavior. But acceptance does not mean that you never have problems with your spouse's behavior. Indeed, certain behavior may ultimately bring about the ruin of the marriage. Adultery and alcoholism are just two of many such problems.

In stressing acceptance I have been attempting to show that we cannot solve our differences in marriage by convincing our spouse that he or she is a bad person in need of reform. God can do that. The Bible can do that. Preachers can do that. The court system and judges can do that. But in the everyday affairs of husbands and wives, the behaviors that need change are usually not critical enough and are too numerous to require authoritative outside intervention. And because a husband and wife are peers and equally the objects of God's grace, it is unwise for either to become the authoritative voice in the marriage (1 Peter 3:7; Gal. 3:28).

Instead of attempting to convince your spouse that he has a problem and is a bad person, perhaps the solution is to own the problem yourself.

"Owning the problem" is a non-condemning way of expressing your inability to accept your spouse's behavior. It is done by seeing it as your problem, not his.

Owning the problem is necessary when (1) your spouse's behavior blocks the fulfillment of your needs, and (2) you cannot accept his behavior without modification.

AVOID CONDEMNATION

When our spouse's behavior bothers us, we tend to handle it by condemning it. And the better our knowledge of the Bible, the greater the temptation to bring the authority of Scripture to bear on that behavior. Now it may be true that the behavior is questionable in biblical terms. But are *you* the one to invoke the authority of Scripture? What is more, unless it is a clear case of sin, your interpretation will be challenged by the offending spouse. It may be challenged even in the case of sinful behavior. Husbands and wives resent it when the other becomes the authoritative guide in matters of morals or ethics. Indeed, I have seen right and righteous husbands and wives invoke the authority of Scripture only to lose an embittered spouse in divorce.

We easily fall into the trap of judging the behavior of other people. If they do what we want, they are good. If they don't, they are bad.

Recently I took my grandson Collin, age three, and granddaughter Stacy, age nine months, for a walk. I was pushing Stacy in her stroller and Collin was running ahead of us on the sidewalk, pretending he was driving a car.

As we approached a cross-street I began to get anxious because I was afraid that he would run across the street ahead of me. So I called out, "Collin! Stop there and wait for papa."

He dutifully applied the brakes and stood there with his

motor idling. When I caught up to him I said, "That's a good boy, Collin."

Then it hit me. Whether Collin's compliance with my wish was good or bad was beside the point. He simply was giving me what I needed to ease *my problem of anxiety.* As far as Collin was concerned, there was no problem! Grandpa had the problem. And when I recognized that it was *my* problem, I responded differently.

At the next street the same thing happened, and I made the same request: "Please wait for me." But this time when he complied I said, "Thank you, Collin." And then said to myself, "Grandpa needed that."

It's true that Collin's safety was at stake and that was what made me anxious. But even then Collin was aware of no danger, and he might have waited for me at the cross-street without my asking. So really, the problem wasn't his; it was mine.

Now let's go back to my original description of "owning the problem." The situation with Collin fits: (1) His behavior was blocking the fulfillment of my need—the need to be free of anxiety. His running ahead of me blocked that need. (2) I could not accept his behavior without modification. He could run ahead, so long as it was not too far ahead, and he could do if it he waited for me to cross the street with him.

Collin's compliance in this case was not so much goodness or badness, smartness or dumbness. It had to do with *my* need. Because Collin loves and respects me he gave me what I needed.

WHAT TO DO WHEN YOU OWN THE PROBLEM

In order to deal with the problem in this example, I used the technique of "requesting."[16]

Requesting. When mutual respect and caring has been established between two people, a respectful request is one way to deal with the problem. It is important that the request is framed in such a way as to make it sound like a respectful request. By that I mean that there should be no blaming, condemning, or judging. The tone of voice should convey respect.

Once again we are attempting to avoid setting up a judgmental situation. We are attempting to avoid the implication, "I have every right to expect this because I am right and you are wrong." Quite apart from right and wrong the message must be, "I need this for me. Will you give it to me?"

Suggesting Alternatives. Perhaps your spouse's behavior might be more acceptable to you under different conditions. Earlier I used the illustration of sailing. Fay was not against my sailing. She could handle my being away from her doing my thing so long as I reserved time and energy for her. So she suggested I come home a little earlier. And this alternative has worked well.

Direct Sending. When all else fails, direct sending is useful. Direct sending is a direct expression of your *feelings* about the unacceptable behavior. Note that I emphasize *feelings.* Moralizing and judging the behavior will lead to conflict. But the expression of your feelings in a nonjudgmental way is much less threatening, and you are more likely to be heard. When you do this you don't judge your spouse. But you do let him know that you can't help having negative feelings about his behavior.

The direct sending of feelings is done in the form of "I" messages. An "I" message is a *report* of the impact of the spouse's behavior on you. I emphasize *report* because we must distinguish between judging the behavior and sharing our feelings about the behavior. Or, to put it another way, it's reporting the problem in terms of where *you* are and not in terms of your spouse's badness. Often I preface "I" messages with "Honey, I have a problem."

"I" Messages. Here's how to do it.

BEHAVIOR ("When")	EMOTION ("I feel")	IMPACT ("Because")

Husband comes home late with no prior explanation. Wife says:

"When I don't know where you are ..."	"I feel anxious ..."	"because I'm afraid something has happened to you."

Wife does not keep house neat. The husband says:

"When the house looks cluttered ..."	"I feel annoyed ..."	"because I think I'm working harder at my job than you are at yours."

In neither case is the spouse accused of being a bad person. In both cases the problem is expressed as though the problem is his own. The second example may open the sensitive subject of role expectations. But it does so in a nonattacking way.

WHY "I" MESSAGES?

The *ICT Manual* has some good things to say about parent/child communication that can be adapted to husband/wife communication.[17] "I" messages are important because:

1. They show ownership of the problem.

2. They communicate honesty and openness.

3. They communicate to the spouse the effect of the behavior, which is far less threatening than the suggestion that something is bad about him because he has engaged in certain behavior.

4. They place a responsibility on the spouse for modifying his behavior and provide opportunities to be considerate of the needs and feelings of others.

5. They demonstrate respect for the spouse and at the same time show that your needs are important, too.

6. They provide a means for being honest. When you share your feelings, your spouse will be more willing to do so when he has a problem.

7. They tell your spouse how you *feel*, which is less threatening than accusing him of causing those feelings.

8. They deal with actions or behavior, not his self-esteem. They do not attack personality or character. We have a right to question a spouse's behavior. But we have no right to question him as a person or his worth as a creature made in God's image.

9. They communicate trust—trust that the spouse will respond to negative feelings which change when his behavior is blocking the fulfillment of the other spouse's needs.

10. They encourage the spouse to help with and share in the problem.

11. They provide a way for the spouse to know the limits of your acceptance.

12. They demonstrate that personal worth is not dependent on performance. Personal worth is not subject to cancellation with every misstep. A person with high self-esteem knows that his behavior does not always please, but knows that his spouse loves him. We can modify our behavior. But it's difficult to correct feelings of low self-esteem.

13. They build high self-esteem by reinforcing positive behavior. Direct "I" messages should express acceptable behaviors as well. For example, "When I hear you set aside the requests of others in favor of my requests, I feel loved, because it makes me feel as if you're willing to put me first."

COMMUNICATION BREAKDOWN

We don't always send our messages effectively. Instead of "I" messages we often send "you" messages. A "you" message results in communication breakdown because the use of "you" implies that the other person is wrong and the speaker is right. These include blaming, name-calling, sarcasm, and analyzing.

"You" Messages and Sending Errors. A "you" message is any message that conveys the idea that I am the normal one, I am right, and you are abnormal, defective, or wrong. Consider the following:

SITUATION AND MESSAGE

1. Marlene, an attractive young woman is *very* attentive to your husband at a social event, and he is very responsive to her. You are hurt and angry. When you get home you say, "You certainly made a fool of yourself tonight. You acted as if your brain was addled with Marlene's attention."

SENDING ERROR

(Name-calling: "You fool. Sarcasm: "Your brain was addled.")

2. Your wife has criticized your teenage son for poor personal hygiene and a messy room. You are unhappy with the way she has handled it, and you say, "You shouldn't talk to Jeff like that. Don't you know that a lot of his behavior is your fault?"

(Criticism, analyzing, fault-finding)

In these examples the messages clearly are, "There is something wrong with you." How might you correct these sending errors? Give it a try. (1) Tune in to your *feelings* toward the situation; (2) *Express* your feelings in terms of where *you are*. Own the problem as your own. Send an "I" message rather than a "you" message.

Did you try it? How did you do? Here are some examples of how the messages might have been handled differently:

Wife: "When it seemed as if Marlene was exceptionally attentive tonight and as if she was getting a lot of response,[A] I really felt angry and insecure[B] because another woman was getting what I wanted."[C]

Let's examine that message by the phrases marked A, B, and C.

A. *"It seemed. . . ."* The wife is not accusing Marlene or her husband of anything. She is only reporting her view of the situation.

B. *"I really felt angry and insecure. . . ."* She is being honest about feelings generated by what she thought she was seeing. Right or wrong, she was having those feelings, and they were affecting her relationship with her husband.

C. *"Because another woman. . . ."* The report includes the impact of what she was seeing and the reason for her feelings.

Another woman is taking her place (at least this is her view of the matter).

The response shows several things. The wife owns the problem. She expresses it in terms of her perception. She reports her feelings without defense of herself. She gives the reason for her feelings without attack on her husband.

Let's consider the second example, that of the husband who criticizes and blames his wife.

> Husband: "When I heard the conversation with Jeff[A] I was irritated[B] because of the way it was handled."[C]

A. *"When I heard. . . ."* He is not attacking his wife when he talks about his son and the problem.

B. *"I was irritated. . . ."* He is reporting his negative reaction to what he heard without accusing his wife of being a bad person.

C. *"Over the way it was handled."* Again, he does not attack his wife for the way it was handled. He is only saying that it irritated him.

THE ART OF TALKING AND LISTENING

Much communication in marriage is a simple exchange of information. For example:

> *He:*   "What time is the meeting tonight?"
> *She:*   "Eight o'clock."

There's no problem with that kind of exchange. We have seen, however, that conversing about a problem requires a little more of us. Effective communication involves a sender who sends "I" messages and a listener who actively listens. Consider the following example.

> *She:*   ("I" message): "When I saw you and Marlene talking last night, I felt angry because I thought she was getting more attention than I."
>
> *He:*   (active-listening and avoiding defense): "It sounds as if you felt left out and neglected by me."
>
> *She:*   ("I" message): "Yes, but there's more. I felt angry at both of you because it seemed that she was giving a come-on, and you were enjoying it."
>
> *He:*   (active-listening and not taking issue with her interpretation of the behavior): "It looked to you as if some not-so-innocent flirting was going on."
>
> *She:*   "Exactly!"

Even though the husband has not interrupted and has made his wife feel that she has been heard, he may have a view of the problem that is different from hers. How does he get to express *his point of view?* After all, different people have different feelings about the same situation. The answer is that he and his wife "shift gears."

Shifting Gears. Shifting gears is simply the process of change from sending to receiving. He now shifts from active-listening to sending "I" messages, and she shifts from sending "I" messages to active-listening. The sequence might go as follows:

> He: "This opens a subject that I've been wanting to talk about." (He then sends an "I" message): "When we're out in public together, I feel inhibited, because I think you may be jealous of the time I spend with others—both men and women."
>
> She: (active-listening): "It sounds as if you're saying that I tend to throw a wet blanket on social activity when we're out."
>
> He: ("I" message): "Yes. I understand your concern over my behavior with women, but I feel inhibited in getting acquainted with others because I think I should stay by your side for the whole evening."
>
> She: (active-listening): "So you're saying that the issue is larger than just Marlene."
>
> He: "Yes. Exactly!"

At this point we don't have a solution, but by shifting gears— each taking turns at sending and receiving—they both are getting a clearer picture of the problem. It's likely that the husband's input will stir further feelings in the wife that she needs to get out, so they'll shift gears again. She will become the sender and he the receiver.

> She: ("I" message): "It's true that I find myself getting tense when we're out socially, and I think it's because I feel insecure with you."
>
> He: (active-listening): "I hear you saying that I'm doing something to make you feel insecure."
>
> She: ("I" message): "I feel hurt often because it seems I need you more than you need me."
>
> He: (active-listening): "Could you help me understand that a little better?"
>
> She: ("I" message): "It seems that you are content with your own life and your own friends, and I have a very small part in your life so I feel left out, hurt, and angry."

This conversation should be permitted to develop until she has gotten out all her feelings. It may be that the husband will have more feelings to share when she is done, so that means that they should shift gears again. He again becomes the sender and she the receiver.

Shifting gears enables each to clearly and completely state feelings and the reason for them *without interruption.* It provides an orderly process for the sharing of new feelings as the problem unfolds.

Talking out the problem in this manner may not yield an immediate solution. But the husband and wife will know exactly how the other one thinks and feels. This will enable them to propose solutions that both can live with. Many times couples can't solve their problems because *they don't know what the problem is.* They have not tried to *understand* each other. Each is more interested in building his own case and destroying the other's.

Shifting gears is, then, an orderly process whereby two people can share their feelings without fear of interruption and can do it with the assurance that they will be heard. It is done by taking turns at sending "I" messages and receiving as an active-listener.

The three sequences on this page and the previous pages might be diagrammed as follows:

> She sends the "I" message.
> He receives by active-listening.
> *shift gears*
> He sends the "I" message.
> She receives by active-listening.
> *shift gears*
> She sends the "I" message.
> He receives by active-listening.

PROBLEMS TO WATCH WHEN SHIFTING GEARS

Be sure you watch out for these typical problems when you're trying to shift gears.

1. *Be careful not to send "you" messages.* When feelings are hot you might resort to attack. Remember that "you" messages are the language of attack. Good communication demands an "I" message that reports where the speaker is, not a "you" message that tells the listener how bad he is.

2. *Defensiveness.* It's never pleasant to hear that you have made someone else unhappy. You will be tempted to defend yourself by denying the validity of what is being said or by counterattacking.

3. *Fear of anger.* Real feelings need to come out so you can deal with the real problems. Often the presenting problem is only the "tip of the iceberg." The "presenting problem" is the problem that is presented or offered as the cause of the trouble. Sometimes it is the cause of the trouble, but the problem usually goes much

deeper, as was demonstrated previously in the dialogue on Marlene. Shifting gears is an unfolding process that enables a couple to thoroughly explore the presenting and related problems without damaging each other's worth, but this does not preclude the expression of anger.

4. *Telling the other person how he feels.* Sometimes when an "I" message is sent, the listener does not listen, but tells the speaker that he does not feel that way. For example, suppose I tell you that I'm hurt because you treated me badly. Instead of listening to my feelings you say, "You don't feel hurt. You're really mad because you didn't get your way." Don't do that. Listen to how I say I feel. Don't correct me and tell me how I "really" feel.

5. *Rushing the process.* When feelings are hot the temptation is to unload all at once. Unload slowly and pause between active-listening and sending your own "I" message. If you rush in with your own "I" message, the other person will not feel that you have listened.

ROADBLOCK CHECKLIST

Note the following roadblocks to good communication:

- [ ] Directing, ordering, commanding, such as, "You must have my breakfast ready by 6 A.M." ("You have to. . . ." "You will. . . .")
- [ ] Warning, threatening, admonishing, such as, "You had better get yourself home directly after work." ("If you don't, then. . . .")
- [ ] Moralizing, preaching, obliging, such as, "You should tithe regularly." ("You ought. . . ." "It is your duty. . . ." "It is your responsibility. . . ." "You are required. . . .")
- [ ] Persuading with logic, arguing, instructing, lecturing, such as, "Do you realize that well-bred people simply don't do that?" ("Here is why you are wrong. . . ." "That is not right. . . ." "Yes, but. . . .")
- [ ] Advising, recommending, providing answers or solutions, such as, "What I would do is tell the boss that he was unfair." ("Why don't you. . . ." "Let me suggest. . . ." "It would be best for you. . . .")
- [ ] Evaluating, judging negatively, disapproving, blaming, name-calling, criticizing, such as, "You are bad!" ("You are lazy." "You are not thinking straight." "You are acting foolishly.")
- [ ] Praising, judging or evaluating positively, approving, such as, "You're a good husband." ("You've done a good job." "I approve of. . . ." "That's a nice thing to do.")
- [ ] Supporting, reassuring, excusing, sympathizing, such as,

"It's not so bad; things will look different tomorrow."
("Don't worry." "You'll feel better." "That's too bad.")

☐ Diagnosing, psychoanalyzing, reading-in, offering insights,
interpreting, such as, "What you need is to get your life
straight with God!" ("What's wrong with you is. . . ."
"You're just trying to get attention." "You're don't really
mean that." "I know what you need." "Your problem
is. . . .")

☐ Questioning, probing, cross-examining, prying, interrogat-
ing, such as, "Why do you always spend so much time on
the phone with George?" ("Who. . . ?" "Where . . . ?" "What
. . . ?" "How . . . ?" "When . . . ?")

☐ Diverting, avoiding, by-passing, disagreeing, shifting, silence, such as, "Let's not talk about it now." ("Not at the
dinner table." "Forget it." "That reminds me." "We can
discuss it later.")

☐ Kidding, teasing, making light of, joking, using sarcasm,
such as, "Why don't you shoot the boss?" ("When did you
read a newspaper last?" "Got up on the wrong side of the
bed, did you?" "When did they make you president of the
corporation?")

☐ Comparing, such as, "Why can't you be like Martha's
husband?" ("When I was a kid. . . .")

♥ TRY SENDING AND RECEIVING "I" MESSAGES ♥

The obvious application of this chapter is to start checking
yourself when you hear yourself sending "you" messages and to
start sending "I" messages instead. The best approach is to
practice with your spouse. Choose daily situations that might
cause irritation or worry and practice describing the behavior
("when"), the emotion ("I feel"), and the impact ("because").

Once you gain skill at sending "I" messages, take turns in
conversation—"shift gears." Have one mate send an "I" message
while the other mate does active-listening to clarify and understand the "I" message better.

Go over the Roadblock Checklist—note that many of the
roadblocks are filled with the pronoun, "you." If you are guilty of
using several of these roadblocks, make an effort to stop. Ask your
mate to remind you when he or she hears you using a roadblock.

If communication in your marriage is not too strong, it may
be difficult to get your mate to cooperate in practicing "I"
messages, active-listening and avoiding roadblocks. This doesn't
mean that you can't practice using these skills alone. It will just be
more difficult, but every effort you make will still be worthwhile.

Keep in mind that if you and your spouse simply seem to be unable to communicate and "I" messages and active-listening appear to be rather useless, you may need professional help. If the two of you can't talk about your inability to communicate, agree to go to a counselor who can help you deal with your problem.

There are many other areas of concern that provide opportunities for practicing the use of "I" messages and active-listening in order to avoid arguments and conflict. In the next chapter, Dean Merrill talks about how to keep money from becoming a breeding ground for anger.

Chapter 28

THE DANCE OF THE DOLLARS

BY DEAN MERRILL
How To Really Love Your Wife

According to a survey done by two sociologists, the issue that caused the most fights among the seven hundred couples interviewed was money.[18] In the following chapter, Dean Merrill writes primarily to husbands to explain one of the key reasons why money is such a problem in marriages. As you read, ask yourself:

- ♥ In our house is it *my* money or *our* money? Do we have a joint checking account or separate accounts?
- ♥ What is our system for managing money? Do we have a budget, or is that just a joke?
- ♥ How often do we talk about money? Do we really communicate, or is it a time of tension and argument? Why?

MONEY MATTERS

The first twenty-five years of our lives, according to an old sage whose name I've forgotten, our major shortage is *money.*

The next twenty-five years, our major shortage is *time.*

And the last twenty-five years, we're fighting hardest for *energy.*

There's a good chunk of truth in that—but I've got news for the wise man: The money problems don't evaporate on the twenty-fifth birthday. (And the time squeeze starts several years earlier, right?)

A shortage is a natural breeder of tension. We all know how

easily our marriage can sputter, fume, and sizzle over the lack—real or imagined—of enough money to do what we and/or our wives want. Long after our sexual lives have been harmonized, our major career choices have been agreed upon, and the size of our family has been determined, we can still be hassling over money, with no solution in sight.

Our difficulty is usually a classic example of worrying about individual trees instead of the forest. How come groceries are so high? Why did she buy that new coat when she *knew* things were tight this month? A hefty six-month insurance premium is due, and there's no nest egg to take care of it.

And we react. We shoot from the hip. We launch into a harangue about holding down expenses. We bemoan the rising cost of living. We curse the Democrats, or the Republicans, as the case may be. To handle the current brushfire, we write a hot check and hope for the best. Or we run out to the friendly household finance corporation for a quick loan—at highway-robbery interest rates.

There has to be a better way.

WHOSE MONEY?

The Bible, as you know, does not say that money is the root of all evil. (What it says in 1 Timothy 6:10 is that "the love of money is a root of all kinds of evil.") Money itself ought not to be a headache. It ought not to be a source of contention. Instead, it is one of our resources (along with time, energy, air, water, etc.), part of the raw material with which we build our lives. Money, I happen to believe, is another "good and perfect gift . . . from above, coming down from the Father of the heavenly lights" (James 1:17).

Don't think of God as too holy to touch the stuff. The Scriptures often speak of him as the Creator and Owner of the entire cosmos. His barrage of questions in Job 38–41 is essentially a litany of all that he controls.

And he has chosen to assign a few of his resources to you and your wife to administrate. He has given the two of you a combination of energy and intelligence, which you convert for forty hours or so each week into earnings.

You do a number of other things with your allotment of energy and intelligence, of course, which don't translate into cash, e.g., mowing the lawn, fixing breakfast, playing racquetball, doing the laundry, etc. Each has its place.

Thus, we come to some premises:

1. Money is a good thing—it's one of God's gifts to us.
2. Since it's one of God's gifts, it needs to be used with care and thoughtfulness.

3. The gift of money is a *joint* gift, a joint asset. It belongs to the household, the unified life that you and your wife have set up.

And the practical question for the two of you boils down to: What shall *we* do with *our* money?

I'm not just talking about whether you file a joint income tax return each year. And it's more than a matter of both of you signing the house mortgage papers. It is of strategic importance that at the very core of your two brains you *think* and *feel* in terms of common money. It belongs to both of you, and you're answerable to each other as well as to the Giver for how it's used or abused.

You don't have trouble thinking *our refrigerator.*

Or *our TV.*

Or *our children.*

Why not *our money?*

True it implies that you and your wife have given up your independence. You're totally vulnerable to each other. She can run the household straight into bankruptcy. And so can you. But you love each other . . . you're committed to each other . . . you're watching out for each other's good . . . and that makes the crucial difference.

Lurking in the back of everyone's mind, of course, is *who actually earned the money.* Whose name was on the paycheck? Who actually invested his blood, sweat, and tears to generate that income? I have not only my energy but, unfortunately, a piece of my ego in those dollars. *I* did it. Other people may have been loafing the past two weeks, but *I* was getting things done, and here's the proof. I am a productive person. I'm carrying my own weight in this world.

So what's this bit about *our* money?!

If you are the sole wage earner of the household, you and your wife have simply made a decision that you will venture into the world of commerce and invest a major portion of yourself earning dollars while she invests a major portion of herself on other nonremunerative but equally important tasks. This arrangement, my friend, does *not* make you better than her. It says absolutely nothing about your value to the household or society at large in comparison with hers.

Your neighbors, friends, and business associates may *think* it does. Ours is such a money-hungry culture that the ability to earn money has become a popular gauge of one's worth. The more you earn, the more you're esteemed.

That is a particularly demeaning as well as non-Christian concept. If my value as a person rises or falls solely on my commercial value in this world, I'm in deep trouble. What happens if I get fired . . . or sick . . . or past sixty-five? I'm suddenly a nonperson.

We Christians have trouble resisting this pagan value-system.

My wife continues to fret occasionally about the fact that she currently isn't generating any dollars. She was a teacher the first six years of our marriage, including a year when I was in graduate school and she was the sole dollar-producer. She may well return to the classroom in a few years when our children are in school, but for now, she's a full-time mother. We keep reminding each other that mothering is an extremely important and valuable part of our life together—more important than earning dollars, in fact. We'd give up my job and try to subsist off the land before we'd ever give up our kids. But Grace still keeps thinking about the days when she used to bring home a paycheck. So she has a ways to go to make her feelings match her Christian values.

I shouldn't talk—not until I've put myself to the test by turning the tables again as we did in graduate-school days, only on a permanent basis. Mike McGrady, a Long Island newspaper columnist, tells about such a life in his delightful book *The Kitchen Sink Papers*. After reaching a fairly high plateau in his profession, McGrady decided to shake things up and trade places with his wife, whose growing home furnishings business had the potential of supporting the family. Mike became the househusband, caring for their three children, while Corinne became the breadwinner. He describes how it felt to be handed his first weekly "allowance" of a hundred dollars for groceries, etc.

> It is an unpracticed exchange, accomplished awkwardly. I don't know which of us has more difficulty, which of us is more embarrassed. I guess Corinne handles her side of the exchange more smoothly than I do. . . .
>
> It is the easiest hundred dollars I've ever made. But the reversal feels strange. . . . This ritual, the giving of allowance by one human being to another, bespeaks whole planets of meaning; it has to do with independence, gratification, reward, punishment, resentment. The feelings are so intertwined that I doubt whether they can be fully understood until the situation is reversed. . . .
>
> My own reaction on receiving money—this first day and every week since then—has not been what I anticipated. It is not a pleasurable experience, not in the least. In fact, there is on my part inevitably an effort to minimize the transaction, to snatch up the check and stuff it into my wallet as rapidly as possible, to pretend that the transaction doesn't really matter. I can see, in Corinne, opposite tendencies, an effort to ceremonialize the offering, to announce it in advance—"Ah, today is the day you get your allowance"—to make a production number out of locating the checkbook and the pen, to sign it with a flourish, to hand it over with a kiss.
>
> I know her feeling all too well.[19]

Throughout the book, the McGradys (who do not pretend to be Christians) can be seen edging toward an *our-money* concept, although at the end they are still not to the point of a joint checking account, except for certain house expenses.

If both you and your wife work, you may be trapped all the more in the rut of "My dollars are mine and hers are hers." In such a mindset, money often equals clout. And if a highly motivated, successful wife starts bringing home the larger paycheck of the two (which is entirely possible in these times), a threatened husband can go into all manner of traumas.

The leader/servant of a Christian household is the person who refuses to use his or her earning power as a club, or even a small lever. He steadfastly resists the culture's belief that money is power. He thanks God for this gift, along with all others, and works with his spouse to use it responsibly.

Now, back to the question: What shall *we* do with *our* money?

A SIZABLE PILE OF CHANGE

The biggest difficulty for most of us is not that we come up with bad answers to that question. It's that we don't take time to answer it at all. We don't plan; we just spend. And when we don't have money to spend, we call it a cash flow problem and proceed to borrow so we can keep on spending.

A family exchequer is a larger, more complicated thing than we often realize. Many of us are running through the equivalent of a new Mercedes every year. We're spending money in twenty-five to thirty different categories, from housing to utilities to restaurants to gasoline.

The key to keeping control over that rather sizable pile of change . . . the key not only to staying out of financial trouble but *enjoying* God's gift to you as well . . . is for you and your wife to *agree in advance* how you're going to spend it. The process of saying "Here's what we have to work with, and here's what we're going to do with it" is called budgeting. If the word has a nasty odor to it, call it *planning your money* or whatever you like. Just do it.

You begin by finding out your monthly income. If you're on a regular payroll, it's easy. All it takes is a little arithmetic to convert your regular paycheck(s) to a monthly basis. If you're paid biweekly, for example, you simply multiply by twenty-six (the number of paychecks you get each year) and then divide by twelve.

(You had a small excuse for not budgeting before the invention of electronic calculators. But now, the old complaint about "doing all that figuring" is dead.)

Be sure to add any little extra sources of income you've got going on the side. Is your wife tutoring? Do you have a part-time or sometime job? Are there investment dividends to add on?

It gets a little messier if your income is not regular—if you're in business for yourself or if you're a salesman on commission. I know more than one such husband who uses this as an excuse not to budget. "I never know when the money's coming or how much. So I just have to fly by instinct."

Nonsense. If giant corporations can estimate their income on the basis of past records, you can too. You told the IRS what you made last year, didn't you? Take that figure and divide by twelve. Even if your money comes unevenly throughout the year, find the average monthly figure. (There are some tricks you can play in arranging the due-dates of certain bills to compensate for those variances in income. More about that later.)

Before you and your wife go any further—stop and thank the Lord for his gift. Think about all the people in the world making less than you are (there are probably billions of them). Tell the Lord how much you appreciate having this much money to work with, and that you're going to try to use it as responsibly as possible, and that you'd appreciate his guidance as you proceed.

Your first decision is how much you're going to return to the Lord directly. In Old Testament times, as you know, Jehovah set that figure for you: ten percent. The New Testament doesn't lay down any hard quotas; instead, in keeping with its spiritual nature, it rather cheerfully urges us to "excel in this grace of giving" (2 Cor. 8:7). A little further on, Paul says, "Remember this: Whoever sows sparingly will also reap sparingly, and whoever sows generously will also reap generously. Each man should give what he has decided in his heart to give, not reluctantly or under compulsion . . ." (2 Cor. 9:6, 7).

It was during my year of graduate school that Grace and I finally came to an understanding of this concept. We were on a rather stringent budget, and we had dutifully written a tithe into it—a ten percent contribution to our church each payday. It was an automatic thing, the result of years of indoctrination, a bill to be paid along with Standard Oil, Master Charge, and the telephone company.

It wasn't a whole lot of fun, we finally admitted. We could hardly be classified as "cheerful givers." We were conscientiously doing our religious duty, and that was about it.

But we began noticing what the New Testament said about giving. And we began thinking about the word *giving* itself. Giving—the Christmas/birthday kind—was a neat experience. It was a joyful, even emotional exchange. It generated lots of smiles.

So Grace and I decided to play a little semantic game with ourselves. We declared a revolt against any further tithing. "We quit!" we said. "Instead, we're going to begin giving to the Lord. We're going to think of it as giving, and we're going to enjoy it."

We set a minimum size for our gifts of ten percent of each paycheck. We decided we didn't ever want to go lower than that, but would go higher whenever we wanted to.

To make us remember, we established a routine of praying together over the Lord's check each time, usually at Sunday morning breakfast. The envelope would be sitting there between the salt and pepper shakers, and we'd say, "Lord, here's a gift for you. We're going to put it in the offering at church this morning, and we want you to know how much we appreciate you."

You may think this is foolishness, but I can tell you that it has totally changed our feelings about giving. We think it's put things into proper perspective.

We're currently away from the ten percent figure altogether. We've set a different percentage and, with the aid of the handy calculator, it's just as easy to compute every time we plan a new budget.

However you choose to figure it, give the Lord the first slice out of the pie. And smile when you do it.

GROCERIES, GASOLINE, AND GARBAGE

If you're a budgeting pro, feel free to skip this section. But if you're often coming up short or finding yourself in a financial squeeze, keep going.

Certain expenses are rather unavoidable:

You have to live in some kind of housing.

You're probably making a car payment.

You're probably paying one or more insurance premiums.

You have to heat/cool your home, pay for electricity, water, garbage pick-up, and a telephone.

And you're stashing something away in savings and/or investments. (You aren't? Well, you've heard lots of sermons about how it never gets easier to save, so do it now, and make it an automatic thing. Take heed.)

You may need to be stockpiling for some taxes, if these aren't already withheld from your check.

Somebody in the family may be requiring tuition.

And you may have some loans to keep whittling away.

All these are what the accountants call *fixed expenses*. Once you've committed yourself, there's not a whole lot you can do about them. They're for the same amount every month (except for heating bills, for which you need to find an average, and long-distance phone calls, for which you need to set a quota).

Write down each of these figures. They form a big block of your disbursements.

The remaining money goes toward *flexible expenses:* groceries, home furnishings, home maintenance, restaurants, clothing, laundry and dry cleaning, gas and oil, car repair, tolls, parking, fares, haircuts, trips to the beauty shop, drugstore items, postage, magazines, books, records and tapes, "nights out," sports, babysitters, doctors, dentists, prescriptions, gifts, and general messing around—wow! Hopefully you won't have too many more categories than those.

What's the tab for all of that?

If you haven't kept records up to now, you don't really know. You're going to have to make some educated guesses. Your guesses can be greatly improved six or even three months down the road if you head now for the nearest stationery store and pick up a family expense record booklet. They cost less than two dollars. My favorite is the kind put out by the Ideal System Company, but you choose your own.

The more accurate records you keep, the better you can see your spending patterns. And the more accurate your budget planning can become.

Now comes the fun of adding up your expenditures—your gifts to the Lord, your fixed expenses, and your flexible expenses—and seeing how far you've exceeded your monthly income! It is at this point that you *cannot* afford to throw up your hands and say, "Oh, well, it'll work out somehow." No, it won't. In fact, things will work out a little worse than you've projected, because you've no doubt forgotten some routine expenditures. And some unexpected surprises will be hitting you—perhaps a major illness, or a valve job on your car. You have no choice but to cut expenses down to your income or a little below. If God has given you $900 of take-home pay a month, it is simply wrong to keep cruising at a $1,000 or $1,100 lifestyle. Make the budget balance, no matter how painful.

Actually, a good feeling comes over you when you've marked out a place for every dollar and when every dollar's in its place. You get rid of that vague uneasiness about whether to spend or not. You *know* whether you can afford an item or event. Some of the best feelings I've had have been taking Grace out to dinner, even when some other column of our budget was in excruciating pain. We had allocated a certain amount of money for restaurant dining, and we could go ahead and enjoy it regardless.

You are not finished with budgeting until both you and your wife can look at the figures and say, "That's good. I'm committed to making that plan work." So long as either of you have reservations about the wisdom or the equity of the various allocations, keep talking. Keep figuring. Keep adjusting. Eventually, copy it onto a clean sheet of paper, and keep it where you both can refer to it as often as necessary.

HOW TO OBEY A BUDGET

Right away, you have a couple of procedural matters to care for. How are you going to implement your budget on a daily basis? You obviously can't keep mental track of how much has been spent for what. You and your wife must look each other in the eye and solemnly swear that you'll both begin using the expense record booklet mentioned earlier. That way, for the first time in your life, you'll have an answer to the periodic wail, "How come we're broke?!" It's right there in black and white.

The discipline of writing down what you spend has a couple of other benefits. It makes you face each expenditure twice—the moment when you shell out the cash, and the moment when you record it in the book. Grace and I have found that this acts as a subtle brake on our spending. (One time we decided we were tired of writing; we were mature adults now, and we didn't need to be so picky-picky. Within *four months*, we were in a serious financial hole, unable to tell how or why we'd gotten there—and eager to get back to record-keeping.)

The other benefit of this procedure is that it partially solves the classic question of who shall be the family bookkeeper. If one person is charged with *all* the paperwork, it can get to be a grind as well as an irritant trying to keep track of what the other person is spending. But if the expense record book is always in a handy location—the kitchen, for example—and both you and your wife are constantly jotting down cash outlays, neither of you has to play the role of cross-examiner.

Naturally, somebody has to write the checks every payday. I don't know that it makes a great deal of difference whether it's you or your wife, assuming you both know how to add, subtract, and spell. Whichever of you takes on this responsibility is merely following through on the *jointly* planned budget anyway. So it's no great position of power and glory. Whenever there's not enough to cover the bills due, and hence some bills have to be postponed, the two of you can together decide which ones.

The family check-writer also has the responsibility of keeping the bills and other financial papers organized. Many households have gotten in trouble simply because their payables were scattered in three different rooms of the house. A few years ago my ingenious mother gave me an odd but wonderful Christmas gift: a nicely repainted metal lunchbucket, not for lunches but for household records. It has cardboard dividers inside for "Bills Due," "Charge Slips Waiting," "Bills Paid," "Paycheck Stubs," "Checking Account Statements," and a couple of other things. The checkbook rests in front. It's fantastic! In case of a fire, Grace and I would probably grab our kids and that lunchbucket ahead of anything else, because it has everything we ever want to know about our budget.

Which items are paid by check and which in cash? (Your decision may depend on whether or not you're charged for each check you write.) Here's one workable breakdown:

CHECKS	CASH
The Lord	Groceries
House mortgage or rent	Home supplies
Utilities	Restaurants
Insurance premiums	Clothing
Car payments	Laundry/dry cleaning
Savings	Tolls, parking
Gas, oil, repairs (through charge cards)	Barber, beauty shop
Tuition	Drugstore items
	Miscellaneous
Subscriptions, books, and records, (some through charge cards)	Postage
	"Special events," baby-sitting
Medical	Gifts

The check items, as you can see, are a mixture of fixed and flexible expenses. That makes it nice, in that the checking money becomes a sort of pool in which the big bills and little bills can slosh back and forth. If there's a big car repair bill one month, the medical bills can be postponed slightly, and vice versa. This takes place without bothering the day-to-day activity in the cash columns.

I've deliberately arranged for the car and life insurance premiums to come due at the end of the year, when there's a Christmas bonus to cover them. That way they don't play havoc with our month-to-month flow. If you're "richer" at certain times of the year, you might consider jockeying your annual and semi-annual bills toward those times.

When it comes to cash, Grace is responsible for certain funds, such as groceries, while I'm responsible for others, such as restaurants. You're going to laugh at this, but I'll tell you anyway: We've even gone so far as to set some of the funds aside in separate little plastic boxes so we *know* whether there's any cash in that fund or not. "Clothing" is one of these; "nights out" is another. We've found that we simply can't trust ourselves to keep either of these in line without an actual, visible "kitty." If the greenbacks are there, okay; if they aren't, we don't spend.

This reflects a basic premise of sound financial operation: *Don't spend it until you've got it. Don't jump the gun.* We laugh at little children who bounce up and down and say they can't wait until Christmas; we discipline them for sneaking cookies a half-hour before dinner. Yet we are sometimes just as guilty when it comes to money. We *just can't wait* until we actually have the money in hand. We can see it coming toward us, and so we go ahead and spend it early. Before long, we're going ahead and spending without asking whether the money is soon to come or not—and down that road lies big trouble.

The most enticing form of jumping the gun, of course, is the charge card. I've proven to myself over the years that I can use the convenience of charging gasoline without torpedoing the budget. The monthly total is fairly constant, and there's not much temptation to splurge in this particular area. But we would never put a fund like clothing on a charge basis. The result, we know from experience, would be swift disaster.

Charge cards facilitate the store manager's dream: impulse buying. And impulse buying is what ruins the well-laid plans of a budget. Hence, another rule of sound finances: *When in doubt— wait.* You may miss an occasional hot deal, but it's worth it. Grace and I are still growling about the encyclopedia salesman whose special price was available *only that week* back in 1970. We told ourselves Vickie needed encyclopedias for school (false). We told ourselves all kinds of things as we took the plunge, withdrawing a life insurance dividend to pay for the set.

By the time Nathan and the twins will be old enough to use them, they'll be ten years out of date. The rotten part is that I *knew* that evening we didn't really need a set of encyclopedias right then; I just couldn't muster the courage to tell the guy no and would he please get out of my living room.

A bargain is not a bargain unless you need it.

Of all the areas of a budget that call for maturity on the part of the husband, the greatest is the car. In most households, car expenses are to the husband what groceries are to the wife: a major category about which one spouse knows quite a lot and the other knows next to nothing. You can walk in the door after paying a $78 repair bill, lay three or four sentences of mechanical jargon on her—and she's helpless. She doesn't know what you're talking about, let alone whether the repair was essential or not.

But she does know you just dropped another $78 on the car. And that hurts, no matter how unavoidable it was.

Our household records show that for the past three years I have sunk sixteen percent of the family fortune each year into automobiles—gas, oil, repairs, payments, insurance, license plates, and municipal vehicle taxes. In the same period, Grace has shelled out no higher than thirteen percent for groceries. These two categories, along with housing and our gifts to the Lord, make up the Big Four of our budget. Everything else is minor by comparison.

I have a responsibility to Grace and the children to hold the automobile area in line, even though they don't have the mechanical know-how to question my decisions. This means choosing dependable cars in the first place, finding honest and competent repairmen (which can be quite a trick sometimes), and changing oil and getting lube jobs on schedule.

In my case, I have come to believe that it means something even more basic—and more sizable in terms of dollars. It means controlling my attitude toward cars in general, viewing them as the pieces of machinery they are rather than extensions of my own ego or self-image. It means resisting Detroit's media blitzes every fall that tempt me to trade for the newest, biggest, and best. It means getting rid of the myth that cars are an investment. They are *not;* they do *not* appreciate in value or pay returns on the initial capital. They *cost* money—lots of it. Some of them can be resold for more than others, but never for the full amount of what you've spent on them.

Like most men, I remember with considerable sentiment my first car during high-school days: a black 1950 Mercury coupe. I paid $100 for it. My self-image was tremendously bound up in that car . . . those rear-wheel covers . . . the deep-throated rumble that turned heads in the school parking lot . . . well, you know what I mean.

Next came a long black '48 Dodge limo I bought from a funeral director for whom I worked one summer; it was a campus conversation piece that fall. But its charm was soon lost, and in its place came a flashy '56 Olds Holiday two-door hardtop (with a cracked head, I might add, and poorly patched rocker panels that disintegrated in the salted streets of the first Chicago winter). No matter. I was a taller-than-average guy who needed a big car, right? Next, a pink '56 Cadillac Coupe de Ville, followed by a '63 Mercury Monterey with that classy reverse-slant window in the back.

Suddenly, I realized something: I was spending an awful lot of money on cars, and there was no end in sight. It took a while, but Grace and I finally came to the conclusion that what we needed was a basic means of transportation, not a status symbol. We dumped the ailing Mercury for a used Volvo and drove it for the next six and a half years.

I remember the first year I didn't go to drool and dream at the Chicago Auto Show. It was like giving up an old friend. But I decided I'd be better off without the bombardment. I haven't been back since.

Not that there's anything immoral about an auto show. I'm just saying that for me, it was my annual orgy of automobile covetousness, and I eventually had to deal with that problem, for my own sake as well as for my family's.

HOW TO REVISE A BUDGET

Obviously, every time you get a raise you need a new budget. But there are other reasons as well. Perhaps your expenses change—a son or daughter starts college, for example. Perhaps your long-range goals change. There was a point early in our marriage at which Grace and I decided to stop using her teaching pay for stereo components and bedroom suites and start socking it away toward a downpayment on a house. We knew we'd eventually be living on one income instead of two, so why not now?

Again, we had to trick ourselves into it. We dubbed the salad days of the past the Era of Elasticity. Now we were beginning the Era of Rigidity. (To tell you the truth, I think we've been in Rigidity ever since.) Our goals had changed, and we restructured our spending patterns to match.

The other time when a budget needs revision is when it's just not working. You haven't allocated enough money for utilities, or gifts, or nights out, and you're getting thoroughly frustrated. It's not that you're unwilling to abide by the budget; it's just that the thing is out of whack. Okay; change it. Face the problem. Don't go on gnashing your teeth. Shift some dollars from one of the other accounts. Or find a way to raise income. Naturally, you have to keep the bottom line in balance whatever you do, but if you're in an intolerable situation, sit down with your wife and take a good, hard look at your priorities as expressed by your budget.

WHAT TO DO WHEN THE BUDGET'S BEEN BLOWN

For all your care and discipline, there will be times when you—or she—will simply blow it. You'll misplace a twenty-dollar bill somewhere. You'll get a traffic ticket. A repair service will rip you off. You'll succumb to the allure of a new sport coat and whip out a charge card before you think.

Well, it's not the end of the world. After all, some things in life are more important than money. Confession, for example. It's *her* money that's been squandered as well as yours, remember? So don't keep her in the dark. Tell her what happened, and how you feel about it . . . and don't be surprised if the whole ordeal draws the two of you closer to each other. You may face a tough month or two recovering from the financial loss, but you'll face it together, and out of such ordeals comes the deepening of love and trust.

The Scriptures direct "those who are rich in this present world [e.g., the majority of us North Americans, compared to the rest of the world] not to be arrogant nor to put their hope in wealth, which is so uncertain, but to put their hope in God, who richly provides us with everything for our enjoyment" (1 Tim. 6:17).

Your household and mine need a leader with that kind of attitude.

♥ HOW DO YOU HANDLE "OUR" MONEY? ♥

Take inventory of your money managing system. Do you have one that is working for both of you? Does it include a budget that is a realistic guide and not a rigid dictator?

Do you and your spouse agree on money, or is one of you a spendthrift while the other is much more frugal? How do you score on the following "Money Matters Quiz"?

Yes   No

_____ _____ We agree in advance about how we will spend our monthly income.
_____ _____ Our giving to God is voluntary and enjoyable.
_____ _____ We are both committed to making our budget work.
_____ _____ We never "spend it" until we've "got it."

If you had to answer no to several of the above statements, maybe it is time to do some sending of "I" messages and active-listening to try to work out a better system. Even one no on any of the above questions can cause plenty of anger in a marriage.

DON'T LET ANYTHING DRIVE YOU APART

Don't let money or any of the other "daily responsibilities" eat at or destroy the intimacy you are both trying to attain. Keep the two dynamic forces in your marriage in balance. Love is drawing you together and anger tends to drive you apart. As David Mace points out, anger is actually a healthy emotion that can play a part in keeping a balance between the independence of each mate as a separate person and their interdependence on each other. While it is true that in marriage "two become one," that does not mean that either person's personality is eroded or destroyed. A wife and her husband are separate and distinct personalities who seek to develop a oneness that the poet, Kahlil Gibran, described this way:

Let there be spaces in your togetherness.

David Mace points out that anger draws attention to areas in the relationship where two personalities don't fit each other. If you do not deal with this anger, it remains your enemy and erodes your marriage. But if you can process it according to the many suggestions in the previous chapters, you can make the necessary changes in behavior in order to keep your intimacy and oneness intact. Mace writes: "The final achievement of intimacy, therefore, comes when husband and wife can make themselves totally vulnerable, with no need to maintain a guard against the possibility of an angry attack or a disapproving rejection. All marriages do not achieve this degree of intimacy, by any means. But some do. And the experience of total trust that develops out of total intimacy, and assures both partners of total love, is marriage at its very best.[20]

WHAT HAVE YOU LEARNED ABOUT COMMUNICATION?

The following checklist of communication principles will be helpful in thinking back over what you have read in Part V (as well as Part IV) of this book. If you feel you understand each concept and are trying to implement that concept in your life, put a check mark. If you are still fuzzy on the concept or not ready to accept it, put a question mark. Fill in your individual answers, then talk together about each of these concepts.

☐ Christian husbands and wives must communicate as equals as far as God's grace is concerned.

☐ *Differences* are the result of *differentness,* and each spouse's differentness is to be respected.

☐ If there is a difference of opinion, our first job as husband and wife is to understand the other's viewpoint before attempting to come to an agreement.

☐ To understand each other, we must learn to actively listen to each other—listen for feelings, not just facts.

☐ We can show respect for each other and our differentness by using the "I" message to communicate feelings.

☐ To communicate effectively, we must be aware of what's going on inside of ourselves and be willing to share those feelings.

☐ Feelings are valuable clues to what really tried to divide us and we should always use our feelings to get to the root issue (or issues).

☐ Our marriage is always subject to review by one or both of us, and we can honestly share our feelings about what we need to change to make things better.

☐ Change in a marriage of equals is best accomplished by knowing what specific changes must be made and agreeing to change because we both care. To achieve real and positive change, we must work to show each other mutual respect, understanding and good will.

It takes two to process anger; it takes two to communicate.[21]

HOW TO GET HIM/HER TO CHANGE

1. I can change no other by direct action.

2. I can change only myself.

3. When I change, others tend to change in reaction to me.[22]

PART VI

SEX:
BLISS OR
BATTLEGROUND?

In our marriage, sex is:
♥ Bliss
♥ A battleground
♥ Boring

Obviously, the desired answer is "bliss," but many couples would have to admit battleground or boredom comes closer to describing what happens in the bedroom. The statement in Genesis 2:24, "and they will become one flesh"—once a promise of physical/spiritual bonding—becomes a mockery or worse. Christians have never been guaranteed total immunity from extramarital affairs, but lately they are falling victim to them with alarming frequency.

Dr. Willard Harley, author of *His Needs, Her Needs* (Revell, 1986), is a clinical psychologist with twenty years of marriage counseling experience. He has specialized in trying to help people caught in the entanglements of an affair, which he defines as "two persons becoming involved in an extramarital relationship that combines sexual love-making with feelings of deep love."[1] According to Harley, an affair is so dangerous because it combines passionate sex with what both participants believe is real love. The result is that one (or both) partner experiences intimacy that develops as needs are met in the affair that were not met at home in the marriage.

Harley believes that partners in an affair literally become addicted to each other as their relationship builds on fantasy but not reality. Using the second person "you" because he believes anyone, under the right conditions, could fall victim to an affair,

Harley lists why affairs are so exciting and enjoyable to the participants:

1. You and your lover seem to bring out the best in each other.

2. You ignore each other's faults.

3. You get turned on sexually as never before.

4. You feel no one else could ever be as exciting a sex partner as your secret new lover.[2]

The reason Harley feels that anyone can be caught in an affair is because of the basic needs in all of us. He lists the five basic needs in men as: sexual fulfillment, recreational companionship, an attractive spouse, domestic support, and admiration (by his partner). The five most basic needs in women are: affection, conversation, honesty and openness, financial support, and family commitment. When any of these needs is not met, a spouse is ripe for an affair and usually gets involved in a deceptively simple way. Often the frustrated husband or wife meets someone at work or in some other mutual setting and strikes up a friendship. The new friend is "someone I can talk to"—which usually isn't happening at home. Soon, without really anticipating it, the "friends" are in bed together.

This cycle can happen in a few short months or over a period of years, and Harley has seen the toll it can take among Christians and non-Christians alike. He believes the most important need for most women is affection; the most important need for most men is sex. It is here the battle lines are drawn. A man mistakenly thinks his sexual advances will meet the woman's need for affection, and the woman can't understand why "all the beast wants to do is take me to bed."

Achieving sexual fulfillment for husbands (and wives) is a vital goal in every marriage. The following excerpts by Zondervan authors have been chosen to help you and your spouse evaluate your relationship regarding sex and affection. For some couples, this material may be unnecessary, but for others it may shed light on where problems lie and how to begin solving them.

In chapter 29, Dr. Ed Wheat (*Love Life for Every Married Couple*) describes three crucial requisites for developing a positive sexual relationship: complete medical information, the correct biblical view, the right approach.

In chapter 30, Dr. Herbert Miles (*Sexual Happiness in Marriage*) covers basic steps toward sexual adjustment in marriage and discusses the two problems that can often block a happy sex life together—time and space.

In chapter 31, Dr. Miles (*Sexual Happiness in Marriage*) covers a major problem in sexual adjustment: lack of orgasm on the part of the woman. He covers basic reasons for a lack of orgasm, including conflicts between husband and wife, personal problems of the husband or wife, and other blocks to fulfillment.

In chapter 32, Shirley Cook (*The Marriage Puzzle*) links sex and marriage to bearing the Fruit of the Spirit and develops a creative apologetic for romance in marriage.

Because a Christian is, by definition, someone indwelt by the Holy Spirit, (see Rom. 8:9), it would seem to follow that Christians would be less susceptible to sexual dysfunction and the temptations of an affair. But Willard Harley's experience does not bear this out. His counseling practice is centered in the Minneapolis/St. Paul area, with fifteen satellite clinics in other communities throughout the state of Minnesota. Many of his clients are church-going, Bible-believing Christians who wind up in his counseling offices, ridden with guilt and desperate for help. The more Harley works with Christians and other people of deep moral convictions, the more he believes that spiritual faith must include knowledge and wisdom, especially in the area of sex. The following chapters can help you reach that goal.

God himself invented sex for our delight. It was his gift to us—intended for pleasure.[3]

Dr. Ed Wheat

Chapter 29

HOW TO LOVE YOUR PARTNER SEXUALLY

BY DR. ED WHEAT AND GLORIA OKES PERKINS
Love Life for Every Married Couple

How much time do husbands and wives usually spend each week in physical love-making? According to research studies, the average couple makes love two to three times per week for approximately thirty minutes each time. That means that they spend one to two hours per week in meeting what Dr. Willard Harley (*His Needs, Her Needs*, 1987), believes is the major basic need of most men—sex.

What about the amount of time husbands and wives spend in fulfilling the woman's basic need for affection? No studies are available on time spent showing affection, but Dr. Ed Wheat believes there is little doubt that the success of the one to two hours spent on sex depends in great part on what happens the rest of the week in regard to the quality of affection displayed between partners. He maintains that sex and love are not interchangeable terms.

A little girl put it all in proper perspective as she was being told the facts of life by her mother. "Oh," she said, disappointedly. "I thought you were going to explain about love! I already know about sex."

You may already know about sex, but to have good sex you need to have good love (affection). As you read Dr. Wheat's description of the components of good love-making, ask yourself:

- ♥ Do we have all the right medical information?
- ♥ Do we have a biblical view of sex (see chapter 1)?
- ♥ Do we use the right approach?

INTENDED FOR PLEASURE

In order to develop a lifetime love affair, you and your partner must maintain a *positive* sexual relationship. The old Johnny Mercer song comes to mind: *You've got to accentuate the positive, eliminate the negative, latch on to the affirmative.* That is what I hope to help you accomplish through the counsel of this chapter. Even if you have a good relationship, it can be better. A mutually fulfilling sex life will enrich your entire marriage, and it is within your reach!

So let's begin with the affirmative. You have good reason to anticipate increased sexual pleasure year after year. Some people dread the loss of their youthful vigor, or they fear their sex life will become boring and empty through much repetition. But this need not be the case. People growing together in love find that their sexual relationship provides more meaning and enjoyment all the time. In middle age and later years, overabundant sexual energy can be exchanged for mature, sensitive, skilled love-making with a beloved partner whose responses are understood intimately. I urge you to read this chapter with a sense of expectancy concerning the positive sexual relationship you and your mate can enjoy throughout your marriage.

But perhaps you are concerned about negatives in your relationship. If you are to eliminate them, you must first understand them. Physical desire with its sexual expression is without doubt the most complicated aspect of love in marriage. So many potential causes of difficulty exist, and problem-solving is complicated by silence, suspicion, anger, hurt, misunderstanding, fear, or guilt, which are often hiding in the shadows. The physiological mechanisms of sexual expression are intricately complex and can be shut down at any stage; yet, when hindrances are removed, they work together smoothly, without conscious effort, to transmit an experience of tremendous thrill leading to fulfillment and complete relaxation.

God's physical design for the one-flesh relationship is amazing! I refer you to our book, *Intended for Pleasure* (Revell, 1977), for a thorough explanation. However, you need to understand this about the sexual experience as it relates to negatives: The entire love-making episode involves three phases of physical response that are interlocking but separate and easily distinguishable. They are desire, excitement, and orgasm. To use Dr. Helen Kaplan's metaphor, these three phases have a common generator, but they each have their own separate circuitry. Sexual desire comes from a special neural system in the brain; excitement is indicated physically by the reflex vasodilatation of genital blood vessels; and orgasm depends upon the reflex contractions of certain genital muscles. These two genital reflexes are served by separate reflex centers in the lower spinal cord.

Problems arise when an inhibiting "switch" turns off any one of these physical responses in your system. Leading therapists are trying to determine and treat specific causes of inhibition in each phase. As Dr. Kaplan explains, "One set of causes is likely to 'blow the fuses' of the orgasm circuits, another type of conflict may 'disconnect the erection wires,' while a different group of variables is likely to cause interference in the 'libido circuits' of the brain."[4]

For example, fear and hostility are two chief inhibitors of the desire phase. Sexual anxiety for any of various reasons impairs the excitement phase. Excessive self-consciousness will short-circuit the orgasm phase. This is not meant to be a quick diagnosis of sex problems, but a reminder that your sexual relationship will always mirror the larger context of your life, revealing personal fears and tensions, and almost always serving as a barometer of the total relationship between you and your partner—which can fluctuate, depending on how well you are getting along in other areas of your marriage. Negative feelings in a marriage will often show up first in a couple's sex life.

I saw a couple recently who made an appointment for sex counseling because of the wife's inability to enjoy sex. It became apparent that the real problem was a seething hostility on the wife's part that had little to do with sex technique. In a short time, when the real issue was recognized by both partners and dealt with, the couple reported that their sex life was far better than ever before.

Another man told me, "My wife and I have a good, if not excellent, sex life together. But when other problems come up, we use sex in a negative way against each other." He added with a rueful smile, "You need to give a seminar on how *not* to use sex!"

Ironically, negative feelings are easily vented through the very act that God designed to bring two people together as one flesh. Sex can be used to frustrate, disappoint, reject, or "pay back" the mate when the individual does not even realize what he or she is doing, or what has caused the "turn-off." Often, of course, it is done deliberately.

Sexual problems sometimes reflect your feelings about yourself, or negative attitudes toward sex that you will have to unlearn. Many sexual problems stem from ignorance of basic medical facts and can be remedied easily by proper counsel. Any of these negatives we have mentioned can short-circuit some phase of the sexual response so that desire is inhibited, a physical dysfunction occurs, or orgasm seems hopelessly out of reach. That, in turn, can give rise to a whole new set of negatives that will further trouble the couple's love affair.

This is why I stress that you must aim for a *positive* sexual relationship with your mate. To do this you will need three things: (1) correct medical information; (2) a biblical understanding of sex that dispels false fears and inhibitions; (3) the right personal approach to sexual love-making in your own marriage.

CORRECT MEDICAL INFORMATION

No one should expect to be a natural-born expert! Fortunately, more people today are recognizing the importance of understanding all that God has built into their bodies for sexual delight. My prescription for you is to read our book, *Intended for Pleasure,* or to listen together in the privacy of your own bedroom to our counseling cassette series, *Sex Technique and Sex Problems in Marriage.* These materials contain an enormous amount of medical instruction, explanation, and counsel that cannot be included in this book. For instance, you will learn how to solve the most common sexual problems and precisely how to give your partner sexual release—a necessity. There is a unique advantage in listening to the cassettes together with frequent stops for discussion. It will open your communication lines on this delicate subject, and for most of you this will be better than a session at a sex counselor's office.

You owe it to yourself and your partner to be fully informed. There is no reason why you cannot be a great lover. (I say this to both husband and wife.) Just make sure you know all you need to know. When the aura of mystery is removed from the physical process, you are in a position to understand and resolve the negatives within your sexual relationship.

A BIBLICAL VIEW OF SEX

Most wrong attitudes toward sex are conditioned by early training, but an understanding of God's view of sex that comes directly from the Scriptures can bring freedom to fearful, inhibited individuals. Hebrews 13:4 proclaims the fact that the marriage union is honorable and the *bed* undefiled. The word translated "bed" in the Greek New Testament is actually *coitus,* the word meaning sexual intercourse.

Those Victorians who claimed that sex was something shockingly distasteful that husbands did and wives endured were tragically far from the truth, but they left a legacy of error that is still around. Queen Victoria wrote to her daughter, "The animal side of our nature is to me—too dreadful." There are Victorians of the same mind today who have trained their children (both sons and daughters) to recoil from sex with repugnance or guilt. The result has been acute suffering in marriage for both partners.

One wife in frustration asked me, "How can I help my

husband see sex as something *good* . . . that my body is touchable, meant to be seen and enjoyed by him? I know he was brought up to believe that sex was dirty and wrong, something to be ashamed of and done in secret. He's kind and thoughtful. *But I wish he loved me sexually.*"

Another wife told me of the "training" that brought her and her husband to the edge of divorce. She said,

> I knew nothing about sex except that my mother disapproved of it. So I borrowed a medical book from a doctor just before I got married. I couldn't believe what I read! The idea that married couples would do such a thing was so hard to accept that I almost broke off the engagement. But I loved my fiancé very much, so I went ahead with the wedding. I spent my honeymoon trying to avoid sexual contact. When we got back I tried to talk to my mother about it. She couldn't conceal her disgust that her little girl was involved in something as terrible as sex. Then she assured me that most men did expect it, but it would never be any fun for me. For the first several years I tolerated it and pretended to respond quickly so that we could get it over with as fast as possible. After the birth of our baby, I told my husband I did not ever want to have sex again. I still loved him—but not in that way.

> I hated the thought of sex. He tried to be kind and understanding with me, but the tension and resentment grew between us. The time came when he said it was all over unless I was willing to change. We had tried a counselor once before, and it was an upsetting experience. This time we went to a Christian counselor who began by showing me what the Bible teaches about sex in marriage. I understood enough at the first session to see how far my attitudes were from the truth and to realize that I could trust God to help me change. My husband and I just fell in each other's arms that night and cried and prayed and asked God to help us love each other sexually. It was the beginning of something good. I am learning what sexual fulfillment means, and my husband and I are so much closer.

The Scriptures tell us clearly that the joyous sexual expression of love between husband and wife is God's plan. It is, as the writer of Hebrews emphasizes, *undefiled,* not sinful, not soiled. It is a place of great honor in marriage—the holy of holies where husband and wife meet privately to celebrate their love for each other. It is a time meant to be both holy and intensely enjoyable. Uninformed people have actually considered the Victorian view to be biblical because they think the Bible forbids all earthly pleasures. Certainly not! In fact, the Bible is far more "liberated" concerning sex than untaught people realize. In God's view there is a mutuality of experience between husband and wife. Each has an equal right to the other's body. Each has not only the freedom but also the responsibility to please the other and to be pleased in return.

These basic principles concerning the enjoyment of sex in marriage are found in 1 Corinthians 7:3–5. Bible teachers have called them: the principle of need; the principle of authority; and the principle of habit.

The principle of need. Scripture tells us, not as a suggestion but as a commandment, to meet our mate's sexual needs because we both have these needs. When husband and wife take hold of this concept and begin to do everything they can to meet their partner's need, they are sure to develop an exciting relationship.

The principle of authority. Scripture tells us that when we marry, we actually relinquish the right to our own body, and turn that authority over to our mate. This amazing principle is certainly an indication of the lifetime scope of marriage as God designed it. It applies equally to husband and wife. Obviously, it requires the utmost trust. People should understand this principle before they decide to marry, for on the day they wed, in God's sight, they relinquish the right of control over their own body. We quickly learn that one of the easiest ways to hurt our mate is to withhold our physical affection. But we do not have this right! To put it bluntly, the wife's body now belongs to the husband. The husband's body now belongs to the wife. This means that we must love our mate's body and care for it as our own. Thus, unreasonable demands are totally excluded.

The principle of habit. Scripture tells us that we must not cheat our partner by abstaining from the habit of sex, except by mutual consent for a brief period of time. Why? Because if we break this commandment and *defraud* our partner by withholding habitual sexual love-making, we will surely open our marriage to satanic temptations. Our Creator knows this; that is why he tells us to participate actively and regularly in sex with our own mate. This is not a debatable issue, biblically. It is an inherent part of the love-life of marriage.

To apply these principles on sex in the most practical terms, I suggest that you make every effort to provide your mate with a good sexual release as an habitual part of your life together. Specific instruction is available to you through biblically-oriented books such as *Intended for Pleasure* and Tim LaHaye's *The Act of Marriage* (Zondervan, 1976).

THE RIGHT APPROACH

I suggest that you begin by looking on sex in your marriage as an opportunity for genuine love-making (the making or building of love) through giving and receiving in ways that are physically and emotionally satisfying for both of you. Don't worry about fireworks and shooting stars; the thrills will come later when you have learned the highly personalized art of sexual love-making. For now, just concentrate on the essentials: physical/emotional closeness and a positive response that may include sexual release.

To develop a real closeness, you will need to view your sex life in the context of your total relationship. A woman at our Love-Life Seminar asked me this question: "What can a Christian wife with a Christian husband do when the husband seems only to want sex and doesn't care about her during the remainder of the day? He forgets her birthday, doesn't care when she has emotional needs, and won't take any spiritual leadership in the family." The lesson is obvious. Sex without signs of love is sure to create resentment, not response, from your partner.

One thing that will always hinder emotional closeness is criticism. You will find it impossible to establish a series of pleasing physical experiences to build on unless you decide to quit criticizing and, instead, begin expressing in the most positive terms your love, your caring, and your desire to please your mate and meet his or her needs. It is not your responsibility to lecture your partner on the biblical commandments we have just discussed, or to insist upon obedience to them. If your mate disappoints you, you must be careful not to say by word or action anything that will make him or her feel like a failure. Even one slip of the tongue can undo weeks of progress, so emphasize your verbal appreciation for your partner. Words are particularly important in this situation. Husband, one sentence of criticism directed at your wife in any area may well drive away the desire she would otherwise feel that day. On the other hand, one sentence of praise and approval (the more specific the better) is going to do wonders for her and for your sense of closeness in the sexual relationship.

Husband, begin showing your wife in other ways that you love her. Give her romantic caresses at times when you are not preparing for sex . . . admiring glances . . . affectionate pats . . . a smile and a wink across the room . . . small attentions that tell her she is a very special person in your sight. Wife, you can do the same for your husband!

All of this sets the stage for the sexual experience. It could be called "before foreplay" technique. Researchers tell us that without affectionate pre-foreplay time together, sexual interest tends to wane. So plan with time as your ally in the development of satisfying closeness in sex. It must be relaxed, enjoyable time. In the busyness of American life, you may find it necessary to plan ahead and to set aside special times for each other. Think of it as a date to take place in the privacy of your own bedroom.

Once you are together, the world should be shut out. Have a lock on your bedroom door and use it. Make sure the children are settled for the night and do all you can to prevent interruptions.

You should be able to concentrate on each other completely in a relaxed, pleasant, and *romantic* atmosphere. I receive from wives scores of comments similar to this one: "How do I convey to my husband my need for romance and tenderness before the act of making love? It is seldom there, and without it I just don't enjoy sex!"

WOMEN FANTASIZE ROMANCE

A recent survey of women's fantasies revealed that they fantasize romance—not just sex—more than anything else, and most often a romantic interlude with their own husband.

Husband, your wife needs a romantic prelude to sexual intercourse. You may not realize how much your wife desires this or what it means to her. Women must be aroused emotionally as well as physically. They enjoy the closeness and intimacy of sex; they enjoy gentle touching and total body caressing done in a meaningful, not mechanical, way. They want their husband to appreciate their entire body, not just to provide some breast or genital fondling as a means of quick arousal.

The physical side of love rests on the human need for close personal contact, especially the need to be touched in a way that expresses warmth, gentleness, softness, and caring. Men have this need for warmth and affection in addition to sexual satisfaction, but they are much less apt than women to admit it or even to be aware of it. Therapists have found that men often misunderstand this need and seek sex when what they really crave is the physical reassurance of loving closeness.

Husbands who are preoccupied with physical gratification should know that even for their own maximum enjoyment of sexual release, they need to have at least twenty minutes of sexual arousal beforehand. We sometimes call orgasm a *climax* and it should be just that: the highest point of interest and excitement in a series of happenings. How do you reach the high point? By *climbing* to it. *Climax* is a Greek word meaning "ladder." You move to a climax with a slow, progressive build-up resulting at the highest point in a sudden, thrilling release—something like a roller-coaster ride with its long, slow climb and then its exciting plunge downward from the peak.

So when you come together, take time to wind down from the outside pressures of the day. Take time to build desire. Take time to enjoy physical closeness and sensuousness. Take time to love each other without words. You don't have to worry about saying something clever or original. Your partner will not be bored with the same loving phrases over and over when it's obvious you mean them. Treat yourselves to pleasure!

When couples strive to obtain an orgasm without regard to

enjoying their time together, sex becomes work rather than pleasure. Remember that orgasm lasts only a few seconds. Emotional satisfaction and gratification occur during the entire episode. Women tell me that they do not *always* need or desire an orgasm during sexual encounter, but their husbands cannot understand this and feel like failures unless an orgasm always occurs.

ROOM FOR IMPROVEMENT, HUSBANDS

A recent study was made of the techniques that wives report as hindrances to their enjoyment of sex. Husbands can use this list to see if there are areas where their technique can be improved.

- The husband's stimulation of his wife during foreplay is mechanical rather than spontaneous.
- The husband is more interested in perfecting physical technique than in achieving emotional intimacy.
- The husband seems overly anxious for his wife to have an orgasm because that reflects upon his success as a lover, instead of simply wanting to please her and give her enjoyment whether it results in orgasm or not.
- The husband fails to provide manual stimulation for his wife to have another orgasm after intercourse, even though she desires it.
- The husband is repetitious and boring in his approach.
- The husband is not sensitive to his wife's preferences.
- The husband seems too deadly serious about sex.

So, husband, if you want to build love in your marriage, you will try to avoid these common mistakes in approach and technique. Concentrate on pleasing your wife rather than anxiously pushing her toward a sexual release. If she thinks you are pressuring her, she will begin to dread the possibility of failure rather than relaxing and surrendering to her own physical response. There is no need for you to ask your wife if she has had a good sexual release. Most women will find the question inhibiting. Simply give your wife manual stimulation for additional release after intercourse. If she does not feel a need for it, she can lovingly let you know. Many women who enjoy manual stimulation are afraid their husband will tire of it just as it is becoming pleasurable. Or they are afraid it is boring to their husband. Let your wife know how much you enjoy giving her pleasure and complete satisfaction. If she believes this, she will feel free to show you what pleases her at a particular time.

By all means, be sensitive to your wife's sexual preferences. It may be difficult for her to state her sexual likes and dislikes directly. If she does manage to communicate them and then they go ignored, she is sure to feel resentful and frustrated.

Finally, don't take the sex relationship so seriously. It will be best if you can establish an easy, comfortable camaraderie in the bedroom with laughter as part of your love-making. At times, sex should be light-hearted fun—recreation for husband and wife planned by the Creator.

Ask yourself these questions about your love-making. Any *no* answers will suggest areas for improvement:

- Is it positive?
- Is it relaxed?
- Is it pleasant?
- Is it romantic?
- Is it physically satisfying?
- Is it emotionally satisfying?

WHAT WOMEN DON'T UNDERSTAND

We have discussed what the wife desires from the relationship. The husband greatly desires *response* from his wife. She can give him this beautiful gift and delight his heart. However, judging from my mail and counseling appointments, many women do not understand how important, both physically and psychologically, the sexual relationship is to their husband. They do not seem to realize that their avoidance of sex or their lack of response will affect their entire marriage in the most negative way. To the indifferent wife I must give this caution: When there is no physical intimacy between you and your husband, whatever emotional and spiritual closeness you have had will tend to fade as well.

This is how one husband expressed the painful feelings resulting from his wife's lack of response. He wrote,

> My wife and I need help. I feel that all our troubles stem from one cause. My wife does not want to have intercourse with me and I cannot accept this. The situation has existed all of our eighteen years of marriage. We currently have relations about once a month. This occurs normally after many days of my frustrating attempts to have her respond. Then it is not a loving affair, but a surrender or duty on her part. I love my wife. She is an outstanding wife, mother, and friend. Except that she does not physically love me. I'm afraid to face up to the fact that maybe my wife just doesn't love *me* and cannot respond to *me*. I have asked myself many times, What are you still married for? I have no answer. I don't know what to do.

We are not speaking now of a wildly passionate response on the part of the wife, but only of a positive response. When a wife responds, she gives an answer by word and action to her husband's love-making. It can be gentle, simple, and loving. It may be enthusiastic; it need not be dramatic. But a wife should meet her husband with open arms and a warm acceptance. A lack of response means that you are ignoring one who in some way is reaching out to you, and there is no worse treatment to give to one who cares for you. Indifference is the enemy of love. So I counsel you to respond to your husband in these simple ways, at least (remembering that your varied spontaneous responses will delight him), and to regard sex with him as an opportunity to build more love into your marriage.

Some interesting studies have been done to determine underlying emotional factors that hinder a partner's response. A primary finding indicates that failure in women to attain orgasm is linked to the feeling that the "love object" is not dependable. All the data gathered seems to suggest that orgasmic capacity in woman is often tied to her feeling concerning the dependability of her relationship with her husband. In other words, the highly orgasmic wife feels she can trust her husband; the low responder fears that her husband will let her down. Since she feels she cannot depend on him and may have to stand on her own, she finds it almost impossible to trust him in the sexual act and to relax and let herself go in his arms. Her deep-rooted apprehension robs her of her ability to respond fully to her husband. Further studies indicate that as her anxieties diminish over a span of time, the potential for sexual response is increased.

What does this mean to the husband who longs for his wife to become sexually responsive? If he wants her to respond passionately with a beautiful relaxation and abandon in love-making, he needs to give her the absolute security of his love in the context of permanent commitment. When he convinces her that he will not let her down, he will find her becoming increasingly responsive.

One of these studies also showed that highly orgasmic women have had fathers who were not passive toward them—fathers who strongly cared about them and their well-being. These fathers were not permissive; instead, they set standards and well-defined rules for their daughters' protection in their growing-up years.

Obviously, you cannot change the way your wife's father treated her, but you can give her what she may have needed from her father—a strong, loving concern from a man who is leader, protector, and example to her. If she believes you actively care about every detail of her welfare, and if she can respect you as the spiritual leader of your home, the chances are very good indeed that you will see improvement in her sexual responsiveness over a period of time. (That is, if you also treat her as a lover should in your sexual relationship.)

Those of you who are familiar with Ephesians 5, will realize that these scientific findings bear out the counsel God gives to the husband to provide his wife with a permanent, sacrificial love, a protective love, a nourishing, cherishing love. This is not just something you do in order to gain God's approval. It works! It brings about the kind of marriage God wants every husband and wife to enjoy—a marriage that includes keen sexual desire on the part of the woman as well as the man.

What about the husband whose response to his wife is, for some reason, hindered? The wife whose husband is indifferent should answer the following: Do you respect your husband's leadership as a man, as the head of your home, as the father of your children, and as your lover? If you indicate to him by word, action, or attitude that you do not respect him in some area of his life, you will diminish his desire for you. While this is a biblical principle, it also is a principle emphasized by secular experts in the sex-therapy field. When a husband's self-esteem is reduced because he feels his wife does not respect him, their sex life is sure to suffer.

HUSBANDS NEED TLC, TOO

Also consider this: Have you misused your sexual relationship in the past? Have you used sex as a tool of manipulation or as a weapon against your husband? Have you rejected him on a whim? Have you withheld physical favors to get even with him? Have you been dishonest with him, playing games? Have you battered his sexuality through hostility or criticism or ridicule?

You should realize that your husband is psychologically vulnerable to injury in the area of sex just as he is physically vulnerable to injury. If you have damaged his sense of manhood and participated in producing an attitude of failure within him, you will have to start all over again and build him up by your tenderness, your sensitivity, your respect, and your responsiveness.

Although we have been discussing how your total relationship can affect your sexual adjustment, the opposite is also true. A sexual problem sometimes affects your entire marriage in ways that cannot and should not be ignored. It is most often true of marriages where the wife has never (or almost never) enjoyed an orgasm. This threatens the couple's love relationship when it becomes an issue, and a chain reaction of negative emotions occurs.

Here is what usually happens. The wife begins to feel like a failure because no matter how hard she tries, she cannot work up the right physical response. Of course, the harder she tries, the more the natural reflex action of orgasm eludes her. This lowers her self-esteem and her confidence in herself as a woman. She also senses her husband's disapproval or disappointment, and the sex act becomes increasingly painful for her emotionally. So she begins to avoid sex. If her husband persists, she feels used, and resentment enters the scene. If he tries to woo her with compliments and caresses, she cannot believe he is sincere because of her low self-image. She thinks he has an ulterior motive in being nice to her.

The husband's confidence in himself as a man is shaken first of all by the sense of failure in being unable to bring his wife to sexual release. It is more deeply shaken as she begins to dislike and avoid sex altogether, and he feels that she is no longer interested in *him*. He wonders if she even loves him. Resentment enters in as he begins to feel that she is not trying to find a solution. The wife's rejection evokes tremendous emotions of depression, as the husband does everything he knows to do to adjust to his wife, believing it is going to work, but rejection still comes. A down draft of anger and discouragement says, Why try anymore?

Actually, both are longing for love and the assurance of love from each other and both are inwardly convinced that they are not loved.

Those of you who are in this situation should realize that this is always a couple problem that has built up over a period of time, so you should not count on an immediate solution. Your belief that the situation is hopeless stands between you and the solution. Once the barriers of persistent discouragement, rejection, and sense of failure are gone, skilled sexual stimulus *will* provide sexual release as a natural result. So both of you need to turn away from concentration on those few seconds of sexual climax and learn to enjoy the whole experience of love-making with all its warmth and closeness. Orgasm may be the end of the experience, but your goal should be to please each other, to satisfy the emotional need you both have to know that you are loved and accepted exactly as you are.

Right now you should begin to move toward each other through the uncomplicated avenue of physical touching. As your problem developed, you moved apart. So now come together by warm physical contact, by cuddling and snuggling and holding hands just as you did when you were teen-agers. Sit close to each other every time you have the chance. Sleep close to each other. One couple I counseled held their marriage together by choosing to sleep nude in each other's arms while they were still working out other problems. Take the focus off the sex act altogether for a while and avoid much discussion of your problem. At the same time begin learning *physical* communication as described in *Intended for Pleasure*.

MEET YOUR WIFE'S EMOTIONAL NEEDS FIRST

Husband, take positive steps to meet your partner's emotional needs. Your wife longs to be encouraged, built up, and praised. She wants to feel close to you emotionally. This will come as you love her in the way the Bible describes. A husband can always meet his wife's deepest needs by loving her as Christ loves us, and as a wife begins to respond to that love, she is ready to respond sexually.

The husband's love has been compared to a warm coat he wraps around his wife. As long as she feels encircled and sheltered in his love, she can give herself completely to him. In this safety, she can accept herself as a woman and value her femininity. Then she will be able to entrust herself to her husband in the sexual relationship as the bird gives itself to the air or the fish to the water.

We husbands may not be able to fully appreciate the deep longings that influence our wives, but if we love them with the sheltering love that is described in Ephesians 5:28–29 we will see results! Our wives reflect the love or lack of love we have provided.

As you move toward each other physically or emotionally, you should also move closer in the spiritual dimension of marriage. Sharing in warm personal Bible study and prayer together will help prepare the way for sexual fulfillment as a natural result of the spiritual union that is occurring daily. Then you will find that your sexual union can bring you still closer to God, so that you often want to pray together after making love. Love produces love in all directions!

The principles described in this chapter, when reinforced by a practical knowledge of physical technique, will enable you to build love in your marriage through the avenue of sex by establishing a physical/emotional closeness that is good and satisfying. Remember that this sense of closeness develops best in the atmosphere of security and stability. Within this setting you can give each other the opportunity to be beautiful and varied and unpredictable; open and vulnerable and receptive. Try it. If you are afraid to try it because you are afraid you will be hurt, consider this: The risk of pain is always the price of life.

As we consider how to build the other kinds of love in marriage, we will find that all of them will enhance the sexual relationship. As Dr. Kaplan has observed, "Love is the best aphrodisiac discovered so far!"

♥ TO EVALUATE YOUR LOVE-MAKING ♥

Go over the list on page 353 that names seven areas where the technique of the husband can be improved. Are any of these problems yours? In addition, ask yourselves:

♥ Is our love-making positive?
♥ Is our love-making relaxed?
♥ Is our love-making pleasant?
♥ Is our love-making romantic?
♥ Is our love-making physically satisfying?
♥ Is our love-making emotionally satisfying?

A no or a "sort of" answer to any of these questions can suggest need for improvement. Dr. Herbert Miles explains the art of love-making in the next chapter.

Chapter 30

ARE SKILLED LOVERS BORN OR MADE?

BY DR. HERBERT MILES
Sexual Understanding in Marriage

One of the worst mistakes made by many of the millions who march down the wedding aisle each year is that they think they understand love-making because they know something about the basic act of sexual intercourse. This is particularly true of men. As the following chapter points out, however, lovers are made, not born, and they must develop the art of making love. As you read the following chapter by Dr. Herbert Miles, note that it talks about love-making on the honeymoon. You may be long past the honeymoon stage, but the information provided may be useful in keeping the honeymoon alive for the rest of your life together.

As you read, keep these questions in mind:

- ♥ What does Dr. Miles mean by "time" in sexual love-making?
- ♥ What does Mr. Miles mean by "space" in sexual love-making?
- ♥ How well do we do as a couple in controlling time and space in our love-making?

TWO MAJOR PROBLEMS IN MAKING LOVE

There are two major problems that tend to block good sexual adjustment in marriage. To make it easy to remember these two problems, we will call them "time" and "space" and discuss them in order.

By "time," we refer to the fact that, sexually, male and female bodies are "timed" differently. Sexually, man is timed quickly. He can become aroused through sexual stimulation with his wife and usually reach an orgasm in a very short time—two minutes, one minute, or even in less time. This is normal for him. He will gradually learn to control himself, but he will always tend to be "quick on the trigger" until he gradually slows down during middle age and the years that follow. His wife should never say to him, "Why don't you control yourself?" She should understand that God created him this way and that all other husbands are equally quick to respond sexually.

On the other hand, a woman is sexually timed more slowly, sometimes very slowly, as compared with a man. We can safely say that it takes the average women ten to fifteen minutes or longer from the time she starts sexual arousal with her husband until she experiences an orgasm. This is after she is married and is experienced in regular sexual relationships. Sometimes she may have an orgasm in ten minutes, five minutes, or even less. A few women on special occasions may have an orgasm in one or two minutes. This is the exception. At other times it may take twenty or thirty minutes, or even longer. It may vary according to where she is in the menstrual cycle. Also, other circumstances such as personal, family, or community problems may affect her.

A young wife will gradually learn how to move toward orgasm a little more quickly, but she cannot change the fact that her sexual arousal timing mechanism is built differently from her husband. Her husband should never say to her, "You iceberg, why don't you hurry up?" He should understand that this is the way God, in his wisdom, created her. Sex in woman is as definite, as real, and as satisfying as it is in man, but it is something deep down inside of her, a spiritual gold mine. The young husband must, with patience, love, understanding, and tenderness, uncover her sexual interest, layer by layer, and gradually bring it to the surface, allowing her to express her love for him in an orgasm. This simply takes time.

TIMING DIFFERENCES CAN BE A BLESSING

When a young couple understands the difference in sexual timing and when they accept it and cooperate with it, it is no longer a major problem, but actually may be a blessing. Let us repeat, a couple must *understand it, accept it,* and *cooperate with it* for it to be a blessing—that is, this period of sexual stimulation and arousal, lasting ten or twenty minutes, may become one of the sweetest, most meaningful and spiritual experiences in husband-wife relationships. It is only when a couple does not understand or does not cooperate with their differences in sexual timing that it becomes a problem.

The second major problem that tends to block good sexual

adjustment we have called "space." "Space" refers to the distance on the body of the wife between the clitoris and the vaginal passage. The clitoris is the external arousal trigger that sets off the orgasm in woman. It is made up of many nerve endings designed by the Creator to arouse a woman to an orgasm. These nerve endings must be stimulated directly by physical contact for a woman's sexual arousal to peak in orgasm. The clitoris is located somewhat out in front, at the upper meeting point of the inner lips, or labis minora. Please note that on the average-sized woman the distance from the clitoris to the vaginal passage is approximately one and one-fourth inches. This is the space we are discussing.

Now, visualize the position of the vaginal passage. Note that in the process of sexual intercourse in the man-above position, the penis moves into the vagina, not from an angle above the vaginal opening, but actually from an angle slightly below it. When this fact is visualized and understood, it should be clear that in normal sexual intercourse the penis does not touch or contact the clitoris. This fact is of major importance. Since the penis does not move back and forth over the clitoris in intercourse, the wife may not become fully aroused and thus will not have an orgasm.

A couple may use other positions for intercourse in which the penis can be forced to move back and forth over the clitoris and stimulate it directly. However, there are two problems involved in doing this. First, these positions may not be very comfortable for either the wife or her husband. Secondly, many husbands cannot control themselves for ten or fifteen minutes of this type of intercourse without reaching an orgasm before their wives are fully aroused.

Since the clitoris is the arousal trigger of the wife, and since the penis does not contact the clitoris in normal intercourse, marriage counselors recommend what is called "direct" stimulation. That is, the husband, in the process of love-play before intercourse starts, will gently stimulate all the erotic zones of his wife's body. This includes kissing her lips and breasts and using his hands and fingers to explore and stimulate her total body, including the inner thighs, her labia minora, the opening of the vagina, and finally her clitoris. He will continue stimulation of the clitoris for ten or fifteen minutes, or whatever time it takes, until he is certain she is fully aroused sexually and ready for intercourse. There is nothing wrong in this procedure. It is normal in the love-play and arousal period for a couple to touch and handle each other's sexual organs. This is a pleasant and meaningful part of love expression. It was planned this way by the Creator.

THE KEY TO ORGASM

The important point to remember here is that the *clitoris is the external arousal* trigger; that there must be uninterrupted stimulation of the clitoris and the area close to the clitoris for a wife to have an orgasm. The *method* of stimulation of the clitoris is not so important. Any one of several different methods may be satisfactory. The fact that the clitoris *has to be stimulated* is the *important thing* to remember. If a couple can give the wife sufficient stimulation simply through the process of intercourse alone to experience orgasms regularly—fine, wonderful! But few can do this during the first part of their marriage. We have simply said that direct stimulation in the arousal period is one of the surest ways for a young bride to reach an orgasm in the early part of marriage. Our research shows that forty percent of wives, after they have gotten used to sex life in marriage, are able to become aroused and experience orgasm through intercourse only, and no manual stimulation of the clitoris is necessary. It took several weeks for most of these couples to learn how to succeed in this manner. All couples would do well to work toward this goal. However, we need to be reminded that sixty percent of all women need direct stimulation of the clitoris in the arousal process before they can reach orgasms in intercourse. Couples should not hesitate to use this method when there is need for it.

There are two types of sexual experiences that are normal for married couples to enjoy. The first type is sexual intercourse. This, of course, involves the vaginal passage and the penis. That is, after a period of love-play and sexual arousal, including direct stimulation of the clitoris, the husband and wife attempt to reach orgasms together, or one following the other by the movement of the penis back and forth in the vaginal passage. This full embrace is the most complete and meaningful sexual experience possible. Couples should *always* have this type of sexual experience *whenever possible.*

WHEN YOU CAN'T HAVE INTERCOURSE

However, there will come times in marriage when couples cannot have sexual intercourse. During these times they will both have their regular and normal sexual needs. Let me discuss three examples. First, we will assume, at this point, that intercourse will not take place during the menstrual period. This period involves four to six days per month. During this time a couple would normally have intercourse one or two times, but because of the menstrual period, they would have to refrain, which they could do.

Let us imagine a husband and wife who normally had intercourse every three days, but because of a special set of circumstances over which they had no control, had gone five days without intercourse. By this time they would probably be very anxious. Let us assume that they had planned intercourse on the night of the fifth day, but during the afternoon the menstrual period shows up two or three days early. Suppose the period lasts for five days. This means the couple would have to wait ten days before being able to have intercourse. Normally they would have sexual intercourse two or three times during ten days. It is true that under these circumstances a couple can refrain. However, this is not necessary.

A second example involves the time before and after a baby is born. Normally a doctor will instruct prospective parents not to have intercourse during the six weeks before a baby is born and the six weeks after it is born. The time will vary according to the condition of the prospective mother. It is well for a couple to ask the doctor for instruction about when to stop having intercourse before a baby is born, and when to start after birth. The doctor must instruct on this matter. However, on the average, there will be a period of at least three months when it will be necessary to abstain from sexual intercourse. During this time normal sexual needs will continue. It is possible to abstain from all sexual relations during this time, but this is unrealistic and unnecessary.

A third example is when a couple wants to express their love in a sexual experience but do not have adequate contraceptives available, and feel strongly that they cannot run the risk of a pregnancy at this time. Reason would dictate that under these circumstances a couple should refrain from sexual intercourse. But it does not follow that they would avoid all sexual expression.

Marriage counselors recommend that during these and other similar times when couples cannot have intercourse, they practice a second type of sexual experience in which they do not have intercourse and do not use the vaginal passage. This second type of sexual experience is called "sexual interstimulation." That is, husband and wife simply bring each other to orgasms through love-play and direct stimulation. The husband will stimulate the wife's clitoris with his fingers until she is aroused to experience an orgasm. At the same time, the wife will stimulate the husband's penis with her fingers until he reaches an orgasm. Through skillful love-play, stimulation, and response, the husband and wife lying in each other's arms can often have orgasms at the same time or nearly so. Let us repeat that no other type of sexual experience can take the place of sexual intercourse. However, when husband and wife cannot have intercourse for justifiable reasons, sexual intersti-mulation—stimulating each other to orgasms—can be as mean-ingful to both of them in this limited set of circumstances as having orgasms in sexual intercourse.

Let us hasten to say that there is nothing about this

experience, under these circumstances, that is evil or a violation of Christian concepts. It is not a type of masturbation. This experience is not self-stimulation. It is the process of a husband and wife, who are in love with each other, stimulating each other to express their love for each other in a mutual sexual experience. This makes it possible for a couple to have a sexual experience, either by intercourse or by interstimulation, whenever they need to, all of their lives, except when they are spatially separated from each other or one or both of them is ill. Most doctors recommend that couples return to regular sex relations (either sexual intercourse or interstimulation) as soon as possible after surgery or major illness. They further recommend that normal sexual relations between husband and wife not be interrupted during many minor illnesses. Lack of interruption tends to reduce much strain on the marriage and promotes emotionally healthy love relationships between husband and wife. When in doubt, couples should seek advice from their doctor. Peter Dickinson, in his book *Fires of Autumn* (Drake Publishers, Inc., 1974), has a chapter dealing with the extent to which surgery and major and minor illnesses should affect a couple's sexual life. We have discussed this because some couples in marriage hesitate to practice this second type of sexual experience, having a vague idea that it might be wrong. We are safe in saying that all responsible Christian marriage counselors would approve this type of experience in marriage as being normal and good.

"*How many orgasms are normal for husband and wife in one sexual experience?*"For young married couples, one orgasm is usually sufficient per sexual experience. When a man has one orgasm, he cannot have another until some time has passed. This is natural for all men. Generally, for young women, one orgasm is sufficient. However, some women need multiple orgasms—two, three, or more—to give them a full sexual release. This need may increase after a few months or years of marriage. When a wife cannot relax and seems to be rather nervous after one orgasm, this may be an indication that she has only had a partial sexual release. Our research indicates that for seventy-nine percent of wives one orgasm is sufficient to meet their needs, while eighteen percent say that more than one orgasm is needed sometimes, and only three percent seem to need more than one orgasm most of the time. If a couple plans multiple orgasms for the wife, stimulation for the next orgasm should begin not later than a few short seconds after the completion of the previous orgasm.

"*How often should couples have sex relations?*"The best answer is, as often as they want to, can, and have the opportunity. During the first weeks of married life, couples have relations more often. This is normal. However, after the first few weeks, intercourse about every three days or twice per week is generally sufficient. A few have relations every two days, and some every four to five days, according to their needs. If a husband and wife have been separated from each other a week or two, when they get back together, they may have intercourse twice in one day or three days in a row.

Our research shows members of our sample having a sexual experience (intercourse or interstimulation) on the average of every 3.3 days. Three percent have a sexual experience every day, 30 percent every two days, 34 percent every three days, 21 percent every four days, and 12 percent every five days or longer. When asked how often they would like to have intercourse and orgasms if they could have this experience every time they wanted to, the husbands' replies averaged every 2.7 days and the wives' replies averaged every 3.2 days. Thirty-nine percent of husbands wanted this experience more often than their wives, while 8 percent of wives wanted this experience more often than their husbands. In 53 percent of the cases, both husband and wife had the same needs. This means that 61 percent of wives wanted a sexual experience as often or more often than their husbands. These findings indicate that the traditional concept that women are not really interested in sex life is not in accord with reality.

During the first twenty or twenty-five years of married life, the husband will probably want intercourse more often than the wife. During the last twenty or twenty-five years, the wife will probably want intercourse more often than the husband. Both husband and wife should adjust themselves to meet each other's sexual drive and needs. When both are motivated by love and Christian principles, this seldom presents a major problem. Restraint and intelligent control is always better than excessive indulgence. It is well to avoid routine, such as having relations only on Tuesdays and Fridays. Often the regular course of daily life forces routine into love life, and a couple simply have to plan the experience. Couples should avoid sameness and routine, if possible. Love and sex expression thrives on spontaneous experiences. Let us repeat, in marriage it is normal for husband and wife to have intercourse whenever they both want to, can, and have the opportunity.

"Who should bring up the matter of having sex relations, the husband or the wife?" The answer is, both of them should bring it up. Many times the experience will be spontaneous and, thus, they both will bring it up together. This is excellent. Our research shows that in the first part of married life sixty-eight percent of sexual experiences are spontaneous and only thirty-two percent are pre-planned. But as life moves on, many times circumstances will be such that experiences will have to be planned and either the husband or wife will have to bring it up. In marriage, if either would like to have a sexual experience, they should not hesitate to bring it up. When both husband and wife face frankly their sexual

needs and turn to each other for satisfaction, this is excellent marriage adjustment.

*"What about experimenting with different positions in sexual relations?"*We recommend that couples feel free to experiment with other positions in intercourse. Some experimentation in the love-play period adds variety to love life. Although most couples use the "man-above" position most of the time, they enjoy other positions some of the time. A few couples adopt other positions regularly because it seems to meet their particular needs.

Our research indicates that ninety-one percent of couples use the man-above position all of the time or most all of the time. Fifty-four percent of couples experiment frequently with other positions, but usually finish with the man-above position. Only four percent use some position other than the man-above position more than half of the time, and only five percent use some other position all of the time.

It is important to the husband to have his feet firmly against the foot of the bed or some solid object to aid him in giving full expression to his sexual orgasm. In case of a bed that has no footboard, the couple may reverse their position so that his feet rest against the headboard.

The wife-above position allows the husband to relax and control himself, and permits the wife to initiate the movement necessary to give her the most stimulation by forcing the clitoris to move over the penis. The disadvantages are that the position is often not comfortable for the wife, the husband may have difficult in controlling his arousal, and neither are in proper position to give fullest expression during orgasms. For some couples the advantages outweigh the disadvantages. This position is often advantageous for a large husband and a small wife.

Another useful position is for both husband and wife to lie on their sides facing the same direction with the husband back of the wife. The penis is moved into the vaginal passage from the rear. The disadvantages are that the penis cannot contact the clitoris and the couple cannot kiss during the experience. The advantages are that the position is very comfortable, the husband can easily use his fingers to stimulate his wife's clitoris, and he can control his own arousal. There are other slight variations of this approach. Many couples use this position for the arousal period and shift quickly to the man-above position for orgasms.

In interpersonal relationships in the community and society, modesty is a queen among virtues, but in the privacy of the marriage bedroom, behind locked doors, and in the presence of pure married love, there is no such thing as modesty. *A couple should feel free to do whatever they both enjoy which moves them into a full expression of their mutual love in a sexual experience.*

At this point it is well to give a word of caution. *All sex experiences should be those which both husband and wife want. Neither, at any time, should force the other to do anything that he does not want to do. Love does not force.*

*"What is the best procedure for the love-play and arousal period?"*There is no one set standard or procedure that should be followed. Actually, there are many possible procedures. In general, the love-play period begins with spontaneous, endearing conversation, with love pats, with hugs, and with kisses. Gradually, couples undress each other. The husband may caress and kiss his wife's body, her lips, her breasts. Finally he will caress her sexual organs. In this process, the husband will want to stimulate his wife in the manner she enjoys and loves the most. A couple should be extremely frank with each other about what they enjoy and what produces sexual arousal.

After the period of relaxed love-play, it is generally efficient for the wife to lie down in the center of the bed on her back, pull her feet up to her hips, open her knees wide, and place her feet flat on the mattress. This puts her in a comfortable and relaxed position. Her husband should lie down on her right side placing his left arm under her neck. In this position he can hug her, kiss her neck, lips, and breasts, and at the same time, his right hand is free to reach down and stimulate her clitoris. Her hands are free to fondle his penis. Or she can place her hand on his hand and direct his stimulation of her clitoris. This position of sexual arousal is described in the Bible in the Song of Solomon 2:6 and 8:3. These two verses are identical. They read as follows: "Let his left hand be under my head and his right hand embrace me." The word *embrace* could be translated "fondle" or "stimulate." Here in the Bible, in a book dealing with pure married love, a married woman expresses herself with longing that her husband put his left arm under her head and that he uses his right hand to stimulate her clitoris.

This position of sexual arousal seems to have been the position used by many people back through the centuries. We do not hesitate to say that the general arousal procedure described here is a part of the plan of God as he created man and woman. Therefore, mankind has used this procedure because it is the plan of God and because it is efficient.

During the arousal period, it is an extra stimulus for the wife to fondle the husband's penis. This adds to the mutuality and fullness of the arousal method as described above. However, often this is too much stimulation for the husband. Self-control is necessary at this point for him. Only experience can determine whether or not a couple can use this part of the procedure.

In this whole arousal process the couple should take their time and concentrate on the arousal of the wife. She should turn herself loose and the husband should control himself. This process should continue until the wife is aroused near orgasm and ready for intercourse.

The art of love-making isn't mastered during a honeymoon or even in a few months or years. There is always something you can learn, and the following tips from Tim and Beverly LaHaye may help.

FOR MEN ONLY

The following suggestions will guide husbands in helping to create in their brides a wholesome appetite for love-making:

Concentrate on your wife's satisfaction. Since a woman's orgasm is much more complex than a man's, it takes her longer to learn this art. A wise husband will make his wife's satisfaction a major priority early in their marriage so they can both benefit from her accomplishment.

The modern research of Masters and Johnson has revealed some interesting feminine responses that a husband should understand. For instance, the intriguing creature known as his wife does not regard foreplay as "a warmup before the game" as men often do; rather, to her it is an integral part of the big game. No husband should rush this activity just because his instincts suggest it. Instead, he should be aware of the four phases his wife goes through in the love-making process. Then he can devote his attention to bringing her through each stage.

Remember what arouses a woman. The sight of his wife getting ready for bed is sufficient stimulation for most men to be ready for the act of marriage. By contrast, the wife at this point is probably only ready for bed! Why is this so? Because men are stimulated by sight, whereas women respond more to other things—soft, loving words and tender touch.

Although not registering on a decibel tester, the auditory mechanism of a woman seems uniquely responsive to the male voice. For instance, teen-age girls are more actively stimulated to emit screams and groans at rock concerts than are their male escorts. Rarely does one hear a man say, "Her voice excites me," whereas it is common to hear a woman exclaim, "His voice turns me on!" That auditory mechanism can be likened to the thermostat on the wall of your home. Entering the house at night, you can turn her thermostat up by speaking reassuring, loving, approving, or endearing words. You can likewise turn her thermostat down through disapproval, condemnation, or insults. In such cases it is safe to conclude that the louder your voice, the more rapidly you turn her down. It is a wise husband who, from the time he gets home from work until he goes to bed, uses his voice and his wife's auditory receiver to turn her on consistently.

Many a wife can identify with Mary: "My husband criticizes

me from the time he walks in the house at night until we go to bed, and then he cannot understand why I'm not interested in love-making. I'm just not made that way!" If only more husbands were alert to this strong influence on their partner's emotions!

Beware of offensive odors. The power of smell is one of our primary senses. Unfortunately, some people experience more difficulty in this area than others, but today there is little excuse for bad breath, body odor, or any other offensive smells. A thoughtful lover will prepare for love-making by taking frequent baths, using effective deodorant, and practicing good oral hygiene.

On the subject of odors we share an observation made in the counseling room about extremely sensitive men. A melancholic man is a perfectionist, a very sensitive idealist. Consequently, he may become "turned off" by the odors emitted by his wife's natural vaginal fluids. Women have a unique problem, not shared by men, for the strong odor of a man's seminal fluid is usually not detected because it remains inside him until he ejaculates it into his wife's vagina, where it is not easily detected until after the resolution phase. But for the wife to permit penile entrance, she must secrete a vaginal lubricant that usually gives off an odor. A husband should simply learn to disregard that odor.

Don't rush love-making. Occasionally, when an experienced wife's monthly cycle causes her to be unusually passionate at a time when coitus is convenient, you both may sustain exciting orgasms in a matter of two minutes or less. When it happens, enjoy it—but don't expect it to be the norm. Most couples find that time in love-play is a major key to feminine response. Therefore the husband who would be a good lover will not advance too quickly, but will learn to enjoy love-play. He will not only wait until his wife is well-lubricated, but reserve his entrance into her vagina until her inner lips are engorged with blood and swollen at least twice their normal size.

The time spent in love-making varies with the culture. The more masculine-oriented the culture, or where sex is viewed as existing purely for male satisfaction, the shorter the time spent in the experience. In such a case, wives view it as a wife's "duty" or as an unpleasant function of life. In cultures where women are cherished and their satisfaction is sought, love-making is a time-consuming art.

Love your wife as a person. No human being likes to be considered an object, for in the quest for identity, everyone wants to be accepted as a person. A young man wins the affection of a young woman because he loves her as a person, showering his attention and affections upon her. After the wedding he too often becomes involved in business and work while his wife is busy raising their children. The two gradually become preoccupied with activities that do not include each other. Consequently, the wife soon feels that the only thing they share is their bedroom life. That is always unacceptable to a woman. This is what gives rise to the complaint often heard in the counseling room, "The only time my husband is interested in me is when he wants sex"; or "I am no longer a person to my husband; I am just a sex object"; or "When my husband and I have relations, I don't feel it is a natural expression of love. Instead, I feel used."

It is interesting that when confronted with the wife's discontent, most husbands admit the validity of her complaint. But they are mystified as to how it occurred so gradually, and they are not always sure what to do to correct it.

There are many things a man can do to express his love for his wife as a person. As he does, he will find them mutually therapeutic. Such expressions not only reassure his wife of his love, but also reaffirm it in his own heart. The little thoughtful things that he does or does not do confirm to his wife's heart that he loves her as a person.

For example, when a man comes home at night, he should indicate a personal interest in her and what she has been doing during the day, rather than become obsessed with the sports page, what is cooking for dinner, or what is on TV. In the evening, giving a hand with the children, relieving her of some of the responsibilities she has borne all day, is a further expression of his love. His spending time with the children rather than being enslaved by the boob tube does as much for the wife as it does for the children.

Moreover, a weekly night out for dinner away from the children is vitally important to the wife, even though the husband's yearnings may be for a quiet evening at home. Then occasionally there are those little birthday and holiday remembrances and, most of all, verbalized expressions of love and approval all through the evening.

A man who treats his wife as someone very special will usually find her eagerly responding to his expressions of love. When his words and actions together convince her that he dearly loves her, their intimate love-making is the natural, culminating expression of that love.[5]

FOR WOMEN ONLY

Relax! Relax! Relax! But like anything else in life, repetition leads to relaxation. It is vitally important that a wife learn to relax in the act of marriage, for all bodily functions operate better under such conditions.

This need for relaxation may be illustrated in a woman's production of vaginal lubrication. Almost all women have the glands necessary to produce this needed fluid that makes possible the entrance of the penis without pain. But when she is tense or nervous, the glands will not function adequately, and she will experience some friction that may be painful. Actually the very fear of that pain can restrict the normal flow of fluids the next time.

Most counselors recommend using a lubricating vaginal jelly during the first few weeks of marriage, which will eliminate the probability of pain and help attain more relaxation. The less tension in the wife, the easier her reproductive organs cooperate with her in the accomplishment of an orgasm.

A wife's relaxation is important to her loving husband, because if he senses that she is tense or afraid, he may interpret that to signify her fear of him. Her relaxation inspires his own.

Chuck your inhibitions. Though modesty is an admirable virtue in a woman, it is out of place in the bedroom with your husband. The Bible teaches that Adam and Eve in their unfallen state were "naked and not ashamed" (Gen. 2:25). Frankly speaking, that means that even in their nakedness they were uninhibited. It may take time for a chaste woman to shake off the inhibitions of her premarriage days and learn to be open with her husband—but it is absolutely essential.

An attractive couple requested guidance for what they called "sexual frustration." The wife of twelve years was too embarrassed to let her husband watch her disrobe at night. "My mother taught me that good women never do that kind of thing," she explained.

I responded, "Just because your mother made the lifetime mistake of failing to make her husband and your father an exception to her modest standards, there is no reason for you to perpetuate that error." I suggested that she let her husband help her undress and encouraged her to relax and enjoy it. It took a while, for she even felt guilty when she found it exciting; but gradually she overcame her acute reticence.

Remember that men are stimulated by sight. Our Lord said, "Whosoever looketh on a woman to lust after her hath committed adultery with her already in his heart" (Matt. 5:28). Has it ever occurred to you that he made no such directive concerning a woman lusting after a man? The reason is clear. Men are quickly stimulated visually, and the most beautiful object in a man's world is a woman.

Many women counselors urge wives to make the daily homecoming of their husbands the most significant time of the day. By bathing, fixing their hair, and putting on fresh attire, they are prepared to give their husbands an enthusiastic welcome home each night. A contented husband is one who is assured that the loveliest sight of the day greets him when he opens the door at night.

Some women resent making their husband's homecoming the object of such attention. Others greet Prince Charming in their work clothes and curlers in an attempt to impress him with the grievous nature of their daily chores with "his kids." The sight of a bedraggled wife may engender sympathy (though it's doubtful), but it will rarely inspire love. A woman has more assets than she thinks, so she might as well take advantage of them. "Clean up, paint up, fix up" is a good motto for every loving wife to remember just before the time of hubby's arrival. We have observed that the women who go that extra mile seem to avoid the problem of "How can I get my husband to be content to come home at night and spend the evening with the family?" If he is provided with a good reason to come home, he usually will.

Never nag, criticize, or ridicule. Since we have already noted that most young men are insecure and desperately need the loving approval of their wives, we will not belabor the point here. Nevertheless, it is important to remember that nothing turns a man off faster than motherly nagging and criticism or ridicule of his manhood. No matter how upset a wife may become, she should never stoop to such conduct, or she may jeopardize a beautiful relationship.

A brilliant doctor with a beautiful, cultured wife had an affair with a woman who had almost no education and was not nearly so attractive as his wife. In fact, he admitted that she was not as sexually enjoyable as his wife. When asked to explain his behavior, he replied, "She makes me feel comfortable." Upon reflection, his wife realized that she had gradually become very critical of his actions and nagged him about the long hours he spent at the office. Not being gifted with ready speech, he had responded by staying away in pursuit of a haven of peace. The other woman was the way he found the peace and quiet he had longed for.

Remember that you are responder. God has placed within the feminine heart the amazing ability to respond to her husband. Most women admit to having exciting experiences they would never otherwise have attempted except in response to something initiated by their husbands. This is particularly true of their love lives.

Except for those occasions when a wife is particularly amorous and initiates love-making, the husband makes the first approach most of the time. Since men are quickly stimulated visually, on many occasions a husband will approach his wife with amorous intentions when love-making is farthest from her mind. The nature of her response often determines the outcome. If she reacts with a sign of indifference (perhaps a groan or yawn), it will probably end right there. On the other hand, if she cuddles close to him for a few minutes and accepts his advances, however passively at first, she will gradually find her mood beginning to match his as her own motor ignites.

Many a wife has cheated herself and her husband out of

countless love-making experiences because she did not understand the unique responding ability of a woman.

Observe daily feminine hygiene. When Beverly was in high school, her girls' physical education instructor told the class that men have a stronger sense of smell than women. That made such an impression on her as a teen-ager that she has always been exceedingly careful in this matter.

Whether that girls' coach was right I do not know, but every woman must be careful of body odors for two reasons: first, in some women the vaginal fluids, especially those which have dried on the outside, can emit a strong odor unless there is regular bathing; and second, she may become immune to her own body smells. In this day of various special soaps, lotions, and deodorants, body odors should never be a problem.

Communicate freely. One of a woman's biggest sexual misconceptions is that her husband knows all about sex. That is rarely, if ever, true. Men may be interested in the subject from the day after they graduate from kindergarten, but they may also be too embarrassed to go to the right sources for the proper information.

Unless a man has read the right books or sought knowledge in the right places, much of what he thinks about women is likely wrong when he enters marriage. The wife should not feel discouraged about this; she should look on this as an exciting opportunity to inform him about the one woman in the world whom he should know intimately. She must learn to communicate freely. Besides telling him how she feels, she should guide his hands to show him what gives her pleasure. Unless she tells him what excites her, he may never know. A wife will probably have to teach only one man in her lifetime about her intimate self. She should do it thoroughly and make it an exciting experience, rewarding to both herself and her husband.

When all else fails, pray. That may sound strange for a minister to say, but if you understand my meaning, I think you'll consider it a valid suggestion. I am convinced that God never intended any Christian couple to spend a lifetime in the sexual wilderness of orgasmic malfunction. He has placed within every woman the sexual capabilities which he meant for her to enjoy. His only real prohibition relates to their use outside of marriage. When kept within the confines of that sacred institution, these capabilities should provide mutual pleasure for both partners.[6]

Understanding the factors of "time and space" in love-making doesn't always lead to automatic success. In the next chapter, Dr. Miles discusses lack of orgasm in more detail.

Chapter 31

DEALING WITH LACK OF ORGASM

BY DR. HERBERT MILES
Sexual Happiness in Marriage

A major problem that causes lack of sexual fulfillment is lack of orgasm in the wife. As Dr. Miles points out, there are answers, if both partners are willing to work lovingly and patiently to solve them.

GOD'S PERFECT PLAN

A married woman who has not experienced a sexual orgasm wants to know, and rightly so, why she has not had the experience. What are some possible conditions which could prevent her from having orgasms? Usually it can be said that there would not be any one single cause, but rather *many small interrelated causes* working together that explain why a wife has not achieved orgasm. If a couple can locate these possible causes, understand them, and accept them as real, they are halfway to victory. These causes may include the following:

A Conflict Relationship Between Husband and Wife. There may have been conflicts between the husband and wife during their courtship days which have been carried over into married life. During courtship, these conflicts may be played down or ignored, but in marriage they tend to grow and become very real. They may consciously, or unconsciously, block a good love relationship.

There may have been conflicts or misunderstandings on the honeymoon in the initial stages of sexual intimacy. These could cause lingering emotional scars and more conflict.

There may be further conflicts in other areas. Five or ten years difference in age may cause unconscious disagreement and strife. If a husband feels that his mother, sisters, or relatives are better cooks or housekeepers than his wife, this could be a major source of conflict. Differences in other areas, such as education, finances, religion, social life, and cultural background may cause conflict.

There may be secret dislikes for each other's habits, attitudes, ideas, and tastes which could tend to block an effective love relationship.

There may be a feeling of competition or jealousy between husband and wife, instead of a feeling of mutual reciprocal love, trust, and confidence.

Personal Problems of the Husband. The husband, who often has a very strong sex drive, and normally so, may tend to be selfish in seeking sexual satisfaction. It is difficult for him to comprehend the slow arousal nature of his wife. Most couples who have not developed a happy adjustment do not take enough time in the arousal period. The husband's hasty approach may unconsciously be crude, bold, and tactless, instead of an approach characterized by gentleness, kindness, patience, tenderness, understanding, and humility.

Sometimes an insecure husband is a dominating husband. No human being likes to be dominated. If a husband tends to dominate his wife, this develops in her secret fears that may block their love relationship.

A few young husbands go into marriage with secret fears about their own sexual capacity, such as feeling they are under-sexed, their penis is too small, or that they will not be able to satisfy their wives. Most of these fears are purely imaginary and have no basis in fact. Yet they are real in the minds of some young husbands and they may hinder a man from meeting the total sexual needs of his wife.

There may be strong guilt feelings about the past such as compulsive masturbation or other attempted sexual outlets.

Personal Problems of the Wife. The young wife may have developed inner fears about sex which are rooted deeply in her childhood and youth experiences. This is sometimes caused by a lack of proper parental guidance. Often, girls secretly feel they are undersexed because their sex drive is not manifested as is that of boys or some exaggerated, imaginary stories they have heard about the sex lives of some women. It is common for girls to feel that they are undersexed. Actually, they are not. God does not create undersexed persons.

Sometimes young girls enter marriage with ascetic ideas, i.e., they feel that sex is not "spiritual," that nice girls just don't "stoop to such." This *utterly false* and *un-Christian* idea can easily block a woman's sexual progress in marriage.

Some girls go into marriage with major feelings of insecurity and inferiority. These feelings tend to block sexual adjustment. Lacking self-confidence, young women are often too passive to become aroused to a full sexual experience.

Sometimes girls go into marriage with guilt feelings about the past. During teen-age years a driving curiosity leads some girls to limited experimentation. Guilt feelings about this experimentation may condition their minds against sex.

Sometimes a wife is simply happy with things as they are. Her main concern during courtship was marriage, a husband, a home, and a baby. Now she has them all. She is thrilled with her life situation. She enjoys meeting her husband's sexual needs. She enjoys her home, her baby, and her friends. She lives unselfishly for them and simply neglects her own sexual needs.

Other General Problems. In a few cases poor sexual adjustment in marriage may stem from some health condition, such as a poor diet, hormonal deficiency, or glandular disturbance. Most of these problems can be corrected by skilled medical guidance.

Some couples simply go into marriage with a lack of knowledge about the nature and function of the sexual organs and about normal sexual techniques. This would not be true of many college graduates or others who have had thorough pre-marital counseling by a qualified marriage counselor.

One of the major hindrances to sexual adjustment in marriage is the lack of time for sexual experiences. Many couples hurry, hurry, hurry through life and through their sexual experiences. It is difficult for a young wife to give herself fully to a sexual experience with her husband during hurried circumstances.

Equal to the lack of time is the lack of privacy, which is often experienced in the first part of married life. Unlocked doors, curtainless windows or doors, squeaking beds, and thin walls are problems. These problems can generally be solved by a couples' creative ingenuity. For example, many couples have made pallets on the floor in order to avoid squeaking beds.

Some couples, before marriage, assume that perfect sex adjustment in marriage would be easy, quick, and automatic. When this does not happen, they develop fears, guilt feelings, and often panic. They become over-anxious, are too serious, and try too hard. In their determined effort to succeed, they often antagonize each other. They need to realize that their experience is rather universal, and that it may take weeks and months to effect good adjustment.

Some have asked, "Can all women achieve sexual orgasms in marriage?" The answer is "Yes . . . if." A significant percentage do not achieve orgasm. In fact, ten to twelve percent of married women in society do not achieve orgasm. However, as a result of our eleven-year research findings, we contend that all women can achieve orgasm in marriage; that is, if they (1) do not have a biological handicap which prevents orgasms (which is very rare), (2) are in reasonably good health, (3) do not have some major mental or emotional disturbance, (4) are in a reasonably good marriage relationship, and (5) apply the principles, attitudes, and techniques advocated later in this chapter, then the answer will probably be *yes.* All women can learn love expression in sexual orgasms. Thorough pre-marriage counseling on sexual adjustment in marriage is of major importance in helping women to realize this high ideal.

A wife who has not achieved sexual orgasm in her marriage is usually in an unfortunate situation. In her sexual experiences with her husband she is sometimes slightly aroused, but never satisfied. Secretly she is disappointed but does not admit it. Sexually, she had expected much in marriage and rightly so, but she has received little. She is careful to help meet her husband's sexual needs, but secretly wonders if there is something wrong with her. As the weeks pass into months, and the months pass into years, the same pattern prevails—slightly aroused, but never satisfied. Gradually she becomes nervous, irritable. The experience becomes distasteful to her. She puts it off as long as possible. When she does submit, it is routine, formal, mechanical. She still loves her husband, but her love is not in the one-sided sexual experiences. This affects the husband's experience. It is not at all satisfactory for him. Unless they are both rather mature Christians, they may drift into a twilight zone of conflicts, frustrations, and emotional scenes. Small molehills may be expanded into mountains. There may be conflict over how to spend their money. Relationships with in-laws may become a major problem. As time moves on such a wife falsely imagines she is undersexed. She feels rejected sexually. She fears that she cannot command her husband's love. She becomes suspicious and jealous. Her husband becomes restless, ill-tempered, impatient, and sullen. When this type of husband-wife relationship is allowed to continue across the months and years, only tragedy can result.

IF A WIFE HAS NEVER EXPERIENCED ORGASM

Any couple who has been married three to six months and has not adjusted sexually should make positive plans toward achieving good adjustment. They must take the initiative. All marriage counselors are familiar with couples who achieved success after one, two, ten, twenty, or more years. It is always obvious that these couples succeeded because they were *trying* to succeed. On the other hand, marriage counselors are familiar with people who have not succeeded and it is obvious that they *have not tried* to succeed.

Any married couple who has not achieved sexual adjustment must set out on a carefully charted plan in which together they move in the direction of victory. Both husband and wife will have to get a fresh start as if they were just now getting married. The past must be forgotten, and each must give the other a chance to perform without demand or criticism. Both should be very clean, and the husband should have a fresh shave and his fingernails trimmed and smooth. All sexual attempts should be in a very private, warm place with no chance for interruption. Both should be rested and as free as possible from stress and tension. The effort is logically divided into two periods of time involving progressive types of sexual arousal techniques.

During the first period, involving approximately one week, sexual effort would be as follows: Both husband and wife should take off all their clothing, and the husband should use his hands and fingers to touch, massage, and fondle his wife's body anywhere she lovingly directs him, while she simply relaxes and becomes conscious of the pleasure gained from his caresses. The wife should avoid any thought of hurrying or of any feeling of need to satisfy her husband, or any effort to experience her own orgasm during this time.

Both husband and wife should avoid negative ideas, such as "I am inadequate"; "I am undersexed"; "I am ugly"; "God is punishing me"; "My parents neglected me"; and "Society has rejected me." They should think positive ideas, such as "God is infinite and good"; "Sex is God's idea"; "I have qualities, abilities, and talents like other people"; "Sex is a central part of me"; "I must use all that God has given me (including sex) to develop my personality and grow spiritually"; "We are equals"; "We need each other"; and "We must meet each other's needs."

The couple should repeat these unhurried, relaxed episodes for whatever period of time gives the wife pleasure—for at least one week. During this period they will avoid touching each other's genital organs. During these sessions, the wife is learning to enjoy her husband's caresses and what her body needs and that she does respond to loving stimulation.

Following the above practice sessions, the wife should now be ready for more intense arousal, moving toward maximum sex pleasure. This should involve all of her body, including her genitals. The next sessions during the second period follow these procedures: Probably the best position for the couple to use (as previously described) is for the wife to lie on her back on the bed with her knees wide apart, her feet pulled up near her hips, and her feet resting flat on the mattress. Her husband should be on her right side with his left hand under her head (Song of Sol. 2:3; 8:3).

This position allows the husband freedom of access for creative exploration and stimulation of her entire body. As the husband explores her body, the wife should place her hand slightly on his so that she can encourage him in specific directions, with the amount of pressure needed to meet her "where and how" desires at any particular time or place. This will allow both husband and wife to learn precise physical communication without verbal request or detailed explanations. The wife should direct his every movement, and he should refrain from any of his own ideas as to what may be stimulating to her. Most women seem to achieve much more pleasure by well-lubricated stimulation along the sides of the clitoris, the inner lips, and around the opening of the vagina. Rarely is there pleasure in introduction of fingers deep into the vagina.

In these sessions, there should be no hurry, and the wife should not at this point attempt to force herself to reach an immediate orgasm. These sessions should extend over a period of several weeks, two or three times per week. Each week the couple will learn a little more about how to excite the wife sexually.

A wife should avoid feelings of fear or dread; fear must be banished because "There is no fear in love" (1 John 4:18). She should think in terms of adventuring, seeking, exploring, giving, and receiving. A couple should be content to learn a little at a time. As the weeks' move by, the couple will gradually move closer to success. Success depends equally on husband and wife. At any time during these efforts that a wife is highly aroused sexually, she should try to continue increasing the intensity of the stimulation with his hand or her hand until she experiences an orgasm. The wife should feel complete freedom to stimulate her own clitoris, if needed, to produce her first few orgasms. Her role in this process must be active, not passive. Both husband and wife must be persistent. Both should be conscious of the fact that with this kind of love-making in marriage is completely within the will and plan of God and is pleasing to him.*

Sexual feelings may be very meager for the wife at the beginning of the arousal period. As the stimulation continues, pleasant sex feelings will gradually grow, build up, develop, and rise higher and higher. This should be continued for five minutes, ten minutes, twenty minutes, thirty minutes, an hour, or longer, if necessary. If stimulation has continued for ten minutes, if the wife is to the highest possible level, usually called the "plateau" stage, and if the stimulation is interrupted for even one minute, her arousal will go down quickly. So the stimulation must be uninter-

---

*Much of the material in these paragraphs concerning lack of orgasm in the wife follows ideas expressed on the tape cassettes *Sex Problems and Sex Technique in Marriage* by Dr. Ed Wheat, M.D., Springdale, Arkansas. Used by permission.

rupted. When the wife is aroused near an orgasm, she will begin to breathe a little faster, heavier, and deeper. Sometimes a woman may get close to her orgasm but it will seem difficult for her to move on into it. If the couple will simply continue this arousal procedure, eventually it will happen. *Many couples fail to bring the wife to an orgasm simply because they stop the arousal procedures before the wife is fully aroused. The right attitude, the right technique, and persistence will result in success.*

Sometimes the wife's sexual feelings will seem to come and go. Now she has it—now it is gone. Sometimes the build-up comes in waves, each wave growing a little more intense. The waves gradually get closer together until the last one "flows over the top," which is the orgasm. At other times instead of the sexual arousal coming in waves, there is a gradual continuous sexual build-up to the orgasm. As a wife moves into her orgasm, her faster, deeper breathing, her mental concentration, her intense sexual ecstasy will culminate in a slight jump of the body, and a short quick gasp for breath. This is actually a muscular explosion, an extremely pleasant spasm of the clitoris, the vagina, and all of her body from the top of her head to the bottom of her feet. Her body, arms, and legs stiffen, she breathes still faster, heavier, and deeper, and she shakes inside and out with waves of pleasure for six or eight long, fast, deep breaths which take only fifteen seconds or less. It may be that the most intense sexual enjoyment in this process of having an orgasm is the period just before the stiffening of the body and the final fast deep breathing.

A woman's orgasms may vary in intensity from time to time, depending on the circumstances. It is obvious that it would hardly be possible for a woman to have an orgasm without knowing it. The husband usually does know when his wife has an orgasm, but at times he may not. He may not know during the first few experiences. As soon as his wife is experienced in having orgasms regularly, he will know all of the time. Under no circumstances should the wife tell her husband she has had an orgasm when she has not. This could set up problems that are difficult to overcome. It is better for husband and wife to face total reality together from the beginning and work things out together.

Confidence in themselves and confidence in and love for each other is important. By all means, a couple should make their love-making a matter of prayer. We should remember that sex originated in the infinite mind of God, that it is God's creation, and that it is God's plan that it be central in all of our lives. Mutual sexual experience in marriage is the focal point of love expression between husband and wife. It tends to relieve anxiety, lessen guilt, and prevent the formation of conflict, tension, and hostility. Also it tends to increase and fortify love and affection. Unquestionably, it is an experience that gives inner poise and security.

Sexual expression in marriage is a function of the total personality at the highest and deepest levels. It makes possible tender understanding and communication between husband and wife that cannot be expressed in language. Through one-flesh sexual experiences in marriage, the spiritual and the physical unite in their highest and most pleasant relationship. Husband and wife are sublimely fused into complete unity and identity through their one-flesh sexual experiences. Truly, sex is the servant of marriage and of Christianity.

♥ FOR FURTHER READING ♥

For a complete discussion of lack of orgasm, be sure to obtain copies of *The Act of Marriage* by Tim and Beverly LaHaye, and *Sexual Happiness in Marriage* by Herbert J. Miles. In *The Act of Marriage*, see especially chapter 8, "The Unfulfilled Woman," and chapter 9, "The Key to Feminine Response," which discusses in detail the Kegel method which calls for the woman to exercise her PC muscle—a muscle that has a strong effect on her ability to have an orgasm.

Another serious problem for some husbands is impotence. For a helpful discussion on how to deal with impotence, see chapter 10 of *The Act of Marriage*.

Chapter 32

S-E-X IS SPELLED
R-O-M-A-N-C-E

BY SHIRLEY COOK
The Marriage Puzzle

In his book, *Belonging* (Zondervan, 1985), Professor S. D. Gaede observes that sexual intercourse has been around for some time and that every human being is a "living testimonial to its timeless popularity." Professor Gaede feels, however, that too many modern marriages have shifted their emphasis from sexual fulfillment to sexual gratification. For today's couples, sexual possibilities abound. "These possibilities," writes Professor Gaede, "are presented as avenues to sexual enjoyment and are intended to prevent boredom, routine or failure. Especially failure. Few things are more dreadful in our era than sexual bankruptcy."[7]

So now we are urged to talk about sex, read about sex in endless manuals and how-to books, and even listen to sex talk shows, absorbing the often questionable wisdom of the likes of "Dr. Ruth."

All of this information and discussion is supposed to guarantee that no one should go without being sexually gratified, but there is a catch. If you achieve a certain level of sexual enjoyment, is it possible that you could be having a better experience? TV, films, books and magazines continue to feed the fantasy. The result is:

> The modern couple is faced with a deadly combination: unreachable sexual goals and unlimited sexual options. Always under the assumption that a better sexual experience is possible, we moderns are on a perennial hunt for new techniques and superior methodology. As a result, we discover option after option, each one heralded as an hedonistic savior, but each one failing to live up to its billing. Unfortunately, in

the process of searching for the ultimate sexual experience, it is easy for us to forget the purpose of sexuality. When this happens, the gift of love is replaced by the goal of self-gratification, and the act of love becomes merely an act.[8]

In the following chapter, Shirley Cook reminds us of the purpose of sexuality in keeping the act of love loving by centering it around the fruit of the Spirit. As you read, ask yourself: "Is our sex life bearing the fruit of the Spirit? Is there Love? Joy? Patience? Gentleness? Goodness? Faithfulness? Meekness? Self-control?"

ROMANCE IS IN

S–E–X, combined with marriage and faithfulness and spelled R–O–M–A–N–C–E, is beautiful.

I like perfume and soft lights and my husband next to me. I like his freshly shaven cheek against mine and his strong arms around me and . . .

It makes me angry when I read the foolish comments of nonbelievers who insist that sex was the devil's idea and that when Adam and Eve yielded to temptation, it was the act of married love that God called sin.

My Bible doesn't read that way. Sex was God's idea. *Illicit* sex is Satan's. Sex as the ultimate interest of life—as god over a man and woman's relationship—robs them of their humanness.

It brings them down to the level of the lower animals.

But in its proper place, sex can be one of the great pleasures shared by husband and wife. A time when each is given up to the other. A fulfillment of the oneness God planned when he created the man-woman puzzle to fit together.

The Bible is clear in its teaching against sexual immorality. "The body is not meant for sexual immorality, but for the Lord, and the Lord for the body. Flee from sexual immorality. All other sins a man commits are outside his body, but he who sins sexually sins against his own body. Do you not know that your body is a temple of the Holy Spirit?" (1 Cor. 6:13, 18–19).

How totally opposed the world is to this teaching! Even you may think it a little straight-laced. Why did God put such restrictions on us?

Recently I heard a young man in a tirade against God's rules. "God doesn't want us to have any fun," he raged. "He says everything fun, like sex and drinking, is bad!"

Later I learned this young man had been the cause of his girlfriend's suffering through the pain and emotional trauma of two abortions. If that couple had saved their sexual powers for marriage, neither would have experienced the shame or guilt of having destroyed two human beings.

Teenagers and adults alike indulge their quest for physical satisfaction through sex outside of marriage.

Self-gratification.

Shame.

Murder.

Disease.

And God wants to take away our "fun"?

The Bible also speaks clearly against adultery, which is "the act of voluntary sexual intercourse by a married person with someone other than his or her own spouse."

"You shall not commit adultery" (Ex. 20:14).

"But a man who commits adultery lacks judgment; whoever does so destroys himself" (Prov. 6:32).

Other types of sexual sin are brought to the light and judged by God's Word. For example:

Homosexuality—Romans 1:26–28.

Incest and perversion—Leviticus 18.

But let's turn our attention away from Satan's misuse of sex to God's plan, which is marriage. How can a couple find the right-shaped puzzle piece to fit their sexual relationship? Physical intimacy is so personal; what is good for my marriage may not suit yours; the part sex plays in your life may be unacceptable to me.

HOW DOES ROMANCE RELATE TO SEX?

This chapter doesn't claim or vaguely aspire to compete with *The Joy of Sex* or *The G Zone*. You will have to find mechanics and "how-tos" elsewhere. I want to delve deeper into human feelings and longings.

What is romance?

Where does it stand in relation to sex?

Is the act of married love only a physical function, or is it a spiritual experience?

How can we learn to relate sexually to our mates in a way that will strengthen and build our relationship in other areas, too?

As I thought about these questions, the command of God to Adam and Eve came to mind, *"Be fruitful and multiply."*

In Galatians 5:22–23, we read about the fruit of the Spirit, the natural product of a Spirit-filled life. This is the fruitfulness we need to satisfy the oneness we long for as a couple. If our marriage puzzle is incomplete or disjointed, it may be that we have left out the fruit of the Spirit. What can we do about the sex-romance part of our marriage puzzle? How about preparing a scrumptious fruit salad?

We are going to taste the fruit of the Spirit one by one, then as we share these morsels with our mates, we can lean back and wait for dessert.

Although some men and most women know this, it bears repeating: Sex doesn't turn on when the lights turn off. It begins at the breakfast table and continues throughout the day—or it doesn't really begin at all. I'm talking about real sex, the kind God intended, the kind that is a result of *love*, not *lust*.

Love. This has to be the first fruit of the Spirit because God is Love.

When a boyfriend argues, "If you really loved me, you'd prove it," he shows he doesn't know the meaning of love at all. Love doesn't have to prove itself. It pours out its favors naturally on the loved one. Look at Calvary.

"God so loved the world" that he *proved?*

No. "God so loved the world that he *gave.*"

That's what love is. Giving, giving, giving.

God gave his Son.

We give ourselves.

Do I love my husband? How much of myself have I given? What do I give him today?

Does he love me? He may say he does, but how much of himself does he give?

It is interesting that although love needs an object on which to spend itself, it is not dependent on reciprocation (although that helps).

God loved us while we were still sinners—even his enemies, the Bible says.

Do I love Les when he is mean and grumpy? Is my love evident when his words are sharp and cutting?

I can't love him then. I can only love when I'm loved in return. I know that. God knows it, too.

So God gives me his love. The fruit of the Spirit is love. I don't have to manufacture it because love is not made with human hands. I have only to enjoy it. God's love for me. In me. Through me.

For my husband.

When he is sweet.

When he is not.

Unconditionally.

Love has a way of expressing itself through the day. A gentle touch on the shoulder and a nibble on the ear. "Wake up, honey." A nice warm breakfast. "Only one egg. We have to watch your cholesterol." Freshly ironed shirts so his colleagues will admire him as much as I do. A little note in his lunch. "I love you and can't wait till you get home tonight." An intimate dinner for two (the kids can go to Grandma's) in front of the fireplace. Candles, best dishes, slinky dress, perfume.

"Hmmm, you smell good!"

Joy. Is there joy in your sexual relationship? Or is it a bother, a bore? Is it something you have to endure? I believe Adam and Eve thoroughly enjoyed each other among the trees of the garden. They gave themselves willingly and totally to one another. Sex was not only warm and loving, but fun and joyful.

Because of the overexposure through films, books, and television, we have lost our spontaneity and naturalness. Sex has become a grim reality, a list of "you do this, and I'll do that." The mystery and pleasure have been reduced to either disappointment or pride. Sex books and manuals may be helpful at times, but they can also promote never-reached expectations that lead to a sense of failure or a lack of fulfillment. The human body begins to look like a machine with buttons and levers instead of a beautiful house.

We can put joy into our love-life. Like love, joy is a gift from God. "That my joy might remain in you, and that your joy might be full" (John 15:11 KJV).

Pluck this fruit of joy and taste it. Fear withers it. Shame covers it. There is no need for either in married love. Joy in sex is God's gift, and his gifts are good and perfect.

Warning: Your joyful response to your "lover" may catch him off guard, but he will be thrilled. Be willing to discover each other in a new and glorious way.

Peace. In our frenetic, agitated world, we are tempted to rush and hurry up our romantic interludes with the same attitude in which we pack the kids off to school. God gave sex to married folks to help them unwind, relax, and get in touch with themselves.

Sex outside of marriage cannot experience the peace of God or any of the other spiritual fruit, but I regard peace as especially impossible because of guilt.

"'There is no peace,' says the LORD, 'for the wicked'" (Isa. 48:22).

What peace a man and woman can enjoy when their union is ordained of God! He is there. He is pleased. His peace envelops the husband and wife in their act of loving and giving. "Live in peace with each other" (1 Thess. 5:13).

Patience, or *Long-suffering,* is the next delicacy—an all-important attitude in our loving-giving times. Patience with "headaches." Patience with "I'm too tired tonight, honey." Patience to wait.

I suppose patience is one of the hardest qualities to attain, but it is right at our fingertips. Yes, patience, too, is a special God-trait, a characteristic freely given to those willing to *wait* for it.

Patience in love-making is essential. For each partner, especially for the woman to reach full satisfaction, patience is the key. Be patient with your mate. Be patient with yourself.

Be patient with God. You have plenty of time. Remember, this is a lifelong commitment. Relax.

Gentleness. To me, gentleness and romance are almost synonymous. Soft kisses, a fleeting look, a warm embrace.

As refreshing as a gentle rain is my lover's touch to me.

Gentle words.

Gentle hands.

A gentle man.

Roughness and severity, the opposite of gentleness, leave me cold. Wounded in heart. Is that because I'm a woman? Or do men like gentleness, too? I think they do. Even the hurly-burly macho-man appreciates the softness of a gentle woman as a contrast.

Some associate gentleness with weakness. Not so. Jesus—the most powerfully masculine man of all time, the exact image of the Father, who created the Universe with the word of his mouth—was known for his gentleness. For his accessibility to the sick, the aged, and the very young.

"A gentle answer turns away wrath, but a harsh word stirs up anger" (Prov. 15:1).

Goodness—"Morally correct, virtuous, kindly." Even though we may have brought some bad memories from our past into our marriage, we can forgive and forget. When we ask, God forgives our sins and cleanses us so that in his eyes, we are as good as Jesus.

If we have been in the habit of reminding each other how "bad" we are, is it any wonder we have problems with this piece of our marriage puzzle?

See yourself as good in Christ.

See your mate that way, too.

Jesus said, "Only God is good."

And he shares that goodness with us.

Fantastic!

Faithfulness, or *Faith.* Remember, even if your eyes have a tendency to stray, and your thoughts to wander, God will give you a faithful heart. It is a delicious fruit. Eat it every day to keep trouble away.

Meekness. The definition of this word to married people is found in Ephesians 5:21: "Submit to one another out of reverence for Christ."

Think not only of yourself and your needs for fulfillment—think of your mate. Submission is *not* just for the wife. It is commanded for both husband and wife. Mutual submission equals marital satisfaction, whereas menial suppression equals slavery.

Jesus said the meek will inherit the earth. Maybe they also inherit the blessings of married love.

Temperance or *Self-control.* This last fruit of the Spirit keeps sex within the bonds of marriage and for times you both want it.

People who have not learned to control their sexual urges are problems to themselves, to those around them, and to society in general.

Nightly our newspapers report crimes of rape and incest. Sickening. Disgusting. Horrifying. These out-of-control people need the power of God to restrain them.

Unfortunately, we sometimes read stories of well-known, respected Christians who have been caught up in sexual sins, too. And all of us Christians suffer as a result of it.

Let's allow God to satisfy us with his self-control so we can enjoy the full cluster of the fruit of the Spirit—love, joy, peace, patience, gentleness, goodness, faithfulness, meekness, and self-control.

What a good thing God has given us—what a happy lifestyle! "Marriage is honorable in all, and the bed undefiled" (Heb. 13:4 KJV).

"Dear God, help me to keep the romance in marriage. It's all too easy after many years to become lazy and disinterested in sex. Cause me to see my mate of thirty-five years with a fresh awareness—then show me how to incorporate my new interest into our lives."

♥ "HMMMM, YOU SMELL GOOD!" ♥

Remember, God has made marriage honorable and the marriage bed is undefiled, so there is nothing wrong with being romantic, desirable or "sexy" if the motive is to glorify God and seek sexual fulfillment, not sexual gratification. Shirley Cook has given several suggestions for putting the right kind of romance into your marriage. Here are some more:

- ♥ Maybe you and your mate need to discuss your sexual relationship. If you have difficulty communicating verbally, get out pencil and paper and write each other a love letter.
- ♥ Don't be self-conscious about the shape of your body. Maybe you think it is too fat, or too thin, but it is yours— and your mate's. You belong to each other. Just keep your body clean, dress it neatly, and then, as the occasion arises, give your mate *all of you*. Love him for himself. Love that person who lives inside the body. Love covers a multitude of sins—along with the lumps and bumps of an imperfect shape.
- ♥ Start your love-making in the morning. Brush your teeth, comb your hair, dab a little perfume behind your ears, and sit across the breakfast table in something colorful and attractive instead of that ugly old bathrobe. Be as attractive

to your partner at home as you are to the people in your place of work.

♥ Husbands can inspire or turn off their wives to romance, too. Use a deodorant regularly. And it is not sissy to apply hand cream on rough hands that can chafe a woman's tender skin. Hold her chair when she sits down. Hug her a little longer than you would a hot coal. If men only realized how far a gentle and kind word goes, they wouldn't be so quick to ignore or bark at their wives. Listen when she talks to you. Stroke her hair. Tell her she's beautiful.

Sexist?

Maybe.

But that is what romance is all about.

Romance is a secret society—with just two members.[9]

♥ BLISS, BATTLEGROUND, OR BOREDOM? ♥

To come back to the question that opened this section, which word best describes your marriage? Battleground or boredom are definitely conditions you want to avoid. Bliss would be nice, but perhaps you would settle for exciting or stimulating, possibly even satisfying or contented.

Following is a list of suggestions by Anne Kristin Carroll for making your sexual life more stimulating. Mrs. Carroll gathered these twenty-seven ideas from hundreds she read or heard about while working on her book, *Together Forever* (see pp. 160–162). Some of them may appeal, while others might appall. What this list proves is that sex is a very personal journey for every married couple. Suggestions, tips and techniques are useful, but only if used to make sex a means, not an end.

1. Be sure you always have privacy. If you have children, the door to your bedroom should have a good lock. Use it.

2. Be sure you start your romance in the morning.

3. Once a week, call and tell your husband, or your wife, how exciting and desirable he or she is to you.

4. Always be prepared for sex, mentally and emotionally.

5. Never forget that praise goes both ways, and is certainly a strong cornerstone as you build a healthy sexual relationship.

6. Ladies, buy some new nighties, and before you do, see what your mate prefers.

7. Guys, surprise her with a get-away weekend for the two of you. Pick a romantic setting. Make this a very special time—and I mean in a pretty motel, with hot and cold water, not in the back of a fishy-smelling camper!

8. Ladies, consider the meals he really prefers and begin to

prepare a very special one, farm the children out for the evening, and have a candlelight dinner alone, perhaps in front of the fireplace.

9. Don't let your sexual life become routine. Why not try some different rooms, the pool or hot tub (if they are private), or (at night) a secluded beach.

10. Set the mood. Some evening, in lieu of the radio, I'd like to suggest two albums or tapes which have soft mood music and the sound of rain falling in the background. They are recorded by the Mystic Moods and are entitled "One Stormy Night" and "One Stormy Weekend." Let me state very clearly, I neither like nor approve of the Mystic Moods' record jackets; on the other hand, why throw the baby out with the bath water?

11. Depending on your personalities, and your size, and the size of your bathtub, try a double-bubble bath before retiring.

12. Guys, when you are ready to go out for the evening, try noticing your wife for a change; really give her one of those long stares, the kind you used to give her before you married her. Tell her she's attractive, or her attire is stunning.

13. Flirt with her in public. I promise you that the reaction when you get home will be beautifully rewarding.

14. Remember, God created sex for our pleasure and enjoyment. *Don't* make it a time of trying to be absolutely perfect; allow for mistakes. Don't make it a workout in calisthenics; relax and enjoy. In other words, don't keep a sex manual under the bed and pull the thing out every few minutes to be sure you are proceeding on schedule!

15. Men, please remember special days—Valentine's Day, birthdays, Mother's Day, anniversaries. If you really want to get a loving and devoted response, bring a small present home in remembrance of the day you met, or the day you proposed!

16. I realize that God created flowers first, but I think maybe he fashioned Eve right beside a flowerbed. It doesn't have to make sense to you, but one of the quickest ways to a woman's heart is through a surprise bouquet of flowers! Try it, and let me know the results.

17. Ladies, remember the song that was popular a few years ago, "Wives and Lovers"? Get a copy. Those words hold a mountain of truth. Wives should always be lovers, too. In fact, a good wife is, as the old saying goes, "a lady in the parlor, and a tiger in the bedroom."

18. Ladies, if your husband travels, as my Jim does, every so often slip little love notes in his suitcase or briefcase before he leaves town.

19. Both of you take a minute every month or two and drop a romantic card to your mate.

20. As you probably know by now, men are usually more

stimulated by sight and smell than women are. Check with your man before investing in some erotic perfume guaranteed to have him chasing you around the house. Let him smell it first. And you might tell him what kind of after-shave turns you on. Jim and I have learned the hard way that some fragrances not only didn't have us chasing each other, but almost made us sick to our stomachs.

21. How about buying some new sheets, perhaps satin or nylon? They are a change for most people and an invitation to more than television watching.

22. Ladies, in particular (but gentlemen, too), there is nothing that relaxes a tired guy, revitalizes him, like a good massage.

23. Some couples have found that soft lights, candles, black lights or smoky mirrors on the ceiling are their forte. The black lights and smoky mirrors are usually preferred by the younger set. Please let me warn you, if mirrors are your thing, have them professionally installed. Improper installation can cause serious injuries.

24. I have a friend who has made a fake fur throw for her bed. Her husband thinks it is delicious—particularly when she is on it.

25. Ladies, leave the curlers and facial cream for nights when hubby is out of town or after he leaves for work.

26. As we have discussed before, for both of you, give your mate a new body to respond to, a new you. Take off any extra weight. You'll look better, feel better and certainly be more confident.

27. If your city is large enough, you probably have a club of some sort that for a small fee supplies you with discounts at many of the best restaurants, theaters, and dinner theaters. This is a good way to stay within the budget, and still have a special evening out—one a week if possible.

♥ SOURCES OF ADDITIONAL INFORMATION ♥

Obtain complete copies of:

Sexual Happiness in Marriage, Herbert J. Miles (Zondervan, 1982).

The Act of Marriage, Tim and Beverly LaHaye (Zondervan, 1976).

Other good sources of information are the writings and tapes of Dr. Ed Wheat. Obtain a copy of *Intended for Pleasure,* Dr. Ed Wheat (Fleming H. Revell, 1977), or Dr. Wheat's two-tape cassette albums: *Sex Technique and Sex Problems in Marriage* and *Love Life for Every Married Couple.* These may be obtained from your local Christian bookstore or ordered from Bible Believers Cassettes, Inc., 130 North Spring Street, Springdale, Arkansas 72764.

In Loving Memory of Martha Shedd
January 15, 1916—April 2, 1988

Her first concern was for me. She'd been in the fog of anesthesia for eight hours. This was her first operation ever. The doctors had gone into her lungs to answer the question "Does she really have cancer?" She did.

It was the worst kind. Violent. Malignant. Now she was coming to and we were alone. I was holding her hand when she opened her eyes and asked how *I* had done through the long hours.

That was so like Martha. She lived in grace and now she would die in grace. Thinking of me, thinking of others, thinking of the Lord.

How does a person face both life and death without crumbling, without growing bitter?

For Martha there could be only one answer. She read her Bible, prayed, and tuned to the inner Presence daily. Always high on her agenda she kept this purpose: to develop a personal friendship with the Lord. Friendship with the Lord for life, and for death. That's a lofty goal for everyone of us, isn't it?

Charlie Shedd

PART VII

SPIRITUAL GROWTH:
HOW'S YOUR SOUL COMMUNICATION?

If you and your mate both claim Christ as Lord and Savior, you must answer the same question every day:

"I'm a Christian, you're a Christian, but are we Christians *together*?"[1]

And to take the question one step further: "Is God at the center of our marriage?"

In his book, *The First Years of Forever*, Ed Wheat observes: "We discover that if we try to keep our love separate from God— jealously guarding our relationship, even from the Lover of our souls—our love will turn into something else." He quotes C. S. Lewis in *The Great Divorce*:

> No natural feelings are high or low, holy or unholy, in themselves. They are all holy when God's hand is on the rein. They all go bad when they set up on their own and make themselves into false gods.
>
> We realize that no earthly love, no matter how wonderful and intimate and beautiful, can replace our need for closeness to God. He has created us so that there is a place within which can be satisfied only by intimate fellowship with him. In the shelter of his love, our love for one another can safely grow and flower until it is transformed by heaven into something even more wonderful.[2]

Dr. Wheat's words are lovely, but we may read them with a twinge of guilt. We say we desire God's hands on the reins of our marriage, but in truth we often take the bit in our teeth and run.

There just isn't enough *time* to accomplish all that must be done! And, ironically, those with whom we should spend time together are left out. Perhaps the most squandered commodity in any marriage is time. The following questions can give insights to how much you value the most important time of all.[3]

Are you using time in a way that blesses your marriage? For example, do you thank God for his daily gift of time to you as man and wife? Time is, after all, the invaluable raw material of your marriage. You wake up in the morning and it's always there— twenty-four precious hours to spend as you choose. But do you live and love one another as if it were the last day to enjoy your gift of time? What would you do if you knew you were spending your final twenty-four hours together? What would you say? How would you act toward one another?

Do you regularly invite God into your precious slice of time together? Have you gained his vision of what he wants to do with your marriage?

Do you practice mutuality each day? That is, do you adapt, accept, forgive, always making all things mutual in the spirit of loving give and take? In Paul's words, "Be merciful in action, kindly in heart, humble in mind. Accept life, and be most patient and tolerant with one another, always ready to forgive if you have a difference. . . . Forgive as freely as the Lord has forgiven you. And, above everything else, be truly loving, for love is the golden chain of all the virtues" (Col. 3:12–14 PHILLIPS).

Do you value the ordinary days—even the dull routine—of living together? Would you trade one ordinary day with your partner for ten "exciting" ones without him or her? Be careful how you answer. Perhaps you have already been doing just that and calling it "working extra hard at the office" or "pouring myself into the children."

Do you flee from the greatest sin of all—wasting your time together on self-centeredness, self-justification, self-advancement, self-pity, self-aggrandizement and self-righteousness? Your time is far too precious for that. In the words of a character who speaks from the grave in the Pulitzer prize-winning play, *Our Town,* "Yes . . . that's what it was to be alive. To move about in a cloud of ignorance; to go up and down trampling on the feelings of those about you. To spend and waste time as though you had a million years. To be always at the mercy of one self-centered passion, or another. . . ."[4]

Do you spend time in a way that helps you hold fast to that most important thing of all—love? In describing that greatest thing, Henry Drummond said, "Covet, therefore, that everlasting gift. . . . Ye will give yourselves to many things; give yourself first to love. Hold things in their proportion. *Hold things in their proportion.*"[5]

"Proportion" has to do with relationships, comparative size or extent. As you seek to hold the many facets of your marriage in proper proportion, is the spiritual part of growing together receiving due attention? To give God his proper place in your conversation and deepest sharing is the goal of the two Zondervan authors who are the sole contributors to this section of "The Growth of Your Marriage"—Charlie and Martha Shedd.

In chapter 33, the Shedds ask how any couple can be "absolutely sure our marriage will last." Their answer is "soul communication" and they include a questionnaire to help you rate your marriage in that area.

In chapter 34, they share the secret of a no-fail marriage—never failing to study Scripture and pray together.

In chapter 35, they share their personal system of Bible study, which is based on marking their Bibles with three special signs: candles, arrows and question marks. The candles denote new light shed on their lives; the arrows denote new convictions they have achieved together; and the question marks suggest areas they want to discuss and learn more about.

In chapter 36, the Shedds give their ideas for what they call "talk-starters" and "meditations" that may stimulate thoughtful conversation of your own.

In chapter 37, they switch gears to share their thinking on the other half of soul communication—prayer. They know the familiar problem of going through start . . . after start . . . after start.

In chapter 38, they go on to the next logical concern: how to keep prayer going and sharing their own unique methods of praying, including "javelin prayers"—the short, quick thrust of a single thought upward to the Lord.

In chapter 39, they focus on the big question: "Is it worth it?" The Shedds' enthusiastic reply is yes and they support this declaration with nine reasons, plus a guarantee to anyone who wants to try it in their own marriage.

Be assured that these brief pithy chapters will not be some kind of guilt trip designed to prick your conscience for "not praying or studying enough together." The Shedds write with an infectious enthusiasm as they speak from over forty years of experience. They make the unabashed claim that they have seldom missed a day of personal devotions or a weekly time of sharing and prayer and study together. There were exceptions due to illness or other circumstances, true, but very, very few. Their consistency was not motivated by teeth-gritting determination nor white-knuckle commitment. They were faithful in Bible study and prayer because they knew that the more faithful they were, the better their marriage—and everything else—would go.

The soul communication that you and your partner are developing is quite possibly the most important kind of communication you can ever work on in your marriage, but be warned of two dangers: lack of time and lack of mutual respect. Even as you read these chapters, you will find yourself saying, "All this is nice and idealistic, but how would we ever find the time?"

The answer is a familiar one, "You never *find* the time to do anything; you *make* time."

But even if you make the time, beware of coming together with the wrong attitude. Nothing will kill soul communication between husband and wife faster than a lack of mutual respect. The following quotes from letters the Shedds have received say it all:

> Whenever we sit down to talk about the Bible, my husband has all the answers. He doesn't pay attention to what I think. Why? Because he thinks he's so brilliant. How long would you study the Bible with someone like this?[6]

> You want to know why my wife and I don't pray together? Study the Bible together? Or even why I don't go to church with her any more? Because that group she got into two years ago, that's why. . . . They've taken a perfectly wonderful woman and changed her into a spiritual snob.[7]

The Scriptures speak much of being alert for Satan who prowls about like a lion, seeking everyone he can devour. If you get serious about soul communication, you can be sure he will be there, ready to prowl and pounce. The best way to resist is to do what Charlie and Martha Shedd advise. Two are always stronger than one and when two come together in his name, he is there, also.

Please—
Come take my hand
Let's walk!!

Give me you—
    Eyes saying—Hi!
    Glances saying—I care!
    Handholds that let me know you were only teasing;
    Hugs saying—Thank you for being you!
    Kisses that—gently want me;

Then Love—
    That says, I'll be here tomorrow
     and everyday hereafter.[8]

Chapter **33**

ARE WE CHRISTIANS TOGETHER?

BY CHARLIE AND MARTHA SHEDD
Bible Study Together

W hat are the three most important words in any marriage? The answer Charlie and Martha Shedd give in the following chapter may surprise you. Strangely enough, those words aren't "I love you" or "Please forgive me." As you read, ask yourself:

- ♥ How close are we to the dream we started with when we were married?
- ♥ Around what and whom do we center our communication as husband and wife?
- ♥ How easily do we dispense grace to one another?

BIBLE STUDY TOGETHER

How close are we now to our original dream of the perfect marriage?

Good question any time for any couple. But for the Christian husband and wife there is an even more important question:

How close are we to the dream our Lord dreamed when he brought us together?

Would he rate us higher today than one year ago? Five years past? Twenty?

Is there any way to be sure our marriage is growing in its divine potential? Are there certain secrets to a no-fail union?

We think the answer is yes, and one of these certain secrets for us has been "Bible Study Together."

So this is our claim, our promise, the exciting news from forty years' experience—

Any couple who will commit themselves
together for a life-long sharing of
God's Word will be brought to exciting
new discoveries in their love
plus exciting new discoveries with the Lord.

How could this happen? The answer is that Bible Study Together brings with it two basics of marriage at its best. And the first of these is:

TALK, TALK, TALK

What are the three most important words in any marriage?

"I love you"?
"You are beautiful"?
"Please forgive me"?

All ultra-important. But our nomination for the three most important words in any marriage:

TALK, TALK, TALK

Why? Because without talk, talk, talk, "I love you" will not come through. Neither will "You are beautiful" nor "Please forgive me" nor any of the other basics.

From both sides we hear these noncommunication complaints, "My husband won't talk." . . . "You've heard of the Sphinx? Well, I married it." . . . "There he sits! The great stone face." . . . "If all the silent husbands of the world were laid end to end, it would be a good thing."

In workshops, personal consultation, letters, phone calls, casual conversation, we hear the same sad lament from lonely wives. Less often, but still too often, comes the same low moan from a puzzled husband.

Ask the average engaged couple, "What do you like best about your relationship?" Almost always, high on the list of answers is some song of praise to their communication. "We can talk about anything. . . ." "No hiding places. . . ." "I can tell him everything I'm thinking. . . ." "Super sharing."

So what happens to these open roads?

To be sure, some of the answers are psychological. But for us, and for most couples we know, there is another plain vanilla reason.

Time for talk gets away from us. Almost before we know it our priorities are rearranged. Secondaries take first place and we find we're becoming strangers.

Here then is another all-important question for every one of us:

In our marriage how much time do we spend talking together about the deeper things?

How many minutes per week do we share what we *feel?* How many hours do we spend discussing the goings on inside?

If that is too sensitive for starters, ask it another way: How many minutes in-depth communication (per week) do we estimate for the average couple?

We've asked this question of husbands and wives by the thousand:

> Eliminating budget, children, neighbors, relatives, weather, happenings, events, things you see on television, what you read in the newspaper—all these aside—how much time per week do you spend communicating in depth?

The answer: *Six minutes!*

There are ten-thousand-eighty minutes in seven days, and the average couple is reporting spending six minutes communicating feelings!

An Eastern university conducted a professional survey on this same theme. They asked one thousand couples: "How much time do you spend each week in 'serious discussion'? And you define the word *serious.*"

Their finding? Amazing coincidence—six minutes.

A statistical accident, chance happening, quirk of the figures? Or could it be that no matter who is doing the testing, no matter who is being tested, this is a fact . . .

> In too many marriages
> bridges have broken down,
>   the expression of real feelings,
>   sharing of all things serious
>   has been crowded out.

*   *   *

LISTEN, LISTEN, LISTEN

> Those who have ears to hear
> Let them hear.*

*   *   *

> Blessed is the marriage where both husband and wife
>   are learning the art of
>   TALK, TALK, TALK.
> Blessed, too, are they who train themselves to
>   LISTEN, LISTEN, LISTEN.

*   *   *

In personal Bible study we adhere to the principle of "escalating attention."†

Principle: Any statement of our Lord which appears twice, we will read twice and ponder twice.

Three times? Triple attention.

Does he say it four times? Quadruple.

But some statements of Jesus are repeated again and again. What do we do with these? These we inscribe on our minds until they become a natural part of our thinking.

Wise, then, the couple who will consider eight times the words: "Those who have ears to hear, let them hear."

Modern translations open up new vistas:

"The man who has ears to hear should use them!"
Matthew 13:9 (PHILLIPS)

"Be listening."
Matthew 13:43 (AMPLIFIED)

"Let him who has ears, listen."
Mark 4:9 (WILLIAMS)

"Take note of what you hear."
Mark 4:23 (NEB)

---

*Matthew 11:15, Matthew 13:9, Matthew 13:43, Mark 4:9, Mark 4:23, Mark 7:16, Luke 8:8, Luke 14:35

†Editor's note: For those interested in the origin of word combinations, the principle of "escalating attention" is a term developed by the Shedds for their own Bible study together. In workshops and in their writing, Charlie and Martha have often advised, "Your Bible study together will have more meaning and be more fun if you develop your own vocabulary."

"Be careful how you listen."
Mark 4:23 (PHILLIPS)

"Give your minds to what you hear."
Mark 4:23 (RIEU)

"Be sure you really listen."
Mark 4:23 (C & M)

Is there any Christian who would disagree with this statement: Jesus was the number-one Communicator of all time?

There may be others who would argue that claim, but not the believer. Nearly two thousand years after his life on earth, he is still communicating. Still speaking. Still listening.

Why would the Great Communicator eight times emphasize and reemphasize the importance of listening?

One sure answer is that most of us too often have our focus wrong. In too much of our conversation, we operate on this delusion: Our thoughts are more important than the thoughts of others. Our words have the better sound. Our feelings matter more than their feelings. Our ideas take precedence over theirs.

Not so. Always, without exception, one hundred percent of the time, no variance—to other people, what *they* think *is* number one to them.

How can we reverse this human predicament? How can we break the cycle of conversational selfishness? Our answer: Bible study together.

As we share the Scripture, we learn to talk, talk, talk.

Through this talk, talk, talk, we sense an amazing fact. "My mate is honestly interested in what I think, how I feel, what I say. The Spirit of the Lord has touched our marriage with divine concern."

But that is only half the miracle. Through Bible study together, his Spirit is reshaping *our attitudes*. More and more *we* really *do* care with his kind of caring. It actually *does* matter to us what our loved one thinks, feels, says. So because it matters, we listen. We hear what we have not heard before. We even hear what the older translations call "groanings of the Spirit." Later scholars labeled these "mysteries," "whispers," "deeps of the spirit."

Does anyone know all the vocabulary of the Spirit? Of course not. But we know this. . . .

*   *   *

The more we are faithful to our Bible study together,
   That much more the Spirit comes to reshape
      our attitudes;
   He frees us to talk, talk, talk;

He breaks up our selfishness
   that we might truly listen, listen, listen.

Then he provides another all-important ingredient for maximum marriage.

"GRACE"

If I should show you who I am, and you don't like it, what have I left? Nothing. There I am—all the weaknesses, the strange, and the evil in me—all exposed!

Is there any couple anywhere, any husband, any wife who hasn't felt touches of this?

So here we are with another reason couples do not talk and listen—*fear!*

What is the answer? The answer is that beautiful biblical word *grace.*

Grace is theologically defined as "the free, unmerited love and favor of God." Which being interpreted in everyday vernacular means, "God loves us not because we deserve it; not because we've earned it; he loves us because we're his!"

All-important questions for any marriage:

What is the grace quotient in our love?

Do you understand that I accept you as you are right now? Faults and peculiars and funnies and odds, show me all you want to show me. Tell me all you want to tell me. Whatever you've done, whatever you dream, past, present, future, facts and fantasies, you can count on my love.

This is grace, and only grace leads us to feel, "Surely the Lord is in this place. This is none other than the house of God and this is the gate of heaven."

♥ IS OUR MARRIAGE REALLY CHRISTIAN? ♥

You're a Christian. Your spouse is a Christian. But what about the most important question: Are you Christians *together*—blending in the Lord? Following is a list of questions used by Charlie and Martha Shedd in one of the most popular sessions from their marriage workshops. The subject is "soul communication," and it always begins with this questionnaire. They recommend that each spouse take it individually and give a rating on each question between 0 and 100. After marking each question from 0 to 100, compare your ratings with your partner's. (Seventy is "passing" for each question.)

Search for a Better Marriage

1. When it comes to vital, livable religion, I rate our marriage overall _____.
2. In theological understanding, early training, and genuine caring for the things of God, I rate myself _____; my mate _____.
3. Our church life together can be rated _____; my own _____; my mate's _____.
4. At the point of sensitivity and service to the needs of other people, I rate my mate _____; myself _____.
5. "I want you to be you." "I respect your individuality." "Let freedom ring." Because God made us unique, these sounds will be heard often in a good marriage. At this point I rate our marriage overall _____; my own attitude _____; my mate's _____.
6. The time I give to Bible reading and study of the Scriptures rates _____; my mate's _____.
7. I have my own personal prayer time. Yes _____ No _____.
8. My spouse and I pray together regularly. Yes _____ No _____.
9. When it comes to mercy, grace, forgiving, and forgetting, I rate my attitude _____; my mate's _____.
10. If it is true that the family is the "number-one theological seminary," for overall relationship to the Lord, including family devotions, I rate our family _____.

If you didn't score too high on some of these questions, don't be discouraged. You are just getting started. Soul communication is a lifelong process and you don't achieve instant perfection. In the next chapter, the Shedds discuss the way to have a no-fail marriage.

Chapter 34

HOW CAN WE BE SURE OUR MARRIAGE WILL LAST?

BY CHARLIE AND MARTHA SHEDD
Praying Together, Bible Study Together

After achieving the highest divorce rate in history in the 1970s, Americans began asking a new and vital question in the 1980s: "How can we make our marriage last?" The National Center for Health Statistics reports that divorces in the United States most often occur within six and a half to seven years of marriage, which has led to the well-known euphemism, "The Seven-Year Itch."[9] But, according to one researcher, the peak time for danger of a divorce comes even earlier.

Anthropologist Helen Fisher of the American Museum of Natural History, New York City, gathered divorce data from 58 countries, regions, and cultures between 1947 and 1981 and came up with an average that suggests a "four-year itch." She studied married couples from Greenland to Australia, who lived in cities, farms, and suburbs. Her data came from 150 different studies and her conclusion is that more marriages end after four years than any other time.[10]

As all too many Christians are well aware, being believers in Christ and members of a church doesn't guarantee you that you won't fall victim to the four-year itch, too. In fact, according to Helen Fisher's studies, in the United States there was strong evidence for a two-year itch among many couples in the period covered by her study. In the following chapter, Charlie and Martha Shedd claim there is a guarantee against divorce for the Christian home, if Christians will use it. As you read, consider these questions:

♥ How sure are we that our marriage will last?

♥ What part does prayer and Bible study together play in
our marriage now?

♥ If we do little Bible study or praying together now, what
are the reasons? Could we change this pattern if we
wanted to?

EVER AFTER?

"What can a couple do to be *absolutely* sure their marriage
will last?"

Constantly this same plaintive query continues to surface. It
surfaces in our workshops, in personal consultation, over the
phone, and by letters beaucoup. Dozens, hundreds, thousands of
times we hear it asked, in many versions, against many backgrounds.

> There is this one couple in our church who seemed to have a
> good thing going between them. They even taught our couples'
> class together for a while. Now, we can hardly believe it! They
> are getting a divorce and we are all simply stunned. I mean,
> really in shock about it.
>
> And do you know why?
>
> I think it's because we're scared. What if that happened to us?
> Most of us think we have a good marriage most of the time, but
> don't you imagine they must have thought so, too?
>
> Well, we talked it over and decided to write you with this one
> question:
>
> What can a couple do to be *absolutely* sure their marriage will
> last?

For us there are two answers.

Almost everyone we hear on marriage and many of those we
read tell us that better communication is the secret to a healthy
marriage. They're right. Too many couples we know walk away
from their marriages because whatever communication they had
was the exchanging of surface data, and the question stands:

> What is the point of establishing channels of communication
> between husband and wife if there is no life-giving message to
> fill the channels?*

> For us, both Bible study together
> and praying together
> Become the answers to

---

*From the foreword of *Bible Study Together: Making Marriage Last,* Dr. Eugene Nida,
Former Executive Secretary for the United Bible Societies of the World, Consultant
for the American Bible Society.

communication at its best.
We also believe that for all husbands and wives
everywhere
They are the *absolute* answer
to this oft-repeated question:
"What can a couple do to be *absolutely*
sure their marriage will last?"

THE ONLY BASE FOR NO-FAIL MARRIAGE

When we married forty-five years ago, we were already well-acquainted with the Bible. We had heard it read in church, in Sunday school, even at family devotions. It had also been a part of our wedding—a beautiful white Bible.

So we had determined the Word of God would have a prominent place in our home. And it did. Every day we saw it on our nightstand. No way we could miss it there. We couldn't miss the other copy either—the one on our coffee table.

Yes sir! Yes ma'am! Ours would be a Bible-based home. . . .

There is an interesting story of a very old church in Mexico. Every Sunday as the people entered, they bowed to a crevice in the wall. There, beside the outside door, they nodded to the hole, and many of them crossed themselves.

Why? That was exactly what some reporter asked one day at a funeral. Curious, he began to inquire of the worshipers, "Why do you bow to this hole in the wall?" Nobody knew the original reason. But almost everyone said, "We bow because our fathers and mothers bowed, and crossed themselves. Our grandparents did. Everyone *always* bows."

More curious than ever, the reporter went back to his office and began extensive research. Finally, in an old, old picture from the newspaper morgue, he found the answer.

There in that faded picture, beside the door, a crucifix was clearly visible! Since those days the old church had undergone complete refurbishing, and in the process of remodeling, the workmen had apparently plastered over the crucifix. Yet still today the people bowed, and some of them still cross themselves—the reason long since lost.

So Martha and Charlie nodded to their Bibles. We nodded to the one on our nightstand and the one on our coffee table. Not quite so often we nodded to others on our shelves. And that's the way it was around our house for much too long.

Most of us believe our God is a personal God, and that is one terrific assurance. The Creator of our universe did not go away and leave us. After the days of his creation, he stayed around. For what? One reason: He stayed to congratulate himself and see that it was good.

That's what we're told before chapter 1 of his Book is done. But as we read on, we discover another reason:

God stayed with us because he loves us.

Then as our New Testament begins, we see him coming to share himself, giving himself completely for us . . . birth, crucifixion, resurrection, that we might know his living presence personally and in our relationships.

> Amazing truth—
> The same God who sets out his stars each night
> He who says to the sun each morning,
>   "Rise, shine,"
> This very same God is a personal God
> He wants to be our God
> And if we give him a chance,
> He will speak to us
> He will meld us
> He will bless us
> He will make our marriage what it should be.

We have heard it said that year five is the bad year for marriages. Others point to seven or eleven. For us, every one of those first years had too many negatives. Sometimes they came with shouting and crying and loud banging. Sometimes they came unannounced on padded feet. And these for us were the real uglies, because they also left on padded feet. But in their going, always they seemed to leave behind more uglies—hurt and a sense of rejection—anger and slow burning—feelings unexpressed.

When we first began to sense that our love was heading for trouble, we made a decision. Since we weren't doing well by ourselves, we would ask the Lord for his help. And where better to get his help than directly from his Word?

So we made a commitment. Every day we would read the Bible together. We would agree on a book and then we would take turns reading one chapter to each other . . . every day.

How did that go? It didn't. How could that possibly go? One of us is up at the crack of dawn, sometimes earlier. The other barely believes in God before 8:30 in the morning and two cups of coffee.

Then, too, there were days we didn't see each other until the evening hours. So we would do our reading at bedtime? Great way to get ready for sleep. Fill the mind with good things. But if the mind is weary, the body tired, concentration level zero, commitment level also zero, what then? "What then" was a total collapse of one more good intention.

What can we do when our good intentions collapse?

We can quit. Give it up as a great idea which never got off the ground. Or if we're still believers, we can back up and come at it again. So once more we committed ourselves to daily Bible reading. But this time we altered our approach.

Because we were not synchronized in those early morning hours, we would have our quiet times at different hours. And we still do.

Every day for forty years, we've read our Bibles and had our quiet times ... each at our own time.

Every week for two thousand-eighty weeks, we've come together (at least once) for sharing.* "What did the Lord say this week to you, to me, for us together?"

♥ WHERE DO YOU STAND TOGETHER? ♥

As you read these first chapters on soul communication, your marriage falls into one of three categories:

- ♥ You are already having prayer and Bible study together as a couple, and enjoying it.
- ♥ You haven't been doing much prayer and Bible study together, but you are open to the idea and would like to discuss it further.
- ♥ You don't do prayer and Bible study together and it's doubtful that it would be easy to begin, usually because one spouse, or perhaps both, is reticent for one reason or another.

If you fall into the first two categories, talk together about the claim the Shedds make for prayer and Bible study as an absolute guarantee for a no-fail marriage. Why did this work for them? Why can it work for you?

If you fall into the third category and are the spouse who would like to do more Bible study and prayer, begin praying now, asking the Lord to show you how this might happen. Then read on to get more ideas for how soul communication can become a reality in your marriage.

Every day? No exceptions? Of course, there have been exceptions, but very few. *Every* week? Very, very few exceptions. Almost zero. And the reason? The more we are faithful to Bible study together, the better our marriage goes. But that's only reason one. Reason two: the more we are faithful to Bible study together, the better *everything* goes.

Chapter 35

CANDLES, ARROWS, QUESTION MARKS

BY CHARLIE AND MARTHA SHEDD
Bible Study Together

Suppose you have decided you would like to study the Bible together. What method can you use? In the following chapter, Charlie and Martha share their special Bible marking system, which features candles, arrows and question marks. As you read, think about how you might adapt their system to your own study.

OUR OWN SECRET CODE

"Isn't it sacrilegious to mark in a Bible?" Surprising how many times we are asked this question. For us the answer is a resounding No!

The Charlie-Martha Bible study method is based on three specific marks:

CANDLES

ARROWS

QUESTION MARKS

Each morning as we read our Bibles individually, we underline and mark.

When we come to an entirely new thought, a new insight, we underline and put a candle in the margin—a candle for new light.

When we read something we don't understand, have doubts about, something we can't believe, we underline and place a question mark in the margin.

Then there are the places that convict us. These make us

realize we are not what we should be. Here we underline and use an arrow in the margin. (We do not place arrows for each other. We allow each the dignity of discovering his/her own sins.)

CANDLE   New light!
                 Fresh thought!
                           Something we've never seen before!
                           Exciting!

QUESTION MARK
                 I do not understand.
                 Vague
                           Whatever could the meaning be?

ARROW   This convicts me.
                 This points to a flaw.
                           There is a weakness in me here.
                           I am a sinner.

Then once each week, sometimes more often, we sit together and share our marks. Straight out of God's Word comes the impetus for talk, talk, talk.

Where do we begin?

If one of us has a mark at the first verse in Chapter 1, we begin there. A candle? "This is a new thought to me. What do you think?"

Perhaps it's chapter 5 before we come to a mark. Or there may be four marks in chapter 3.

At the same verse one of us may have a question mark; the other, a candle. Here we help each other.

If we both have a question mark, we go to our commentaries. What does the commentary say? Biblical scholars give us more inspiration for talk, talk, talk. Yet this we learned early in our pilgrimage: What the Lord says to us is more important than what he says to the scholars!

That being true, we discuss our questions for our own conclusions before we go to the wise men.

Candles for enlightenment
Question marks for further study
Arrows for self-analysis.

Anyone who needs a psychiatrist should find a psychiatrist. But those of us who are wrestling only with oddities or neurotic trends may require nothing more than the help of a friend. For us, Bible study together provides that caring friendship. In the interchange of arrows, we share our quirks and foibles. With the tender touches of love and with God's help, we unbraid some tangled skeins. We help each other and he helps us to a new peace.

If communication
(real depth communication)
is the key to marriage at its best
AND

If it is true that God
instructs and guides
out of his book
then this has to be one no-fail
method for no-fail marriage.

Why? Because by this system two great things are happening—

We are sharing* our discoveries with each other
and with the Lord.
But this is only half the miracle.
He is sharing himself with us.

Now to some specific candles, arrows, question marks, with a thought-starter for each.

CANDLES FOR NEW LIGHT

In the year that King Uzziah died, I saw the Lord . . . high and lifted up (Isa. 6:1 RSV).

Sometimes when things are hardest, we *do* see the Lord. What negative experience in our lives has brought certain positives?

To see your face is, for me, like seeing the face of God (Gen. 33:10 C & M).

What a goal! Are we reflecting the Lord for each other?

Avoid stupid arguments (Titus 3:9 C & M).

Flash! Some things are not worth even the slightest fuss. Are we reserving our energies for the important differences?

We must not be proud or irritate one another (Gal. 5:26 C & M).

Let us now have an honest sharing time on: "The thing you do that irritates me most."

Elkanah [her husband] answered [Hannah], "All right, do whatever you think best" (1 Sam. 1:23 GNB).

As far back as the Old Testament a fine part of a fine marriage has been the granting of individual freedom.

---

*Sharing is the key word. Our dictionaries define *sharing* as: "Giving and taking" . . . "enjoying together" . . . "exchange of ideas" . . . "developing with another" . . . "accepting" . . . "sharing the good and the bad."

Where do we tend to box each other in?

Where would the ring of some liberty bell sound a plus in our love?

Would we have more genuine togetherness if we allowed each other more freedom at certain points?

ARROWS FOR CONVICTION

In quietness and confidence is your strength (Isa. 30:15 LB).

In times of rush, rush, rush, are we learning to listen for the still small voice?

Do the noises of this world steal too much of our sharing time?

I will help you to speak, and I will tell you what to say (Exod. 4:12 GNB).

What a promise—a promise for every public contact, and a promise for our sharing with each other. Are we letting the Lord bring us to a fuller sharing?

That's enough! Don't mention this again! (Deut. 3:26 GNB).

Should we write this verse on our minds for touchy subjects, embarrassing moments, delicate matters, certain historical boo-boos?

And I sat among them, overwhelmed, for seven days (Ezek. 3:15 LB).

Always, getting behind the scenes in other lives prepares the way for more understanding, more love. Do we honestly try for the other person's view?

Don't hide your light. Let it shine for all (Matt. 5:16 LB).

Do we tend to let our light shine for people outside the home and fail to turn it on for each other?

Men, you should have listened to me (Acts 27:21 LB).

If ever a verse applied to us, this is it.

"I told you so" . . . "Didn't I warn you?" . . . "Why didn't you pay attention?" . . . Shouldn't these lines be on our "never-say" list?

QUESTION MARKS

The Lord called me before my birth. From within the womb he called me by my name (Isa. 49:1 LB).

What do these words mean to us: "Sacredness of life" . . . "the rights of the unborn"?

With all the talk about abortion these days, do we have a solid theological position here?

For the eyes of the Lord search back and forth across the whole earth (2 Chron. 16:9 LB).

Is this an awesome warning or a beautiful promise?

As a couple, are we doing anything we'd rather the Lord did not see?

For it is written, "As I live," says the Lord, "every knee shall bow to me and every tongue confess to God" (Isa. 45:23 C & M).

Can this be true?

When . . . ?

The Bible has it all. Every subject we need to discuss, every problem we need to face, every place we need to grow—it's in The Book. That being true, every couple who will commit themselves to Bible study together is sure to grow, to be taught, to be entertained. And one certain reason is that God speaks to us out of his Word as he speaks nowhere else.

All this is why we call the Bible—solid base for no-fail marriage.

♥ TRY IT, YOU MIGHT LIKE IT! ♥

Why not try the Shedd method of Bible marking for a few days and share your results with each other? What seems to come up most for you as you study—the candle, the arrow, or the question mark?

Establishing a Bible marking system is only a rudimentary step in Bible study. For what the Shedds call "talk-starters" (words and questions for discussion and meditation), see the next chapter.

Chapter 36

STARTER IDEAS FOR BIBLE STUDY TOGETHER

BY CHARLIE AND MARTHA SHEDD
Bible Study Together

For many married couples, finding the right material for Bible study and soul communication is no small chore. On the following pages, Charlie and Martha Shedd offer some ideas that have worked for them. As you read, keep in mind that you need topics and "starter ideas" that will keep you both interested and at the same level of concern. Avoid heavy theology and sticky doctrinal issues. Focus on areas where the Bible can speak directly to your relationship.

A PLACE TO START

"Will you give us some suggestions for launching talk, talk, talk?"

Following are what we call "talk-starters."

These come from our own private collection of helpful texts. Each began with one of our candles, arrows, question marks. Each has contributed to our love.

ANGER

Let all bitterness, and wrath, and anger, and clamour, and evil speaking, be put away from you (Eph. 4:31 KJV).

There will be flashes of anger in even the best relationships. Do we need to develop a more effective way to handle hostility when it surfaces? How can we "put away" these things of Ephesians 4:31?

Additional verses for meditation:

Proverbs 15:1   Matthew 12:25
Romans 12:19   James 1:19–20

Our own thoughts on these verses:

_____

_____

_____

_____

FAITHFULNESS

Be thou faithful unto death, and I will give thee a crown of life (Rev. 2:10 KJV).

Some scholars say God is promising a crown to those who will be forever loyal. But isn't our loyalty to each other a part of our loyalty to him?
Are we absolutely loyal to each other? Verbally?
Are we thoroughly committed to physical fidelity?

Additional verses for meditation:

Genesis 2:23 (Matthew 19:5)
Ephesians 4:29

Our own thoughts on these verses:

_____

_____

_____

_____

FORGIVENESS

Therefore as God's people consecrated, and dear to him . . . be merciful . . . just as the Lord has freely forgiven you, so must you do also (Col. 3:12–13; phrases from TWENTIETH CENTURY, KJV, and WILLIAMS).

Does either of us tend to carry a grudge?
Or do we both harbor hurts too long?
What can we do to live more like genuine Christians at this point?

Additional verses for meditation:

Matthew 5:7
Matthew 6:14
Matthew 10:21–22

Our own thoughts on these verses:

_____

_____

_____

_____

JEALOUSY

Wherever you find jealousy and rivalry, you also find disharmony and all other kinds of evil (James 3:16 PHILLIPS).

In any way are we in competition of a negative nature?
Are we mature enough to face these problems, discuss them, and then surrender them to the Lord?
Do we know where our jealousies originate?

Other verses for meditation:

Galatians 5:26
1 Corinthians 13:4

Our own thoughts on these verses:

_____

_____

_____

_____

MONEY

Be not highminded, nor trust in uncertain riches, but in the living God, who giveth us richly all things to enjoy (1 Tim. 6:17 KJV).

Are we too much concerned with money?
Does it dominate us?
Would we do better with a better philosophy of spending, saving, giving?

Additional verses for meditation:

Ecclesiastes 5:10   Luke 6:38
Malachi 3:10   2 Corinthians 9:7

Our own thoughts on these verses:

_____

_____

_____

_____

PRAISE

A word at the right time is like apples of gold in a network of silver (Prov. 25:11 C & M).

For compliments, praise, and verbal affection, our rating is:

Superior _____
Average _____
Low _____
Zero _____

Are we satisfied with things as they are?
What could we do to improve?

For meditation together:

Song of Solomon

Our own thoughts on praise to our lover from this beautiful psalm:

_____

_____

_____

_____

SELFISHNESS

Love does not insist on its own way (1 Cor. 13:4–5 rsv).

Would ours be a better marriage if we disciplined ourselves to think *first* of our mate?

Are we growing in the unselfish love described throughout all of 1 Corinthians 13?

How can we become more Christlike in our concern for each other?

Other verses for meditation:

Matthew 7:12 and Luke 6:31
Romans 12:10
Galatians 5:13

Our own thoughts on these verses:

_____

_____

_____

_____

TROUBLE

The Lord is good, a strong hold in the day of trouble; and he knoweth them that trust in him (Nah. 1:7 kjv).

Anyone can smile when success is certain and the sky is blue! But what will we do when the shadows come?

Will the troubles we face drive us apart or draw us together?

Additional verses for meditation:

Psalm 30:5
Psalm 138:7
Psalm 46:1
Romans 8:28

Our own thoughts on these verses:

_____

_____

_____

_____

TRUTH

You desire honesty from the heart . . . sincerity . . . truthfulness (Ps. 51:6 LB).

On a scale of zero to one hundred, our grade for absolute honesty with each other is _____.

Since the Lord desires honesty from the heart, are we growing in that direction?

Additional verses for meditation:

John 8:32
Philippians 4:8

Our own thoughts on these verses:

_____

_____

_____

_____

_____

_____

_____

_____

MORE IDEAS FOR MEDITATING TOGETHER

At times we find it especially helpful to listen quietly together for a time. When we do this prayerfully, we can almost hear the Lord saying, "Now that you have had your discussion, here are some questions from me!"

We share now some more of the Lord's questions to us.

Each of the following meditations came together like this: One of us marked the verse with which the meditation begins. Following our discussion we quieted ourselves and listened. Then came more talk, more ideas, more surfacing of selves, more questions.

As noted, somehow for us these questions that seem to come from the Lord have about them an awesome holiness. "Holy" in the sense of "whole"; "wholeness" . . . "constituting an undivided unit" . . . "sound and healthy" . . . "complete" . . . "total."

Our hope is that, by introducing you to our methods, you will work out your own methods. But by whatever method you develop, we know you will find this true: *If you will include some listening time together at the passage, some waiting together, you will hear him!*

Then when you follow even the smallest light he gives you, he will lead you to more light.

HOW GOOD ARE WE AT SAYING "THANKS"?*

We will think now of our marriage as an old-fashioned scale—on the left, negatives; positives on the right.

Most of the time our scale tips right ☐
                       left ☐

We will set aside time for thanksgiving now. We'll make a list of things (about each other) for which we are grateful:

Thoughts on gratitude from a California husband:

I am writing you because this is Thanksgiving month, and I want to tell you what happened to my wife and me last year about this time. Up until that time our marriage was only average, and some of the time below average.

For the first year or two we had a good thing, but then it began going downhill. The reason was that we had fallen into the habit of putting each other down.

This year when school was out for the holiday, we sent the children to visit my wife's parents. Then later she and I drove to their home for Thanksgiving dinner and to bring the children back.

I don't know who thought of it, but on that drive one of us suggested we start telling the things we were grateful for, the good things that had come our way during the past year.

Then my wife began to tell me some things about me she was thankful for. Wow! This was something new. So I told her some, and it had been a long time since we had exchanged compliments. We could hardly believe this was happening.

Well, the whole thing was absolutely great. In fact, it was so great we decided that from then on we would do it more often—like every week.

Since then, we've hardly missed a week, and we both agree this past year is the best year we've ever had.

We thought maybe there might be some other couples who would like to hear what happened to us. Like I said, just telling each other what we are thankful for does make a difference, and especially it does if we keep it up.

---

*Illustrations for this section have been selected from two sources: (a) the letters we receive; (b) input from our Fun in Marriage Workshops.

Assignment: This week we will go to the commentary and count how often the words *thanksgiving* and *gratitude* are mentioned in the Bible. Then we will select seven of these verses and discuss one every day for seven days.

A word fitly spoken is like apples of gold in a setting of silver (*Proverbs 25:11* RSV).

DO WE OVER-RESPOND TO EACH OTHER'S MOODS?

Subjects and happenings which tend to depress the mood in our marriage are: (Check one or more)

- [ ] Money
- [ ] Weather
- [ ] Criticism
- [ ] Too much to do
- [ ] Worry
- [ ] That let-down feeling after success

- [ ] Disappointment
- [ ] Change of plans
- [ ] The news
- [ ] Houseguests
- [ ] Disagreements
- [ ] Others

Who sets the mood around here? Do I "go down" when my mate is down?

Comes now an interesting letter from Iowa. Joe is a high school teacher. His wife is an accountant, and from Joe's report, they must have an unusual relationship.

> Thelma is a beautiful person, but she's one of those moody people—up one day and down the next. This hasn't always been easy, but lately I decided to do something about it.
>
> I used to get up in the morning waiting to see how Thelma felt, and then I felt like she felt. If I sensed she was feeling good, I'd feel good. If she was out of sorts, I'd be out of sorts, too.
>
> But not anymore. I came to the conclusion that this was ridiculous. Why should I let her determine how I was going to feel? So now I ask myself, "Who sets the mood around here?" Then I decide how *I* feel.
>
> Almost immediately I began to see some changes, because Thelma started reacting to my feelings. She noticed it right away, too, and even thanked me. It is almost as if she needed direction and was waiting all this time for me to take a position so she could follow.
>
> Anyway I can tell you since I decided to take the lead, things have been a lot better for both of us.
>
> Then there is one thing more. I also began to notice a difference in my classroom. It was as if my opening tone not only affected my whole day, but the students' as well.

What couple couldn't profit from a discussion of Joe's question: "Who sets the mood around here?"

Sensible people will see trouble coming, and avoid it, but an unthinking person will walk right into it and regret it later (Proverbs 27:12 GNB).

CAN WE HONESTLY DISCUSS OUR TEMPTATIONS?

For us, this beautiful line from Longfellow is another goal in our love:

> Straight between them ran the pathway,
> Never grew the grass upon it
> Singing birds, that utter falsehood
> Story tellers, mischief-makers,
> Found no eager ear to listen,
> Could not breed ill-will between them,
> For they kept each other's counsel,
> Spake with naked hearts together.*

Check one:

In our marriage are we hiding more and more from each other? Yes _____ No _____

Are we moving toward more thorough surfacing of all our feelings, including the ultra-sensitive? Yes _____ No _____

From a tempted husband:

> Do you know anyone who ever cheated on his wife without getting caught? I have heard of men who say they did, but seems that every one of my friends who tried wound up in a peck of trouble, and I don't want that.
>
> Most of the time my wife and I have a pretty fair thing going. But that doesn't mean you never think of anyone else, does it? Right now someone is throwing it at me, and to be one hundred percent honest, I'm thinking it over.
>
> What I really wish is that I could talk to my wife, but we've never been that open. So that's what I'm asking, "Does anyone ever get by? No problems?"

A most unusual letter, and he must be a most unusual person to be so honest. But that unusual honesty is the very reason he wouldn't be getting by even if he had that one hundred percent clandestine affair.

In the long run people as honest as he is will respect themselves more if they are honest all the way.

The honesty questions come often. "Should we always tell all?" "When?" "How?"

Caring mates learn the art of timing. Some days it takes all the strength we have just to go on breathing. To unload at low energy levels might be devastating.

We're also wise to ask this caring question: "Would it hurt my mate more right now to hear it all than it would hurt me to carry it by myself for a time?" In most marriages the Golden Rule of Jesus is without equal.

The Song of Hiawatha, sc. VI, ll. 8–15.

But the fact still stands: Total honesty is a goal toward which we must keep our love moving. Any husband and wife studying the Bible together will hear it over and over: Personal honesty, honesty with each other, honesty before God is the ultimate.

But now I tell you; anyone who looks at a woman and wants to possess her is guilty of committing adultery with her in his heart (Matthew 5:28 GNB).

ARE WE DOING ENOUGH FOR OTHER PEOPLE?

Would we love each other more if we took more time to love other people?

1. In our marriage are we really "other-oriented?" Yes _____ No _____

2. How much thought, time, effort, money do we give to the needs of people outside our home?

3. What could we be doing in our neighborhood, community, state, the whole world to make things better for somebody who needs what we could give?

   Thoughtful story from a lady in New Hampshire:

   Most of us have been residents here a long time, and I suppose like they say about New Englanders, we are a bit standoffish at first.

   A year ago this fall, a new couple moved in across the street from us. Of course, I took the usual plate of cookies over and found out a few things about them. They came from South Carolina. I didn't ask why they moved here, but I had my own thoughts.

   Our winters are sometimes severe, and this winter was no exception. Anyhow, we all noticed a peculiar thing. The wife did their snow-shoveling, carried the wood for their fireplace, and ran most of their errands. I guess we wondered about that, because her husband was a big, strong, healthy-looking man.

   Now I almost hate to tell you. In February, the husband died, and naturally we all went to visit the widow. Then we learned the full story. He'd had a serious heart attack and doctors agreed his condition was inoperable. This made it necessary for him to take early retirement. Since the house belonged to an old aunt, they could live here rent-free.

   Why am I writing you? Maybe this is my way of going to confession. All that time, we were doing nothing, and we are ashamed of what we didn't do. We're even ashamed of each other. My husband and I agree we would be feeling better now if one of us had said, "Come on, let's extend ourselves a little."

   Fine words for improving relationships at home and other places: "Come on, let's extend ourselves a little."

I tell you, whenver you did this for one of the least important of these brothers of mine, you did it for me! (Matt. 25:40 GNB).

ARE WE SPENDING TOO MUCH TIME WITH TV?

"Where are we spending too much first-class time on second-class items?" In our workshops, this two-letter answer comes through like a flashing red light:

TV

What difference does it make how many hours we spend watching TV?

Here is a letter which says it well:

> We have a question for you. It is a question we ask ourselves regularly and we pass it along. There might be other couples who need to ask: Are we falling into the trap of believing that, because there is a lot of talk going on at our house, we are really communicating?
>
> This is our story:
>
> We have been married three years and, at first, things were good. Then lately we realized something was wrong. It seemed somehow we were losing touch. No, it wasn't that we were angry, or afraid to talk, or not spending time with each other. It was rather that we just were not getting things said.
>
> Well, we sat down to analyze and we found the trouble all right. The trouble was our TV. At breakfast, it was our favorite newscast; in the evening when we got home from work, the news again. After dinner, it was back to the tube for our regular programs. Weekends, too, a lot of TV—games, golf, even church services.
>
> You can see there was plenty of talk, but it wasn't talk *between us*. In one of your books you wrote that we need to check whether we are communicating, not only with our heads, but with our souls, too. Well our problem was all eyes, and too little soul as in "Too much television!"
>
> When we located the trouble, we determined to make some changes in our lifestyle. We decided to set aside time for talking about important things and for getting our feelings across to each other. I guess you would say we made the decision that there is nothing on television as important as what goes on between us.

Always this is super loving: Face facts, analyze what's wrong, and then do something to make things right again.

In any way does this story apply to us?

But seek ye first the kingdom of God and his righteousness; and all these things shall be added unto you (Matt. 6:33 KJV).*

---

*As we go through the Bible together, one verse brings to mind another. We have learned to be particularly attentive when this happens. For us double direction may be doubly effective, as in the verses above.

WHAT IS OUR COURTESY QUOTIENT?

Essay on "What Makes Marriage Great" (by small girl):

> I think to make marriage great you have to treat each other like
> company a lot of the time and be polite and stuff like that.

How much difference would it make in our marriage if we
gave more thought to treating each other like company and "stuff
like that"?

1. For "please" . . . "thank you" . . . "excuse me" . . . and other
phrases of common courtesy, we grade each other (zero to 100)
_____.

2. Do we sometimes treat other people better than we treat
each other? Yes _____ No _____

Words of a young wife:

> I am slowly losing respect for my husband. Why? He's
> becoming so careless about his personal habits. Sometimes I
> think he is almost vulgar. I've talked to him about this and told
> him he's turning me off, but I don't think he hears me. Is there
> anything I can do?

Words of a young husband:

> I'm getting worried about my wife and what she is becoming. I
> don't like to say it, but sometimes she's downright crude.
> Never a "please" or a "thank you" anymore. I know things are
> different today from the day I grew up, but shouldn't manners
> be "in" for every generation?

*   *   *

> There's one sad truth in life I've found
>   While journeying east to west,
> The only folks we really wound
>   Are those we love the best.
>
> We flatter those we scarcely know,
>   We please the fleeting guest.
> And deal full many a thoughtless blow
>   To those we love the best.

(Author unknown)

*   *   *

From Genesis to Revelation the Bible bears down hard on this
fact: Real religion is tested by our treatment of others. Shouldn't
this especially include those at our own address?

Love is not ill-mannered (1 Corinthians 13:5 GNB).

I'M SORRY

1. The last time one of us apologized was _____

2. Have we discussed thoroughly why it may be hard to apologize? Yes _____ No _____

3. When one of us apologizes, the other accepts that apology graciously. Yes _____ No _____

4. Does either of us tend to be a bit pious? Yes _____ No _____

According to our mail, resistance to apology is a common problem.

This letter comes from Illinois, but what the lady says might have application anywhere.

> My husband has a very hard time admitting he is wrong. All the men in his family are like that. So it meant something special to me when you wrote in *Letters to Karen* that it doesn't matter who starts the fuss. What matters is that someone will start the apologies.
>
> It was almost uncanny that I read those words at a time when we were into a big one. He wouldn't give in, and I wouldn't. So I asked myself, "How do we get out of this?"
>
> Then I got an idea. I wrote him a note and, before he left for work, I slipped it in his pocket where I knew he would find it. Now, you should understand, I still felt he was more wrong than I was. He even admitted that later, but what I said in the note was:
>
> I am honestly sorry we aren't getting along.
> Please, can't we be friends again?
>
> That's all I said, and would you believe when he found my note, he called me to tell me he wanted to be friends again, too. He said he was as sick and tired of the fuss as I was. Then he even said he was sorry—two or three times! That might not sound like much to you, but if you knew him, you'd know it was a miracle.
>
> I thought maybe you'd like to know about this. I really think it's true that the most important thing is not who is to blame, but who will start somewhere trying to make things right again.

I confess my sins, I am sorry for what I have done (Psalm 38:18 LB).

DOES ANYONE AROUND HERE NAG TOO MUCH?

In our marriage workshops one theme sure to raise its ugly head is "nagging." We find it wise on occasion to do some personal research on frequently asked questions from other marriages.

Is there a specific point in our relationship where we should quit nagging? Yes _____ No _____

One of us? Yes _____ No _____

Both? Yes _____ No _____

Who's most prone to nag? _____

Psychologists tell us almost all nagging comes from background factors. The mind experts also say many of the problems in any relationship started long before that relationship began. If they are right, then knowing the ancient origin of any problem will have a positive effect on any marriage.

Letter from an appreciative wife:

I thought you might be interested in something which happened with us. For several years I've been twenty pounds overweight. Sometimes thirty. Wally's reaction was to nag, and the more he nagged, the more I ate. Well, three months ago on my birthday, he wrote me a nice note in which he told me he was giving me an unusual gift. His gift was *that he would never say another word about my weight.*

Now that was really something for Wally. In fact, it was sensational coming from him, because, as long as I can remember, he's been on my case. So now he said he was through, and I can still hardly believe it. Sure, he slips sometimes, but when that happens, all I have to do is look at him a certain way, and he tells me he's sorry.

Can you guess what happened?

When I saw he really meant it, something changed in my attitude. I decided I would try my best to make him the gift of a wife like the one he married. No, it hasn't been easy, but I'm determined, and I've lost fifteen pounds. I still have several more pounds to go, only now I feel confident that I'm on the right road. Some day I'll get it off. There is simply no way I can tell you what this has meant to both of us.

Three more words to go along with *talk, talk, talk,* and *listen, listen, listen*—

hush, hush, hush.

Assignment: Individually and together we will consider places where we tend to nag. Then we will try to track these to their origin and discuss our findings.

A nagging wife is like water going drip-drip-drip on a rainy day (Proverbs 27:15 GNB).

ARE WE EXPECTING TOO MUCH TOO SOON?

The children of Israel were sometimes impatient. Their leaders were forever calling them to understand that the Promised Land could not be reached in one giant step. "Little by little"—these three words can become a motto for our relationship. In serious Bible study we hear this note again and again.

Examination for patience factor:

1. Do we push too hard sometimes for changes and corrections? Yes _____ No _____

2. In order to better both myself and our relationship, I am willing to change, but in these areas I feel you pressure me too much:

_____

_____

_____

3. Can we agree on one place (or several) where we should begin easing off?

_____

Jerry and Sue had come for counseling. The very fact that they were having trouble surprised them. Theirs had been an ideal courtship. Everyone said they made a perfect couple. But now, only a few months down the road, things weren't going well.

In all the flow of their talk, Jerry kept returning to this one-liner, "I guess we expected too much too soon."

Many of us make that mistake. We assume that, by the mere act of mounting those chancel steps, we are climbing heaven's stairs.

Yet those of us who have been married a long time know it isn't that way. The heavenly marriage is more like a kit to be put together slowly, carefully. Sanding, fitting, gluing, hammering, varnishing, waxing, polishing. "I do" does not mean "we did it."

One of our friends is a hobby craftsman. He carves mottoes with his router and he makes interesting plaques of his favorite sayings. Most of his mottoes are done on polished wood—pine, mahogany, walnut, oak, maple. But one he inscribes on tough-looking boards from the beach or from an old barn. And that motto is:

> Radishes mature in a few weeks.
> Oaks take years to grow.

I will drive them out little by little (Exodus 23:30 GNB).

♥ IF YOU WANT MORE HELP ♥

Be sure to obtain a copy of *Bible Study Together* by Charlie and Martha Shedd. It contains many other suggestions for studying Bible texts and characters, as well as spiritual and devotional issues that are crucial to a marriage relationship.

Studying the Bible together is only the first half of developing soul communication. The other half is prayer. In the next several chapters, the Shedds share what they learned in over forty years of praying together.

Chapter 37

THE REAL PURPOSE OF PRAYER IN YOUR MARRIAGE

BY CHARLIE AND MARTHA SHEDD
Praying Together

Do you pray to get or to give? You say you do both? That's an honest answer. In this next chapter, the Shedds explain what prayer has meant in their relationship. As you read, try to keep one question in mind: "What is the real purpose of prayer in our marriage?"

THE PURPOSE OF PRAYER

It was a great day for us when we caught the meaning of Revelation 3:20: "Behold, I stand at the door and knock," saith the Lord. "If any man will open the door, I will come in" (Revelation 3:20). Until then our dominant thought was turned in the wrong direction. We conceived of prayer first as an effort to bring the Lord in. Seeking, pleading, asking, we must draw his attention to our needs.

Then gradually came the light. Prayer, at its finest, is not beating on heaven's door. It is rather opening inner doors to the Lord. Always in the divine-human encounter, the first move is God's move.

Until the arrival of his Son, mankind had thought of God off there in the distance—Creator, Judge, Credential-checker. But now came Jesus with an entirely new picture. "Behold," he said, "I stand at the door and knock." Always knocking, always hoping, always ready to enter any door.

Sounds idyllic. We open. He comes. But is it so idyllic? No! Always at the center of our faith is the Cross.

THE CROSS

The Cross means many things, but one thing it means for sure is that God wants his way in our lives. He wants to live in us, think through us, act through us, reshape us. For most of us that means a thorough overhaul. Individually and together there must be some changes made.

The divine Presence does not come as a courteous guest. He makes demands. He goes through every room, looks under the rugs, opens drawers. Up to the attic, down to the basement, into all the closets and storage places. Everywhere he wants to know, "What's this? What's that?" And if we let him stay, some things will have to go, some changes will need to be made. Changes in ourselves, changes in attitudes, changes in our relationship to each other.

Small wonder the ancient mystics sometimes talked of "agonizing" in prayer. Prayer with a cross at its heart could never be all gladness and good times.

Why?

Because the first purpose of prayer is not our getting what we want from the Lord. It is first his getting what he wants from us. This will be true for us, both individually and as a couple.

And when we understand that, we find him leading us straight up the hill to a cross. Yet wherever did we get the idea that marriage must be a posy patch for our enjoyment?

For the Christian couple, marriage means the Lord shaping this relationship to his design.

Hard sometimes. Traumatic. But if we do yield ourselves to his shaping, then comes joy we could never know in any other way. And isn't that exactly how it was with him? *He for the joy that was set before him endured the cross (Hebrews 12:2).*

At the conclusion of *Bible Study Together* we offered this absolute guarantee:

> That couple who will keep the Scriptures central
>   in their relationship
> By any method, ours, or one of their own making,
> That couple, in even thirty days, will experience
>   positive changes in their love.

Now comes another promise, this one straight from the Lord himself—

"Call to me and I will answer you:
I will tell you wonderful and marvelous
things."
Jeremiah 33:3 (GNB)

Other translators make *wonderful* and *marvelous* : "remarkable secrets" ... "great mysteries" ... "hidden things" ... "joys of which you have no knowledge."

All of these from biblical scholars. And then the lingual experts add this veritable fantasmagoria: "exciting surprises" ... "incredible" ... "thrilling vistas" ... "awesome" ... "things to shout about" ... "to celebrate" ... "limitless possibilities" ... "the dream come true" ... "truly divine."

So the more we study Jeremiah 33:3 word by word, the more it explodes with meaning.

Plus the more it comes clear that his "exciting surprises" and "things to shout about" do not come free. These gifts are not like some lucky number on some lucky card. These he gives us by his grace, but we must earn them by our efforts.

Every day we hear the many casual calls of routine living: ... "Call me some time for coffee" ... "I only called to say hello" ... "Call and let me know when the meeting starts."

But in the original language the "call" of Jeremiah 33:3 is not at all casual. Here the meaning is "earnest calling, the call of commitment, the call of ongoing lifestyle."

This is the call to which he promises all the good bound up in "wonderful" and "marvelous."

So the secret is
day by day
week by week
month by month
and year by year
to call and keep on calling

How long?
Forty-seven years?
This is our witness and this is our experience—

For forty-seven years we have been studying the Bible
together,
learning to pray together
and out of those forty-seven years
these things we know for sure:
I. With or without prayer your forty-seven years are sure
to pass anyway.
II. If you will make your days and weeks and months a
pilgrimage of tuning in upward together

The Lord himself *will* one day bring you
   where the blessed are—
and you will experience
   your own unique and very special
      heaven on earth with him.

♥ CALL AND KEEP ON CALLING ♥

Talk together about the place of prayer in your marriage. Is it hard to pray together? Many couples find it to be so. In the next chapter, Charlie and Martha share a simple discovery that helped them over that hurdle.

Chapter 38

HOW TO START AND KEEP IT GOING

BY CHARLIE AND MARTHA SHEDD
Praying Together

Praying together sounds like a great idea, but just how do we get started? I feel a bit awkward praying with my spouse and, besides, what would we pray about and when would we find the time?"

These are typical questions which Charlie and Martha Shedd have heard hundreds of times over many years of conducting marriage workshops. In the following chapter, they talk about getting past the problem of "praying aloud" together and then give several different kinds of prayers and subjects to pray about.

WHEN YOU PREFER TO PRAY ALONE

I'd rather talk with God alone
than to talk with God with you.

Most couples who have tried praying together will understand that statement. Praying together has such a pleasant sound, a winsome and amiable ring. "Come, let us be best friends, friends with each other, friends with the Lord." But in actuality the prayer together does not come off like this, not at first.

It didn't for us. Married in our final year at seminary, we were headed for the pastoral ministry. From the beginning we had assumed that we should pray together. Jesus had plenty to say about blind leading blind, and we understood. If we weren't growing spiritually, how could we help our people?

On the wall of our study we had tacked this ancient motto:

441

When diving and finding
No pearls in the sea,
Blame not the ocean
The fault is in thee.

So we tried. We tried this, we tried that, we tried and tried and tried. And almost all of our trying was based on a mistaken assumption.

MUST WE HAVE SOUND?

Wherever did we get the idea that we must pray *aloud* with each other? Is it because our minds are programmed for constant audibles? Television, radio, music, utterance; these we have always with us. Every waking hour, noise. Is this why we fall into the trap of believing that communication can only be vocal?

For whatever reason, all of our experiments were in spoken words, prayer aloud. But no one of our efforts was lasting.

In some way the climate was wrong.

We weren't comfortable. Praying aloud made us nervous.

"Awkward. Embarrassing."

"I have this sneaky feeling I must check everything I'm telling the Lord against 'What will Charlie think?'"

"Suppose Martha doesn't like what I'm about to say. Won't this hurt her feelings?"

. That's how it went, start after start after start. And every new beginning was eventually laid low by that same strange label, "I'd rather talk with God alone than to talk with God with you."

Then one year—somewhere in our first five—our relationship came on one of those "no other place to go" emergencies.

What now? If we *could* get through to the Lord together, would he have some answers for us?

We decided on one more try. Only this time we would *not* give up. This time we would find out, "Can prayer together be for real *any* way?" This time we would study prayer. This time we would dig deep in the writings on prayer. We would begin again and keep on beginning and pray for a major breakthrough.

PRAYER IN SILENCE

Suddenly there it was—a new approach. Why not start our prayer time with the list of things we'd like to pray about? Then when we had shared enough to understand each other, we would go to the Lord together in silence.

So that's how we did it.

We would sit on our rocking love seat. We would take turns

telling each other things we'd like to pray about. Then holding hands we would pray, each in our own way, silently.

This was the beginning of prayer together that lasted. Naturally, through the years we've learned to pray in every possible way, including aloud. Anytime, anywhere, every position, every setting, in everyday language. Seldom with "thee" or "thou." Plain talk. Ordinary conversation. We interrupt, we laugh, we argue, we enjoy. We hurt together, cry together, wonder together. Together we tune our friendship to the Friend of friends.

Do we still pray silently together? Often. Some groanings of the spirit go better in the silence.

> "I've been feeling anxious lately and I don't know why. Will you listen while I tell you what I can? Then let's pray about the known and unknown in silence."

> "This is one of my super days. So good. Yet somehow I can't find words to tell you. Let's thank the Lord together in the quiet."

Negatives, positives, woes, celebrations, shadowy things—all these, all kinds of things we share in prayer. Aloud we share what we can. Without the vocals we share those things not ready yet for words.

Why would this approach have the feel of the real? Almost from the first we knew we'd discovered an authentic new dimension.

> In becoming best friends with each other,
>   we were becoming best friends with the Lord.
> And the more we sought his friendship,
>   the more we were becoming best friends
>   with each other.

PRAYER IS LIKE AN OCEAN

We meet many interesting people on our beach. Friendly, unfriendly, awed, bored, happy, sad. Then there are those extra specials like the "small girl with a bottle."

"Look," she said, "I'm taking the ocean home."

Winsome moment, yet we knew and she would know later, no one takes the ocean home. Not in one small bottle. Not in any way.

As we muse on our little friend, we get the feeling, "Here is a parable of prayer."

Even after centuries of writers writing, after millions of seekers seeking, students studying—still all the knowledge of all the students, all of the wisdom of the scholars—isn't all of it all together like one small bottle of ocean water? Still out there is the real ocean, vast, boundless, infinite.

So with prayer. For centuries and forever, wave after wave, and never an end to the learning.

Did the Apostle mean something like this when he said there are twelve gates to the Holy City? Or if he was thinking of prayer, wouldn't he have said twelve million times twelve million?

Nobody has ever even approached all the gates. Nobody knows all the roads. Nobody has all the answers. And how could we? The more we pray, the more we know what the mystics mean by their quaint phrase, "Many and myriad are the ways of prayer."

This phrase appears often in the language of spiritual pilgrims. We like it. It is a needed reminder that other gates might be every bit as authentic as our own. But here is another exciting fact: The gates we find for ourselves may be every bit as authentic as other people's gates. We must never let others discourage our experiments or put us down or call us off our own discoveries.

In this chapter we present certain approaches to prayer and methods of prayer we've discovered for ourselves. Some of these are oldies, truths others knew long before we heard of them. Then there are those we invented for ourselves, innovations just for us as needed.

Still the Wisdom Writer says, "There is no new thing under the sun" (Eccl. 1:9). Had he been living now, would he have said that?

What does it matter whether he tells it like it is, or was, or will be forever? Isn't this what really matters—that we, in our praying, should be open to the heavenly revelations for us?

Following now are some of the techniques, old and new, that have served as aids in our prayer life. Each of the approaches presented here has been tried, tested, used, and re-used. Each has brought new blessings, positives for our prayer together.

FIRST-THOUGHT PRAYERS IN THE MORNING

How am I doing with this admonition of Paul?
First of all, then, I urge that petitions, prayers, requests, and thanksgiving be offered (1 Tim. 2:1 GNB).

Report from one *Fun in Marriage* workshop. The question for discussion now was, "What do we think about first on awakening?"

"You want the truth? When I first wake up, I'm too stupid to think of anything."

"Where did I leave my cigarettes?"

"The weather. Too hot. Too cold. Too wet. Too dry. Why should my first thoughts be negative?"

"My wife is up before I am, so she wakes me. I know it sounds weird, but my first thought is, 'Why is this woman plaguing me?' "

"I rush for the morning paper. First thought? What did the stock market do yesterday?"

"If you feel like I do when you wake up, you'd think you deserved a medal if you refrained from hitting someone."

Both Old and New Testaments point to the importance of our early-morning thoughts:

"Early will I seek thee."

"Those that seek me early shall find me."

"And in the morning long before daylight, Jesus got up and went out to a deserted place, and there he prayed."

Almost without exception praying people say this is true: What we think at the outset of our day will make a difference in how we handle that day's happenings. Morbid leads to the morbid. Gladness ushers in more gladness.

This has been our experience. If we discipline ourselves to pray first, our day does go better. But the same daily discipline also affects our long-term prayer life.

It is almost as though we hear the Lord saying,

"You give prayer top priority in your day,
I will help you keep it top priority
    through the years."

Such top-priority thinking of the Lord does not come at a bargain price. This is a discipline. And for starters, is there any finer Scripture verse than that familiar affirmation of the Psalmist? *This is the day the Lord has made. We will rejoice and be glad in it (Psalm 118:24).*

*   *   *

The sign on our printer's wall read "PF." Nothing more. Large sign. White sheet. White frame. Two big black letters: "PF."

When we asked, "Why the PF?" he explained, "The meaning is PRAY FIRST. I put it there, because I'm trying to break old habits. My natural tendency seems to be to think about me first and all my problems. Worry first, fuss first, panic first, blow up first, act first. But now that I've become a Christian, I'm trying to live by The Book."

PRAY FIRST!

JAVELIN PRAYERS FOR ANY TIME

The saints have an interesting term for flashing our thoughts upward. They call it "javelin prayer."

The Bible is replete with this kind of praying, and who of us hasn't done it? Especially in emergencies we pray javelin prayers. Sudden danger, catastrophe, calamity, pain, bad news, storm signals without and within . . .

"Oh God!"

"Lord, help me!"

"Please! Please! Please!"

"Bless him!"

"Bless you!"

"Heal me!"

"Protect her!"

Yet this is only one small part of javelin praying at its best. When we decide to make prayer top priority on our agenda, a fine thing happens. Each day all day seems to be filled with opportunity for the quick upward thrust.

The telephone rings, and who is this? The good news we've been awaiting? Friend? Foe? Someone between the plus and minus? An unknown?

Haven't we done a good thing when we use the phone as a call to prayer? "Bless whoever it is." "Lord, speak through me."

Such prayer does more than help us keep our equilibrium. It blesses others. Our Lord did say he could bless others through us. Why not through us via the telephone?

Other sounds too can be reminders of another moment for prayer.

The sirens: police, fire, ambulance . . .

"May they feel you near."

Airplanes overhead . . .

"Keep them safe."

The doorbell, a knock, the cry of a child . . .

"Use me, Lord."

The chime of a clock . . .

"Thank you, for your gift of minutes and hours."

First Timothy 2:3 says of its call to "prayer, petition, intercession" . . . "Such praying is good and right, and it is pleasing and acceptable to God, our Savior" (AMPLIFIED).

Most of us need all the help we can get to change our prayer life from "me, me, me" to the higher forms of intercession. Promise:

> When we develop the art of javelin prayer
> we will know "Such praying *is* good and right."

Good for us.
Good for others.
Good for the known and unknown.
Good and right too for the Lord,
"pleasing and acceptable to him."

THANK-YOU PRAYERS FOR NEW FRIENDS

On television recently we saw an amazing performance. Some memory expert was ushered into the studio with thirty strangers. Row by row the Master of Ceremonies introduced each person. Name, where they were from, and what they did for a living.

Then our hero proceeded, row by row, to repeat each name. First name, last name, hometown, occupation. No mistakes.

How did he do it?

"Association," he said. "Blue necktie, white hat, bright lipstick, horn-rimmed glasses, gray hair, etcetera." Unbelievable. Especially unbelievable with so many gray heads, several horn-rimmed glasses, and ever so much bright lipstick.

"How can I remember names?
I don't have much trouble recognizing faces, but I
can't seem to recall who this is."

These are common complaints, and all of us must have our own version of the problem along with solutions. *We* have *our* own version of how to remember names—javelin prayer.

We meet someone new. We pray, "Lord, bless Mike Martin, Mary Jean Johnson, Tom, Bob, Susan, Jane." Almost one hundred percent of these people we will remember by name. Why? Our secular psychologist friends say, "Clever mental trick." But isn't there something more happening here? The Christian believes that we are all related in the Lord. Then why not this explanation of a javelin prayer for remembering names?

He relates us,
not only for this moment,
but for moments to come
when we meet each other again.

Foolproof? No. Dependable? Yes, if we remember the javelin prayer. Unbelievable? Not for the believer. Scripture says, "All things cohere in him" (Colossians 1:17 MOFFATT).

For us, javelin prayer to remember names and thank the Lord for new friends has become one more witness of this truth—

There is a heavenly network
and we are all related in him.

The Bible admonishes us to remember one another before the Lord. Couldn't this also mean to remember one another's names?

CELEBRATION OF LIFE'S GOODNESS

What is the highest form of prayer?
From one of our most mature praying friends:

> "My highest form of prayer is simply three words:
> THANKYOU. THANKYOU. THANKYOU."

Prayer for ourselves—good. Prayer for others—one step up. But haven't we reached an even higher level when we move from "What have you done for me lately?" to "Thank you, Lord, for all you've done."

Important question for any couple:

> Is the tone of our marriage
> negative _____ positive _____
> downbeat _____ upbeat _____

If the tone does need re-doing, how can it be changed? One answer is for husband or wife or both together to learn one thousand different ways to pray, "Thank you, Lord. Thankyou. Thankyou. Thankyou."

PRAYER ON OUR KNEES

Knee praying is almost a lost art in today's Christian homes. We've quit asking those couples who do pray together, "How often do you pray on your knees?" And the reason we quit asking is to avoid the put-down answer, "Never."

But on those rare occasions when someone in our workshops gives witness to praying on their knees, we find their report is exactly like ours. "Knee praying brings a contribution no other kind of praying brings."

TRY "WORD FOCUSING" PRAYERS

Among the innovative approaches to prayer none has done more for us than Word Focusing.* It is based on Jesus' promise in Matthew 6:22, "If therefore thine eye be single, thy whole body shall be full of light."

---

*Word Focusing was described at length in two previous publications, both out of print. *Word Focusing: A New Way to Pray*, Upper Room, and *Getting Through to the Wonderful You*, Revell, 1976. In each of these books we included additional words and texts that have been especially helpful to our prayer together. Word Focusing as a spiritual practice adapts itself to personal prayer. Families and groups have found it useful, too.

Generally, words we find for ourselves will be most enlightening. However, for those who wish them, an extensive list of both words and texts are available from the authors. Write Charlie Shedd, c/o Zondervan Corporation, 1415 Lake Drive, S.E., Grand Rapids, Michigan 49506.

"Singling the eye" in prayer calls for serious mental discipline. But like so many things in the spiritual life, after the discipline comes pure enjoyment—plus new appreciation of words and the language in general—plus fresh insights into the mind of our mate—plus a sorting out of things in our own mind that need adjustment—plus a deeper relationship with each other—plus a purer oneness together with the Lord—plus the ever-growing appreciation that he does want us to be joyful. "These things have I spoken to you," he said, "that my joy may be in you, and that your joy may be full" (John 15:11 RSV).

Far back in the Middle Ages there were groups who called themselves Contemplatives. They spent one hundred percent of their time concentrating on spiritual things. Their procedure was to take a single phrase and repeat it constantly:

"Thou art my all in all."

"In him is our peace."

"Praise his holy name."

These and other phrases opened up new roads to God for them. That's what they claimed, and we believe their claim. We believe it because we tried it, and it worked for us.

Then another wonderful thing happened. We discovered that sometimes focusing on a single word would put us in touch with The Inner Presence.

Various approaches to meditation have run the gamut in our day. From ultra-popular to ultra-passé, they come and go. One reason for their passing, we think, is that many of them aim to empty the mind. In Word Focusing we are doing the opposite. We are asking The Inner Presence to fill our minds with his Spirit.

This is the *how* of Word Focusing:

- We begin by selecting a word from our Bible reading. In our morning quiet time a single word leaps out at us. It stands there on some mental road demanding our attention.
- When we have chosen a word to incorporate in our prayer life, we look it up in various dictionaries. Amazing how different dictionaries provide different shades of meaning to a single word.
- We agree that in our quiet time we will try to "single" our minds on the chosen word.
- Then we will retain this word until it has accomplished its purpose in us.
- We ask the Lord to apply it to our lives where needed.
- Many times during the day we concentrate on our word. When we are together, we exchange ideas and what the

word has meant ... how it blessed us ... what new
meanings came to us and how these can apply to our
relationship. All of which, it is easy to see, will lead us again
to those three most important words in any marriage: talk,
talk, talk.

• How long do we continue our use of a single word? It
might be one day, one week or two, a month. So long as it
continues to provide new insights, we continue with this
word.

Suppose our word is *patience*. One morning in our quiet time
it has come alive for one of us. Reading again in the New
Testament, there it is, "For ye have need of patience" (Heb. 10:36).
How right can you be, Lord! We need it badly. So we write down
the verse on a slip of paper where we can refer to it often.
(Eventually, of course, the slip gives way to memory; we learn this
verse by heart.)

Our second move is to the dictionary. Patience: "1. Possessing
or demonstrating quiet, uncomplaining endurance under distress,
longsuffering. 2. Tolerant, tender, forbearing. 3. Capable of tran-
quilly awaiting results."

Having pondered the Bible verse, then having seen it through
the light of several dictionaries, we now make this word a focal
point of our meditating.

All this is no panacea. We still lose patience, blow up, say
things we shouldn't say. What do we do? We pray:

> Lord, I need your holy patience.
> Control this eager beaver in my soul.
> How can one heart like mine hold enough patience
> for all these problems, big and little?

Answer, straight from the Source: "It can't. But Christ living in
us can."

And when we do let him live in us, he does fill the gaps in our
patience with his patience. He can do what we cannot do as
individuals and as couples.

Again:
We select a word from Bible reading.
We study its dictionary meaning.
We ponder.
We ask the Lord to apply it where we need it.
We exchange ideas ... talk, talk, talk.
We continue the word as long as it continues blessing our
love.

Here, now, are some of our favorite words. With the first
group we have included text, dictionary definition, and a prayer.
Then comes a list of words, with texts. These we include for those

who wish to experiment with Word Focusing. In praying together, for us there has been no finer way to reach the deeps.

ABUNDANCE

And God is able to provide you with every blessing in abundance, so that you may always have enough of everything and may provide in abundance for every good work (2 Corinthians 9:9 RSV).

* * *

Abundance: an ample quantity . . . relative degree of plentifulness . . . full supply.

* * *

Prayer:

> Lord, why do we fuss so much about your goodness
>   running out before it gets to us?
> Why do we worry that we may be shortchanged
>   Or miss our share of treasures from
>   Your storehouse?
> Have we been straining for things instead of
>   reaching for you?
> Help us to exchange our poverty complex for
>   an abundance complex.
> Teach us to move our eyes from intake to outgo—
> We know that when we give what we should,
> You will provide what we need.
>   We know too that you can provide what
>   other people need through us.
> Write it on our hearts:
>   You are the Lord of "ample quantity, plenty,
>   full supply."
> Thank you for choosing us as your trustees.

MATURITY

Therefore, let us leave the elementary doctrine of Christ and go on to maturity (Hebrews 6:1 RSV).

* * *

Mature: highly developed or advanced in intellect, moral qualities, outlook . . . perfected, detailed . . . being completed or ready.

* * *

Prayer:

> Lord, do you need us on a higher plane?
> Teach us to open our minds for fresh thoughts.
> Grow us up.
> Expand our understanding.

*   *   *

Check questions for frequent review:

1. Can we increasingly tell the important from the unimportant?
2. Are we growing in the wisdom to keep silent when we should?
3. Is it easier now for us to apologize when we are wrong?
4. Do we have new courage to stand for what we believe?
5. Are we more able to pray for those who do not like us?
6. Are we continually moving to higher levels, deeper places, in our prayer life?
7. Together are we "leaving the elementary doctrine of Christ and going on to maturity"?

INFLUENCE

A wise man is esteemed for being pleasant; his friendly words add to his influence (Proverbs 16:21 MOFFATT).

*   *   *

Influence: "An emanation of spiritual or moral force . . . the act or power of producing an effect without apparent exertion of force . . . changing the nature of."

*   *   *

The writer of Proverbs opens a two-way road for us here. The things we see, voices we hear, thoughts we entertain—these will influence us. But that's not all. Our words, our acts, our touch, our thoughts—all these, for good or bad, will influence others.

*   *   *

Prayer:

> Lord, we can hardly believe it—
> We are a part of your influence.
> Help us to remember that others are reading you
>   by reading us.

Filter the forces flowing into our hearts that
we may be the finest kind of influence for you.

♥ HOW CAN WE START USING ALL THIS? ♥

You may not want to practice everything the Shedds suggest, and they would be the first to say, "Use *only what works for you.*" The following are some suggestions for putting the techniques you just read about into action. Use them, adapt them, or think up your own.

- ♥ If praying aloud together is a problem for you and your spouse, do as the Shedds suggest: Start by sharing a list of prayer subjects or concerns. After talking about these briefly, go to the Lord together silently in prayer.

- ♥ Praying first thing each morning together may or may not be practical. But it's something each of you can do on your own. First-thought prayers don't have to be long. The important thing is to direct your new day toward the Lord and invite him to bless and guide you and your mate.

- ♥ Javelin prayers could be good first-thought prayers: "Good morning, Lord ..." "Guide us this day ..." "Bless our family ..." Javelin prayers may also work well as part of saying grace, and don't forget the telephone. As you answer, or as you make a call, send up a quick thrust for God to hear. His line is always open.

- ♥ Try brief times of thanking God together for blessings (and challenges, too!). Count your many blessings, name them one by one, and then thank God silently or aloud— whatever is comfortable.

- ♥ Word focusing may sound a bit esoteric or ambitious, but you may want to give it a try. Pick a word like *patience.* Talking about its definition, apply it to your own needs and marriage. Confess to each other your own "need of patience." Then pray together, thanking the Lord for patience or asking him for more.

As you have noticed in going through the many techniques and approaches that the Shedds have used, there is a blending of prayer and study of Scripture together. Indeed, this is as it should be. Bible study should naturally lead to talking to God about what he has told you in his Word. And talking to God should naturally lead to looking into his Word for further guidance and wisdom.

Chapter 39

IS IT WORTH IT?

BY CHARLIE AND MARTHA SHEDD
Bible Study Together

Like anything else worth having, soul communication will take time and effort. And be aware that it's the easiest kind of communication to neglect. After all, you and your mate probably attend church, possibly a Sunday school class, and maybe a Bible study besides. You get "plenty" of prayer and Bible study through the week, or so it seems. But the Shedds aren't talking about prayer and Bible study in a church, class or group setting with other Christians. They're talking about *soul communication*—the linking of you, your spouse and the Lord together in a special oneness that can be achieved in no other way.

In this chapter, the Shedds share the rewards they have discovered in doing prayer and Bible study together. They also share some of the letters they have received from other couples who have tried their suggestions. And they give you a thirty-day trial offer with a guarantee. As you read, ask two questions:

♥ Are praying and studying Scripture together activities that could help us grow a better marriage? If not, what seems to be hindering us from trying?

TALK AND LISTEN

Talk, talk, talk. Say them again. Say them often. Say them loud and clear. These are the three most important words in any marriage.

Listen, listen, listen. Say these too again and again, clear and loud.

Talking together—listening together—this is the number-one plus for Bible study together.

But there are other blessings.

1. THE THRILL OF DISCOVERING TOGETHER

The zest and tang of fresh ideas, new thought, surprises. Since boredom is a serious threat to every marriage, Bible study together becomes a built-in guarantee against the "blahs." This is true, because the more we learn, the more we yearn to learn. New light on the Scripture, new light on ourselves, new light on our relationship—all these make for ongoing excitement individually and with each other.

2. SYMPATHETIC UNDERSTANDING

Inevitably, Bible study together leads to a clearer view of two interiors. Mate reactions which seemed peculiar now begin to make sense. Result? A growing sympathy. Compassion.

But that's not all. As we share the deep places, we discover similarities. See how many verses we marked with the same marks. *Thank you, Lord, for sudden harmony sometimes, plus slow blending in your Word.*

3. RESPECT

Has our respect quotient eroded with the passing of time?

Bible study together provides a built-in safeguard against this sad demise. As we listen to our mate, we thank God. Such an incisive mind! See all these fine ideas, superior insights. Out of all the people in my world, see whom I chose? Congratulations to me and how fortunate I am. *Thank you, Lord!*

4. WE BECOME MORE TEACHABLE

Why are some of the wisest folks we know among the humblest folks we know? One answer: The more we learn in any field, the more we realize how much there is to learn.

"He really knows his Bible." . . . "She is a fine Bible student." . . . How often we've heard these compliments. Yet, if ever that kind of praise gets back to the one of whom it's said, he or she might comment: "What I know is nothing compared to what I know there is to know."

So this is another result of our study together, we become more teachable and how much nicer it is to live with someone teachable.

5. PHYSICAL HARMONY AT ITS MAXIMUM

So often in our workshops, in consultation, in letters, we hear the plaintive cry, "If only we had a better sex life, we'd have a better marriage." To which we reply: "You've missed the point. The point is that maximum blending of bodies requires maximum blending of minds and souls."

One more plus for Bible study together.

6. DELAYED BLESSING

Does the Lord have special angels whom he assigns to work in the unawareness?

You struggled with a problem. You prayed, and no answer came. The tension remained, conflict continued, there was no peace. Then one day without your knowing, you realized those clouds had cleared. It may have been weeks later, years later. Suddenly you felt an inner quiet. Somehow, below the surface, God had been sorting things out, putting them where they belonged, making them right.

It is our experience that the more we study together, the more his delayed blessings become reality. And can't we count on this same happening in the future?

The psalmist says, "My times are in thy hands." Won't that be true of tomorrow, too?

> Blessed are they who have learned
>   that today's time,
>   times past,
>   times off there in the future
> are his times too.

7. SURPRISE! WE ARE BETTER PEOPLE!

That is one great day when we can look in the mirror and say, "I really do like what I see." More than ever I can say again and mean it, "Congratulations to me!"

Yet isn't there one greater thrill? This is two of us saying together, "Ours is a better marriage than ever before. Spiritually we really are making progress. Congratulations again; this time to *us!*"

8. WRITING OUR OWN TRANSLATION

As we gain confidence in Bible study comes another exciting plus. The day arrives when we realize, "Here is a message straight from the Lord with our name on it." So this is the meaning of "C&M": To Charlie and Martha it comes through like this.

No serious students of Scripture will play loose with meaning or change texts to fit behavior. But this we can count on: If we commit ourselves to Bible study together, his message does come through with special meaning for us. No question. This is his personalized word for us.

9. INNOVATIVE TECHNIQUES

He brings from his treasure things new and old (Matt. 13:52 c & m).

Innovative techniques

Fresh ideas

These, too, are rewards of Bible study together.

One such for us is what we call, "Release it! Let it go!"

Example—For some months there has been a disagreement between us. Small at first, we thought it might go away. Yet the hard fact is we're getting nowhere!

Give it to the Lord? Yes, but how?

Find a verse and let it go.

PROCESS:

After having agreed we should table the matter, we find a verse which seems exactly right for this particular problem. Next, we write a brief description of the disagreement, perhaps in code. We date the note and place it at the chosen verse. Then we pray, "Lord, we're getting nowhere. We don't like it. We don't think you like it, either. We know you see problems of every kind. We know you see things about this problem we can't see. So here it is. We release it now to you. We leave it in your care. Thank you."

What do we do when we begin chewing on the problem again individually; chewing on it with each other? Back to the chosen verse we go and one more time we pray, "Lord, we really did mean to release it. So here it is again. Thank you for your patience with us."

Psychologists say we should never bury our disagreements. Too many times they push over old tombstones and shake their gory locks again. True. But for us, using the Bible to let our disagreements go temporarily can be a genuine healer.

Question: Do we ever sit together, open The Book once more and look at our problem together? Yes, when we both agree the time is right.

Amazing truth—sometimes when we go back for another look, this lovely fact comes clear. He has touched our problem with some warm memories. Or maybe he gives us some easy-to-understand directions, solutions we could never have seen or managed on our own.

All these "Release it! Let it go!" items are not in the conflict category. They may be burdens, worries, people problems, children problems, economic problems, job problems. These and many more of every trauma are for that all-inclusive invitation: "Cast thy burdens on the Lord."

Recently we had gone to our Bible shelf for reference in a particular translation. As we turned the pages, out dropped a slip of paper dated five years past. Because it was written in code, try as we might, neither of us could remember what this ancient problem was all about.

REVIEW:

Find a verse; release it; let it go.

Step one: Write the problem.
Step two: Select an appropriate verse or passage.
Step three: Place the paper at that verse.
Step four: Pray a prayer of release.
Step five: Leave it with the Lord.
Step six: Review it again when we both agree.

THEY TRIED IT AND LIKED IT

In our workshops and correspondence, we frequently ask for reports from those couples who are studying the Bible together. Here are some reports straight from where it's happening.

FROM CALIFORNIA

Last August we made an in-depth study of the Book of Revelation together and in April we studied Paul's Letter to Galatians while on vacation. These moments of reading and studying the Scriptures together are the most precious moments of the day, and our love and devotion for one another grow deeper and richer as the years go by. Burdens are lifted, problems are solved, peace and serenity are experienced, and we feel God's Presence in these quiet times. We have read the Bible through together from Genesis to Revelation, using different translations, and find we must discipline ourselves to make and take time for study, for personal communication with God.—Ed and Fern

AFTER A COUPLES' WORKSHOP

Our marriage was in the process of strangulation from lack of communication, verbal affection and the glue that holds it all together—God. We'd gone from seminar to seminar, from counselor to counselor, and we seemed to be getting nowhere. Well, we thought, one place we haven't been is into the Bible together. What have we got to lose? So we started reading, marking, sharing.

At first it was awkward. Awkward like two kids on a first date. But we stayed with it and one day, would you believe, we began to sense some good things happening. We really were starting to communicate. Like beautiful! Super! Praise the Lord!—Jerry and Beth

TEXAS WIFE

Result of our Bible study? It's as if we are "walking the hills together" with the third guest. It's exalting in an extraordinary way, an intimacy of spiritual togetherness. We experience a natural outpouring of feelings, a consciousness of spiritual duet that grows steadily and imperceptibly. No way without our day-to-day studying could our exchanges flow so deep.— Lawrence and Helen

WITNESS FROM A FLORIDA HUSBAND

My wife and I are both employed and fortunately we can ride together to work. Since it's almost forty-five minutes from our house to our jobs, we decided to put this time to good use by reading the Bible to each other. Every day we take turns driving and reading. We read a chapter or several chapters. Then we talk about what we've read. Sometimes we break in on the reading to have a deep discussion. You can't believe all the good things that have happened to our marriage since we began doing this.—Bruce and Josephine

FROM AN ILLINOIS HUSBAND AND WIFE

In our home the two of us have Bible reading each morning after breakfast. We have read the Psalms and in the New Testament, the Gospels. Recently Romans has been our inspiration. Just now it is Hebrews. We use The Living Bible and have also used the Revised Version and the King James. We each have a commentary. We have a lot of fun. We laugh and joke. We express our love for each other often, hug a lot. Fifty-nine years we've been married. That is a good long stretch. But because of our study together, we think our love and fun with great amounts of laughter keep us young. They also keep us in love with the Lord and with each other.— Harold and Alice

THE SHEDDS' THIRTY-DAY TRIAL WITH GUARANTEE

Some sage describing a speaker said, "He edified and electrified, but never specified."

Here we specify.

We challenge you to commit yourselves for thirty days trying our method. Read an agreed book of the Bible individually. Use our marks or others of your choosing. Include in this commitment at least one weekly time for discussing your marks; sharing ideas; getting acquainted; letting the Lord have his say. Talk, talk, talk. Listen, listen, listen.

And at the end of thirty days?

We guarantee you will see an improvement in your marriage.

This guarantee can be tripled if you commit yourselves for three months.

Try it.

You'll see.

Your marriage will move from ordinary to good.

From good to better

> And for any couple who will continue on and on
>   The Lord himself will move this marriage
>   From better to the very best . . .
>   HIS BEST!

♥ QUESTIONS AND ANSWERS ON SOUL ♥ COMMUNICATION

Following are the most frequently asked questions the Shedds have received in years of doing Soul Communication sessions in their marriage workshops.

1. *Where is a good place to begin Bible study together?*
We do not think it's wise to start with Genesis and work straight through the Bible. In some marriages one is more biblically

advanced than the other. But starting with Genesis, even the most experienced Bible student could become discouraged. All those lineages, the fighting, the cruelty, the hate passages might be a bit much. For us, a good launching pad in the Old Testament has been the Psalms, or Proverbs. The Gospels make a good starting place in the New Testament. And who could go wrong beginning with 1 Corinthians 13?

2. *Do you recommend that we both use the same translation?*
Some of our most productive times have come from using different translations. Right now one of us is reading the Bible in Basic English which limits itself to 850 words. The other is reading Lamsa's Translation based on the Syriac rendering of the Greek original. The variance here is fascinating—the simplest—the most erudite. For us, it's like looking through a wide lens telescope.

We think one of the best modern translations is *Good News for Modern Man.* Both scholarly and simple, this is the work of the American Bible Society. Since the American Bible Society is part of the United Bible Societies of the World, scholars are brought in from everywhere. The clever little drawings scattered throughout the text help us "see" meanings.

We try to keep up on all the new translations and incorporate these in our study. Particularly with our question mark verses, we find it helpful if we refer to the newer translations. Comparing this fresh insight with older versions invariably opens up new thought.

One of the newest versions we're using for supplemental insight right now is our own publisher's *The Holy Bible: New International Version.* Compiled by more than one hundred scholars, no serious student of Scripture could fail to be stimulated to think new thoughts.

3. *Is there a difference between a version and a translation?*
No, there is no basic difference between a version and a translation. The word *translation* is the more modern usage, while *version* is the more traditional term. However, today they mean the same thing.

4. *Is it true that the King James Version is nearer to the original than any other? I was brought up in a Sunday school where there was something special about it. What do you think?*
No question—it *is* special. For beautiful phraseology the King James cannot be duplicated. However, after using many versions and translations, we have concluded that some of these newer versions are closer to the original. Makes sense, doesn't it? In every field experts are continually coming closer to the truth.

Our catechism tells us the Bible was written by "good men taught of the Holy Spirit." Christians believe that the Holy Spirit is every bit as active today as yesterday. Contemporary scholars can be and are channels of his ever-growing truth.

5. *Should we skip some passages?*

Yes, at first. Later on you may prefer to read from cover to cover. As we study for help with problems and moods, we soon learn what passages lift and bless. When we ask for his guidance, the Lord will lead us to verses, chapters, whole sections which meet our special needs for special times.

6. *In using your system, what if one gets too far ahead of the other?*

There is a built-in safeguard in our approach. When either of us has finished a book, we wait for the other to complete it. In our case one of us is a naturally fast reader; the other, slow, making flexibility important. It is never our intent to proceed together, chapter by chapter. On any given day one of us may read only a few verses. The next day we may take two chapters, or five. Our weekly sessions keep us somewhere in the same general range.

7. *Do you think it's important to read books about the Bible before we begin the Bible itself?*

No. We think it's important for serious students to read books about the Bible, but not before beginning the Bible itself. Books on "how the Bible came to be" can provide excellent background. Books on individual books of the Bible are also helpful. Since individuals have different needs and different couples have different needs, too, we recommend browsing through Christian bookstores. Most of these carry a line of materials on the Bible. The term we use for this general reading and study is "our helicopter ride over biblical terrain." In no way, however, is the helicopter ride a must before getting directly into God's Word.

8. *Will you give us some thoughts on commentaries and other helps?*

For those who wish to go deeper, individual commentaries are available on each book of the Bible. Or, if you prefer the simple approach, there are some excellent one-volume commentaries covering the entire Bible. There are many Bible dictionaries which will make good additions to any library. Advice from your pastor or browsing again in your bookstore may be helpful in the selection of commentaries and other aids.

9. *How long will it take us to go through the Bible together?*

There are 1,189 chapters in the Bible. Beginning with Genesis and reading through Revelation will take a little over three years, reading at the rate of one chapter per day. We don't set that kind of pace. Our speed has varied from reading through the Bible in two years to much longer.

Because we are all so different, there is no definite answer to the "how long" questions. Yet since there is no prize for speed, hurrying is not imperative. What is imperative is that we stay with our reading faithfully and take plenty of time to talk, talk, talk, and listen, listen, listen.

10. *What if we make a mistake in interpreting Scripture. Couldn't this be dangerous?*
We don't think so.

If we are into ongoing Bible study, God has a way of correcting our errors. He leads us from the byways back to the main road. We can count on the biblical promise, "If it is of God, he will bless us. If it isn't, he'll protect us."

11. *Do you ever use other marks in addition to the candle, question mark, and arrow?*
Yes, but the candle, question mark, and arrow are our special marks, our own original development by us for us. Yet, are they ours? Ecclesiastes 1:9 tells us, "There is nothing new under the sun" (rsv). That statement, by our experience, is much more than the observation of an Old Testament cynic. Almost everything has its duplicate in some day long gone.

After we began making our marking system, we discovered other similar systems, mostly historical. From monks and nuns in the Middle Ages, we learned of their methods. From more current groups in other lands—Sweden, Italy—we read of their developments, their approaches also based on certain marks.

But, yes, we have some subsidiary marks we use sometimes:
Thumbs down—Negative. Isn't this the antithesis of a Christian attitude?
Exclamation point—Startling . . . unusual!
Star—Ultra-important . . . don't ever forget it . . . write it on the heart, the mind.
Plus mark—For some positive note we need right now.
Rippled lines at the side—Read these sections to get the meat of the coconut.

How often do we use these subsidiary marks? Not often. If you were to look through the Bible on our shelves, you would find thousands of candles, question marks, and arrows, but only occasionally other marks.

12. *Do you keep a record of your discussions?*
Yes, some thoughts we file. But the most important record is right there in our Bibles. Every day, in our reading time, we write the date. This way the Bibles on our shelves, marked and dated, become a record of our spiritual pilgrimage.

Marriages are not simply "consummated"; they are worked at, hammered out, prayed through, suffered through. Often the starry-eyed dreams of romance give way to the harsh realities of diapers, drudgery, debt, and despair; however, where there is a measure of maturity, a willingness to face facts, and the humility to recognize that both may be at fault, a good marriage can usually be worked out.[11]

Cecil Osborne

PART VIII

STEADFASTNESS:
HOW TO KEEP IT GROWING

We started with the question: "How do we grow a good marriage?" To find the answer, we have looked at:

- ♥ Intimacy—how two separate personalities become "one"
- ♥ Love—keeping romance alive with *agape*
- ♥ Understanding and accepting your individual needs and differences
- ♥ Communication—talking *and* listening
- ♥ Processing anger and conflict
- ♥ Sex—fulfillment for both partners
- ♥ Spiritual growth—soul communication.

In this final section, we will focus on steadfastness, having the grit, pluck, and creativity to keep the marriage growing and glowing with the joy and satisfaction that come only when two people commit themselves to working full-time at making life together work.

The secret of remaining steadfast is called by many names: intimacy, fulfillment, contentment, oneness. And, of course, we cannot forget love. Whatever you call it, the goal is never to let that wall of rejection, hurt, and loneliness rise between you. There are ways to be sure that, somewhere between the oldest child's front tooth and the youngest one's graduation, you do not lose each other. Instead, your goal is to find each other, discover each other anew every day as the years dissolve with what seems to be the speed of light.

In every marriage, time is the great paradox. "Time is on our side," says the young couple just starting out. "We have all our lives to spend together. No more parting, no more waiting to be one."

But then something happens. Time is no longer "on their

side." All too quickly time is the enemy—mocking their noble efforts to squeeze in all the activities, tasks, and responsibilities. Yes, especially those responsibilities which stack up like cord wood with each passing year. The following letter, written by a lonely wife seeking counsel, says it all too well:

Dear Dr. and Mrs. Shedd:

Jerry and I used to be such good friends. At least that's how I remember it, and he says he remembers it that way, too.

I do think that's how it was. Before we married, one of the great things we had going was the way we could discuss everything. I do mean everything, our hopes and our hurts, our love for each other, things we liked and didn't like, our guilt, everything.

So what happened? One thing that happened is three kids. Do you know what that means? What that means is time consumption, almost total time consumption. Car pooling, music lessons, bumps, bruises, fussing, fighting, little questions, little answers, big questions, big answers, and on and on forever.

But that's not all. There are neighbors to keep up with, friends to see, and oh yes, our jobs! I forgot to mention that we both work. Jerry is sales manager for his company, real good at it, but he gets so tired. I'm a nurse, also real good at it, and I get tired, too.

So we come home and wouldn't we like to sit down to talk, to hold hands, share, make love? But there is dinner to cook, dinner to eat, dinner dishes to do, meals to plan for tomorrow, the house to straighten, homework, phone calls, and have you ever counted all your evening interruptions?

So we fall in bed, Jerry and I. Fall? That's exactly the right word—fall, as in fall exhausted.

Then in the morning it's do it again. Breakfast, lunches to pack, schedules to check, dinner to plan, good-byes, "take care," "I love you," plus a million more last-minute thises and thats.

Anyway, I tell you true, sometimes I could just cry the way Jerry and I look at each other. It's almost as if some lonesome part of us was calling, "You seem like such a nice person over there. I wish I could know you. I mean I wish I could know you again."[1]

Charlie and Martha Shedd believe a major delusion in most marriages is what they call Mental Error No. 1:

Some day off in the future, darling, we will stumble onto big chunks of time. When we get caught up a little . . . when the car is paid for . . . when we work the mortgage down a little . . . when we get another promotion . . . save more . . . when the

kids are a little older . . . when the strain is off . . . then we can
relax, then we will take it easy, travel, have fun, just be together.[2]

But it won't happen. That voyage to "Some day I'll" never takes place. The days become too crowded with much-ness and many-ness. Where did all the flowers go? Who knows? We couldn't even find time to smell the roses!

Of course not. You don't *find* time for the important things like intimacy, friendship, romance, communicating, making love. You have to *make* time—carve it out of what seems to be an impenetrable and overpacked schedule. In the following chapters, you will find another cornucopia of ideas for growing a good, yes, a great, marriage together, but they will all be quite useless if you do not make time to use them.

In chapter 40, Gary Smalley (*The Joy of Committed Love*) talks about how husbands can so easily fall into that deep pit they seem so gifted in digging for themselves. Included is a list of 100-plus ways a husband can offend his wife and five tips he can use to build a lasting and loving relationship with her.

In chapter 41, Smalley (*The Joy of Committed Love*) explains how a husband can give his wife first place and shares his own ten-year struggle before he learned to do just that.

In chapter 42, Dr. Bruce Narramore (*Why Children Misbehave*) and Melodie Davis (*You Know You're a Mother When . . .*) team up to discuss the effect of parenting on marriage and how to plan time for one another.

In chapter 43, Charlie and Martha Shedd recommend making mini-covenants to support the major covenant you made when you got married. All of these mini-covenants deal with making time for one another in special ways.

One characteristic above all others
Distinguishes marriages that last:
The willingness of husband and wife to testify
In public in each other's behalf[3]

Chapter 40

ONE HUNDRED WAYS TO OFFEND YOUR WIFE (AND FIVE STEPS TO MAKING IT RIGHT)

BY GARY SMALLEY
The Joy of Committed Love

Without question, this next chapter is for the men. Much of Gary Smalley's writings are directed at men because he has discovered over many years of counseling (and personal experience as a husband) that it is the man who usually needs advice on how to be sensitive and loving. As you read the following chapter, ask yourself:

♥ In what ways might I be offending my wife?
♥ What specific steps can I take to change this behavior now?

THE (ALMOST) UNPARDONABLE SIN IN MARRIAGE

It was 4:00 P.M. on Valentine's Day when I remembered my basketball game. I reached for the phone to call Norma, my bride of less than a year.

"Honey, I forgot to tell you I have a basketball game tonight. We're supposed to be there at seven o'clock. I'll pick you up about 6:30."

Silence hung heavily on the line before she answered, "But this is Valentine's Day."

"Yeah, I know, but I need to be there tonight because I promised the team. I don't want to let them down."

"But I have a special dinner prepared with candles and—"

"Can you hold it off until tomorrow?" She didn't answer, so I continued. "Honey, you know how important it is for a wife to submit to her husband." (Little did I know that one of the worst things a husband can do is to demand submission from his wife.) "I really need to be there tonight, and if we're going to start off with good habits in the early part of our marriage, now is the time to begin. If I'm going to be the leader of this family, I need to make this decision."

"Ice" perfectly describes the reception I received when I picked Norma up. It was easy to see I had severely offended her, but I figured she had to learn to be submissive sometime, and we might as well start now.

The lifeless expression on her face grew worse as the evening wore on. When we returned home after the game, I noticed that the table was all set for a special dinner—candles, our best dishes, and pretty napkins. She still wasn't speaking to me the next day, so I rushed to the florist to gather a variety of flowers which I put in various spots all over the house. That warmed her up a little. Then I gave her a giant card with a hand on the front that could be turned thumbs up or thumbs down. "Which is it?" I asked her. She turned it thumbs up. I never said whether I was right or wrong, only that I felt badly about the night before. And so began a history of offenses I never cleared up with her.

Had someone not shared with me a year later the secret of developing a lasting and intimate relationship, we might have joined the millions who seek divorce each year. *End every day with a clean slate—no offenses between the two of you.*

Couples often ask me, "Where have we gone wrong?" "Why don't we feel romantic toward each other?" "How come we argue so much?" "Why do we avoid touching each other?" These problems are not primarily attributable to incompatibility, sexual problems, financial pressure, or any other surface issues. They are a direct result of *accumulated offenses.* If a husband and wife can understand how to maintain harmony by immediately clearing up every hurtful offense between them, they can climb out of such common problems and even marriage's deepest pit—divorce.

HOW DID I GET DOWN HERE ANYWAY?

When a man treats his wife carelessly, she is usually offended far deeper than he realizes. She begins to close him out, and if he continues to hurt her feelings, she will separate herself from him mentally, emotionally, and physically. In other words, she doesn't want any contact in any way with him. Haven't you noticed how your wife clams up after you have insulted her? She not only avoids conversation, but also avoids being touched. *A wife simply will not respond to her husband when he continually hurts her feelings without "clearing the slate."*

Some people justify their reactions by saying, "But he/she

hurt my feelings." There's no such thing as hurt feelings, according to psychologist Dr. Henry Brandt. He says, "Let's call hurt feelings what they really are—anger." It may not be right for your wife to react in anger, but that's not the point of this book. Our goal as husbands should be to adjust our behavior so our wives won't have to react in anger.

To understand why your wife naturally "clams up" when you offend her, imagine yourself the proud owner of a new car. When you first drive that classy model into your driveway, every part of you says, "I love it." You love the smell, the feel, the look. Because you love the car, you polish it until it sparkles. You devote special time and care to it. When the engine starts knocking, or the oil leaks, or the gleaming paint job suffers a few scratches, or the windshield wipers quit right in the middle of a rain storm, you become irritated with this "lemon" that you've bought. Soon you can think of seventy-two reasons to get rid of it. As long as it treats you right, you like it. But as soon as it starts to fall apart, you wish you'd never bought it, and soon you don't even want to be near it.

The same thing can happen with a job. Did you ever quit because you weren't happy with the boss or working conditions? I remember how much I loved one job until the boss offended me deeply. At that moment, my mind became tangled in a web of reasons to leave. Although I knew what was going on inside me, I couldn't seem to control my emotions. They had changed, and I wasn't as fond of the work as I had been. I eventually didn't want to show up or have anything to do with that job.

We tend to follow a natural pattern when we've been offended. Mentally, we are more alert to the flaws of the offender. Emotionally, we feel estranged. Physically, we avoid that person. And spiritually we close out the person (Prov. 15:13).

I have watched my wife go through this process many times. When I played basketball that Valentine's evening instead of going home to her romantic candlelight dinner, she was so angry that she didn't want to talk to me. She didn't want to touch me or have me touch her. Have you ever put your arm around your wife after provoking her and felt her tighten up? You may have criticized her when that happened. But you need to accept the responsibility for her coldness and say, "I understand how you feel, and I don't blame you for not wanting me near you right now." If your wife does not want you to touch her, if she has lost some of that romantic "spark" she once had for you, or if she is plotting ways to get away from you even for short periods of time, *you can be sure you have offended her and possibly crushed her spirit.*

A not-so-funny thing happened on the way to a party one evening. Norma teasingly said she planned to play a joke on the company president, a joke that would have embarrassed me. I couldn't believe she would consider such a thing, and I said,

"Norma, you can't do that. I'm not going tonight if you really plan on doing it."

I stopped the car and with harshness and impatience yelled, "I would be too embarrassed to go!" She kidded around with me a little more and admitted she really wasn't serious, but my persistent harshness was too much for her (Prov. 15:4). Because I was so abusive, she began to cry. Realizing I had done the wrong thing, I tried to make it right. But the more I talked, the worse it grew. At the party, whenever I glanced at her, she looked away. She was thinking of all the reasons her husband wasn't such a "good guy" any more. It took days for me to reestablish harmony.

What does a man have to do to clear up offenses against his wife? How can he maintain harmony with her?

Harmony can be defined as the absence of unsettled offenses between the two of you. When a real harmony and oneness exist between you and your wife, the two of you will want to relax and spend time talking. Your wife will be more agreeable. She will feel emotionally and physically attracted to you. But when you have offended her, she will probably *resist* you and *argue* with you.

Wives are often accused of being strong-willed and rebellious when, in reality, they're simply responding to their husbands' thoughtless abuses. They are sometimes accused of wrecking marriages because they have lost affectionate or romantic love for their husbands. Of course, husbands seldom realize that their insensitive behavior is what ushered the affection out the door.

Many a man has labeled his wife sexually frigid for not wanting to be touched or have sex. But wives have often told me that when a woman is mistreated, she feels like a prostitute having physical relations with her husband. Sex is more than just physical—it involves every part of us. A woman must first know she is valued as a person and be in harmony with her husband before she can give herself freely in sex. She has to feel romantic love before *wholeheartedly* entering the sexual union in marriage. Without harmony, the sexual relationship between husband and wife will most certainly deteriorate.

Have you ever known the futility of trying to reach a woman mentally, emotionally, and physically after offending her?

Gary tried to reach out to Laurie, his estranged wife, but she wanted no part of him. He kept saying to her, "I miss you so much. I want to be near you. I love you." But she was *closed* to him emotionally. "Don't you see how you're hurting our daughter?" he said. "Don't you see what kind of reputation we're going to have by being separated?" He tried to appeal to her mentally, but she wouldn't listen. He had already gone too far—he had offended her too often and too severely—so her spirit completely shut him out of her life.

I asked him, "Are you willing to forgo touching Laurie for the time being, to forgo wondering if she will ever again have emotional feelings for you, to forgo trying to reason with her mentally? Will you concentrate on clearing up your past offenses?

"If you will accept my counsel and reestablish a harmony with Laurie, she will mentally open up to you again. She'll gain new romantic love for you. Finally, she will desire to be near you again.

"This is the reality of life," I advised Gary. "In cases where a woman has fallen in love with another man or has been *severely* mistreated, it may take a little longer to win her back."

A man often becomes disgusted when his wife doesn't sparkle with romance any more, not realizing that he killed that sparkle with his hurtful ways.

FIVE WAYS TO BUILD A LOVING RELATIONSHIP

What steps can a man take to rebuild a harmonious relationship with his wife?

1. *Endeavor to understand the ways you have hurt or offended your wife.* To help you avoid hurting your mate, we have included a list of common offenses. [This list is in Gary Smalley's book, *The Joy of Committed Love.*] In the past, perhaps you haven't realized how your actions were hurting her.

Ken and Sharon's story is a good example of how a man's insensitivity damaged a marriage. After eight years of marriage and three children, Sharon's once-petite figure was a little on the chubby side. Since Ken couldn't understand why she had not regained her slender figure after the birth of their third child, he found a number of "creative" ways to point out the extra poundage to Sharon. He tried to make her lose weight by lecturing, demanding, and bribing. He even threatened to cancel their vacation unless she lost weight. But nothing worked. She seemed powerless to comply.

Ken's continually critical, harsh attitude wounded Sharon. As a result, she slowly began to close him out of her life. She shut him out emotionally, and resisted when he demanded sex, excusing herself because of headaches or fatigue. His occasional jabs, "Do you realize you had two desserts for dinner tonight?" and his overbearing personality continually pressured her, making her more nervous and increasing her desire to eat. Ken was totally unaware of what he was doing to her. There was no way he could really understand her. "If you want to lose weight," he said, "you just decide and do it!"

Since Sharon had little or no interest in pleasing Ken, she might have been subconsciously punishing him by staying over-weight. Quite by accident, Ken did one thing that finally motivated Sharon to lose weight. He called her long-distance while on a business trip and said, "I've been a lousy husband to treat you the way I have. From now on, I'm going to love you—you alone—no matter what. I've been the one out of control."

Sharon responded, "You know, every time you demanded that I lose weight, your attitude was so pitiful that if anything, I wanted to run to the refrigerator and empty it out. I never had any desire to please you. But now that you say I'm free to do whatever I want and I sense you mean it, I actually have a greater desire to lose weight."

Ken became more sensitive and gentle when Sharon explained that she really didn't want to be overweight. She felt ugly around her friends, and the new fashions only made her look *fatter*. Sharon had said so many times, "If only you would accept me for who I am instead of demanding that I be slender and sexy . . . your rejection is almost more than I can take." Rejection is one of the deepest pains a human can suffer. It cuts right to the core.

When Ken began to recognize that his criticism was wounding his wife, he was on the path to a restored relationship.

2. *Admit your major part in weakening the marriage.* At this point I'm about to prescribe the most bitter medicine I have ever had to swallow. When I first heard about it from my friend Ken Nair, I resisted it strongly. I thought he was crazy! I couldn't believe what he was telling me. I squirmed and kicked, fought and argued for an entire month. In spite of my initial opposition, I ultimately became a "believer" because I have not been able to come up with a single exception to this rule, and I have spent long hours laboring to think of even one.

I want you to experience whatever emotions are natural to you as you read the statement in the box below. If you react strongly, I understand why.

IF A COUPLE HAS BEEN MARRIED FOR MORE THAN FIVE YEARS, ANY PERSISTENT DISHARMONY IN THEIR MARRIAGE RELATIONSHIP IS USUALLY ATTRIBUTABLE TO THE HUSBAND'S LACK OF GENUINE LOVE.

I am not suggesting that the husband is solely responsible for all disharmony in marriage. Some day-to-day conflicts may be the result of his wife's physical exhaustion, health problems, overextended schedules, etc. On any given day, she may respond negatively to her husband due to a headache, a disturbing phone call from her father, or any number of other temporary upsets. Certainly, the husband is not to blame for these occasional problems. However, I have found that after five years of marriage, a husband can eliminate prolonged disharmony in his marriage by knowing his wife's needs and meeting them on a consistent basis.

This is very hard to believe, isn't it? It took me months to even imagine that it was true, let alone accept it.

During a lecture one man reacted to this concept violently, saying, "When a woman gets out of line, I think you ought to knock her up against the wall."

"Throw him out!" a woman in the meeting shouted.

His reaction took me by surprise at first, but I later discovered he and his wife were in one of those "marriage pits." Since he was trying to convince his wife that all the problems in their marriage were *her* fault, accepting my statement would have destroyed his line of reasoning.

I know of at least three types of men who resist accepting this concept:

1. *A man whose wife has left him.*

2. *A man with a relative or close friend whose wife has divorced him.* "It couldn't have been my brother's fault. You never met his terrible wife." (Don't forget, though, most of what you know about that "terrible wife" you learned from your brother.)

3. *A man having an affair.* It is just too hard for him to blame himself for a frigid or nagging wife. He feels she was enough to drive him into another woman's arms.

I tried in vain to find an excuse to get out of this *principle* with the phrase, "What would happen *if* . . . ?" Don't follow my example. If you base your objection on hearsay or hypothetical situations, *your* objection is unfounded. Before you excuse any husband, you have to hear both sides of the story firsthand, and the story can't be fiction.

MUST IT ALWAYS BE ONE-SIDED?

I knew by Norma's facial expression that I had offended her one morning. I immediately said, "I understand what I just said was too harsh, and I shouldn't have said it. I would like to ask you to forgive me."

"Okay, I'll forgive you," she said.

I thought to myself, *It seems like all the pressure to act right is on me. What about her?*

So I said, "Hey, how come I'm always the one asking your forgiveness? Why don't you ask me to forgive you any more? This thing is kind of one-sided, isn't it?"

Then she looked at me. "I'd be happy to admit where I am wrong and seek your forgiveness *if* I have offended you."

"Well, that's just too much! What an arrogant statement. What a terribly selfish thing to say," I sputtered. "There are lots of things you have done to offend me. I can't remember the last time you admitted you were wrong and sought my forgiveness."

"Well, what are some of my offenses?" she asked.

"Give me a minute and I'll think of a lot of them."

"Well, what are they?"

"Just a minute and I'll think of some," I said, stalling for time.

I thought and thought, but I couldn't come up with even one. I told myself, *This can't be true.* But I couldn't think of a thing she had done to offend me.

Finally I said, "But I can think of some things I'd like to see you change about yourself."

"Well, what are they?"

"Even though we've been married five years, I'm going to come up with the first exception to this thing of it being all my fault." (I was pleased with myself.) "There are some times when you don't respect me and you don't honor me as a special person in your life. Sometimes your words are cutting and disrespectful . . . *now how is that my responsibility?*"

We sat down at the kitchen table and started going through each item. It took only ten minutes for us to figure out that every time she had been disrespectful to me, I had either rolled out of bed grouchy or been critical of her most of the day. I hadn't earned her respect. It was amazing. All three things I had felt *she* should change were a direct result of *my* failure to love her in a genuine way.

Now I have to admit the whole episode left a bad taste in my mouth. Even today, when I'm tired or a little down, I think to myself, *This is crazy. I shouldn't even tell people this because it'll make wives run all over their husbands.* But just the opposite is true. When a man treats his wife with gentleness, when he is loving and understanding, and when he does most of the things we describe in this book, she will respond to him on every level. She'll desire intimate conversation with him, she'll feel emotional love for him, and she'll respond to him sexually. The only exception, as I mentioned before, occurs when a wife is romantically involved with another man.

I know how *difficult* it is to admit we are wrong. One night Norma and I were lying in bed when I said something obnoxious to her. She closed me out, and though I wanted to restore our relationship, I was too proud to say anything. The words stuck in my throat. I wanted to say, "Norma, I was wrong about what I just said." I tried, but it just wouldn't come. So I decided to go to sleep, thinking in the morning it would be easier to admit my mistake. Throughout the night I woke up, feeling more and more eager to admit I was wrong and feeling worse and worse about what I had done. By morning, I could admit my mistake, and our relationship was restored. But do you realize what I had done? I let my wife suffer with the feelings of a broken relationship all night long.

3. *Express sorrow to your wife whenever you offend her.* My wife has told me time and time again how much she appreciates

seeing my genuine sorrow when I have hurt her. "How do you put up with me? How do you live with me? You deserve the medal of honor for staying with me. You deserve the purple heart. You are an amazing woman to live with such an insensitive man." Sincere words like those express my repentant spirit and soothe our relationship.

I asked a wife, "After your husband has verbally abused you, would you appreciate if it he admitted he was wrong and expressed sorrow that you were hurting? What would you do if he said, 'How do you put up with such a crumb like me, as insensitive as I am?'"

"I'd call the cops," she said.

I repeated in amazement, "You'd call the cops?"

"Yes, because I'd know that there was an imposter in the house," she replied.

I have had wives say to me, "My husband will never admit when he's wrong. He's too proud." Yet I meet husbands everywhere who are willing to admit their offenses if their wives are patient enough to help them understand *how* they have offended them.

4. *Seek her forgiveness for your offensive behavior.* A woman needs a man who *understands* the *depth* of her grief after his hurtful behavior. Wives have said to me, "If only my husband knew how much I feel those words that he says so glibly and harshly. If only he knew how long they stay with me." Harsh words can stay with a woman for years.

A woman loves to hear her man say, "Will you forgive me?" And when she verbalizes, "Yes, you're forgiven," she is freer to restore her side of the relationship. However, if her husband simply says, "Oh, honey, I'm sorry," it's not always enough. He might be able to get away with it if he says it in a tender and gentle way, but a woman really needs to hear, "Will you forgive me?" That proves her husband values her half of the relationship. A flippant "I'm sorry" may mean "I'm sorry I got caught" or "I'm sorry to have to put up with your sensitivity." It usually doesn't restore the relationship to oneness and harmony.

5. *Let her see your consistent and sincere efforts to correct offensive actions or words.* This is another way of saying "repent." It simply means changing our way of thinking or acting to the way Christ thought and acted (Luke 17:3–5).

A woman isn't impressed with a man who seeks forgiveness or admits he is wrong and then continues to hurt her year after year in the same areas. Words are nice, but they are not enough.

Attitudes, not words or actions, often harm a woman the most. When she *sees* her husband's attitudes changing, she is more willing to open herself to him and accept him into an intimate relationship. Otherwise, she'll keep him closed off for fear of being offended again.

IS IT ALWAYS THE HUSBAND'S FAULT?

I want to emphasize the fact that *only after five years* of marriage is a husband responsible for the prolonged disharmony in his marriage. When you marry a woman, you inherit the way she was treated by her father, her mother, her brothers and sisters, and even her friends. She is the sum total of her environment, her associations, and her life as a single person.

The main problem that we men have to overcome is our *lack* of knowledge and skills to nurture (Eph. 5:28–29) our wives to a level from which we can enjoy a growing, loving, and intimate relationship with them. We, too, are the sum total of our environment, etc.

You may be thinking thoughts similar to those Mike had when he challenged me on this whole concept.

"Now wait a minute," Mike said. "That can't be true."

I assured him, "I know, it's hard to believe."

"Well, take my wife, Carol, for example," he said. "She has divorced me, but you can't tell me that the problems we had in our relationship can all be traced to my failure to love her. I just can't buy that."

To prove my point, I said, "Give me an example—something you didn't like about her—and we'll see if we can check this thing out."

"Take this one example," he said, confident that he could disprove this concept. "On our wedding night we had sexual relations. She was turned off by the whole experience and from that day on, for over twenty years, she never really enjoyed our sex life. She never initiated it. She didn't even want to be involved. It was always at my initiative.

"I felt she was more of an object that wasn't really involved in this relationship. How would I be the cause of that? On our wedding night, she changed on me!"

Mike had dated Carol for three years. So I asked how he treated her during those years.

"Well, okay," he said.

"Mike, I happen to know that it wasn't okay. You and I both know that you had a reputation of being mean and extremely insensitive to her. Do you remember some of the things you did?"

When he admitted that he did remember, I said, "You really hurt her feelings. During all those years that you dated her, did you ever clear up your offenses with her?"

"No, I didn't. I didn't know how to do it. I didn't know what to do," he said.

"Why did she marry you—to get away from her family?"

"Right."

"Then the first night she realized that sex wasn't that great. And do you know why?" I asked. "Because you two weren't in harmony. Besides this fact, did you prepare her for sex?" I explained that many women tell me they need as much as three days' preparation for sex, romantically and emotionally, before they can respond to their husbands. A woman is sort of like an iron and a man is like a lightbulb. She *warms up* to the sexual expression, while he *turns on* immediately.

"Did you ever clear your conscience with her? Did you ever clear those past offenses when you were married?" I asked him.

"No, I never did." Mike had never admitted he was wrong.

"Did you criticize your wife a lot?" I asked. Mike's head sank lower and lower. He even admitted that he once told her all their problems were her fault. After a few minutes, tears appeared in his eyes because he realized how insensitive, cruel, and harsh he had been for all those years.

The chart on pages 86–87 will provide some additional illustrations to help you discover how you might have contributed to a weaker marriage relationship. (This chart was devised by Ken Nair, a marriage and family lecturer/counselor). If you need help, you have an expert in your own home—your wife. You may be amazed at how well she remembers your unloving words and actions. However, many wives say they are afraid of their husbands, afraid to be honest for fear they'll be *rejected* or *criticized* for being illogical, too sensitive, or unforgiving.

IF YOU REACT NEGATIVELY TO THIS IDEA, YOU'RE NOT ALONE

I explained this concept to an older woman whose husband had left her, after many years of marriage, for a younger woman. She resisted the idea that I could trace their broken relationship to her husband's failure.

"Oh, this is ridiculous. Everyone knows it's a fifty-fifty deal. I'm just as much responsible as he was," she argued.

"Well, I'm looking for my first exception. I would certainly appreciate it if you would explain to me where you were wrong in the relationship," I told her.

An hour later, she realized that if her husband had treated her differently, she would have responded much differently during those years. We traced everything he had accused her of to his failure to love her.

Some men (including me) have said this material is dangerous because it will make women irresponsible. They panic because they are afraid their wives will accuse them of things their wives really are guilty of in their marriage relationship. I can understand the panic. In general, the concept provokes us to rage because it reveals our irresponsibility as husbands, and we just can't take it—especially at first. Believe me, I know and understand the fight that might be going on inside you at this moment.

Some single women also react negatively to this concept at first. For example, I overheard two of my editors discussing the concepts in this book; one was single and the other married.

"I just can't believe that some of the ideas in that book are good," said Debi, a twenty-five-year-old single woman. "I don't believe part of it—like women are more emotional."

"Just wait until you're married," Judy told her. "In a year and a half of marriage, my husband and I have run into many of the problems discussed in Gary's book."

"Some of the generalizations bother me, though," Debi continued. "I don't feel that women in general are more sensitive, because I've seen you at work. I know you."

"But it's different in a marriage," Judy said. "Just the other day when my husband was reading a chapter I had edited, he said, 'Hey, I think you're letting your thoughts creep into this book!' because the example was almost an identical account of a discussion we had recently."

If this section of the book doesn't do anything more than stimulate you to try and find an exception to the rule, it will be worthwhile. And if five years from now we discover hundreds of exceptions, the experience will still not have been damaging, because you and I need to become more responsible, loving partners, no matter what our wives do. That is the basis for genuine love—*doing what is right no matter what the other person does or says.*

Genuine love motivates us to build a relationship primarily for the other person's sake, and when we do that, *we* gain because *we* have a better relationship to enjoy.

Listed below are some of the ways (100-plus) a husband can offend his wife. When a husband recognizes that he has offended her in any one of these ways, he needs to clear it up to restore the relationship. Why not ask your wife to check the ones that are true of you?

1. Ignoring her.
2. Not valuing her opinions.
3. Showing more attention to other people than to her.
4. Not listening to her or not understanding what she feels is important.
5. Closing her out by not talking or listening to her (the silent treatment).
6. Being easily distracted when she's trying to talk.

7. Not scheduling special time to be with her.
8. Not being open to talk about things that you do not understand.
9. Not being open to talk about things that she does not understand.
10. Not giving her a chance to voice her opinion on decisions that affect the whole family.
11. Disciplining her by being angry or silent.
12. Making jokes about areas of her life.
13. Making sarcastic statements about her.
14. Insulting her in front of others.
15. Coming back with quick retorts.
16. Giving harsh admonitions.
17. Using careless words before you think through how they will affect her.
18. Nagging her in harshness.
19. Rebuking her before giving her a chance to explain a situation.
20. Raising your voice at her.
21. Making critical comments with no logical basis.
22. Swearing or using foul language in her presence.
23. Correcting her in public.
24. Being tactless when pointing out her weaknesses or blind spots.
25. Reminding her angrily that you warned her not to do something.
26. Having disgusted or judgmental attitudes.
27. Pressuring her when she is already feeling low or offended.
28. Lecturing her when she needs to be comforted, encouraged, or treated gently.
29. Breaking promises without any explanation or without being asked to be released from the promise.
30. Telling her how wonderful other women are and comparing her to other women.
31. Holding resentment about something she did and tried to make right.
32. Being disrespectful to her family and relatives.
33. Coercing her into an argument.
34. Correcting or punishing her in anger for something for which she's not guilty.
35. Not praising her for something she did well, even if she did it for you.
36. Treating her like a little child.
37. Being rude to her or to other people in public, like restaurant personnel or clerks.
38. Being unaware of her needs.

39. Being ungrateful.
40. Not trusting her.
41. Not approving of what she does or how she does it.
42. Not being interested in her own personal growth.
43. Being inconsistent or having double standards (doing things you won't allow her to do).
44. Not giving her advice when she really needs it and asks for it.
45. Not telling her that you love her.
46. Having prideful and arrogant attitudes in general.
47. Not giving daily encouragement.
48. Failing to include her in the conversation when you are with other people.
49. Failing to spend quantity or quality time with her when you're at a party.
50. "Talking her down"—continuing to discuss or argue a point just to prove you're right.
51. Ignoring her around the house as if she weren't a member of the family.
52. Not listening to what she believes is important as soon as you come home from work.
53. Ignoring her at social gatherings.
54. Not attending church as a family.
55. Failure to express honestly what you think her innermost feelings are.
56. Showing more excitement for work or other activities than for her.
57. Being impolite at mealtime.
58. Having sloppy manners around the house and in front of others.
59. Not inviting her out on special romantic dates from time to time (just the two of you).
60. Not helping her with the children just before mealtimes or during times of extra stress.
61. Not volunteering to help her with the dishes occasionally—or with cleaning the house.
62. Making her feel stupid when she shares an idea about your work or decisions that need to be made.
63. Making her feel unworthy for desiring certain furniture or insurance or other material needs for herself and the family.
64. Not being consistent with the children; not taking an interest in playing with them and spending quality and quantity time with them.
65. Not showing public affection ,for her, like holding her hand or putting your arm around her (you seem to be embarrassed to be with her).

66. Not sharing your life with her, like your ideas or your feelings (e.g., what's going on at work).
67. Not being the spiritual leader of the home.
68. Demanding that she submit to you.
69. Demanding that she be involved with you sexually when you are not in harmony.
70. Being unwilling to admit you were wrong.
71. Resisting whenever she shares one of your "blind spots."
72. Being too busy with work and activities.
73. Not showing compassion and understanding for her and the children when there is real need.
74. Not planning for the future, making her very insecure.
75. Being stingy with money, making her feel like she's being paid a salary—and not much at that.
76. Wanting to do things that embarrass her sexually.
77. Reading sexual magazines in front of her or the children.
78. Forcing her to make many of the decisions regarding the checkbook and bills.
79. Forcing her to handle bill collectors and overdue bills.
80. Not letting her lean on your gentleness and strength from time to time.
81. Not allowing her to fail—always feeling like you have to lecture her.
82. Refusing to let her be a woman.
83. Criticizing her womanly characteristics or sensitivity as being weak.
84. Spending too much money and getting the family too far into debt.
85. Not having a sense of humor and not joking about things together.
86. Not telling her how important she is to you.
87. Not sending her special love letters from time to time.
88. Forgetting special dates like anniversaries and birthdays.
89. Not defending her when somebody else is complaining or tearing her down (especially if it's one of your relatives or friends).
90. Not putting your arm around her and hugging her when she's in need of comfort.
91. Not bragging to other people about her.
92. Being dishonest.
93. Discouraging her for trying to better herself, either through education or physical fitness.
94. Continuing distasteful or harmful habits, like coming home drunk.
95. Not treating her as if "Handle With Care" were stamped on her forehead.

96. Ignoring her relatives and the people who are important to her.
97. Taking her for granted, assuming that "a woman's work is never done" around the house.
98. Not including her in future plans until the last minute.
99. Never doing little unexpected things for her.
100. Not treating her like an intellectual equal.
101. Looking at her as a weaker individual in general.
102. Being preoccupied with your own goals and needs, making her feel like she and the children do not count.
103. Threatening never to let her do something again because she made some mistake in the past.
104. Criticizing her behind her back. (This is really painful for her if she hears about your criticism from someone else.)
105. Blaming her for things in your relationship that are clearly your failure.
106. Not being aware of her physical limitations; treating her like a man by roughhousing with her or making her carry heavy objects.
107. Losing patience or getting angry with her when she can't keep up with your schedule or physical stamina.
108. Acting like you're a martyr if you go along with her opinions.
109. Sulking when she challenges your comments.
110. Joining too many organizations which exclude her and the children.
111. Failing to repair items around the house.
112. Watching too much TV and therefore neglecting her and the children.
113. Demanding that she sit and listen to your point of view when she needs to be taking care of the children's needs.
114. Insisting on lecturing her in order to convey what you believe are important points.
115. Humiliating her with words and actions, saying things like "I can't stand living in a pigpen."
116. Not taking the time to prepare her to enjoy sexual intimacy.
117. Spending money extravagantly without helping those less fortunate.
118. Avoiding family activities that the children enjoy.
119. Taking vacations that are primarily for your pleasure, like fishing or hunting, while preventing her from shopping and doing the things she enjoys doing.
120. Not letting her get away from the children just to be with friends, go shopping for special items, or have a weekend away with her friends.

121. Being unwilling to join her in the things she enjoys like shopping, going out for coffee and dessert at a restaurant, etc.
122. Not understanding the boring chores a wife does: picking up clothes and toys all day long, wiping runny noses, putting on and taking off muddy boots and jackets, washing and ironing, etc., etc.

♥ SEPARATING THE MEN FROM THE BOYS ♥

This wasn't an easy chapter for husbands to read and think about. It almost sounds as if Gary Smalley and his wife are ganging up on them. Actually, however, Gary is simply speaking the truth in love. There could be some truths here that would change your entire relationship to your wife. Go back over the 100-plus ways that a husband might offend his wife. Which ones have you been guilty of lately? If possible, discuss the list with her and let her give her opinions without ignoring her or refusing to value her opinions.

By going through the list and thinking about how you may have hurt or offended your wife, you have already taken the first step toward building a better relationship with her. The next four are a little tougher.

♥ Admit your part in weakening your marriage. Be humble enough to say "I am wrong."

♥ Show real sorrow whenever you offend your wife. Again, this will be hard on your pride but good for your marriage.

♥ Seek your wife's forgiveness when you offend her. It is good to say, "I am sorry," but it is infinitely better to add, "Will you forgive me?"

♥ Repent—that is, really turn around and try to change. As the Scriptures say, "Love isn't just words, it's action" (see 1 John 3:18).

HOW TO PLAY MARITAL DOMINOES

The following game is an effective way for a husband to cause a negative chain reaction in his wife. The "benefits" of this game are double. Not only does the husband enjoy his own sins, but he also gets to put up with his wife's. Everybody loses!

Husband is unreliable and lets time slip by unnoticed. This leads to nagging by his wife as she repeatedly reminds him of things that need attention as well as his past wrongs and forgetfulness.

Husband is untrusting and condemning with an attitude of superiority in finances. He demands control of all the money, won't let his wife know their financial status. This leads to impulsive spending by his wife. She goes through money as if it grew on trees, uses credit cards without concern.

Husband is angry and demanding, particularly with the children. Hates being inconvenienced by the family and sets standards too difficult for the children to meet. This leads to permissiveness by his wife who makes excuses for the children's disobedience and keeps secrets from the husband about their conduct.

Husband is insensitive and unkind, using hurtful words and often making his wife and others the butt of humor that is in poor taste or sarcastic. This leads to overemotionalism on the part of his wife who cries often, is easily hurt and keeps careful score. She can recall past offenses in minute detail.

Husband is inattentive, thoughtless and untrustworthy, often preoccupied with personal concerns. Dismisses feelings of others as unrealistic or invalid (if he acknowledges them at all). This leads to domination by his wife who makes a habit of answering all questions, even those directed to her husband. Wife makes decisions in the home and assumes responsibility for disciplining the children.

And so the weary game continues—until all the dominoes fall down.[4]

Chapter 41

IF YOUR WIFE DOESN'T WIN FIRST PLACE, YOU LOSE!

BY GARY SMALLEY
The Joy of Committed Love

Gary Smalley continues to talk to husbands about how they can get past the "What's Wrong?—Nothing, You Wouldn't Understand Anyway" syndrome. What if you want to tell your wife she's the most important person in your life, but she doesn't believe you? Smalley writes from personal experience as he explains how a husband can always win by putting his wife in first place. As you read, ask yourself:

♥ Is my wife the most important person in my life?
♥ Does she really know this?
♥ How do I show her she is important, and how could I improve in this area?

IS YOUR MARRIAGE "GOING TO THE DOGS?"

"Even our dog is more important to him than I am," grumbled a wife in a recent interview. "My husband comes home and plays with the dog and then it's more of a when's-dinner-going-to-be-ready? attitude," she sighed.

A woman's sparkling affection toward her husband is diminished when he begins to prefer other activities or people over her. Many times he is not even aware of the way his misplaced priorities damage her and their relationship. For a marriage to flourish, a wife desperately needs to know she has a very special place in her husband's heart.

Many husbands are shocked when their wives leave them "for

no reason" after twenty or even thirty years of marriage. They feel they provided everything their wives could have possibly needed— a nice home, a good car, enough money to raise the children. Yet that wasn't enough. Why? A woman needs much more than things.

I have met creative businessmen who make large sums of money with their business skills and who keep their employees satisfied with respect and an awareness of their needs. Isn't it ironic that such intelligent men can go home at night and not even know how to apply the same principles to their wives? Could it be that their most important accomplishments are over at 5:00 P.M.?

Without meaning to, a husband can communicate nonverbally that other people or activities are more important to him than his wife. Haven't you heard of golf widows? Whether it is golf or tennis, club activities or community leadership, your wife and your marital happiness will suffer if most of your time and efforts are directed toward some other interest, with only cold leftovers for her. A wife can feel less important just by comparing the amount of time her husband spends with her to the time he spends elsewhere. Women notice how our eyes light up and our entire personalities change as we become excited about fishing or hunting or other activities. If your wife doesn't sense that same excitement in you when you're with her, she has a gnawing sense of failure because she feels she isn't as attractive to you as are your activities or friends. This can be devastating to a woman's sense of personal worth.

My own wife graphically illustrated this very important concept to me during our fifth year of marriage. I arrived home for lunch to find her standing quietly at the kitchen sink, not even interested in talking when I tried to make conversation. In a moment of insight, I perceived that I was in hot water. I remembered her coolness toward me during the previous few days which I had mistakenly attributed to some sort of "hormonal change."

"Is there anything wrong between us?" I asked her.

"It doesn't matter. You wouldn't understand anyway," she replied.

"Funny thing, I'm losing my desire to go back to work right now. I can see there are some real problems here. Wouldn't you like to talk about it? I'm not sure what I'm doing wrong."

"Even if I told you, either you wouldn't understand or you wouldn't change, so what's the use? Let's don't talk about it. It's too painful. It discourages me and disappoints me when you say you're going to do something and then you don't."

But I gently resisted, telling her that I wished she would share it with me, that I just didn't understand. Finally, she was able to verbalize what actions during the past five years had driven an impenetrable wedge between us and were causing me to violate an important biblical principle.

"You'd really rather be at work, or with your friends, or counseling people than spending time with me," she said.

I asked her to explain.

"If someone calls you when we have plans, you're liable to say 'Let me check with my wife and see if I can't postpone our plans.' I just can't believe you would do that to me over and over again."

I explained how it was easier for me to turn her down than to say no to other people.

"What about when I cook a special dinner, sometimes even with candlelight? You'll come home or call and say you've had to make other plans. You go off somewhere with other people as if I didn't even exist, as if it didn't even mean anything that I've gone to extra-special effort for you."

She continued, "I don't care any more. I don't even want to do these special things for you. I've been disappointed so many times that I just can't handle it emotionally."

She made me realize that although I always had time for someone in need of counseling, I made no effort to spend time with her. When I did spend time with her, she said, I didn't have the same concentration or excitement about being with her.

I listened as she revealed her innermost feelings for several hours. I really didn't know what to do, and I wasn't sure I'd be able to change. But I could understand her complaints. I had neglected her and offended her with my unloving ways. However, when I agreed with her, she was unresponsive, and I could tell she had given up.

She helped me discover how I was violating the biblical principle found in 1 Peter 3:7, and since then I've come to realize that it's the cornerstone of all relationships! *Grant her honor.* Honor basically means to attach high value, worth, or importance to a person or thing. Norma felt less important than my vocation and activities. Without realizing it, I was not honoring her as the most important person in my life, second only to my relationship with Christ.

"Could you forgive me for the way I've treated you?" I asked. "I'm willing to change. I'll really plan on changing."

"Sure, I've heard that song before," she said skeptically.

I didn't know how long it would take for me to reform. But I knew the next time someone called right before dinner I would have to ask, "Is this an emergency, or can we work it out tomorrow?" I had to show her I really meant business about meeting her needs *first.*

I *wanted* to tell her she was the most important person in my life. I really *wanted* to feel that way. At first I didn't have those feelings, but I *wanted* to have them. As I tried to make her more important to me than anyone else, I soon began to *feel* she was top priority. Feelings *follow* thoughts and actions. In other words, the warm inner feeling I have for Norma began to burn *after* I placed the "queen's crown" upon her head.

My pride was broken, my ego bruised, and my feelings wounded in numerous falls from marital harmony during the first two years of living these principles. Because I tried so hard to make it work, Norma finally believed I was earnest in my endeavor to change. But it took two years to convince her.

I learned from Norma and other wives that women need to see effort and not hear mere promises. Give your wife time to watch you climb the mountain if she doesn't believe what you say initially. Show her you are learning to scale the cliffs and hurdle the crevices. The more *consistently* loving we are as husbands, the more trustworthy we become to our wives. Soon they will join us as we climb hand over hand toward the goal of a loving marriage.

The most important way I've ever expressed my love to Norma was when I finally attached a high value to her; she is worth more to me than anything on this earth—and she knows it.

HOW TO GIVE YOUR WIFE THE PROOF

Wives need proof of change in at least three areas before they will believe their husbands' commitment.

CAREFUL LISTENING WITHOUT ARGUMENT

Can you imagine a husband being able to justify everything he ever did to hurt his wife? Wayne thought he could. He and his wife couldn't talk for more than fifteen minutes before falling into a heated argument. Inevitably, through his logical deductions, the argument ended up being her fault.

Finally, Wayne told Cathy he really wanted to change, and to love her. A few hours later she suggested a quiet little vacation, just for the two of them to get reacquainted.

"Are you kidding?" he replied, crushing her hopes for better understanding. "You mean you want me to pay rent here at the apartment and then pay for a motel too? That's double rent!"

The topic developed into a fight that led to more fights as the months went by, until their relationship deteriorated and she finally left. He had refused to listen to her needs without arguing and lost her as a result.

It is often difficult for a man to converse with his wife without challenging the meaning of various words she uses to explain how she feels inside. If a husband can *overlook the actual words* his wife uses to express herself and instead actively pursue *what she means*, fewer arguments will take place. One man I know finds it almost impossible to do this. When his wife uses phrases like "You *never* do this," or "You *always* do that," he will inevitably say, "Now, dear, I don't *always* do that." Or he begins to analyze her statement to prove its fallacy. In ten minutes, they're off on another hot discussion. It is essential in communication to *look past the words* to the real meaning.

Everyone has his or her own definition for a given word. We attach meanings to words based on our own unique experiences. So when we attempt to communicate with another person, we use words we believe will accurately convey our thoughts. For instance, in this book I may use words that you enjoy or words that irritate you. You might even be indifferent to my words because you have another frame of reference or because my definitions might be different from yours. That is why I try to illustrate all the important points I make, probing for our common point of reference.

If we can stop justifying our actions and quit arguing about the words our wives use, we can get down to the heart of the matter. We can try rephrasing our wives' statements until they say we have grasped their meaning. "Is this what you're saying, dear?" or "Is this what I'm hearing?" At all cost, avoid sarcastic questions like, "Is this what you're having trouble saying?" A budding relationship between husband and wife can be stunted by an attitude of male superiority.

QUICKNESS TO ADMIT ERROR

Countless wives and children have told me how their family relationships were weakened because of a husband's or father's unwillingness to admit his errors. Though husbands sometimes think admission of error reveals their weaknesses, the opposite is true. Just think back through your own life to the times when someone admitted his or her offense to you. Chances are, your respect for him or her increased, not decreased.

A friend of mine told me about the time he made a racially derogatory statement to an associate during the day. The man was offended; however, the situation was not discussed. My friend drove away feeling somewhat uneasy and guilty for what he had said. Before he reached his home, he turned around and drove back to confront the man.

Walking into the room, he said, "A few minutes ago I said something very offensive to you. I know it was wrong, and I have come back to ask if you could forgive me for what I said."

The man nearly fell over. Of course he forgave him, and I'm sure his respect for my friend doubled. A humble admission of wrong produces positive results. When a husband admits he has hurt his wife, she feels better just knowing he understands. His admission of wrong produces a much stronger marriage.

PATIENCE WHEN SHE DOUBTS HE HAS CHANGED

What if you've been doing everything within your power to let your wife know she has first place in your life, and she still doesn't believe you've changed? Do you throw up your arms in disgust? Or do you gently persuade her over a period of time? I hope you choose the latter. Her initial respect for you wasn't lost overnight, and it can't be regained in a day. Show her that no matter how long it takes, you want to earn her respect.

TWO REASONS WHY A WIFE BECOMES LESS IMPORTANT

What causes a man to come home after work, pick up his young son, and kiss and cuddle him without even greeting his wife? How can a husband walk straight to the garage to begin a project without even acknowledging his arrival to his wife as he passes by her in the kitchen? *Why* does a man *lose* affection and enthusiasm for his wife after marriage? I think there are two major reasons.

1. A man will pursue and charm a woman with words or flowers or whatever he needs to do to *win* her. But after the wedding, he feels he has conquered her. She is his, so he doesn't have to maintain the same level of enthusiasm and creativity as he did before they married. She is his emotionally and legally. The husband may say to himself, "I have my wife. Now I need to conquer my business . . . become a better hunter . . . begin a family.. . ." Each frontier is viewed as a new conquest, a new experience.

2. Almost anything is sweet to a starving man, but when he's full, even honey nauseates him (Prov. 27:7). In a very real sense, a man is filled up when he marries because his wife is now a part of him. He believes he has experienced knowing her in every way—spiritually, emotionally, mentally, and physically. He may feel there is nothing left to know about her. He is satisfied and, therefore, has a tendency to look for other potential "frontiers."

It is healthy for a husband and wife to put a creative sparkle into their relationship by remaining a challenge to each other. I remember this was the motivating factor in my attraction to Norma. We had been dating casually for three years when I heard she was getting serious with someone else. At the moment I visualized losing her, I became far more creative, challenging myself to restore our relationship. But, like so many other men, after we married I focused upon other conquests such as school and my career. Since it was no longer a priority to earn her affection, I simply went on to oil whatever wheel squeaked the loudest.

Now, I find when a wife can learn to put a little mystique back into the relationship, it tantalizes her husband. That mystique is not simply "playing hard to get"; it is more a matter of self-confidence. It's letting her husband know she is not totally dependent upon him. Other areas also satisfy her, like her relationship with God.

HOW TO GAIN YOUR WIFE'S LOVE AND MORE

If it came down to an evening with your friends or a night with your wife, she needs to know you would choose her company just because you enjoy being with her. In the same way, if the choice were between the children or her, she needs to know you would choose to spend time with her. She needs to know she's Number One. When she is satisfied that she's in first place in your life, she will encourage you to do the other things you like doing. For example, I am taking six weeks away from my wife and children to write this book. Several years ago my wife would have been crushed by the mere suggestion of such a long separation. Yet today she is as enthusiastic about it as I am because she knows I will be able to fulfill *our* dream of writing our inner convictions about marriage. More importantly, she knows I would rather be with her than with my typewriter and editor.

Putting your wife in the Number One slot doesn't shackle you to the house; instead, it frees you of the dread of going home.

"Why don't you let me go to the meeting alone tonight so you can go to the basketball game?" Mary said. Her husband was pleasantly shocked. Not so long ago they had had misunderstandings about his unsatiable appetite for basketball. In fact, they were thinking about separating because he did not have the knowledge or skills he needed to treat Mary right, and she did not have the emotional strength to continue living with him or loving him. Today he regularly puts her before his work, his activities, etc. And Mary is now free to encourage his outside interests, knowing she's at the top of his list.

My wife also encourages me to enjoy my interests in hunting and fishing because she feels secure in her position of importance. If an emergency arose, she knows my first commitment would be to taking care of her or the children, not to my recreational enjoyment.

> The more important a woman feels she is to her husband, the more she encourages him to do the activities she knows he enjoys.

Do you wonder whether your wife feels she is more important to you than other people or things in your life? Complete the following exercise, and I think you will find out.

First, list, your favorite spare-time activities.

_____

_____

_____

_____

_____

What is an enjoyable after-work activity for you?

Monday _____

Tuesday _____

Wednesday _____

Thursday _____

Friday _____

Saturday _____

Sunday _____

Where do you enjoy taking your vacations?

_____

_____

_____

Now, look back over these three lists and ask yourself, *"Is there anything on the lists I would rather do than be with my wife?"* Probably so. And if so, chances are you have already "communicated" to your wife that she is not as important to you as your activities, even though you have never uttered those words. Since a woman has tremendous perception, she knows where your heart is, even when you haven't said a word. . . . But that doesn't mean it's too late to change.

YOUR WIFE'S "RADAR" CAN DETECT YOUR SINCERITY

What a man values, he takes good care of. Or as Christ said, "Where your treasure is, there will your heart be also" (Matt. 6:21). If your hobby is fishing, you probably hesitate to loan out your rod and reel. If you enjoy hunting, you probably know how to carefully oil and polish guns. Based on the amount of time you spend on each activity, your wife can sense which is most important to you. If she doesn't feel that you are as careful with her as you are with your other interests, she will know she is not as important. That feeling shatters her self-worth and can result in physical as well as emotional problems. The emotions she struggles with now may surface years later in the form of serious and expensive physical problems.

However, some husbands feel threatened by the thought of giving their wives special treatment, fearing they will lose out with their friends, career, or hobbies. They falsely believe if they give up other activities for the sake of being with their wives, they will give them up forever. Remember, when a wife feels she is the most important, she gets excited about her husband being able to do the things he wants to do.

HOW I GAINED MY WIFE'S LOVE AND EVERYTHING ELSE

After ten years of marriage, I felt I was finally becoming a success in my work. I was privileged to speak regularly for various organizations in our city and throughout the country. My wife and I had a beautiful home and two children. What more could a man want? Then from my point of view, a tragedy occurred in my marriage. Norma became pregnant with our third child. I was not enthusiastic. If anything, I was depressed, realizing our youngest had only been out of diapers for two years. I was just starting to enjoy my children, and the thought of another little baby around the house was almost overwhelming.

Although I tried to be nice to Norma, I couldn't hide my disappointment. I was afraid I might not be able to travel as much and would be forced to take a less prestigious position in the company. My work load increased as the months passed, and I warned my wife I would not be able to help her with the children because of job demands. Even on the day our son was born, I worried about the added hardships he would add to my vocational dreams.

Norma's health suffered during the first year after our son's birth because of the long night hours and the responsibility of taking care of two other small children. Our baby had to have surgery and was often sick, adding to her burden. How cruel I was during that year! Whenever the baby would cry at night or need special attention, I would quickly remind Norma he was her child. She had wanted another baby, not I.

A year passed in this way before Norma finally said to me, "I can't take it any more. I wish I had the emotional and physical strength to take care of the kids, discipline and train them, but I just can't do it with an absentee father."

(Norma had actually come to a new spiritual level by realizing that her hostility toward my schedule was really her resistance to Romans 8:28—God can work all things together for good to those who love him, and especially to those loving others [called according to his plan]. She had never thanked God for my schedule and asked him to work it for good in her life. With the added responsibilities she finally broke before God and confessed she could not fight him any longer about my schedule. This new calmness on her part, as described in 1 Peter 3:1–6, greatly motivated me.)

She wasn't demanding. She wasn't angry. She was simply stating the facts. She had had it. I could see the *urgency* and *calmness* in her facial expressions and realized that she desperately needed my help. I faced a major decision. Should I go to my boss and ask for a different job in the company? Ask for a job that would allow me more time at home? It was a struggle because I knew I would get a less prestigious job. I felt I would have to sacrifice some of my career goals. Inwardly, I felt resentment toward my son and my wife for being weak. But I gave in. In nervousness and embarrassment, I approached my boss to explain I needed more time at home because of the children. "Is there any possibility that I could have a different job that would allow me to stay home more?"

My boss graciously cooperated by giving me another job. But to me the new job was a demotion. I was asked to do some things which only a few weeks earlier I had been training my subordinates to do. What a blow!

I was devastated for a while, but soon I became interested in home life. I actually looked forward to five o'clock. My family and I began doing more things together, like camping and other special activities. Before long, a new love blossomed within both Norma and me. Norma began to feel more physically alert which, in turn, made her more cheerful and outgoing. She changed some habits I disliked without any pressure from me. My "big" career sacrifice seemed smaller every day in comparison to the richer relationship we were developing.

Within a few months, my boss gave me a new position in the company that I liked much better than the one I had given up. By this time, Norma was so secure with me that she had no resentment toward my new job or any necessary travel that went with it. I gave in and gave up at first, but I won in the long run. That's almost exactly how Christ explains the principle of exchange in Mark 8:34–37.

Even to this day, if I ask our son Michael, "Why are you so important to Dad?" he'll say, "Because I brought you back to Mama and the family."

♥ TRUST ISN'T BUILT IN A DAY ♥

Review what Gary Smalley says about earning your wife's trust by proving that you've changed. He lists three areas where your wife will need proof that you are committed to putting her first.

- ♥ Listen carefully, don't argue or justify your position (review the material on active listening in Parts IV and V).
- ♥ Be quick to admit your own errors or mistakes. "I was wrong, will you forgive me?" are some of the hardest words any of us can say, but they can bear the most fruit.
- ♥ Be patient if she remains skeptical. Distrust is usually built over a period of years; trust won't be rebuilt in a day. Sit down with your wife and ask her:

> Do you feel you are the most important person in my life?
> Are there any activities in my life you feel are more important to me than you are?
> Are there any special ways you believe I could better communicate how important you are to me?

Making each other the most important thing in life is a constant challenge, especially when the little feet start to patter (thunder?) through the house. In the next chapter, Bruce Narramore and Melodie Davis discuss caring about each other while you care for the children.

Chapter 42

GO AHEAD—BUY THAT LOCK FOR THE BEDROOM DOOR

BY DR. BRUCE NARRAMORE
Why Children Misbehave

AND MELODIE M. DAVIS
You Know You're A Mother When . . .

For many couples marriage naturally leads to parenthood, which brings joy mixed with responsibility, frustration and possible heartache. As many parents know, it is all too easy to let children fracture the marriage relationship, or at least cause both partners to neglect it. The following chapter includes two parts. First you will hear from Dr. Bruce Narramore, a psychologist who has written many fine books on parenting, and then you will hear from Melodie Davis, free-lance writer and homemaker who knows a great deal about being a mother as well as a wife. As you read, keep one question in mind:

♥ What do either or both of these authors have to tell me about blocking out more time for *us*?

PARENTS ARE PEOPLE, TOO!

Most books on rearing children contain a lot of good advice on meeting children's needs. They help us understand our children's needs for love and limits and offer practical ways of guiding children to maturity with a minimum of psychic damage. This advice and understanding can be very helpful. In fact, a significant portion of this book is written for that very purpose. But if we aren't careful, we can focus so intently on our children's needs that we forget that parents are people, too. We have our own needs, our own feelings, our own desires, and our own responsibilities. We are not simply our children's guardians. We existed as individuals and couples before our children were born and will continue to do so long after they leave the nest.

Consequently, before looking at our responsibilities to our children, let's take a few minutes to look at our responsibilities to ourselves and our spouses. If we are unable to meet our own needs, it will be impossible for us to find fulfillment in our roles as parents—and both we and our children will suffer for it. One of the saddest situations I encounter as a psychologist is that of a parent (usually a mother) who has totally thrown her life into her children only to wake up in her forties with the children gone, a sterile marriage, and no sense of who she is as a person. She has been so busy trying to be a good parent that she has lost sight of the fact that she is a person first! Let's look, then, at a few of our own rights and needs.

TIME FOR YOURSELF

One of the greatest frustrations mothers of young children face is the lack of time alone. Caring for even one child is a big responsibility and a time-consuming task. But if we happen to have two or three preschool children, we can really encounter a problem. Where, in the middle of all of our responsibilities, do we find any time alone? How can we gain even a few minutes of peace and quiet? And how can we get out of the house without feeling guilty for abandoning them? In short, how can we be both a person and a parent? As Julie, the frustrated parent of a seven-month-old baby told me, "I seem to spend all day taking care of one end or the other! There is never time for me!"

When I asked a group of parents to discuss the most frustrating problem they faced, one mother replied, "My biggest frustration was when Penny was small and so demanding. Every time I turned around she thought she needed something. Sometimes I just felt like stuffing her under the bed or tossing her out the window—not to hurt her, but just to make her shut up!"

These mothers expressed feelings many parents would hestitate to admit. But they are entirely normal. Everyone has a legitimate need for time alone, and none should have to apologize for it. It is impossible to meet our own needs fully if we spend twenty-four hours a day assuming responsibility for our offspring.

In our society it is usually the mother who encounters this particular conflict. Since men generally work outside the home, they have a convenient escape from the ongoing demands of young children! If you are feeling these frustrations, it would be very good to stop now and have a long talk with your husband. Explain your need for a little time and space. A sensitive husband will understand. If he doesn't, ask him to change places with you for several days or a week. I am sure he will see your point of view before the time is up!

While discussing your needs with your spouse, be honest with your feelings. Let him know you "love the kids but sometimes they get on my nerves." Let him know you aren't ready to run off and abandon the family, but at times you need to be alone. And let him know you still need time with your friends. Then plan with your husband how it can be done.

Can your husband relieve you of some of the responsibilities? Do you have grandparents nearby who can help? Is there a baby-sitting co-op you can join? Is one of the children ready for nursery school? Can you hire a baby sitter a couple of days a week? Or would a housekeeper coming in for a half-day each week improve the situation? These are just a few of the many possibilities for making a little time for yourself.

Once you decide how to provide the time, you can decide how to spend it. Would you like just to be left alone? Do you need some time to shop? Would you enjoy a Bible study group or a weekly tennis match? Or would you even like a part-time job? While there are some real difficulties in trying to hold down a job and be a responsible parent, some women find relief and a fulfillment in their work that makes them better mothers. If this is true of you, don't be afraid to consider the possibility. It is one way of getting relief from some really difficult responsibilties and having a bit more time just for yourself. And when you feel better about yourself, you will do better with your children. A tense, bored, overworked, or stifled woman is in no condition to be a happy parent!

TIME FOR YOUR SPOUSE

Close on the heels of our need for time alone is the need for time with our mate. God created marriage before he created children, and we must not forget that marriage is the basic institution of society. It is likely that we were married for a significant period of time before we became parents, and if we follow the statistical average, we will have a full three decades of married life after our children reach adulthood and leave home.

We must not assume we can take a twenty-year vacation from working on our marriage while we are rearing children. All of us need regular communication. If we don't have these times with our mate, tensions begin to build and problems surface. Husbands can easily feel left out when wives spend most of their time with the children, and wives can feel unloved when husbands fail to make a habit of finding time to be together without the children.

Carol, the mother of a baby girl, described her experience as a parent and a marriage partner. She wrote:

I had no idea babies could be so time-consuming. I felt like a stranger to my husband because there just was no time for us to be alone. Keith wasn't the kind to get involved with feeding, bathing, or that kind of thing, so I began to put all of my energy into Kimberly.

This caused us to drift apart even more and I found myself loving and hating Kimberly at the same time. One day I had a talk with a good friend and realized what was happening. Kimberly was becoming the center of my attention, and Keith was being pushed aside.

Carol's experience is common. Fortunately she realized she was falling into a trap and began to break out. She talked the problem over with her husband, and they found ways of meeting both their needs and those of their young daughter.

A weekly evening out, a regular time together after the children are in bed, and an occasional weekend away from home can all help keep our marriages alive and make us better persons and better parents. When our children are old enough to sleep over at a friend's home, arrange for them to be out for a night or two. Some couples take turns keeping each other's children for a weekend. This frees them up for a weekend trip, a night at a fine hotel, or just a quiet evening together at home.

The possibilities are endless, and the principle is simple. When we become parents, we do not cease to be partners. If we are going to enjoy a happy family life, we must give attention to our own needs and the needs of our mates as well as those of our children.

*   *   *

HOW TO KEEP THOSE LITTLE PEOPLE OUT

(Melodie Davis continues this chapter with her homemaker's-eye-view on how to keep a strong relationship with your husband.)

One night while I was writing in the kitchen after the girls had gone to bed, Stuart kept coming out during television commercials to check on what I was doing. I was wondering about all this uncharacteristic attention when he finally blurted, "You hardly ever pay any attention to me anymore. When you're not busy with the girls, you're busy working."

Ouch. At first I was mad. "You're an adult. I guess I was expecting you to take care of yourself. I'm really not interested in that TV program anyway."

Regardless of how true my statements were, he had a point I couldn't deny. When we were dating and spending an evening in the other's home, I wouldn't have gone my own way while he went his. The natural desire is to be close—physically close—to the one you love. Circumstances and responsibilities change: children, extra work from the office, different interests on TV, or hobbies. But one thing should never change: the desire to be close to the one you love.

Now, how can a busy mother find a way to be close to her husband? In titling a chapter in my book (*You Know You're a Mother When . . .* "You Decide to Buy a Lock for Your Bedroom Door") I was really thinking of a figurative lock rather than a real one. Oh sure, a lock is nice insurance against having your four-year-old show up at 11 P.M. in the middle of "you know what." But I suspect that such scenarios happen more often in magazine stories than in real life. Too often, however, kids stumble into our marriage relationship in far more threatening ways.

"Little people can easily dominate the whole scene," admits Dorothy, mother of two. "We have to remember that children are just passing through; a spouse is (we hope) permanent."

But let's face it. Having kids drastically alters the amount of time parents can spend gazing into each other's eyes. And I think that physical contact with the children—hugs, kisses, and having them climb all over you—fulfills part of our need for touching.

I've heard mothers say that they felt less need for physical contact with their husbands, especially during the nursing period.

But there are physical needs our children can never fulfill. If we want to maintain a strong marriage, we must be as committed to *making* time for our spouses as we are to making time for the children.

SURVIVING THE INFAMOUS DINNER HOUR

It's true that the best thing a wife can do for her children is to love their father (and vice versa). But how does it work out practically? Take, for instance, my very worst time of the day: supper. The kids are acting as if they have Oscar the Grouch hangovers, Dad's ears are humming from working in an 85-decibel environment all day, and Mom is trying to get supper on the table with a whiny two-year-old leech on her leg. It's definitely not the right time to greet husband at the door in pink baby doll pajamas. But I *do* try to break away from the leech and the scorched gravy long enough for at least a peck and a smile. You could call it perfunctory, force of habit, or a sentimental holdover from newlywed days. All I know is that if I *don't* bother, Stuart feels as though he should have gone ahead and joined the guys at Bob's Pizzeria.

No matter how much we love our husbands, the duties of motherhood and the needs of children sometimes make it seem otherwise. Stuart may be talking about his day when one of the children interrupts to ask for more water. We're trying to teach our kids *not* to interrupt, but my immediate response is to stop listening to Stuart and attend to Michelle's request. "I can see where I count around here," mumbled Stuart one day. "Right about number 100, after the dog, the kids, and the termites."

Judy pointed out that the reason we moms listen to our children over husbands is because that's what we *do* all day. We're programmed to respond right away to our children's voices. "If I don't answer Janelle right away, she'll repeat it until she gets an answer. So I might as well respond and save my ears." My mind and body are as programmed to respond to the call of a child as any factory worker is programmed to respond to the quitting bell.

That doesn't make it right to allow children to interrupt parents or other adults. But it's hard not to let them. I want to teach Michelle not to interrupt by being a good example. More likely, however, children learn to be such expert interrupters from our bad example. Combine childish immaturity with bad role models and it's no wonder children have a hard time learning not to interrupt.

How can we pay adequate attention to our children, our spouses, and ourselves? How can families juggle it all?

Couples who have a few years alone to establish a good relationship have an advantage. Joanna says, "I'm *so* glad we waited as long as we did to have children." She and her husband know that suppertime, when everyone has low energy for coping, won't always be so tense.

Jan and her husband had a son within a year of their marriage, followed by another baby about eighteen months later. "You try harder," she said simply, "if you *don't* have the luxury of waiting several years to have children." Not too long ago, couples rarely postponed parenthood more than a year or two. But society has changed, so now many couples feel they need four or five years alone together before taking on the responsibilities of a family.

Joanna and Duane make their relationship a priority by going out together once a month. On a school teacher's salary it's not easy to afford it, but Joanna claims it's "well worth the money."

"Kids like their parents to go out if they know why," agrees Judy. If they understand that it helps Mom and Dad love each other more they won't have such a hard time accepting it. They also understand it better if they, too, have special "dates" alone with Mom and Dad regularly.

Judy remembers one couple who had a policy of never allowing a child to sit between them when they were all in the car. My own Mom and Dad often hold hands as they walk, or Dad puts his arm around Mom while they sit in church. Are these just silly, token gestures done for show? With some they may be, but I remember what a nice feeling it gave me as a child to see Mom and Dad show affection for one another.

KEEP YOUR BEDROOM KIDPROOF

I've heard some marriage counselors suggest that the parents' bedroom be one place where no toys, no children's books or clothes, nor any children's paraphernalia be allowed to litter the landscape. Bedrooms, especially when newborns enter the scene, too easily lose the look of a romantic getaway and become a second nursery. But I like that goal: to have one spot in the house that is *not* overrun with baby or children's gear—one spot where I can escape to write, read, or pray.

Our bedroom is not off limits—I think the girls enjoy seeing a different four walls from time to time, and it's a treat to be allowed to nap in "Mom and Dad's" bedroom. Our house is small enough that during the day the kids use our bedroom as an extra playroom. But periodically I have to de-kid it. As I put away their playthings, I focus on "This is our special room, where Stuart and I are still Stuart and Melodie, not Mommy and Daddy. When I close the door before retiring, the click reminds me of my fifth goal: *Keep a strong relationship with my husband.*

What about the family bed? Some writers have recently assured parents that it's okay to let children come to bed with them. Some have gone so far as to say that parents need to allow their children unlimited access to their bedroom or else the parents risk being "detached" from their kids.

Frankly, my sleep is lousy if there are more than two people in our queen-size bed. Little ones wiggle, stick their limbs in odd places, and otherwise make it impossible for me to sleep soundly. However, if we have already gotten our night's sleep and are just dozing, it is comforting and cozy to let the kids climb in bed for a few minutes in the morning. When I was nursing and the baby was having trouble sleeping, we'd occasionally let her sleep with us awhile, too. I never slept very well, but it was better than getting up every hour to see why she was crying.

Anyone reading this book knows by now that I'm not one to make a lot of hard-and-fast rules. So for me, the family bed is okay to use occasionally, but I wouldn't want to make it a permanent fixture.

June remembers having a terrible nightmare as a child and running downstairs to her mom and dad's bedroom as fast as her little legs would go. Her mom heard her coming and had the covers thrown back in anticipation. "Want to crawl in bed with us awhile?" I like that attitude: Mom and Dad are there when kids need them, but ordinarily they sleep by themselves.

No one ever said it would be easy to keep a strong relationship with a husband and raise kids at the same time. Nor is it easy to love God and a family at the same time. Both Jesus and the Apostle Paul warned how difficult it is to serve God and have a family, too. In Matthew 19:12 Jesus said, "Others have renounced marriage because of the kingdom of heaven. The one who can accept this should accept it." In 1 Corinthians 7:34 Paul states, "An unmarried woman . . . is concerned about the Lord's affairs: Her aim is to be devoted to the Lord in both body and spirit. But a married woman is concerned about the affairs of this world—how she can please her husband." Paul and Jesus both say also that singleness is not for everyone and they do not condemn the married person. Certainly, if life is to go on, someone has to have and raise children. These passages from Paul and Jesus say to me: Yes, *you* have a difficult job to balance it all.

Other passages of Scripture remind me that *whatever* I do, I should give it my best. God will be with me, giving me guidance, tolerance, wisdom, and strength.

In my bedroom hangs a favorite photo taken by my cousin: It's of grandmother in her rocking chair, wearing her apron, reading the Bible and praying. I know she prays for Stuart, me, and the girls every single day. So do my parents. It is not their prayers that move the hands of God to be with us. God would love, care for, and guide us out of his own merciful concern. But as I'm aware of my family's support, I'm strengthened to find the way through all the petty problems that arise in married and family life. It's also a reminder to pray for my own children.

Maybe what every marriage needs even more than a lock for the bedroom door is a picture of a faithful grandmother (or parent, teacher, prayer partner, or friend). It's powerful medicine when you're feeling used up.

♥ HOW STRONG IS YOUR RELATIONSHIP? ♥

As this chapter suggests, your relationship to your spouse may be as strong as the lock on your bedroom door. For wives especially, it is all too easy to pour everything into the care of the children and forget to care for the marriage. Here are some questions you may want to think about and discuss with your husband:

- ♥ How have children made a difference in your physical needs for intimacy with your spouse?
- ♥ How do you make quality time together?
- ♥ How do you feel about having the kids sleep with you and your husband?
- ♥ What changes could you make to have more quality time together? Perhaps you already have a lock on your bedroom door. Is that really the answer, or is the real lock in your mind and in your attitude?

Making time for each other is a vital key to keeping your marital covenant of total faithfulness to one another. In the next chapter, Charlie and Martha Shedd share ways to keep mini-covenants to spend the time to keep your marriage strong.

Chapter 43

SO HOW CAN WE MAKE THE TIME?

BY CHARLIE AND MARTHA SHEDD
Bible Study Together

Vowing to make time for one another is good; doing it regularly with a planned approach that becomes a habit is better. In this chapter, Charlie and Martha Shedd describe the "weekly date" they kept throughout the years of their marriage, plus ideas shared by other couples who have written to tell how they mini-covenant with each other to make time for each other.

As you read, be looking for at least one idea you could adapt to make more time for yourself and your spouse.

TO LOVE, HONOR, CHERISH ... AND ENJOY!

The word *covenant* is loaded with special meaning for all religious people. Dictionaries define *covenant:* "Agreement between two or more" ... "a compact" ... "contract" ... "pledge taken together."

When we marry, we covenant to love, honor, cherish and provide for. Some of us even promise to obey, and all of us promise to be faithful.

Good promises, every one! But are they good enough?

No!

One graduate school professor, a real wag, would start us off on test day with, "Define the universe and give three examples." At which, we would smile and then move to question two.

Some things are so all-encompassing we can only nod and say, "Yes. Of course. I agree." And for the two people we know best, the marriage covenant is very much like that. Too grandiose. Too massive. Too far removed from plain vanilla everyday concourse.

So whatever can we do?

One thing we can do is to live the major covenant of marriage by many little covenants.

OUR WEEKLY DATE

Early in our years together we took this pledge:

By whatever means required, we will not let our love be crowded out. Come success, come children, come urgent matters of every kind, nothing matters more than our togetherness. That being true, once each week (at least once) we will go from our home for an old-fashioned "date." A time of romancing. A time for fun. A time to dream, and a time to remember. But above all, this is our time for in-depth communication—sharing our love by talk, talk, talk. Sharing our love as we listen, listen, listen.

Score on this commitment?

One hundred percent. Forty-five years times fifty-two weeks equals two-thousand-three-hundred and forty weekly "dates." Who wouldn't be best friends after investing that much time?

What if we had to miss one week? Then we made it up the next week, or the next. No excuses. None.

Usually we managed a dinner date. But some busy weeks when there simply were no evenings, we would book a lunch together. Some fine restaurant? Occasionally, but never in the early years. Then, and even now, it was and is more likely a favorite simple place. And in those years when the budget was super-tight, we would sometimes make it a long walk; a drive, if we could afford the gas; maybe a picnic in the park.

(Interesting note: The more we grow in love, the simpler grow our tastes. Why? Isn't this because the real thing is not outward decoration? Wherever we're together, the decoration is exactly as it should be. And what we're sharing on our date is not first sustenance for the body, but food for the soul.)

Never did we count those times when we were entertaining or being entertained. Our dates were *our* time for talk, talk, talk. Our time to put our elbows on the window sill of heaven and gaze deep into each other's souls.

So this is another major answer to "How can we make time?"
The weekly date.

Subquestion: What's the matter with regular sharing time at
home?

Answer: Nothing. Great idea. But for us, too often across the
years, this is one more great idea murdered by a gang of brutal
facts. Facts like the telephone. Facts like the doorbell. Facts like
children, large or small. Facts like a light bulb needing replace-
ment, or the hot water heater going out, or "Will you help me with
my schoolwork?"

Interruptions we have always with us. That being true, for us,
week by week, year by year, there is only one answer. This is the
regular observance of a regular special event for regular sharing of
our love outside the home. No exceptions. No excuses. A sacred
covenant for talk, talk, talk, listen, listen, listen.

OTHER LITTLE COVENANTS

HAPPIEST MOMENT

"What was your happiest moment today?"

If every day toward evening (dinner ... after dinner ...
bedtime), you agreed to share your number-one recall of that day's
good happenings, would that be a plus for you?

At one of our workshops a loquacious psychiatrist, when he
heard about "happiest moment," made this statement:

> *Did you ever figure how much of your dinner talk, your after-
> dinner talk, and even bedtime talk focuses on the negative? I tell
> you what, for Ginnie and me this "happiest moment" thing has
> to be one super idea, one sure winner. And what a way to go to
> sleep!*

Paul must have had something like this in mind when he
wrote, "Love rejoices not at wrong, but rejoices in the right" (1 Cor.
13:6 RSV).

What would it mean to our marriage if we were to really bring
these words alive in our love?

Little covenant for major miracle:

What was your happiest moment today?

HOW OTHERS MAKE TIME

EARLY MORNING COFFEE KLATSCH

The Martins live in Virginia. They're a busy couple with three teen-agers. He has a good job in the local garment factory. She works at the bank, and this is their story.

> We've been married twenty-one years and you know what they say? The bad times come in multiples of seven. We really don't believe that, because almost every year for us has had its bad times. Lots of good times too, fortunately. But isn't it sad the way those bad times tend to dominate?
>
> Well, to be perfectly honest, this year we woke up to some real slippage. I mean certain happenings we knew couldn't be anything but bad unless we moved in on them right away.
>
> To make a long story short, when we took an honest look, we knew why these things were happening. The reason was a breakdown in our communication. Why? I'll tell you why. It was three teen-agers—eighteen, fifteen, thirteen. Do you know how many things three teen-agers can be into? Football, drama, clubs, friends, rock music, country music, band music, chorus, church, dating, one broken arm, one broken heart, grades good and bad, and, believe me, that's only for starters.
>
> So, in all this chaos, how could the two of us ever find time for being alone with each other?
>
> Well, we found a way and we thought we should write and tell you in case there are other couples with our problem, or some other problem like it.
>
> What we decided we would do is to set our alarm thirty minutes early every morning. I mean every single morning we wouldn't even leave the bedroom till we had spent one solid half hour together just plain visiting, listening, sharing our love. (I take the coffeepot to the bedroom at night, ready to plug in.) We started this three months ago, and there is simply no way we could tell you what a difference it has made. We both feel this is going to be our best year ever.

Repeat. Say it again. One more time.

> Any way we do it
>   Creating time for talk, talk, talk
>   listen, listen, listen
>   Starts us on the road to our best year ever.

MONDAY NIGHT FOOTBALL FORUM

Dear Dr. and Mrs. Shedd:

Last night after the children had gone to bed, my husband sat me down and told me about an unusual gift he was going to give me. He said this year he was going to give me the first half of every Monday night football game. Not just this week, but every week, he and I would just visit during the first half.

Now that might not sound like much to you, but you see he commutes, so he doesn't get home till 7:30, sometimes later. Every Monday night for years it's been the same routine. I would feed the children early. Then Bob and I would sit by the TV and have our dinner. At first he tried to explain football to me, but I never really could appreciate it, and I think the reason is I wanted to talk. I wanted to hear about his day, to tell him about mine, just plain visit.

Well, I wish you could have heard the speech he made when he told me what he was going to do. Believe me, it was one of the most beautiful things I ever heard. He told me he had been thinking about football and us, and he had decided two things. First, he said he decided it couldn't be good for the children being shoved aside while he watched football. But the best part was the next thing he said (and I know I will appreciate this forever), "In the second place, Lucy, after being with the kids all day, you must need some scintillating conversation, and you know how scintillating I can be." I guess you can see why I'm so thrilled and why I say I think I have the greatest husband ever!

Aside to the male gender:

Why do we think we have to do some big, big thing to make our love what it should be?

A trip to Hawaii, that mink stole, the new home. If only we could manage one of the biggies, then she would love me like crazy.

But would she?

Probably not.

The Book says,

Behold how great a matter
a little fire kindleth (James 3:5 KJV).

HIGH-TECH TALK

Are you ready for this? The Johnsons do most of their talk, talk, talk by cassette recorder. Excerpt from his letter:

Right now we're going through a period when we're absolutely snowed, and I do mean snowed. I'm at the height of my career, and this is the year it's go-for-broke. But would you believe that is exactly how it is with her? She's one rung below the top of her ladder, too, this year. But we do love each other, and as you know, we both love the Lord.

So we took one look at this and decided there is no way we're going to lose touch with each other or with the Lord. Fortunately, we're crazy about our jobs, and even though it means go, go, go, traveling, long hours, we have actually communicated more this year than ever.

How? Are you ready for this? By cassette. It's a great way to stay in touch, and here's how the idea started. One time when we were into one of our own discussions on what could happen if we weren't careful, we remembered one little item from one of your books.

It was about the couple who couldn't express themselves very well, so they talked by tape recorder. And that's exactly how we've done it. Every week we exchange cassettes. Never less than three cassettes. I mean three cassettes each. That's what we promised, and to date we haven't missed a single week.

In a lonely hotel room, in our car (we both commute), any open moment of the busy day we talk to each other, and I simply can't tell you what this has meant to us. It has freed us both to pour ourselves into our jobs without the customary guilt trip. And it's done a lot for those times when we are together, too.

Now I should tell you we both agreed this couldn't go on forever. But we also agreed we'd give it a try for one year and then we'd reevaluate.

Please do tell our story. Sure, it may sound weird, but we are praising the Lord for some unknown couple's brilliant idea.

Brilliant is the right word. Any time any couple can develop any method for talk, talk, talk, listen, listen, listen, there is only one word for this: *brilliant.*

EIGHT HUNDRED HOURS

If you and almost any other person had spent eight hundred hours visiting about everything, you'd be good friends, wouldn't you?

That's what my wife and I have done. We've spent eight hundred hours in what you call talk, talk, talk. Sounds impossible? It would be if you tried to do it all at once. But let me tell you how we did it.

Every Saturday morning for the seventeen years of our marriage, we've gone out to breakfast, just the two of us together. When the children were small, that Saturday morning babysitter money had top priority. Even when we had company for the weekend, we still did it.

Weren't there ever any emergencies and didn't we have to miss some Saturdays? Yes, but do you know what we did? We made it early Sunday morning before church. That's why I can say we have spent eight hundred hours visiting with each other.

Actually, we could double that and not be far off, because many times our Saturday morning session goes on for at least two hours.

We teach the couples' class at our church and this is one thing we tell them. Don't give us any excuses for not taking time to communicate. I'm a traveling man, gone five days a week, and we do it. If you really want to, you can do it.

SANCTUARY ON THE CELLAR STEPS

Since all three of our children are junior-high age, our house is sort of like a zoo, if you know what I mean. Animals, friends, telephone calls, and oh that loud music!

Arnie and I have always been good communicators, and we thought you'd like to know one way we've kept it good. You can see that with us it's not a matter of whether we're going to talk, but where and when.

Some years ago when the house was total confusion and we had a decision that had to be made, we went to the basement steps. Well, from that day we've made it a practice to spend some regular talk time there.

If anybody asks, How do you keep the kids from interrupting? That's easier than you might imagine. We simply told them this is our place, so unless it's an emergency, you leave us alone. It's amazing how you can teach even a small child to respect parents' privacy.

Anyway we call our cellar steps "our sanctuary," and that's what it's been for us.

♥ A FINAL THOUGHT ABOUT TIME ♥

Prescriptions, list of ways, and other tips work only when they are used. *The Marriage Collection* contains literally thousands of suggestions, ideas, principles and concepts for building a stronger, truer, happier relationship. "Making time" for any of these worthwhile ideas doesn't mean hurriedly slipping a communication session or a precious moment of intimacy between your one-hour commute and the seven o'clock news. Take time for the growth of your marriage.

It takes time
to spend
enough time together.

A COLLECTION OF "EACH OTHERS" TO GROW YOUR MARRIAGE

NINE WAYS TO BUILD EACH OTHER UP

The scriptural word for "build up" is "edify." Although the Scriptures teach that Christians can be edified spiritually by preaching, that is *not* the way to edify your mate. Following are nine ideas that will work much better than preaching.

1. Make the irrevocable decision to never again be critical of your partner in word, thought, or deed. This may sound like an impossibility, but it is not. It is simply a decision backed up by action until it becomes a habit you would not change if you could.
2. Study your partner. Become sensitive to the areas where your partner feels a lack and think of ways to build up your partner in those areas particularly.
3. Think every day of positive qualities and behavior patterns you admire and appreciate in your mate.
4. Consistently verbalize praise and appreciation for your partner. Be genuine, be specific, be generous. You edify with the *spoken* word.
5. Recognize your partner's talents, abilities, and accomplishments. Communicate your respect for the work he or she does.
6. Husband, show your wife publicly and privately how precious she is to you. And do not express admiration for another woman. This is never edifying to your wife. Keep your attention focused on her!
7. Wife, show your husband that he is the most important person in your life—always. Seek his opinions and value his judgment.

8. Respond to each other physically and facially. The face is the most distinctive and expressive part of a person. Your mate wants to see you smile, eyes sparkling in response to him or her.
9. Always exhibit the greatest courtesy to each other. You should be VIPs in your own home![5]

TWENTY-FIVE WAYS TO REACH OUT AND TOUCH EACH OTHER

Dr. Ed Wheat emphasizes the tremendous value of physical touching to every human being. And who would need touching more than your mate? Following are twenty-five ideas you can put to work immediately.

1. When dating, young people can scarcely be kept apart. Most married couples have forgotten how much fun physical closeness can be! So set aside practice times at night (at least once a week) to learn the delights of nonsexual body caressing. Make a date ahead of time. Anticipate pleasure and relaxation together.
2. Show each other where you like to be touched and the kind of touch that pleases you. Usually, a light touch is the most thrilling. Be imaginative in the way you caress.
3. Remember the purpose: to establish a good emotional climate of warmth, love, and affection; *not* to initiate sex. If sex results later because you both want it, that's all right. But you need to learn to enjoy *nonsexual* touching during these exercise times.
4. Demonstrate to each other how you prefer to be held. Kiss your partner the way you would like to be kissed—not to criticize past performances, but to communicate something your partner has not sensed before.
5. Use lotion or baby oil in body caressing; use K-Y Jelly when touching the more sensitive areas of the body. Physical caressing should be totally pleasant.
6. Try caressing (not tickling!) each other's feet. For almost everyone this is a pleasurable and nonthreatening form of touch communication. Some people bathe, dry, and oil each other's feet gently and leisurely.
7. Cleanliness is essential for enjoyment of these sessions.
8. Some evenings take your shower or bath together. Make this a light-hearted, sensuous experience.
9. Americans habitually do everything in a rush, including love-making. But to learn the art of expressing warm, sensual feelings, you will have to slow down. If what you

are doing feels good, take the time to enjoy it. This may become the best part of your day.

10. Caress each other's back. Pay special attention to the back of the neck at the hairline and the area just above the small of the back.

11. Maintain a positive attitude (the attitude of yes, rather than no). If some manner of caressing or the area chosen does not feel particularly enjoyable, gently lead your partner on to something you do like. Never say, "Stop doing that!" or similar words. The atmosphere should be delightfully permissive.

12. Practice communicating warmth. Learn to be emotionally aware of your own feelings and those of your partner. Focus on expressing your love through the medium of touch. Caress each other's face in the dark, becoming more aware of your partner and spelling out love through sensitive fingertips.

13. Make sure that both of you are having equal opportunity to give and to receive. Take turns giving pleasure to each other.

14. When you caress, use a slow, tender, appreciative touch, indicating how much you enjoy your partner's body— each part of it. When people feel negative about some part of their body, it is more difficult for them to relate freely to their partner. Help your mate realize that every part of his or her body is pleasing, attractive, and desirable to you.

15. Develop positive feelings toward your own body given to you by God. This is biblical! Meditate on Psalm 139, "I praise you because I am fearfully and wonderfully made; your works are wonderful, I know that full well" (Ps. 139:14 NIV).

16. Communicate verbally during your exercises, telling each other what you especially enjoy and how it makes you feel.

17. Sleep in as few clothes as possible at night. Clothes are only a hindrance during these touching sessions.

18. Practice breathing together in rhythm, both of you lying on your side, the other pressed up against your back, hand on your abdomen to gauge your breathing and adjust his rhythm to yours. Then reverse places and do it again.

19. Try to go to bed when your partner does *every* night.

20. Have a period of fifteen to thirty minutes every night to lie in each other's arms in the dark before you drift off to sleep. Whisper together, sharing private thoughts and pleasant little experiences of the day. Avoid controversial

or negative topics. This is the time to build intimacy and wind down for sleep. You will become used to sharing things with each other that you would not otherwise mention. In each other's arms the hurts and frustrations of the day are healed. You may want to pray together at this time, or just relax in the comfort of physically-felt love.

21. Establish the cozy habit of staying in some sort of physical contact while you are going to sleep—a hand or a leg touching your partner's, for instance.

22. Begin every day with a few minutes of cuddling and snuggling before you get out of bed. A husband can tell his wife how nice she feels and how glad he is to be close to her. A wife can nestle in her husband's arms and tell him she wishes they didn't have to leave each other that morning. Just be close and savor gentle physical contact for a while. It will make the morning bout with the alarm clock far more pleasant, so allow a few minutes in your schedule for this, even though one or both of you must soon be up and off to work.

23. Hold hands often. Think of all the different ways you can enjoy just touching with your hands, and all the different feelings that can be conveyed.

24. Become aware of the many ways you can have physical contact in the course of a week. Touch when you are talking and maintain eye contact. Sit close to each other in church. Kiss each other when there is no occasion for it. Add variety to your kisses, your touches, and your love pats.

25. While you watch television, make sure you sit close together and use the time for some physical communication. A wise wife will cuddle close to her husband when he chooses to watch his football games, even if she is not interested in the program. Since so many people spend so much time before the TV set, it need not be wasted if they are at least together physically.

My final word on touching: even if you practice everything else in this book, but do not touch each other frequently and lovingly, the thrill of romantic love will be absent from your marriage. It's up to you to add the spark.[6]

ONE HUNDRED AND EIGHTEEN WAYS TO LOVE EACH OTHER

1. Communicate with her, never close her out.
2. Communicate with him, never close him out.

3. Regard her as important.
4. Regard him as important.
5. Do everything you can to understand her feelings.
6. Do everything you can to understand his feelings.
7. Be interested in her friends.
8. Be interested in his friends.
9. Ask her opinion frequently.
10. Ask his opinion frequently.
11. Value what she says.
12. Value what he says.
13. Let her feel your approval and affection.
14. Let him feel your approval and affection.
15. Be gentle and tender with her.
16. Baby him just enough to make him feel loved.
17. Develop a sense of humor.
18. Thank the Lord he usually gives mothers a sense of humor.
19. Avoid making major changes without discussion.
20. Avoid giving him surprises—particularly when spending money.
21. Learn to respond openly when she wants to communicate.
22. Learn to send communication signals when he isn't exhausted or distracted.
23. Comfort her when she is down emotionally.
24. Encourage him when he is down emotionally.
25. Be interested in what she feels is important.
26. Be interested in what he feels is important.
27. Disagree with her gently and respectfully.
28. Disagree with him gently and respectfully.
29. Allow her to teach you without being defensive.
30. Allow him to teach you without pouting.
31. Make special time available to her and your children.
32. Make special time available to him without the children.
33. Be worthy of her trust.
34. Be worthy of his trust.
35. Compliment her often.
36. Praise him often.
37. Be forgiving when she offends you.
38. Be forgiving when he offends you.
39. Show her you need her.
40. Thank him for being there.
41. Accept her the way she is.
42. Seek to change yourself, not him.
43. Be willing to tell her, "I was wrong." Don't be afraid to be humble.

44. Be willing to tell him, "I made a mistake." Don't be afraid to be humble.
45. Be the spiritual leader of your family.
46. Encourage him to be spiritual leader of the family.
47. Take time to sit and talk calmly with her.
48. Ask him how his day went before you tell him about the Tonka truck in the toilet.
49. Take her on romantic outings.
50. Help him plan romantic outings.
51. Write her an occasional love letter.
52. Write him an occasional love note.
53. Surprise her with a card or flowers.
54. Surprise him with a special dish or dessert.
55. Express how much you appreciate her.
56. Express how much you appreciate him.
57. Tell her how proud you are of her.
58. Tell him how proud you are of him.
59. Give her loving advice when she asks for it.
60. Give him loving advice when he asks for it.
61. Defend her to others.
62. Defend him to others.
63. Take time to notice what she has done for you and the family.
64. Take time to notice what he does for you and the family.
65. Share your thoughts and feelings with her.
66. Be patient if sharing thoughts and feelings is hard for him.
67. Learn to enjoy what she enjoys.
68. Learn to enjoy what he enjoys.
69. Take care of the kids before dinner—give her a break.
70. If he comes in exhausted, give him fifteen minutes to relax, then give him the kids.
71. Let her take a bubble bath while you do the dishes.
72. Put on a sexy nightie.
73. Get rid of habits that annoy her.
74. Get rid of habits that annoy him.
75. Do not compare her relatives with yours in a negative way.
76. Do not compare his relatives with yours in a negative way.
77. Do not expect a band to play whenever you help with the housecleaning.
78. Always thank him when he helps with the housecleaning.
79. Make sure she understands everything you plan to do.
80. Make sure he understands everything you plan to do.
81. Do little things for her—an unexpected kiss, a neck rub.

82. Do little things for him—breakfast in bed.
83. Discover her anxieties and fears.
84. Let him know it's okay to have anxieties and fears.
85. See what you can do to eliminate her fears and anxieties.
86. Ask how you can help eliminate his fears and anxieties.
87. Respect her need for affection.
88. Respect his need for sex.
89. Find out what makes her insecure, then avoid doing or saying those things.
90. Find out what makes him insecure, then avoid doing or saying those things.
91. Practice common courtesies like holding the door, letting you go first.
92. Don't cut him off when he is trying to talk, especially in a group.
93. Ask if she is uncomfortable about the way you spend money.
94. Ask him if he is uncomfortable about the way you spend money.
95. Take her on dates now and then.
96. Take him on a date now and then.
97. Tell her you love her—often.
98. Tell him you love him—often.
99. Remember anniversaries, birthdays and other special occasions.
100. Help him remember anniversaries, etc., without nagging. Be appreciative when he does.
101. Learn to enjoy shopping.
102. Learn to enjoy football, basketball or whatever he watches on television.
103. Give her a special gift from time to time.
104. Give him a special gift from time to time.
105. Do not criticize or belittle her in private or public.
106. Do not criticize or belittle him in private or public.
107. Call her when you're going to be late.
108. Call him when you're running late.
109. Do not disagree with her in front of the children.
110. Do not disagree with him in front of the children.
111. Take her out to dinner and for weekend getaways.
112. Try kidnapping him for a weekend getaway.
113. Do those little repair jobs she always needs.
114. Do those little mending jobs he always seems to need.
115. Give her special times to be alone or with her friends.
116. Give him special times to be alone or with his friends.
117. Pray for her to enjoy God's best in life.
118. Pray for him to enjoy God's best in life.[7]

NOTES

INTRODUCTION

[1] Author of this poem is unknown.

[2] Cecil Osborne, *The Art of Understanding Your Mate* (Grand Rapids: Zondervan, 1988), 9.

[3] See Dr. Ed Wheat and Gloria Okes Perkins, *The First Years of Forever* (Grand Rapids: Zondervan, 1988), 21–23.

[4] See Margery Rosen, "The Marriage Report: Marriage is Back in Style With a Difference," *Ladies Home Journal* (June 1985), 98.

[5] See "What Really Makes a Marriage Work," condensed from Francine Klagsbrun, *Married People: Staying Together in the Age of Divorce*, *The Reader's Digest* (October 19, 1985), 89. This article is excerpted from Ms. Klagsbrun's book, *Married People: Staying Together in the Age of Divorce* (Bantam Books, Inc., 1985), which is based on her interviews of 87 couples whose marriages had lasted 15 years or more.

[6] See "Now For the Good News," *U.S. News and World Report* June 8, 1987, 68.

[7] Klagsbrun, *Married People: Staying Together in the Age of Divorce*, 8, (soft-cover edition issued 1986).

[8] See "Portrait of Divorce in America," *Newsweek* (February 2, 1987), 78.

[9] See Jane Marks, "Is Love Lovelier the Second Time Around?" part of the "Marriage Report," *Ladies Home Journal* (June 1985), 102.

[10] Ibid., 102, 161.

[11] For exact percentages, see Ethel Gofen, "Divorce and Marriage: A Report," *Current Health 2* (December 1986), 10.

[12] See "Portrait of Divorce in America," 78.

[13] Dr. David Mace, *Love and Anger in Marriage* (Grand Rapids: Zondervan Publishing House, 1982), 94.

[14] Ibid., 95, 96.

[15] Wheat and Perkins.

[16] Herbert Miles, *Sexual Happiness in Marriage* (Grand Rapids: Zondervan, 1967), Appendix V, 198.

[17] Ed Wheat and Gloria Okes Perkins, *Love Life for Every Married Couple* (Grand Rapids: Zondervan, 1980), 16, 17.

[18] See Jane Marks, "Golden Oldies," part of the Marriage Report, *Ladies Home Journal* (June 1985), 100.

[19] Karen Kuhne, *A Healing Season* (Grand Rapids: Zondervan, 1984), 131.

[20] Paul Tournier, *To Understand Each Other* (Richmond, Va: John Knox Press, 1966), 30.

PART I

[1] Lawrence J. Crabb, Jr., *The Marriage Builder* (Grand Rapids: Zondervan, 1982), 7.

[2] Ibid., 8.

[3] Ibid., 8–12.

[4] Ibid., 12.

[5] See Margery Rosen, "The Marriage Report: Marriage Is Back in Style With a Difference," *Ladies Home Journal* (June 1985), 102.

[6] Mike Mason, *The Mystery of Marriage* (Portland, OR: Multnomah Press, 1985), 26.

[7] Wheat, *Love Life for Every Married Couple*, 21.

[8] Klagsbrun, *Married People*. See chapter 11, "Forever II—Some Conclusions."

[9] Osborne, *The Art of Understanding*, 10.

[10] See Jeanette Lauer and Robert Lauer, "Marriage Made to Last," *Psychology Today* (June 1985), 24.

[11] Bustanoby, *Just Talk To Me*, 33.

PART II

[1] See Cris Evatt and Bruce Feld, *The Givers and the Takers* (New York: Macmillan, 1980), chapter 2, "Which One Are You?".

[2] Ibid., 18.

[3] Wheat and Perkins, *Love Life for Every Married Couple*, 57.

[4] Ibid., 58–61.

[5] Ibid., 62.

[6] Quoted by Cecil Osborne, *The Art of Understanding Your Mate*, 215.

[7] Walter Trobisch, *I Married You* (New York: Harper & Row, 1971), 75–77.

[8] Ibid., 77.

[9] Stephen Grunlan, *Marriage and the Family* (Grand Rapids: Zondervan, 1984), 73.

[10] Jay E. Adams, *Christian Living in the Home* (Phillipsburg, NJ: Presbyterian and Reformed, 1972), 100.

[11] Shirley Rice, *Physical Unity in Marriage* (Norfolk, Va: The Tabernacle Church of Norfolk, 1973), 3–4.

[12] Sheldon Vanauken, *A Severe Mercy* (New York: Harper & Row, 1977), 20.

[13] Helen B. Andelin, *The Fascinating Girl* (Santa Barbara: Pacific Press, 1969), 15–16.

[14] Glenn Wilson and David Nias, *The Mystery of Love* (New York: Quadrangle/The New York Times Book Co., 1976), 48.

[15] Mary Ellen Curtin, ed., *Symposium on Love* (New York: Behavioral Publications, 1973), 120.

[16] Vanauken, *A Severe Mercy*, 36.

[17] Mary McDermott Shideler, *The Theology of Romantic Love: A Study in the Writings of Charles Williams* (Grand Rapids: Eerdmans, 1962), 1.

[18] See Connell Cowan and Melvyn Kinder, "Wise Women, Wonderful Marriage," *Redbook* (October 1987), 106.

[19] Adapted from Shirley Cook, *The Marriage Puzzle*, 34, 35.

PART III

[1] Gary Smalley, *The Joy of Committed Love* (Grand Rapids: Zondervan, 1984), 13.
[2] Ibid., 13.

[3] "Heart to Heart," by Lois Wyse, from *Love Poems for the Very Married* (Cleveland: World Publishing, 1967).

[4] Tolstoy, from *The Kingdom of God Is Within You*, 33.

[5] Mike McGrady, *The Kitchen Sink Papers* (Garden City, N.Y.: Doubleday, 1975), 82.
[6] Ibid., 30, 31.

[7] For more on the subject, see *Toward Effective Counseling and Psychotherapy: Training and Practice*, Truax & Carkhuff (New York: Aldine-Atherton, 1972).

[8] Adapted from Smalley, *The Joy of Committed Love*, 32–33.

[9] Osborne, *The Art of Understanding Your Mate*, 11.

PART IV

[1] André Bustanoby with Faye Bustanoby, *Just Talk to Me*, from the Preface, 7.

[2] Ken Durham, *Speaking from the Heart* (Fort Worth: Sweet Publishing, 1986), 17.
[3] Ibid., 91.

[4] Domeena C. Renshaw, M.D., "Communication in Marriage," *Medical Aspects of Human Sexuality* (June 1983), 205.

[5] Martin Goldberg, M.D., "Commentary on Survey: Current Thinking on Why Some Marriages Fail," *Medical Aspects of Human Sexuality* (June 1982), 131.

[6] Renshaw, p. 205.

[7] Anthony Pietropinto, M.D., "Commentary on Survey: Distress Signals in Marriage," *Medical Aspects of Human Sexuality* (April 1984), 87.

[8] Judson J. Swihart, *Communicating in Marriage* (Downers Grove, Illinois: InterVarsity Press, 1981), 19–20.

[9] Carmen Lynch, MSW, and Martin Blinder, M.D., "The Romantic Relationship," *Medical Aspects of Human Sexuality* (May 1983), 155.

[10] Donald G. Ellis, Ph.D., "Listening Creatively to One's Spouse," *Medical Aspects of Human Sexuality* (March 1983), 173.

[11] Czeslaw Milosz, *Selected Poems* (New York: The Ecco Press, 1980), 18.

[12] Anne Kristin Carroll, *Together Forever* (Grand Rapids: Zondervan, 1982), 105.

[13] Based on suggestions by Carroll, *Together Forever*, 105–106.

[14] Truax and Carkhuff, *Toward Effective Counseling*, 284.

[15] Brad Greene, Robert Isenberg, Duane Rawlins, Shayle Uroff, *Intra-Family Communication Training: Parent's Manual* (Simi, Calif.: ICT Corporation, 1971), 3.1.

[16] Ibid., 2.4, 2.5.

[17] Truax and Carkhuff, *Toward Effective Counseling*, 286.

[18] Greene et al., *ICT Manual*, 3.17.

[19] Ibid., 3.1.

[20] Statements adapted from the "Caring Relationship Inventory" by Everett L. Shostrom, published by the Educational and Industrial Testing Service, Box 7234, San Diego, CA 92107.

[21] Greene, et al., *ICT Manual*, 4.13.

[22] Adapted from Shirley Cook, *The Marriage Puzzle*, 59, 60.

[23] Diane Head, *A Precious Bit of Forever* (Grand Rapids: Zondervan, 1976), 91, 93, 94.

PART V

[1] Mace, *Love and Anger in Marriage,* 12.

[2] See Dr. David Mace, "Love, Anger and Intimacy," *Light* (April/May 1980), 2. See also Mace, *Love and Anger in Marriage,* 12–13, 23–37, 38–62.

[3] Henry Drummond, *The Greatest Thing in the World* (Chicago: M. A. Donohue & Company), 33–34.

[4] Jeanette C. Lauer and Robert H. Lauer, "How Fighting Can Help a Marriage," *Ladies Home Journal,* (July 1987), 42.

[5] Ibid., 44.

[6] Ibid., 47.

[7] Ibid., 144.

[8] George Sweeting, Compiler, *Great Quotes and Illustrations* (Waco: Word, 1985), 16.

[9] Barbara E. James, Ph.D., "The 'Silent Treatment' in Marriage." *Medical Aspects of Human Sexuality* (February 1983), 100.

[10] Ibid.

[11] Chuck Swindoll, *Strike the Original Match,* (Portland: Multnomah, 1980), 306.

[12] Pietropinto, "Distress Signals in Marriage," 88.

[13] Emily Dickinson, *The Complete Poems of Emily Dickinson,* ed. Thomas II Johnson (Boston: Little, Brown and Company, 1890), 534–535.

[14] David Hellerstein, M.D., "Can TV Cause Divorce?" *TV Guide* (September 26, 1987), 4–7. Adapted from Wheat and Perkins, *The First Years of Forever,* 73.

[15] Ibid., 73.

[16] Bustanoby, *Just Talk To Me,* 89.

[17] Brad Greene, et al., *ICT Manual,* 4.1. This is one of several techniques suggested.

[18] Ibid., p. 4.3.

[19] Lauer, "How Fighting Can Help," 44.

[20] McGrady, *The Kitchen Sink Papers,* 26, 27.

[21] Mace, *Love and Anger in Marriage,* 120.

[22] Adapted from Bustanoby, *Just Talk To Me,* 173–174.

[23] Osborne, *The Art of Understanding Your Mate,* 24.

PART VI

[1] Willard F. Harley, Jr., *His Needs, Her Needs* (Old Tappan, NJ: Fleming H. Revell, 1986), 11.

[2] Ibid., 13.

[3] Dr. Ed Wheat and Gaye Wheat, *Intended for Pleasure* (Old Tappan: Fleming H. Revell Company, 1977), 16.

[4] Helen Singer Kaplan, *Disorders of Sexual Desire* (New York: Simon and Schuster, 1979), 6.

[5] Tim and Beverly LaHaye, *The Act of Marriage* (Grand Rapids: Zondervan, 1976), 82–89.

[6] LaHaye, *The Act of Marriage,* 96–101.

[7] S. D. Gaede, *Belonging* (Grand Rapids: Zondervan, 1985), 92–93.

[8] Ibid., 93–94.

[9] Shirley Cook, *The Marriage Puzzle* (Grand Rapids: Zondervan, 1985), 79–80.

PART VII

[1] Charlie and Martha Shedd, *Praying Together* (Grand Rapids: Zondervan, 1987), 9.

[2] Wheat and Perkins, *The First Years of Forever*, 172.

[3] Ibid., 174–175.

[4] Thornton Wilder, *Our Town, A Play In Three Acts* (New York: Harper & Row, 1957), from Act III.

[5] Drummond, *The Greatest Thing in the World*, 55.

[6] Charlie and Martha Shedd, *Bible Study Together* (Grand Rapids: Zondervan, 1984), 99.

[7] Shedd, *Praying Together*, 43.

[8] "Just Married—But Will It Last?" *U.S. News and World Report* (June 8, 1987), 68.

[9] Klagsbrun, *Married People*, 8.

[10] Osborne, *The Art of Understanding Your Mate*, 47.

PART VIII

[1] Shedd, *Bible Study Together*, 105–106.

[2] Ibid., 107.

[3] Henry N. Ferguson, *These Times* (May 1983), P.O. Box 7000, Boise, Idaho, 83707.

[4] Adapted from Smalley, *The Joy of Committed Love*, 82–83.

[5] Wheat and Perkins, *Love Life for Every Married Couple*, 190–191.

[6] Ibid., 184–187.

[7] Adapted from Smalley, *The Joy of Committed Love*, 32–35.